The Obama Legacy

PRESIDENTIAL APPRAISALS AND LEGACIES

Bert A. Rockman and Andrew Rudalevige
Series Editors

THE OBAMA LEGACY

Edited by Bert A. Rockman
and Andrew Rudalevige

 University Press of Kansas

Published by the University Press of Kansas (Lawrence, Kansas 66045), which was organized by the Kansas Board of Regents and is operated and funded by Emporia State University, Fort Hays State University, Kansas State University, Pittsburg State University, the University of Kansas, and Wichita State University.

Library of Congress Cataloging-in-Publication Data

Names: Rockman, Bert A., editor. | Rudalevige, Andrew, 1968– editor.
Title: The Obama legacy / edited by Bert A. Rockman and Andrew Rudalevige.
Description: Lawrence, Kansas : University Press of Kansas, 2019. | Series: Presidential appraisals and legacies | Includes index.
Identifiers: LCCN 2018059047
  ISBN 9780700627905 (paperback)
  ISBN 9780700627912 (ebook)
Subjects: LCSH: United States—Politics and government—2009–2017. | Obama, Barack—Influence. | BISAC: POLITICAL SCIENCE / Government / Executive Branch. | POLITICAL SCIENCE / Government / National. | POLITICAL SCIENCE / Political Process / Elections.
Classification: LCC E907 .O2245 2019 | DDC 973.932092—dc23
LC record available at https://lccn.loc.gov/2018059047.

British Library Cataloguing-in-Publication Data is available.

Printed in the United States of America

10 9 8 7 6 5 4 3 2 1

The paper used in this publication is recycled and contains 30 percent postconsumer waste. It is acid free and meets the minimum requirements of the American National Standard for Permanence of Paper for Printed Library Materials Z39.48-1992.

To the memories of Ed Artinian and Barbara Sinclair and to the friendship of Colin Campbell—all were present at the creation, and all inspired it.

Contents

PREFACE AND ACKNOWLEDGMENTS

As Donald J. Trump's presidency approached its midterm, his seemingly scattered policy agenda had one united theme: opposition to anything his predecessor, Barack Obama, had accomplished, proposed, or even thought. In June 2017 *New York Times* reporter Peter Baker wrote, "Rarely has a new president appeared so determined not just to steer the country in a different direction but to actively dismantle what was established before his arrival. . . . Mr. Trump has made clear that if it has Mr. Obama's name on it, he would just as soon erase it from the national hard drive."[1]

Assessing the full impact of Trump's efforts in this regard will have to await the next volume in this series. In the meantime, the chapters that follow lay out the contours of the task he set for himself. What policy achievements have Barack Obama's "name on it"? How do they compare with what Obama sought to accomplish in the first place—and with what he plausibly could have aimed for, given the political contexts and constraints of his eight years in office? That is: what is the Obama legacy—and how much of it is likely to endure?

In this volume, some of our finest scholars assess the consequential years of Obama's presidency. From the Affordable Care Act to the wars in Iraq and Afghanistan and against ISIS, from the Iran nuclear deal to the Clean Power Plan, the policies and politics of the eight years that ended on January 20, 2017, come to life in the chapters that follow. At times, their conclusions buttress those reached in our earlier book on Obama's presidency, published toward the end of his first term; at times, the experience of the second term tempers or even reverses that analysis.[2]

As that suggests, this project represents a continuing, even continuous, conversation, the next stop on a journey that began in 1991 with *The George Bush Presidency: First Appraisals*.[3] But it also marks a new beginning, as stewardship of the series shifts to the University Press of Kansas. This volume marks the first in what we hope will be many entries under the banner of the Presidential Appraisals and Legacies series.

One notable change involves timing. Whereas earlier volumes were commissioned and published before the end of an administration, we believe the virtue of immediacy is outweighed by the risk of prematurity. Examining an administration in its entirety allows our authors to gauge—and engage with—the full range of a president's actions in office, providing a more authoritative analysis. Of course, drafts of the history assessed here will continue to be written, especially as the archival record of a given administration becomes available over time. This book, and indeed this series, is meant to help readers understand the recent past while giving future historians a useful starting point from the vantage of close temporal observation.

We are grateful to all those who helped this book come to fruition. First and foremost, that means the contributing authors: we were delighted that a diverse range of top-notch scholars agreed to lend their time, talents, and judgments to this volume.

Special thanks must also go to the hugely supportive and notably patient editorial team at the University Press of Kansas, starting with Chuck Myers, who brought this series to the press before bequeathing it to Joyce Harrison and then David Congdon. We are grateful to all of you, as well as to all those who worked on the design and production of the book, including but hardly limited to Michael Kehoe, Linda Lotz, and Larisa Martin. Thanks and kudos to Bowdoin College's Lorenzo Meigs, who compiled the index. And we are, of course, particularly thankful for our families and colleagues, whose support and sacrifices are too often unnoted but never unappreciated. Along these lines, Andy Rudalevige offers special homage to his wife Christine's forbearance with yet another book-length project in a non-sabbatical year. Bert Rockman offers special appreciation to his wife, Susan, who kept insisting that he was supposed to be retired, and to their cat, who demanded that petting her should be his principal responsibility.

We are also grateful to Colin Campbell, who began this series as a coeditor assessing the presidency of George H. W. Bush and continued in that role until the most recent edition. He was there at the creation and remains an inspiration. And we want to lift up the memories of two other individuals crucial to this series' quality and longevity: Ed Artinian, founder of Chatham House Publishers, where this series first took root, and Barbara Sinclair, professor emerita at the University of California at Los Angeles. Barbara, who died in 2016, was both a renowned expert on the lawmaking process and a consummate professional—and, not least, a wonderful person. We are proud that she contributed to each previous volume in this series and distraught at her absence this time around. To all of them, we dedicate this volume.

Notes

1. Peter Baker, "Can Trump Destroy Obama's Legacy?" *New York Times*, June 23, 2017, https://www.nytimes.com/2017/06/23/sunday-review/donald-trump-barack-obama.html.
2. See Bert A. Rockman, Andrew Rudalevige, and Colin Campbell, eds., *The Obama Presidency: Appraisals and Prospects* (Washington, DC: Sage/CQ Press, 2012).
3. Colin Campbell and Bert A. Rockman, eds., *The George Bush Presidency: First Appraisals* (Chatham, NJ: Chatham House, 1991).

The Obama Legacy

CHAPTER ONE

Obama's "Long Sweep" and the Fragility of Legacy

Andrew Rudalevige and Bert A. Rockman

On January 10, 2017, ten days before leaving office, President Barack Obama delivered a farewell address to the nation. Standing before a crowd of supporters packed into McCormick Place in Chicago, the city where he had launched his political career, Obama said that while "the work of democracy has always been hard"—sometimes even "bloody"—"the long sweep of America has been defined by forward motion, a constant widening of our founding creed to embrace all and not just some."[1]

The president clearly saw his own eight years in office as part of America's forward motion, and he argued that the vision of hope and change he campaigned on in 2008 had become real. "If I had told you eight years ago that America would reverse a great recession, reboot our auto industry, and unleash the longest stretch of job creation in our history," the president riffed, "if I had told you that we would open up a new chapter with the Cuban people, shut down Iran's nuclear weapons program without firing a shot, take out the mastermind of 9/11—if I had told you that we would win marriage equality, and secure the right to health insurance for another 20 million of our fellow citizens, if I had told you all that, you might have said our sights were set a little too high. But that's what we did. That's what *you* did."

But reciting his version of his administration's accomplishments was not the only point of the speech. In fact, Obama's main theme was "the state of our democracy," a clear reference to the divisive polarization, insult, and spite that had been central to the 2016 campaign. "The future should be ours," the president warned. "But that potential will only be realized if . . . our politics better reflects the decency of our people. Only if all of us, regardless of party affiliation or particular interests, help restore the sense of common purpose that we so badly need right now." Democracy does not require "uniformity," he went on, but it does "require a basic sense of solidarity—the idea that for all our outward differences, we're all in this together; that we rise or fall as one." In this, Obama echoed his speech from more than a dozen years earlier that had, in some ways, made him president in the first place—the keynote address to the 2004 Democratic National Convention that had so abruptly thrust him into the national spotlight. Obama had famously opined then, "There's not a liberal America and a conservative America; there's the United States of America. There's not a black America and white America and Latino America and Asian America; there's the United States of America."[2]

The message of unity was as appealing in 2017 as it had been in 2004. But the very nature of the farewell address suggested that this ideal—and the ways Obama could serve as its messenger—had become a more conflicted proposition in the intervening years. To be sure, the idea of taking an end-of-administration opportunity to bequeath one's hard-won wisdom to the public was hardly new. George Washington began the tradition in 1796 (and said some similar things: "Citizens by birth or choice of a common country, . . . the name of American, which belongs to you in your national capacity, must always exalt the just pride of patriotism more than any appellation derived from local discriminations").[3] Nor was it unusual in the television era to deliver that message as a live address. But doing so *not* from the Oval Office but in a large hall in front of a cheering, chanting audience *was* new. And presenting such a serious disquisition (when *read*) at what looked and sounded like a campaign pep rally meant that Obama's eloquent paean to unity was delivered in a manner that would divide. It nearly guaranteed that thoughts meant to reach out past his more fervent supporters would be ignored by everyone *except* those supporters; that a message meant to distill the lessons of a president would be heard as the platform of a candidate. After all, if Obama supported something, a substantial proportion of the population knew they should reflexively oppose it.

That was where the United States of America found itself in 2017. And fairly or not, that too was part of the Obama legacy.

The Obama Trajectory

This book seeks to explicate that legacy in all its complexity—to explore the policies, politics, polarization, and polemics that marked the Obama years and that will, in turn, be shaped by them for years to come. It is complete in itself, although it can be read in conjunction with an earlier volume we published in 2012 on the president's first term.[4] Obama's prepresidential career is also well chronicled elsewhere, in a collection of magisterial biographies published between 2010 and 2017, not to mention in his own (absorbing but rather more strategic) writings.[5]

As a starting point for the essays that follow, it is worth sketching a high-altitude view of the Obama administration—with special attention to the electorate that brought Obama to office and, with some diminution, reelected him in 2012. Obama left the White House with just under 60 percent of the public approving of his performance as president, a number that had been rising steadily as the 2016 campaign progressed: a sort of buyers' remorse, perhaps, given how widely both presidential nominees were disliked. But even so, the 60 percent figure was somewhat artificial, since Obama's average approval rating for his presidency as a whole was 48 percent. His public standing had declined from his inaugural honeymoon to about 50 percent by August 2009 and more or less stayed there, with the occasional dip (in late summer 2011 and late fall 2014) or spike (surrounding the 2012 election and in 2016).[6]

Thus, for much of his term, Obama was a 50–50 president in a 50–50 nation, and his polarized popularity seemed peculiarly personalized. Democrats lost hundreds of seats at all levels of government from 2010 to 2016, and despite Obama's strong endorsement, Hillary Rodham Clinton could not rebuild his coalition to become a pioneering president in her own right. The result was Donald Trump's election and a unified Republican government in 2017—a confluence of events that, as discussed throughout this volume, posed an immense challenge to Obama's policy legacy.

But if that seemed an improbable outcome even in November 2016, it was dramatically harder to foresee in November 2008. The scenes in Grant Park on the Chicago lakefront were instructive. That site had a history of hosting large crowds chanting about Democratic candidates—but while in 1968 those chants had been profanity laden and interrupted by tear gas, in 2008 the chorus was reverential, the tears welling up from joy and not a little disbelief. Barack Hussein Obama—half white, half black, and all political outsider, with a background that stretched from the Kansas heartland to the Hawaiian Islands to Indonesia to Chicago—had been elected president of the United States.

The process had hardly been foreordained, notwithstanding that evening's rose-colored glow. Yet the campaign had lived up to Obama's own words in Iowa nearly a year earlier, as "the moment when the improbable beat what Washington always said was inevitable."[7] (Namely, the same thing as in 2016: a Hillary Clinton presidency.)

In June 2008, after a protracted primary season, Clinton conceded the Democratic nomination and endorsed Obama. In November Obama carried 28 states and won 365 electoral votes. He received 52.9 percent of the popular vote overall, and his nearly 54 percent of the two-party vote was more than that won by any candidate for two decades and the highest vote share for any Democratic candidate since passage of the Voting Rights Act in 1964. He won "red" states such as Indiana and made inroads into the solid Republican South, winning Virginia and North Carolina as well as Florida. As Gerald Pomper notes, Obama "did not build his victory by simply focusing on the [Democrats'] customary areas of strength. The party did gain popular vote share in its reliable states of the Northeast, upper Midwest, and Pacific Coast. But the largest gains came in areas in which Democrats previously had underperformed."[8] Likewise, in Congress, Democrats netted 21 new seats in the House, building on the 30 they had gained in 2006; their majority now stood at 257 of 435 seats. In the Senate, 8 additional Democrats were elected, and Republican Arlen Specter of Pennsylvania later become a Democrat, ultimately making that caucus 60 (of 100 seats) strong.[9] In late 2008 the Gallup Corporation could rate only four states as "solid Republican," with one more leaning that way.[10] The country seemed united behind dramatic change.

Obama's popularity was widespread in the 2008 general election, as he won votes across a range of income and education levels. Notably, he won among both those who had never attended college (by a 54 to 44 percent margin) and those with postgraduate degrees (58 to 40 percent), and he won more than 40 percent of votes among the "white working class."[11] That was a five-point gain over 2004 Democratic nominee John Kerry, and indeed, Obama outpaced Kerry across most demographics. He won a massive margin among blacks (greater than 95 percent, compared with Kerry's 88 percent) and Latinos (67 percent versus 53 percent). Obama's 43 percent of the white vote overall exceeded Kerry's too, and it was better than that of any Democratic nominee since 1980, with the exception of Bill Clinton.[12] Obama even won a majority of white voters younger than 30 years of age. In fact, an excellent predictor of an Obama vote (or not) in 2008 was the voter's age. Overall, two-thirds of those under 30 voted for Obama (versus 54 percent for Kerry), as did just over half of those in their forties; however, less than 45 percent of those over 65 (and just 40 percent of white senior citizens) voted for Obama.[13] His popularity with younger voters provided his entire margin of victory in states such as Indiana and North Carolina.[14]

Even so, the result was hardly foreordained. Obama may have inspired young voters with his vision of "hope and change" and even organized them with creative usages of new technologies, but the polls indicated a tight race; indeed, by early September, Republican nominee John McCain seemed to be moving into the lead.[15] As political scientist James Campbell put it, "with values considerations on McCain's side of the scale and performance considerations on Obama's side, the election was on course to be narrowly decided—but then all hell broke loose."[16] The financial crisis and subsequent stock market meltdown turned a close race into a referendum on Republican stewardship of the economy. Bush's—and even more so, McCain's—response seemed halting and indecisive. Coming on top of the wars in Iraq and Afghanistan, the failed response to Hurricane Katrina, and other issues, "it was one crisis too many."[17]

By Election Day, more than 70 percent of voters disapproved of the job President Bush was doing. More than nine in ten Americans felt that the country was "on the wrong track."[18] Americans did, indeed, hope for change. Obama—frequently likened to (and, on the cover of *Time* magazine, literally pictured as) Franklin Delano Roosevelt—was ready to deliver some.

Even without the pressing emergencies, Democrats had a backlog of legislation they hoped to enact. The party had been in the minority in both chambers for most of a decade, from 1995 through 2006,[19] during which time their substantive preferences had been largely rejected. What followed was not a "new New Deal," but it did constitute consequential policy change. An expansion of the state children's health insurance program (SCHIP) and an equal-pay law to address gender-related disparities passed rapidly, followed by the administration's economic stimulus proposal: the $787 billion American Recovery and Reinvestment Act (ARRA). The ARRA also included important changes to K–12 education policy (the "Race to the Top" initiative) and student loan reform as well as expanded funding for clean energy technology and support for scientific research. All this happened within a month after the president took office. By the end of 2010, the most comprehensive changes to Wall Street regulation since the Great Depression and an ambitious extension of health care coverage to 30 million uninsured Americans—inevitably termed "Obamacare"—had also become law. The "Don't Ask, Don't Tell" policy restricting LGBT service in the US military had been repealed and the "New START" nuclear treaty with Russia ratified. And two new Supreme Court justices had been confirmed.[20]

Still, this success came at a price. As noted earlier, much of Obama's original appeal flowed from his compelling calls for national unity. The Obama brand of governance was grounded in being post-, or in fact supra-, partisan. Obama invited Republican lawmakers to the White House to watch the Super Bowl and even gave them fresh-baked cookies. But whatever he may have intended, when push came to shove, his legislation was passed nearly entirely by Democratic votes. In part, this was because of organized efforts within the GOP to deny the patina of bipartisanship to anything and everything Obama proposed. Indeed, on January 20, 2009, the very night of Obama's inauguration, Republican congressional leaders decided over dinner to "challenge every single bill" and show "united and unyielding opposition to the president's economic policies."[21] More systematic research shows that in the modern era, presidential leadership is inherently polarizing, driving opposition-party legislators away from bills they might otherwise support.[22] And while presidents claim the mantle of unity, their rhetoric (and, for that matter, the substance of their agendas) normally hews to their partisan base, not to the centrist ideal point of public opinion.[23]

In any case, GOP opposition, however strategic, was overdetermined: it flowed from political (some would add racial) calculations, but also from clear disagreements over policy specifics. And if the Obama victory and Democratic sweep of 2008 were attributable mainly to dissatisfaction with the incumbent administration—and, more proximately, to the financial meltdown—that did not represent a mandate for the party's entire policy agenda.

This eagerly ignored (by Democrats) disjunction was made clear just two years later when the Republican Party achieved widespread congressional, gubernatorial, and state legislative victories, flipping the American electoral map from solid blue to deep red. The GOP netted sixty-three House districts—a "shellacking," as Obama himself put it. It was the largest midterm swing in the House since 1938 and enough for a 49-vote majority in that chamber. Meanwhile, the Democratic majority in the Senate was cut down to 53 votes.

The results were shocking, yet not surprising: the Democrats' moment of good feelings had been a matter of circumstances that cut against the deeper grain of partisan identification. Some fifty House districts had supported McCain in 2008 yet elected Democratic representatives; most of those returned to GOP hands in 2010. If war and economic crisis had spurred an opportunity for revolutionary change, two years later, continued pessimism about the economy and loud doubts about Democratic priorities had stalemated those hopes.

For a time, Obama continued to reach across party lines, at least rhetorically. In his 2011 State of the Union address, the president reminded legislators that voters "have determined that governing will now be a shared responsibility between parties. . . . We will move forward together, or not at all—for the challenges we face are bigger than party, and bigger than politics." But in fact, politics proved stronger than the lackluster economic growth, huge budget deficits, and looming debt limit—not to mention troops on multiple fronts still embroiled in conflict abroad—that still burdened the nation. The now-Republican 112th House fervently, but fruitlessly, attempted to undo the work of the 111th House. The Senate was less fervent but accomplished even less, perhaps in line with Minority Leader Mitch McConnell's admission that "the single most important thing we want to achieve is for President Obama to be a one-term president."[24] Obama was reduced to scolding Congress for its work ethic and his opponents for their unwillingness to compromise.

As efforts to forge a "grand bargain" over the budget fell apart and the statutory limit on government borrowing approached, negotiations largely consisted of accusatory rhetoric leaked to the press.[25] Affirmative answers to Gallup's longstanding question about trust in government plummeted—in October 2011 only 10 percent of respondents answered that they expected Washington to do "the right thing" all or most of the time, just half the number expressing that expectation the year before. Obama's job approval rating dipped well below 50 percent, but approval of Congress skidded to a remarkable 9 percent—so low that veteran congressman John Dingell (first elected to the House in 1955) snarled, "I think that pedophiles would do better."[26] By the fall of 2011, and with his eyes on reelection, Obama effectively washed his hands of legislative change and proclaimed, "We can't wait for an increasingly dysfunctional Congress to do its job."[27] He began an aggressive push toward administrative action instead. That pattern would last, at least intermittently, until the end of his term.

The 2012 election pitted Obama against former Massachusetts governor and businessman Willard "Mitt" Romney. Romney was the clear Republican front-runner from the outset, but he had to traverse a long primary season during which partisan loyalists auditioned an array of mostly undistinguished competitors in a search for doctrinal purity.[28] Romney even found himself traveling to Las Vegas to seek the endorsement of one Donald J. Trump, whose main political credentials at the time were his prominent trafficking of "birther" falsehoods, claiming that Obama had not been born in the United States.[29] Meanwhile, Obama's campaign used the time to define Romney's image among the electorate as a whole. As Franklin Foer later observed, "Obama ran two of the most populist campaigns in recent American history," and in 2012 Democrats hammered home selected highlights of Romney's successful business career to paint him "as the cold-hearted representative of plutocracy."[30] Endless ads claimed that his firms had shut down American factories and moved jobs overseas. Perhaps the Obama campaign's most effective spot juxtaposed scenes of shuttered Rust Belt industrial sites with audio of Romney warbling "America the Beautiful" ("Oh beautiful, for spacious skies") at a campaign rally.

Romney didn't help himself by declaring to a roomful of wealthy donors that "there are 47 percent of the people who will vote for the president no matter what . . . 47 percent who are with [Obama], who are dependent upon government, who believe that they are victims, . . . who believe that they are entitled to health care, to food, to housing, to you-name-it. . . . My job is . . . not to worry about those people. I'll never convince them that they should take personal responsibility and care for their lives."[31] Ultimately, the American National Election Studies found that only 20 percent of voters thought the statement "[Romney] really cares about people like you" described the governor "extremely well" or "very well," whereas more than 40 percent thought the same was true of Obama.[32] The Obama bumper-sticker message was simple: as Vice President Joe Biden crowed at the Democratic National Convention, "Osama bin Laden is dead, and General Motors is alive!"

Four years after the start of the Great Recession, a large majority of voters continued to name the economy as the nation's most important problem (the runner-up, health care, was cited by just 18 percent of respondents).[33] Thus, Romney touted his business acumen and hammered the Obama administration for the country's stagnant economic growth and slow decline in the jobless rate. "Obama isn't working," his campaign stressed over pictures of unemployment lines, borrowing a phrase used against the British Labour Party in the 1979 election.[34]

Exit polls suggested that voters agreed with Romney's diagnosis, but not with his causal logic.[35] Nearly 80 percent of voters thought the economy remained "not so good" or worse, and less than 40 percent thought things were "getting better." Even so, fewer than four in ten voters blamed Obama for this state of affairs; more than half still assigned culpability to George W. Bush. Thus, while gross domestic product (GDP) growth hovered around the same level that had brought defeat to past incumbent presidents, Obama got the benefit of the doubt.[36] Just about half the electorate was at least "satisfied" with the administration as a whole (a quarter was "enthusiastic"), and 54 percent approved of President Obama personally.

That, in turn, translated into reelection. On November 6 Obama captured just over 51 percent of the popular vote to Romney's 47 percent (the two-party vote split was 52–48 percent). Obama became the first Democratic candidate to capture a majority of the national vote in consecutive elections since Franklin Roosevelt, but also the first president since FDR whose reelection margin declined from his original mandate.[37] Obama tallied a healthy 332 electoral votes, but this too reflected a decline from 2008, as Indiana and North Carolina returned to the Republican column.

It was, in effect, a base election. Turnout declined overall from 2008: 58.6 percent of eligible voters cast a ballot in 2012, compared with 61.6 percent four years prior.[38] However, Obama was able to turn out constituencies—notably, young and African American voters—who had undergirded his 2008 win but had been conspicuously absent from the polls in 2010. Indeed, for the first time, black turnout (as a percentage) was estimated to be higher than white turnout.[39] As usual, young people voted at a dramatically lower rate than their elders, and although their turnout dropped off slightly from 2008, this was less pronounced in heavily contested battleground states, where young voters once again provided a crucial margin of victory for Obama.[40] He won the under-30 vote by a 60–40 spread nationally.

However, if age remained one cleavage—and again, Obama's share of the vote declined as voters' age increased—so did race. Obama had won young white voters in 2008, but he lost them in 2012, when even white voters under 20 supported Romney (by about a ten-point spread). Two-thirds of white voters over age 70 gave Romney their vote.[41] But race was inextricable from other variables, too. Obama won a large majority of voters at the lowest and highest ends of the educational spectrum and at lower income levels. Also, Romney won majorities among whites in all educational categories and at all income levels except for upper-middle-class voters earning between $125,000 and $175,000. Thus, one systematic review of the election results concluded that "much of the relationship between social class—in this case, measured by income and education—and the vote is conditioned by race and ethnicity."[42]

Another divide might be defined on an axis of social traditionalism or conservatism. Obama won the votes of more than 80 percent of unmarried women but just 40 percent of those who were married, a margin that held up when controlling for race.[43] Likewise, four in five voters who identified themselves as gay, lesbian, or bisexual favored Obama.[44] Religiosity served as another proxy. Those who identified as Christian broke heavily for Romney, a margin that rose sharply among those claiming weekly church attendance. Protestants in that category (about half the total) voted Republican at a 70–29 clip; Catholics, 57–42. Not surprisingly, white "born again" voters were even more likely to choose Romney (78–21 percent). Those professing Protestant faith with less regular church attendance still voted for Romney, but by a smaller margin (55–44 percent), while similarly situated Catholics voted for Obama 56–42. More than 70 percent of Jewish voters did as well. At the same time, 43 percent of those polled had no stated religious affiliation and thus were not in any of these categories. This more secular group voted 58–39 for Obama.[45]

Finally, as a glance at an electoral map of the United States makes clear, there are large differences in voting patterns between urban and rural America. Since 2000, though, the mix of "red" and "blue" at the state level has changed far less than at the county level, as even cities in red states turned blue. Indeed, the only major cities that voted Republican in 2012 were Fort Worth, Oklahoma City, Phoenix (barely), and Salt Lake City.[46] In rural areas, splits were discernible between what one group of scholars called "recreational counties" and counties still dominated by agriculture; residents of the former (many of them transplants) supported Obama at significantly higher levels than those in the latter.[47] Both these developments suggested a burgeoning divide between the "new" and "old" economies that would return in force in arguments over globalization and cosmopolitanism during the 2016 campaign.[48]

Obama's success, then, rested more heavily than before on an alliance of generally urban, educated, and secular whites and a coalition of what we might call identities of color. To be sure, he never promoted a message grounded in that sort of division: the "one America" theme never wavered, from the 2004 convention speech to his farewell address. Indeed, Obama invested not just message but also time and money in reaching out to rural white counties—if only with the aim of limiting losses there to margins that could be overcome by urban vote totals.[49]

In 2012—unlike in 2016—that worked. Meanwhile, Democrats held on to their Senate majority, despite having to defend the gains they had made in 2006. Senate majority leader Harry Reid's caucus even picked up two seats for a majority of fifty-five (including two independents who caucused with them). Democrats picked up eight seats in the House, too, but that was not nearly enough to regain a majority: the chamber remained Republican by a 234–201 margin. The status quo would hold for two more years.

Polarization and a "Snarly Sort of Politics"

Looking forward to what would be a defining decade, Richard Neustadt predicted in 1960 that "we face a snarly sort of politics, with party followings more likely to be brittle and unstable than secure."[50] The general "snarl" was an excellent description of Obama's second term, but the problem was the reverse of Neustadt's prediction: by then, party followings were rather *too* secure. Even when both parties agreed on the substance of an issue, they could not agree on solutions that would enable effective action. And the problem extended into the partisan public empowered by primary politics. There had been "yellow dog" Democrats in the Reconstruction South—those who said they would vote for a yellow dog rather than a Republican—but in the 2012 Republican presidential primaries, one Ohio voter upped the ante. A Newt Gingrich supporter, he was asked whether he could support Mitt Romney instead. "Look," he said, "I'd vote for a dead dog instead of Obama."[51]

Obama, of course, was not the first president to prompt highly polarized responses from the public. While George W. Bush famously claimed to be a "uniter, not a divider," political scientist Gary Jacobson found just the opposite: Bush prompted "the widest partisan divisions among ordinary Americans regarding any . . . president since the advent of scientific survey research on such questions more than sixty years ago."[52] Until late in his presidency, Bush attracted support from close to 90 percent of Republican respondents, while only one out of five Democratic identifiers approved of the job he was doing for large periods of his presidency.[53] The gap between partisans, then, was often more than 70 percentage points—a record until Obama took office. Jacobson's follow-up research on the Obama presidency showed the same shape of polarized approval, though of course, one that flipped the party labels at each pole.[54] By November 2014, just 9 percent of Republicans endorsed Obama's performance, versus 78 percent of Democrats. On his last day in office, those figures were 14 percent and 95 percent, respectively —a gap of more than 80 percentage points.[55]

This reflected a certain hardening of the nation's political arteries. And such rigidity did not bode well for the grand bargains that remained necessary in so many aspects of American governance. Obama had compiled a list of issues that he thought could attract bipartisan support, including immigration reform, systematic tax reform, infrastructure investments, and the long-overdue revamping of the No Child Left Behind education law,[56] confident that his reelection would break the partisan "fever" and the attendant gridlock. "My hope is," he said, that once "the goal of beating Obama doesn't make much sense because I'm not running again, that we can start getting some cooperation again."[57] But that hope was largely misplaced. After some immediate success in dismantling the "fiscal cliff" of items postponed until after the election, little happened. Worse, in October 2013 efforts by a cadre of Republicans to defund the Affordable Care Act (ACA) led to the first full-blown government shutdown since the mid-1990s. Shortly thereafter, the ACA became a political liability of a different sort, as its bungled rollout— including problems with the healthcare.gov website that served as the law's online portal—prompted the president to unilaterally change deadlines and conditions in the law.[58] By his 2014 State of the Union address, Obama was again talking about using administrative tools—his "pen and his phone"—to make changes, rather than relying on legislative action.

This would lead to a "year of action," Obama said, but the action with the greatest influence on Capitol Hill that year was at the ballot box. In the 2014 midterm elections, Democrats suffered heavy losses as the GOP won numerous state legislative chambers and its biggest congressional majorities since the 1920s. Republicans added 13 new House seats, to claim a majority of 247; more crucially, they netted 9 seats in the Senate to take a slim majority there as well. Political scientists argued that the election served as a nationalized referendum on the economy and on Obama's presidency.[59] If so, it was a markedly negative judgment compared with two years earlier. At just 36 percent, voter turnout nationally was extremely low—down several percentage points from 2010 and, in fact, the lowest since 1942. This in itself was an advantage for the GOP, since demographic groups affiliated with the Democratic Party are generally the least reliable voters in low-turnout elections.

Since the 2010 election, Obama's agenda had been stymied; after 2014, dueling agendas were on show. The last two years of his term were marked largely by foreign policy and administrative initiatives—notably, to advance environmental regulations—even as domestic politics grew more unsettled and unsettling.

There was good news, too. By the end of 2015, the unemployment rate had dropped to 5 percent for the first time since the pre-recession spring of 2008. (During the 2012 campaign, Romney had promised that his policies would reduce unemployment below 6 percent by the end of 2016.) The Federal Reserve raised its interbank borrowing rate for the first time since mid-2006, albeit to just 0.5 percent.

Meanwhile, for LGBT Americans, civil liberties were on the rise. The culmination of a series of legal victories came with the Supreme Court decision in *Obergefell v. Hodges*, which found that state bans of same-sex marriage violated the Constitution's guarantee of equal protection of the law. Obama, a relatively late but enthusiastic convert to the cause, illuminated the White House with rainbow lights mimicking the LGBT rights flag. Still, the Court's decision hardly ended debate or division over the matter—prompting, for instance, some states to adopt new "religious liberty" laws.

And the American racial divide was also at the fore, from the fiftieth anniversary of 1965's "Bloody Sunday" march in Selma, Alabama, to the wave of Black Lives Matter protests over a series of well-publicized deaths of unarmed African American men at the hands of police officers. In June 2015 a young white supremacist killed nine black parishioners at evening prayer in South Carolina in the hope, he later said, of igniting a "race war." Obama eulogized the victims with one of the most memorable orations of his presidency, ending by breaking into song: "Amazing grace, how sweet the sound. . . ." This moment of uplift was temporary, though, with regard to both racial reconciliation and gun violence, which the president went on to deplore. The president had to eulogize a new group of victims in July 2016, when a heavily armed African American sniper killed five police officers and wounded nine others; Obama urged a long-term commitment to "forging consensus, and fighting cynicism, and finding the will to make change." But change came slowly and mass shootings far too frequently. What the FBI called "homegrown violent extremists" killed fourteen in San Bernardino, California, in December 2015 and forty-nine in an LGBT nightclub in Orlando, Florida, in June 2016.

Elsewhere, a far larger terrorist attack in Paris in November 2015 had upped the ante for American foreign policy in the Middle East. Obama had consistently opposed direct engagement in the Syrian civil war, despite the waves of refugees flooding out of the country and the administration's growing frustration with Russian involvement there. However, the administration began military operations against the so-called Islamic State terrorist group (known as ISIL or ISIS) in Iraq and Syria as early as 2014, using airpower and special operations missions. Obama's lawyers argued that this was legal under the post-9/11 Authorization for the Use of Military Force (AUMF), since ISIL had once been affiliated with al-Qaeda; others were far from convinced. Congress showed little interest in taking a stand on the matter, effectively giving Obama the flexibility to act as he wished in the region. He received extensive criticism for other unilateral initiatives in foreign policy, including a multilateral agreement to limit Iran's nuclear program, a global pact signed in Paris aimed at limiting global climate change, and the resumption of diplomatic relations with Cuba. But here too, legislators could not muster a consensus to force the administration to change its policies. Obama also continued to endorse the Trans-Pacific Partnership (TPP) free-trade pact, not least as a brake on China, even as the TPP became a punching bag in the 2016 campaign.

Obama's last year in office, and perhaps even the state of American politics, might best be summed up by an extraordinarily high-profile example of legislative obstruction. When Supreme Court justice Antonin Scalia died unexpectedly in February 2016, the importance of the vacancy, given the tight ideological balance of the Court, was crystal clear. Obama made what he saw as a conciliatory nomination, putting forward DC Circuit Court judge Merrick Garland, a 63-year-old centrist widely respected within the judiciary. Senate majority leader Mitch McConnell, backed by his caucus, refused even to hold committee hearings to consider Garland's nomination. The seat would remain open for close to a year, awaiting the results of the November election.

In short, polarization had reached the point where dereliction of institutional duty was an obvious choice—where, in fact, McConnell could call this "one of my proudest moments."[60] And why not? Substantively, and certainly politically, it worked.

The Conversation to Come

As even this brief summary makes clear, the presidency of Barack Obama will surely be regarded as both consequential and controversial. It will be considered a landmark if only for the president's multiracial background. But the crisis-racked period in which Obama took office, his ambitious responses to those crises, the subsequent substitution of administrative and rhetorical tactics for legislative achievement, the continued backdrop of terrorism, gun violence, racial tension, and changes in cultural mores, and arguments over globalization and immigration—often in disconcerting combination, and all capped by the surreal spectacle of the 2016 campaign (complete with Russian plots to disrupt the election)—meant not just complex policy debates but also strong reactions to them. Obama's critics on the right called him radical, dictatorial, and, quite literally, un-American. His critics on the left, however, wished he had taken far *more* radical stands on issues ranging from health care to entitlement reform to human rights. Obama himself never seemed to doubt his pragmatic course. History will have to judge whether that approach fulfilled the president's early promises of hope and change.

The chapters that follow provide an early but well-considered draft of that history. They illuminate the political and governance strategies that undergirded the Obama administration—strategies of the president and "all the president's men" (and women), as well as of his allies and adversaries in and out of elected office. In so doing, they provide both reference and touch point for the arguments that will continue for a long time to come.

The book continues with four chapters that explore the relationship between Obama's record and his leadership of public opinion, political parties, and particular segments of the mass public (especially African Americans and Latinos). Brandon Rottinghaus kicks off this section by examining the strategies employed by the Obama White House to influence public opinion. Rottinghaus notes that Obama's behavior reflects new political realities whereby presidents intensify the mobilization of their own constituency bases, given a shrinking middle ground and hardened partisan positions. As Rottinghaus observes, presidents used to "go public" on a national scale, but they now find it more useful to "go narrow" by focusing on their own political bases. Thus, it is no surprise that the most recent presidents have been perceived as the most polarizing.

Julia R. Azari also considers polarization in her examination of President Obama's role as a party leader. She notes the highly partisan circumstances that shaped Obama's ascendancy, his personalized appeal to rise above those circumstances, and the political hostility of his opponents as a consequence of his personal "celebrity." Obama may have hoped to transcend party, but as Azari observes, he focused on partisan Democratic audiences and on building, whether intentionally or not, a particular Democratic Party brand. His attention to cultural issues that appealed to an educated party constituency, and to structural issues of inequality rather than macroeconomic issues, mobilized new constituencies for the Democrats but simultaneously mobilized intense opposition and rendered Democratic candidates vulnerable in more conservative locales. Although Obama had little choice but to serve as a partisan leader, he did little to strengthen his party's political and organizational capabilities (in this, he was hardly alone among presidents). Azari concludes that "partisanship without parties has great potential to result in politics that is superficial and divisive and presidencies that are disruptive without transformation."

One of the Democrats' key constituencies, and certainly the party's most loyal, are African Americans. Alvin B. Tillery Jr.'s chapter traces Obama's tightrope walk in this regard. As the first US president of color, Obama carried high expectations and even higher aspirations, but to succeed politically, he needed to navigate a complicated political environment in which racial hostility toward him was a significant factor. The "age of Obama," in this sense, was paradoxical. Inevitably, expectations of Obama's capacity to create meaningful change outpaced his capabilities, and to some critics, his efforts to recognize the concerns of African Americans were at odds with his ability to do much about them. Obama referred more frequently to African Americans in his rhetoric than any prior president, his appointments to the executive branch and the courts were more diversified, and he often spoke of the contributions of civil rights pioneers and the work of succeeding generations. Yet, at the same time, African Americans as a group continued to suffer disproportionately from economic setbacks, from mistreatment in the criminal justice system, and from legal retrenchment eroding their influence at the ballot box.

Latinos are another critical Democratic constituency. As the fastest growing political constituency in the United States, their loyalty is crucial to electoral outcomes. The chapter by Angela Gutierrez, Angela X. Ocampo, and Matt A. Barreto discusses how Obama achieved historically high levels of support from this diverse community. That success was a result of both his actions and his adversaries. Partly, the unpopularity of the evolving Republican nativism and Mitt Romney's self-deportation rhetoric moved Latinos more firmly to Obama's side in 2012. However, Obama himself eased immigration anxieties via his Deferred Action for Childhood Arrivals (DACA) and Deferred Action for Parents of Americans (DAPA) initiatives, and over time, he adopted positions that were more favorable to the various Latino communities. His outreach to Cuba, for instance, made inroads with the traditionally Republican Cuban American population.

A second group of chapters deals with Obama's interactions with American governing institutions: the legislative branch, the wider executive branch, and the judiciary. In her chapter, Molly E. Reynolds analyzes the political context that shaped the often difficult relationship between the president and Congress. Democrats' loss of control of the House of Representatives for the last six years of Obama's presidency and the Senate for the final two years was crucial. The Obama years witnessed a pull of party so powerful that it promoted "oppositionism" even when agreement might have been possible. This resulted in the routine utilization of cloture votes in the Senate requiring a 60-vote majority; brinkmanship tactics over what had once been relatively straightforward budgetary and fiscal matters, including the infamous debt ceiling debacle of 2011; clashes over recess appointments; and bitterness over tactics used to delay or deter appointments more generally.

As Obama himself noted, it is preferable to go through the legislative process because its achievements are harder to undo. But when traditional legislative norms are undone, legislating itself becomes increasingly unlikely. Obama's frustration with Congress inevitably led him to use executive means to accomplish what he could not achieve through legislative means. This brings us to Sharece Thrower's chapter, which examines several dimensions of Obama's ability to manage the executive branch. The president's capacity in this regard is deeply affected by the extent of interbranch conflict or cooperation. For instance, Obama's executive branch nominees were frequently obstructed by Senate Republicans, leading to lengthy vacancies within agencies and on regulatory commissions. Frustrated Democrats, while still in the majority, ultimately eliminated the 60-vote requirement for executive appointments. This enabled Obama to fill vacancies by simple majority vote, but of course, it allowed his successor to do the same. If "politicization" of the executive agencies fails, presidents often turn to centralized White House decision-making, and Obama did just that. His centralization strategy, featuring a large toolbox of unilateral directives aimed at controlling executive branch policy-making, was somewhat more successful but not unconditionally so.

David A. Yalof's chapter on Obama and the courts argues that despite critical claims that Obama wished to bypass the political process to achieve his policy goals, the president was, in fact, reluctant to use the courts to achieve political ends. Similar to Obama's ability to manage the executive branch, his success with judicial appointments was also a function of comity with the Senate or, in this case, its absence. The end of the appointments filibuster in late 2013 gave Obama a single year to move many of his stalled nominees through the confirmation process. Otherwise, the dilatory tactics utilized by the Republican minority to prevent action on many of Obama's judicial nominees were quite effective. And when that Republican minority became the Senate majority after the 2014 midterm elections, its tactics escalated into virtually complete denial of consideration—all the way up to the Supreme Court. Ironically, despite Obama's desire to contest policy issues within the (more obviously) political branches, the fate of many administration initiatives wound up resting on decisions made by the courts. Here, Obama's most prominent legislative legacy, the Affordable Care Act, was largely sustained.

The last section of the book turns to policy-making—domestic, administrative, and international. Alyssa Julian and John D. Graham's chapter on Obama's domestic agenda begins with the basic supposition—well supported in the book over-all—that "under conditions of partisan polarization, . . . the opposing leadership in Congress seeks to deny the president legislative successes." The authors then speculate about counterfactual tactics Obama might have used in various policy areas, exploring how different political approaches to policy in the first term might have affected the second term as well. The Republican gains in 2010, 2014, and 2016 had an immense impact: why did Obama's party suffer so much during this time? Julian and Graham suggest that despite the economy's recovery, Obama failed to obtain sufficient political benefit from it, given its slow progression and the absence of gains for low-income and working-class Americans. Perhaps even more important was Obama's health care reforms. Although Obamacare became more popular once it was genuinely threatened in the post-Obama era, it helped drive the Republican resurgence during Obama's presidency. Given the extreme party polarization and congressional Republicans' unyielding opposition to Obama's policy agenda, the authors conclude that Obama might have been better off choosing executive pathways to achieve his ends, thus protecting the congressional majorities that accompanied him into office.

Andrew Rudalevige's chapter shares many assumptions with Julian and Graham's. But it arrives at different conclusions about the efficacy of taking unilateral action and governing through executive means, regardless of how tempting that may be. Mainly, as Obama himself noted during the transition between his presidency and the incoming Trump administration, it is easier to undo what was easier to do in the first place. As Rudalevige concludes, at least in the domestic arena, "administrative action is inherently fragile compared to legislative change," especially when relying on the statutory interpretation of past laws to achieve policy results. The main question that remains unanswered is whether the "consensus and coalition building [necessary] to achieve permanent reform" was possible in the political environment over which Obama presided.

David Patrick Houghton's chapter title, "Don't Do Stupid Shit," is extracted from a statement Obama made later in his presidency as a guideline for US foreign policy. The Obama years both reflected and extended a series of American interventions that turned sour or inconclusive while incurring high costs. Over time, Obama's instincts became those of a realist and a skeptic when it came to interventions with unclear objectives and potentially limitless commitments. For those with an impulse to involve the United States anywhere and everywhere, especially with hard power, Obama's attraction to minimalism seemed feckless. But to Obama himself and to mass opinion (the "public mood") more generally, the simple if less soaring ideal was to avoid doing stupid, or stupider, stuff.

The book concludes with Bert A. Rockman's chapter on Obama's leadership style, dealing with policy matters in concert with a broader template of presidential decision-making. Rockman notes several elements that influenced both the style and the legacy of Barack Obama as a leader. First, of course, was the highly constraining political environment that affected the last six years of his presidency. Second is the fact that leadership style is influenced by one's predecessor, if only as a form of market differentiation from what came before; one's leadership style is thus inherently destined to have little if any legacy, except to the extent that nostalgia sets in. Bookended by George W. Bush and Donald J. Trump, Obama's deportment and prudence now seem to be overshadowed by his successor's volatile behavior. Even so, leadership style is influenced by events and time. Seeking consensus bargaining and institutional modesty at the outset, Obama became much more skeptical and even cynical of his opponents' motives as his influence became progressively weaker throughout his administration.

Rockman assesses three components—character, temperament, and intellect—in comparing Obama with some other presidents from the modern era. He sees Obama as a president of high character, cautious temperament, and considerable intellect. None of these admirable traits guaranteed good outcomes, but they were more likely than not to promote them—or at least to avoid bad outcomes. Ultimately, Rockman concludes that Obama is best characterized as a progressive president who sought to govern, not always successfully, through conservative means.

What Came Next

Any volume on the Obama legacy must acknowledge his immediate successor's efforts to dismantle it. Early in his presidency, Donald Trump betrayed little interest in the substance of most policy debates, nor in the consistency between his Twitter feed and his campaign pledges. However, the exception that proved those rules was the lodestar of his most fervent supporters: if Obama, then bad. As longtime chronicler of the presidency Peter Baker observed in June 2017, "Whether out of personal animus, political calculation, philosophical disagreement or a conviction that the last president damaged the country, Mr. Trump has made it clear that if it has Mr. Obama's name on it, he would just as soon erase it from the national hard drive."[61] Some policies will be harder to erase than others, but those that were enshrined in administrative directive rather than law are correspondingly more fragile.

At Obama's final press conference, he painted a picture of progress on the economic, domestic, and diplomatic fronts. "By so many measures our country is stronger and more prosperous than it was when we started," said the outgoing president. "It is a situation that I'm proud to leave for my successor."[62] That successor took a rather different view. At *his* first press conference as president, Trump said, "To be honest, I inherited a mess—it's a mess—at home and abroad. A mess. Jobs are pouring out of the country. . . . Mass instability overseas, no matter where you look. The Middle East, a disaster. North Korea—we'll take care of it, folks. We're going to take care of it all. I just want to let you know I inherited a mess."[63]

Which brings us full circle: part of the legacy of the Obama years is a disconcerting difficulty in enforcing Daniel Patrick Moynihan's wise precept that people are entitled to their own opinions, but not their own facts. The rest of this volume provides the latter, so as to help elucidate the former.

Notes

1. "President Obama's Farewell Address," Office of the White House Press Secretary, January 10, 2017, https://obamawhitehouse.archives.gov/farewell.
2. "Transcript: Illinois Senate Candidate Barack Obama," *Washington Post*, July 27, 2004, http://www.washingtonpost.com/wp-dyn/articles/A19751-2004Jul27.html.
3. George Washington, "Farewell Address," September 19, 1796, http://www.presidency.ucsb.edu/ws/index.php?pid=65539&st=&st1.
4. Bert A. Rockman, Andrew Rudalevige, and Colin Campbell, eds., *The Obama Presidency: Appraisals and Prospects* (Washington, DC: CQ Press/Sage, 2012).
5. See especially David Maraniss, *Barack Obama: The Story* (New York: Simon & Schuster, 2012); David Remnick, *The Bridge: The Life and Rise of Barack Obama* (New York: Picador, 2010); David J. Garrow, *Rising Star: The Making of Barack Obama* (New York: William Morrow, 2017). Obama's own books on his prepresidential life include the partly fictionalized *Dreams from My Father: A Story of Race and Inheritance*, reprint ed. (New York: Broadway, 2004) and the policy-oriented *The Audacity of Hope: Thoughts on Reclaiming the American Dream* (New York: Crown, 2006).
6. Figures are from Gallup, "Presidential Job Approval Center," http://www.gallup.com/interactives/185273/presidential-job-approval-center.aspx.
7. Speech from January 3, 2008, quoted in Richard Wolffe, *Renegade: The Making of a President*, paperback ed. (New York: Three Rivers Press, 2010), 102. For a useful discussion of just how far from inevitable the Obama victory was, see chapter 4 of Wolffe's account, as well as Michael Nelson, ed., *The Elections of 2008* (Washington, DC: CQ Press, 2010).
8. Gerald M. Pomper, "The Presidential Election," in Nelson, *Elections of 2008*, 49.
9. That figure was not official until July 2009, when an extended recount process confirmed Al Franken's victory over incumbent Norm Coleman in Minnesota, and it lasted only until January 2010, when Republican Scott Brown won a special election to replace Senator Edward Kennedy, the legendary Massachusetts Democrat who had died in August 2009. Arlen Specter switched parties in April 2009 (he would go on to lose a Democratic primary in 2010).
10. Gallup, "State of the States: Political Party Affiliation," January 28, 2009, http://www.gallup.com/poll/114016/state-states-political-party-affiliation.aspx (accessed June 28, 2017). The states so identified were Idaho, Utah, Wyoming, and Alaska, with Nebraska "leaning Republican." Twenty-nine states were rated "solid Democratic" and six as leaning Democratic, leaving ten as competitive.
11. Figures are from 2008 exit polls, as reported in Pomper, "Presidential Election," 53–55. See also Paul R. Abramson, John H. Aldrich, and David W. Rohde, *Change and Continuity in the 2008 and 2010 Elections* (Washington, DC: CQ Press, 2012), chap. 5.
12. See Abramson et al., *Change and Continuity in 2008 and 2010*, figure 5-1, which shows a very similar result using American National Election Studies (ANES) data.

While exit poll data showed Obama winning 67 percent of the Latino vote and 95 percent of the black vote, ANES figures were 75 percent and 99 percent, respectively.

13. American National Election Studies data for 2008, cited in Patrick Fisher, *Demographic Gaps in American Political Behavior* (Boulder, CO: Westview, 2014), 146; exit poll data in Pomper, "Presidential Election," table 3-2.

14. Fisher, *Demographic Gaps*, 146.

15. See the Real Clear Politics "poll of polls" for September 7–16, 2008, https://www.real clearpolitics.com/epolls/2008/president/us/general_election_mccain_vs_obama-225 .html.

16. James E. Campbell, "Political Forces on the Obama Presidency: From Elections to Governing," in Rockman et al., *Obama Presidency*, 79.

17. Ibid., 80.

18. See the *New York Times*/CBS poll results, https://www.nytimes.com/interactive/proj ects/documents/latest-new-york-times-cbs-news-poll#p=1 (accessed June 28, 2017).

19. The exception was the Senate in 2001–2002, after Senator Jim Jeffords's defection from the Republican caucus in late May 2001 gave the Democrats a narrow 50–49–1 margin.

20. For more details, see Molly Reynolds's chapter 6 in this volume and Barbara Sinclair, "Doing Big Things: Obama and the 111th Congress," in Rockman et al., *Obama Presidency.*

21. Robert Draper, *Do Not Ask What Good We Do* (New York: Free Press, 2012), xiv–xv.

22. Frances E. Lee, *Beyond Ideology: Politics, Principles, and Partisanship in the U.S. Senate* (Chicago: University of Chicago Press, 2009).

23. Applied specifically to the early Obama administration, see George C. Edwards III, *Overreach: Leadership in the Obama Presidency* (Princeton, NJ: Princeton University Press, 2012). More generally, on rhetoric, see B. Dan Wood, *The Myth of Presidential Representation* (New York: Cambridge University Press, 2009); Julia Azari, *Delivering the People's Message* (Ithaca, NY: Cornell University Press, 2014); James Druckman and Lawrence Jacobs, *Who Governs? Presidents, Public Opinion, and Manipulation* (Chicago: University of Chicago Press, 2015). On policy, see Matthew Eshbaugh-Soha and Brandon Rottinghaus, "Presidential Position-Taking and the Puzzle of Representation," *Presidential Studies Quarterly* 43 (March 2013): 1–15; Jeffrey E. Cohen, *The President's Legislative Policy Agenda* (New York: Cambridge University Press, 2012). Of course, some scholars doubt that public opinion is centrist to begin with. See, e.g., James E. Campbell, *Polarized* (Princeton, NJ: Princeton University Press, 2016); by contrast, see Morris J. Fiorina with Samuel Abrams and Jeremy Pope, *Culture Wars: The Myth of a Polarized America*, 3rd ed. (New York: Longman, 2010).

24. Quoted in (one of many places) Sean J. Miller, "Reid: McConnell Comment a 'Road to Nowhere,'" *The Hill,* November 3, 2010, http://thehill.com/blogs/ballot-box/sen ate-races/127517-reid-mcconnell-comment-a-road-to-nowhere.

25. See, generally, Andrew Rudalevige, "'A Majority Is the Best Repartee': Barack Obama and Congress, 2009–12," *Social Science Quarterly* 93 (December 2012): 1272–1294.

26. Quoted in Draper, *Do Not Ask What Good We Do*, 282.

27. Barack Obama, "Remarks in Las Vegas," October 24, 2011, http://www.presidency .ucsb.edu/ws/index.php?pid=96941&st=&st1.

28. See John Sides and Lynn Vavreck, *The Gamble* (Princeton, NJ: Princeton University Press, 2013).

29. Mark Leibovich, "Over the Top Setting, Run of the Mill Endorsement," *New York Times*, February 3, 2012, A14, http://www.nytimes.com/2012/02/03/us/politics /trump-endorses-romney-in-las-vegas.html?_r=0.

30. Franklin Foer, "What's Wrong with the Democrats?" *Atlantic*, July–August 2017, 52.

31. "Full Transcript of the Mitt Romney Secret Video," *Mother Jones*, September 19, 2012, http://www.motherjones.com/politics/2012/09/full-transcript-mitt-romney-secret -video/. The event was held on May 17, 2012, but the covert video was not made public until mid-September. Romney also noted—accurately—that 47 percent of Americans do not pay income taxes.

32. Twenty percent thought the statement described Obama "extremely well," and 22 percent thought it described him "very well." For Romney, the figures were 6 percent and 14 percent, respectively. See Paul R. Abramson, John H. Aldrich, Brad T. Gomez, and David W. Rohde, *Change and Continuity in the 2012 Elections* (Washington, DC: Sage/CQ Press, 2015), 148.

33. Ibid., 153.

34. It must be conceded that "Labour isn't working" was a better pun.

35. Exit poll results from CNN, "President: Full Results," http://www.cnn.com/election /2012/results/race/president/.

36. James E. Campbell, "The Miserable Presidential Election of 2012: A First Party–Term Incumbent Survives," *Forum* 10, 4 (2012): 20–28.

37. For FDR, that applied only to his third and fourth terms; his 1936 reelection far outpaced his 1932 totals.

38. See Michael McDonald, "National General Election VEP Turnout Rates, 1789– Present," United States Elections Project, University of Florida, http://www.electproj ect.org/national-1789-present. Note that "VEP" is a percentage of those eligible to vote. It is somewhat higher and more accurate than the commonly reported "VAP" (turnout as a percentage of the voting-age population), since not everyone old enough to vote is legally allowed to do so.

39. Abramson et al., *Change and Continuity in 2012*, 95.

40. Ibid., 98.

41. Ibid., 118.

42. Ibid., 123.

43. Ibid., 120.

44. Ibid., 121.

45. Ibid., 118–119.

46. Josh Kron, "Red State, Blue City," *Atlantic*, November 30, 2012, https://www.theat lantic.com/politics/archive/2012/11/red-state-blue-city-how-the-urban-rural-divide -is-splitting-america/265686/.

47. Dante J. Scala, Kenneth M. Johnson, and Luke T. Rogers, "Red Rural, Blue Rural? Presidential Voting Patterns in a Changing Rural America," *Political Geography* 48 (2015): 108–118.

48. See, e.g., the discussion of the "open" versus "closed" electorate in Andrew Rudalevige, "The Meaning of the 2016 Election: The President as Minority Leader," in *The Elections of 2016*, ed. Michael Nelson (Washington, DC: Sage/CQ Press, 2017).

49. See Foer, "What's Wrong with the Democrats?"

50. Richard E. Neustadt, *Presidential Power* (New York: Wiley, 1960), 188.

51. Jim Rutenberg and Jeff Zeleny, "Romney and Santorum Court Blue-Collar Voters in Ohio," *New York Times*, March 6, 2012.

52. Gary C. Jacobson, "George W. Bush, Polarization, and the War in Iraq," in *The George W. Bush Legacy*, ed. Bert Rockman, Colin Campbell, and Andrew Rudalevige (Washington, DC: CQ Press/Sage, 2008), 62. More generally, see Gary C. Jacobson, *A Divider, Not a Uniter: George W. Bush and the American People*, 2nd ed. (New York: Pearson, 2010).

53. Jacobson, "George W. Bush, Polarization, and the War in Iraq," 71.

54. Gary C. Jacobson, "Polarization, Public Opinion, and the Presidency: The Obama and Anti-Obama Coalitions," in Rockman et al., *Obama Presidency*, 113.

55. Gallup surveys of November 3–9, 2014, and January 17–19, 2017. Among independents, Obama's approval rating was at 36 percent in November 2014 but 61 percent in January 2017.

56. Barack Obama, interview with the *Des Moines Register*, November 29, 2012.

57. Byron Tau, "Obama: Republican 'Fever' Will Break after the Election," *Politico*, June 1, 2012, http://www.politico.com/blogs/politico44/2012/06/obama-republican-fever -will-break-after-the-election-125059.

58. See, e.g., Steven Brill, *America's Bitter Pill* (New York: Random House, 2015).

59. Gary C. Jacobson, "Obama and Nationalized Electoral Politics in the 2014 Midterm," *Political Science Quarterly* 130, 1 (2015): 1–25.

60. Mike DeBonis, "Will Hillary Clinton Stick with Merrick Garland if She Wins the White House?" *PowerPost* (blog), *Washington Post*, August 16, 2016, https://www .washingtonpost.com/news/powerpost/wp/2016/08/16/the-forgotten-nominee-mer rick-garlands-fate-rests-on-forces-beyond-his-control/?utm_term=.89720f038c76.

61. Peter Baker, "The Anti-Legacy," *New York Times*, June 25, 2017, Sunday Review sec., 1.

62. "Transcript: Obama's End-of-Year News Conference on Syria, Russian Hacking and More," *Washington Post*, December 16, 2016, https://www.washingtonpost.com/new /post-politics/wp/2016/12/16/transcript-obamas-end-of-year-news-conference-on -syria-russian-hacking-and-more/?utm_term=.f80ad86b3eab.

63. Donald J. Trump, "Remarks by President Trump in Press Conference," February 16, 2017, https://www.whitehouse.gov/the-press-office/2017/02/16/remarks-president -trump-press-conference.

CHAPTER TWO

Hope, Change, or Neither?
Reassessing Obama's Leadership of Public Opinion

Brandon Rottinghaus

As Barack Obama strode onto the stage on election night 2008 and steadied himself behind the podium in Grant Park along Chicago's lakefront, millions of people looked on. The president-elect noted his place in history but also the challenges facing his just-born administration. "I will always be honest with you about the challenges we face," he said. He vowed:

> I will listen to you, especially when we disagree. And, above all, I will ask you to join in the work of remaking this nation, the only way it's been done in America for 221 years—block by block, brick by brick, calloused hand by calloused hand. What began 21 months ago in the depths of winter cannot end on this autumn night. This victory alone is not the change we seek. It is only the chance for us to make that change. And that cannot happen if we go back to the way things were.

He ended by proclaiming, "In this country, we rise or fall as one nation, as one people. Let's resist the temptation to fall back on the same partisanship and pettiness and immaturity that has poisoned our politics for so long."[1] For a president with vaunted eloquence and a personal connection to the American voters, a vision of political and policy change seemed momentarily within reach.

Indeed, the White House trusted implicitly in the president's ability to inspire America and lead public opinion. Chief political strategist David Axelrod noted, "I don't think there's been a President since Kennedy whose ability to move issues and people through a speech has been comparable."[2] An Obama presidency would not be satisfied with mere leadership of public opinion. He sought policy leadership, too—indeed, transformational leadership garnering large coalitions looking past race and beyond partisan politics to a spirit of unity toward common goals.

Such optimism was needed. As President Obama entered office, the nation faced the prospect of crippling financial collapse (unemployment figures at 9 percent, wage stagnation, a burst housing bubble) and was involved in two intractable and polarizing foreign conflicts (in Iraq and Afghanistan). Crises in Egypt, Syria, and Ukraine loomed on the horizon. The president also had ambitious substantive goals destined to generate opposition. His signature health care policy was the cornerstone of his campaign and a bellwether of his ability to accomplish big policy changes. He also promised significant reforms of Wall Street to establish rules and regulations that would encourage financial stability and ensure consumer protection. A stimulus package (the American Recovery and Reinvestment Act) was in the offing to boost local infrastructure spending and to extend benefits to Americans caught up in the economic downturn.

Two years after his inauguration, the challenges of communicating with a polarized public—and of achieving large-scale substantive change—were clear. President Obama said:

> I think that one thing that I do need to constantly remind myself and my team is, it's not enough just to build the better mousetrap. People don't automatically come beating to your door. We've got to sell it, we've got to reach out to the other side and where possible persuade. And I think there are times, there's no doubt about it, where, you know, I think we have not been successful in going out there and letting people know what it is that we are trying to do and why this is the right direction.[3]

The challenge of public leadership was real. Former congressman Mickey Edwards was candid when asked how effectively the president used the bully pulpit. He answered: "Poorly. To put it bluntly, the president talks too much. Barack Obama has a power rare among political leaders—he can move audiences with the strength of his words. But it is a resource that diminishes with over-use."[4] Obama himself referenced the elephant in the room: how could a president with such tremendous persuasive skills fail to shift public opinion in favor of his policies? "It's funny—when I ran, everybody said, well he can give a good speech but can he actually manage the job?" the president noted. "And in my first two years, I think the notion was, 'Well, he's been juggling and managing a lot of stuff, but where's the story that tells us where he's going?' And I think that was a legitimate criticism."[5] As a deflated press secretary Jay Carney lamented in 2013, "There are limits to the powers of the bully pulpit on every issue."[6]

That is true for all presidents, of course: even effective communicators have trouble connecting to the public, and most blame "bad communication" rather than their policies. Each presidential administration experiences highs and lows in bridging the public divide, uniting the nation through effective communication, and shifting that support to a positive policy agenda. So how does Obama fit into that pattern? This chapter examines his public presidency with an eye toward understanding the challenges and opportunities facing Obama and how his administration handled its leadership role during its eight years in power. In all presidencies, the scope of presidential leadership is conditional on the president's environment, the makeup of the political process, and the messenger himself. When there is a disconnect among these elements, the White House is often unable to achieve its leadership objectives. Was the Obama White House able to harness its extensive network of political affiliates in leading public opinion? The monumental changes in the media and in the political environment during President Obama's time in office put his optimistic "yes we can" strategy to the test.

Political Context, Partisan Climate, and Presidential Limits

There has been evolving debate about how (or whether) presidents lead public opinion. Richard Neustadt identifies the phenomenon of "president-as-teacher" (as a resource in the "power to persuade"), whereby "a president concerned for leeway inside government must try to shape the thoughts of men outside."[7] Amplifying this assertion, Samuel Kernell argues that presidential efforts to persuade the mass public are directed at persuading members of Congress who are "on the fence."[8] Critiquing presidents' ability to accomplish this, George Edwards suggests that presidents are unable to lead public opinion because of a fragmented media and a polarized public, a disease clearly afflicting the Obama White House.[9] But, contesting Edwards's assertion, Brandice Canes-Wrone finds that presidential appeals to the public about domestic and foreign policy expenditures lead to public-supported spending in the next budget cycle.[10] Elsewhere, I argue that presidents are conditionally successful in leading public opinion and have some effect on members of Congress.[11] Jeffrey Cohen augments the idea of "going public" and argues that "presidents now go narrow; that is, they focus their public activities on building support in their party base, some interest groups, and select localities" while pursuing a persuasion strategy for wavering members of Congress.[12] Dan Wood also claims that partisanship in presidential politics is the norm because of incentives to respond to partisan electorates, challenging the myth that presidents are broadly representative of the public.[13]

Not surprisingly, the Obama White House had its work cut out for it in terms of achieving the same connection to the American public the candidate had enjoyed during the campaign. Recent scholarship has found that the mass public is not inclined to follow the president in most circumstances, primarily because the audience is more partisan than it was before and because the media are less likely to cover the president in general,[14] to cover the president positively,[15] or both.[16] Although presidents continue to dominate news coverage coming out of Washington, this coverage has become increasingly negative, with the media criticizing presidents in nearly every instance, except when the nation is at war.[17] In addition, there are fewer cross-pressured members of Congress with whom the president can bargain. Although President Obama had a unified government for his first two years in office, bitter partisanship remained, and a boomerang effect of ideological extremism (in both parties) reacted to his governing strategy.

Why is this the case? Individual partisans who don't even know one another fear one another. More than half (55 percent) of self-identified Democrats and just about half (49 percent) of Republicans say the other party makes them "afraid." These findings are even more pronounced among those who are highly engaged in politics. Among those who volunteer for or donate to campaigns or who vote regularly, 70 percent of Democrats and 62 percent of Republicans are "afraid" of the other party. Pew polls also posed "thermometer" questions, asking respondents to rate individuals on a scale of 0 (coldest feelings) to 100 (warmest feelings). They found that "Republicans and Democrats give very low ratings to the people in the opposing party. Democrats give Republicans a mean rating of 31—far lower than the average ratings for five other groups on the thermometer, including military personnel and elected officials."[18] Polarization and partisanship have trickled down to the state level as well, where three-quarters of the states are controlled by either Republicans or Democrats. Like their national colleagues, state Democrats have raised taxes, pushed for education and infrastructure investment, and backed the Medicaid expansion enabled by the Affordable Care Act (aka "Obamacare"). Republicans have cut taxes, pushed social issues, and balked at expanding Medicaid through Obamacare.[19]

Given the limits of the White House's reach, the fragmented media, and a polarized public, the Obama White House quickly tucked and transitioned its campaign apparatus from persuading voters to communicating to Americans. Obama, like all presidents, had to be opportunistic as he fought for space in the public sphere and attempted to pierce public discussion on policy issues. Presidents must accurately assess the potential for obtaining support, and they must exploit opportunities by using specific tactics at the proper moment.[20] Changing circumstances call for altered strategies, a lesson that any White House must learn quickly or risk policy stasis.

In reacting to the environment, five elements of the Obama administration's distinctive public communications strategy can be identified: (1) populism through popular culture, (2) strategic avoidance of mainstream media outlets, (3) reflexive partisanship, (4) persuading the persuaded (preaching to those in the front pew), and (5) using unilateral power as leverage in leading public opinion.

Populism through Popular Culture

President Obama and host Zach Galifianakis had this conversation on comedy website Funny or Die's "Between Two Ferns" in March 2014:

> OBAMA: Well, first of all, I think it's fair to say that I wouldn't be with you here today if I didn't have something to plug. Have you heard of the Affordable Care Act?
>
> GALIFIANAKIS: Oh yeah, I heard about that, that's the thing that doesn't work. Why would you get the guy that created the Zune to make your website?
>
> OBAMA: Health-care-dot-gov works great now and millions of Americans have already gotten health insurance plans and what we want is for people to know that you can get affordable health care and most young Americans, right now they're not covered and the truth is they can get coverage all for what it costs to pay your cell phone bill.
>
> GALIFIANAKIS: Is this what they mean by drones?[21]

Squaring off in an adversarial but joking manner with comedian Zach Galifianakis, President Obama pitched the importance of Americans signing up for health care coverage as prescribed by his signature law. That bit, according to the White House, "drew more young people to sign up for health care than any other pitch," with more than 19,000 people visiting healthcare.gov within hours of the episode's release.[22] These activities, along with the use of social media and digital media across other platforms, made it easier to communicate with a wider segment of the American people and encourage their greater participation in government.[23] Candidate Obama's use of technology had been critical to his election, and the White House hoped to capture lightning in a bottle and use those same techniques to communicate while in office. Using social and digital media allowed the president to send a personalized political message to targeted groups that were likely to be receptive.[24]

Before 2000, sitting presidents rarely appeared on popular entertainment venues, except for Richard Nixon's brief appearance on *Laugh-In* and Bill Clinton's saxophone rendition of Elvis's "Heartbreak Hotel" on Arsenio Hall's late-night talk show. But Barack and Michelle Obama were "more conversant in popular culture than any other couple that has occupied the White House."[25] This tactic played to the president's strength at a time when the political impact of social media had reached an apex. The president's ability to communicate with young voters made this tactic attractive and effective. As campaigning and governing bled together over the years, image, commination, and persuasion seamlessly blended. Candidate Obama had used these tactics to demonstrate his appeal and intelligence when he appeared on the *Tonight Show* and *Saturday Night Live* during the 2008 campaign. As president, these platforms allowed him to communicate in indirect ways and say things he might not have said in traditional "presidential" settings, such as using comedian Keegan-Michael Key (part of the comedy duo Key & Peele) as his "anger translator."[26]

These platforms also allowed the White House to diversify its message to targeted audiences. To encourage younger Americans to acquire health insurance under Obamacare, the White House created a series of humorous GIFs for BuzzFeed featuring Vice President Joe Biden.[27] The president also gave an extended interview to comedian Marc Maron on his *WTF* podcast (taped in Maron's Los Angeles garage), where the president spoke openly about race, mental illness, and police violence. The president also granted interviews to websites such as Zillow for housing news and WebMD for health care news. Obama even joined Jimmy Fallon on his late-night talk show to "slow jam" the news in 2012 and to sing-speak some campaign talking points about his legacy, his policy accomplishments, and his observations on the 2016 election.[28] From his "mic-drop" at the White House correspondents' dinner in 2016 to an appearance on *Running Wild with Bear Grylls*, a reality TV adventure show, the president was able to command the stage in a way that set a high bar for his successors.

Significant alteration of the media environment made this possible. The audience reachable by social media or digital formats had expanded rapidly, especially among younger people, providing opportunities for the White House to exploit those dynamics. In 2013 the Pew Research Center found that the vast majority of Americans got their news in digital format (82 percent on a computer, 54 percent on a mobile device).[29] By 2016, 62 percent of Americans got their news on a social networking site, led by Facebook and Twitter. Younger Americans (aged 18–29) were more likely to get news from Instagram, while adults (aged 30–49) were most likely to get their news from LinkedIn.[30] As Obama's senior adviser and longtime communications strategist Dan Pfeiffer noted, "It used to be that Ronald Reagan or, to a lesser extent Bill Clinton could [simply] give a national address. We don't have that option. We have to go where the public is."[31] The nation's first "internet president" established an Office of Digital Strategy to harness the collective cross-platform capability of blogs, Twitter feeds, Facebook, Flickr, and other formats. Obama's Twitter feed had 62 million followers, his Facebook page accumulated 45 million likes, and his internet interviews routinely yielded tens of thousands, sometimes even millions, of votes on questions posed to the audience. In addition, the Obama campaign's operation-cum-volunteer network, Organizing for America, had a list of 13 million email and 4 million cell phone contacts.[32]

Likewise, as attention to politics waned and the mass public became less attentive to the president, the Obama White House attempted to harness alternative means of communicating with the public. It had been shown that attention to daytime talk shows was positively associated with respondents' ability to correctly identify which candidate in the 1992 presidential race supported several different policies.[33] Moreover, consumption of entertainment-based programs and late-night comedy programs had been associated with better recognition of campaign events in the 2004 presidential primaries.[34] Beyond the campaign context, Matthew Baum found that people who were exposed to "soft news" programming paid more attention to certain international crises.[35] This was true even among those who did not follow international affairs in general.

"Soft news" is not a valid replacement for "hard news"; nor would presidents want entertainment to take the place of factual information about politics or policy. Indeed, there may be trade-offs. Exposure to "new media" is weakly and inconsistently related to voters' learning about politics.[36] Some studies point to a negative relationship between exposure to soft or "infotainment" news and political knowledge.[37] Although Obama's use of the media was effective at targeting unique audiences, these types of appearances may have unknowingly diminished the regal nature of the office and, ironically, contributed to the decline of the president's persuasive capacity as a political leader and policy expert. Comedian David Spade joked, "I realize Woodrow Wilson went on *Dancing with the Stars* once. But what president is doing reality shows? It just seems weird to me."[38] The line between reality and fiction may be so blurry that the factual record is compromised, and future presidents may see a shift in persuasion techniques. President Obama was lambasted by Republicans for his media appearances, some suggesting that it cheapened the lofty status of the presidency.[39] But the small seed planted by the Obama administration has grown into a full-blown topiary during the Trump administration, with a president who relies on his crowded Twitter feed to unite his supporters and excoriate his enemies.

Strategic Avoidance

Why would a president with vaunted communication skills and charismatic, climactic performances on big stages avoid the media? Direct delivery methods abound in a post–broadcast television world, and the Obama administration was successful at navigating these trends, setting the standard for future presidents. Obama himself lamented the "balkanized" state of the American news media—splintered by ideology, focused on entertainment, and fact-check challenged. When it came to granting interviews, one scholar noted in 2016 that Obama "very often favor[ed] media that target particular slices of the electorate that are largely aligned with him already: left-leaning comedians, bloggers, YouTubers and podcasters. He [was] more reluctant to submit to questioning by mainstream news outlets and conservative publications that would push back harder on issues on which his opponents disagree[d] with him."[40] Finding a common, baseline set of facts can be a challenge in this new information age. Controlling the message by targeting specialized media pathways or direct avenues of communication has largely supplanted attempts to control the mainstream media.

Evidence of a reluctance to engage with the mainstream media can take several

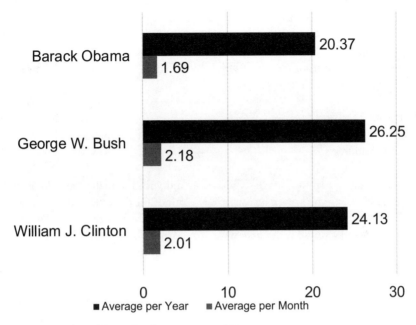

Fig. 2.1. Presidential Press Conferences, 1993–2017

forms. One prominent form is the decline in formal press conferences. As figure 2.1 shows, President Obama held fewer press conferences than either of his two predecessors. Ironically, press conferences were originally televised by the White House because of the fear that reporters were not fully relaying the president's message and the hope that the president could more readily and persuasively convey his own thoughts to the public.[41] As televised press conferences became routine, these events were transformed into "high-risk performances," and the White House looked for ways to "meet the press" without holding a press conference. This is not surprising because, over time, journalists have become less deferential when questioning the president, while their "directness" has increased.[42] The steady (but not linear) decline of the average number of press conferences illustrates this trend.

Presidents in the last few decades have been significantly less likely to speak formally from the White House, choosing more informal settings instead. Ronald Reagan gave a record number of speeches from behind the Resolute Desk in the Oval Office: twenty-nine. Bill Clinton broke into televised programming to address the nation live three times, but Presidents George W. Bush and Obama did so only twice each (for Obama, to address the oil spill in the Gulf of Mexico and to announce the end of combat operations in Iraq).[43] The Oval Office speech, in particular, is thought to be too stilted in its orientation and too uncomfortable for presidents who are used to delivering speeches on the stump. Aides to President Obama called it an "argument from the '80s" that a televised speech could command a majority audience on any given night. Presidents' farewell speeches are traditionally delivered from the Oval Office, but Obama gave his at a massive venue in Chicago in front of a large crowd.

Reflexive Partisanship

CNN correspondent John King said this about President Obama's 2013 State of the Union address:

> He's trying to mobilize his base, just as he did with the inaugural. Mobilizing his base because he knows he can't change minds on the other side. That's one of the problems. . . . But the state of Washington even as the President gets a new beginning tonight, the first State of the Union of his second term, it's still divided. Can the president change any minds on the other side? Probably not, which is why you gin up your own base.[44]

In a short but sharp speech to House Democrats at their annual policy retreat in 2016, President Obama largely abandoned hope that a bipartisan consensus could prevail in Washington. "Our policies rescued the economy from the worst crisis in generations," he exclaimed. "We have now seen the longest streak of private sector job creation in our history. Sometimes I get a little frustrated that we don't run back the tape to what the Republicans said back then. Every single one of the steps we took . . . they wanted to go in a different direction, claimed that our policies would crush jobs and destroy the economy. Do people remember that?"[45] The president chastised Republicans for a narrow focus centered on opposing his agenda—for instance, the Iran nonproliferation deal, voting rights reform, and efforts to combat climate change.[46] Election year partisan mobilization tactics aside, President Obama confronted a new partisan reality that was designed to solidify support among wavering Democrats and set the stage for the electoral battle to come.

Political scientists have charted the effects of rising partisanship for several years. Partisan publics are on the rise,[47] complicating the president's ability to lead mass public opinion.[48] A partisan presidency emerges, as modern presidents experience large "approval gaps" between copartisans and out-partisans.[49] Parties in Congress have become more polarized, complicating the president's ability to "reach across the aisle" and forge bipartisan consensus with the opposition party.[50] First, the mass public has not been inclined to follow the president in recent years because of reduced media coverage and the increasing negativity of the remaining coverage.[51] Second, partisanship has limited the audience for presidential persuasion. The public has also become much less moderate, and partisan identifiers are much more polarized.[52] For instance, Joseph Baufumi and Robert Shapiro argue that the strength of partisan voting is "more ideological and more issue based along liberal-conservative lines" than it has been in more than thirty years.[53] Even independents are partisans in "disguise."

President Obama attempted to raise the flag of bipartisanship after pushback on his health care policy and in advance of the 2010 midterm elections. Obama's speech to the GOP Issues Conference was an effort to show voters that the White House would "engage Republicans rather than govern in a partisan manner."[54] To open the speech, Obama highlighted the importance of "bipartisanship, not for its own sake, but to solve problems, that's what our constituents, the American people, need from us right now."[55] Stressing the need for vigorous debate in a democracy, the president noted, "I hope that the conversation we begin here doesn't end here; that we can continue our dialogue in the days ahead. It's important to me that we do so."[56] The *New York Times* reported the next day: "At a moment when the country is as polarized as ever, Mr. Obama traveled to a House Republican retreat on Friday to try to break through the partisan logjam that has helped stall his legislative agenda. What ensued was a lively, robust debate between a president and the opposition party that rarely happens in the scripted world of American politics."[57] The *Washington Post* reported that the meeting, though often tense, produced "bipartisan comity over the stark policy differences that separate the two sides."[58] This "post-partisan" promise melted quickly: "Two showdowns (one over shutting down the government, the other over defaulting on the country's debt) marked 2011. A grand bargain proved elusive. By the time 2012 rolled around, so too did another presidential campaign. Gridlock persevered."[59] With no way to change the culture of Washington, the White House turned to other mechanisms.

If presidents find themselves in a political environment that prevents them from negotiating directly with Congress or mobilizing or persuading the mass public, they may alter their leadership tactics. One option is for presidents to "facilitate" their leadership of public opinion by reflecting, clarifying, or intensifying the opinions of their existing supporters.[60] In this sense, the mass public is less relevant to the president than his partisans are. Jeffrey Cohen and Ken Collier note that "the president who rests his leadership on going public will be tempted to travel frequently, in search of sympathetic audiences and 'presidential images.'"[61] To use this strategy, "presidents need to tailor their messages to attract those most predisposed to support them, those with 'special interests,' instead of focusing on building support within broad coalitions."[62] Those individuals who are predisposed to approve of the president (those in his coalition) are more likely to support the president on policy issues.[63] Presidents often find success in leading the public preferences of political supporters as they try to rally their base.[64]

Other scholars have found that a "localized" strategy is effective when presidents are trying to motivate partisans. When a president visits a state, the president's partisans in that state become mobilized. This is where presidents "preach to the choir" rather than "convert the flock."[65] Earlier scholarship suggests that recent presidents have been unable to control public opinion from a national perspective, but newer research argues that, rather than focusing on national opinion leadership, presidents have begun a new trend of public opinion leadership: "going local."[66] Cohen argues that Kernell's "going public" model is obsolete and that presidents are now focusing on specific constituencies, interest groups, and localities (e.g., states, regions).[67] Presidents directly rally the partisan base by visiting states to mobilize partisan attitudes and encourage greater partisanship among members of Congress. Edwards notes that slippage in partisan support in Congress "forces the White House to adopt an activist orientation towards party leadership and sometimes devote as much effort to converting party members to support them as to mobilizing members of their party who already agree with them."[68] Cary Covington, J. M. Wrighton, and R. Kinney point out that the president can influence legislative outcomes through the party leadership's influence on rank-and-file members.[69] David Rohde and Meredith Barthelemy argue that "starting out with a substantial level of solid loyalty and shared preferences with his base in Congress is a much easier way for the president to begin a vote than by facing a sizeable opposition or large groups of undecided members with which he must negotiate to change preferences."[70] On presidential initiatives especially, presidential efforts are likely to cause greater cohesion within the party and greater conflict with the opposition party.[71]

Microtargeting: Preaching to Those in the Front Pew

In short, presidents find receptive audiences among partisan publics when attempting to build support for their policies, and when policies are associated with popular presidents, public support for those policies increases. "Leaning" partisans return to the partisan fold after being mobilized by partisan messages from elites.[72] Presidents borrow this partisan "rally" tactic from their campaigns.[73]

But presidents' increasingly local delivery also helps them break through the national media's filter more generally. Presidents are limited in their ability to "go public" on a national scale due to increased party polarization in the public and in Congress and due to the media's fragmentation into a plurality of options for news coverage. This has "forced president[s] to develop a more targeted approach to public leadership and communications."[74]

Thus, recent presidents have taken more trips in their first year in office and have been more likely to travel more frequently.[75] In addition to arguing for "going local," Cohen suggests that "presidents now go narrow; that is, they focus their public activities on building support in their party base, some interest groups, and select localities."[76] They eschew bargaining directly with Congress in favor of persuading constituencies to pressure Congress to enact the president's preferred agenda.

One payoff for presidents is that coverage of local visits (by both local and national media) is more positive than coverage of their national speeches.[77] Jeffrey

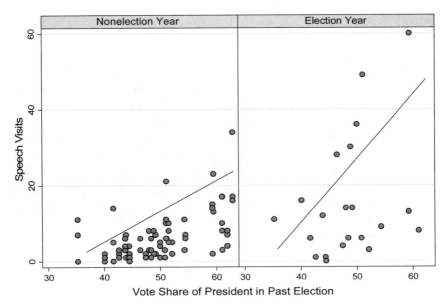

Fig. 2.2. Obama's Visits to States in Election and Nonelection Years and Vote Share in Past Election. *Note*: Line indicates linear fit of data points.

Cohen and Richard Powell determined that presidents can attain a modest boost (1 to 2 percentage points) in their approval rating at the state level when using a localized strategy.[78] Andrew Barrett and Jeffrey Peake concluded that the amount and tone of local coverage of George W. Bush's visits were dependent on presidential support in the community—the wider Bush's margin of victory in the prior election, the more positive the coverage was.[79] Similarly, using the National Annenberg Election Study (NAES), Cohen matched respondents' approval of the president with local newspaper coverage and found that positive coverage increased respondents' approval of the president, especially among those who lacked strong political predispositions.[80]

Obama conducted local assaults on a number of issues. In 2011 the automatic budget "sequestration" was set to cut $85 billion from defense and discretionary domestic programs unless the two sides could agree on a new budget. The president "hoped to spark a public revolt against Republicans over sequester-induced budget cuts," and in early February he did eight interviews with local television stations to outline the dramatic cuts that lay ahead if no action was taken.[81] To promote sign-ups for health insurance before a 2013 deadline, President Obama and his cabinet "hit nine of the top 10 cities with the highest concentration of the uninsured, while senior administration officials have held almost daily reporter conference calls in nearly a dozen states to challenge Republican governors who refuse to expand Medicaid."[82] This "going local" effect is not always successful, but it provides additional venues from which the White House can spread its message.

The president's targeting of supportive states bridged both his campaigns and his administration. Figure 2.2 graphs the number of visits during which Obama gave public speeches in election years (2008 and 2012) and nonelection years in those states with more than 10 Electoral College votes (eliminating smaller states), as well as the percentage of the two-party vote share the president received in the previous election. Both election and nonelection years reveal similar upward-scaling scatter-plot trends: Obama was more likely to visit states where he had gained a higher percentage of the two-party vote in the previous election.[83] The trends for election years are somewhat more amplified—that is, presidents visit states where they had greater electoral success in the previous election. This may be the best option a president has. Supporters are more likely to watch the president and to watch more of the president's speeches than are his opponents. For instance, supporters were 13 percent more likely to watch a State of the Union address than were members of the opposition party—up from 3 percent in the last three decades.[84]

President Obama focused his microtargeted legislative bargaining on his own partisans, especially when his party controlled at least one chamber of Congress. For example, Obama visited Montana in 2009:

> [The intent was to] put even more pressure on the rural state's senior senator, Max Baucus, and his panel to produce bipartisan health care legislation in just a month's time. The president's Friday town hall in a conservative suburb of Bozeman allowed him to speak directly to Baucus' constituents—the same people who are already giving the senator an angry earful during the congressional August recess. The White House supports Baucus' bipartisan effort in hopes of crafting a bill with broader appeal, although Baucus has been given just a month to finish the job.[85]

The president noted that not everybody "'agrees on the public option, but I just want . . . people to be informed about what the debate is about.'" Obama told the crowd of approximately 1,300 people, "'The only point I want to make about this is whether you're for or against a public option, just understand that the public option is not a government takeover of health insurance.'"[86] In this case, there is evidence (although speculative) that President Obama attempted to use the bully pulpit to mobilize support for his plan and indirectly persuade Senator Baucus to side with him on the Affordable Care Act, a cornerstone of the White House's legislative agenda.

Linking Unilateral Leverage and Public Opinion

Unilateral power—the use of executive orders, proclamations, memoranda, and other administrative rule-making—is not strictly a public tool, but the Obama White House transitioned it into a fulcrum to leverage public support for the president's agenda (see also chapters 7 and 10 in this volume). On October 24, 2011, President Obama avowed that, "without a doubt, the most urgent challenge that we face right now is getting our economy to grow faster and to create more jobs. We can't wait for an increasingly dysfunctional Congress to do its job. Where they won't act, I will."[87] Under the banner of "We Can't Wait," the White House trumpeted its ability to act without Congress by issuing unilateral orders to combat domestic violence in the federal workplace, implement a pilot program for workplace innovation, make it easier to refinance government-sponsored mortgages, make funding for Alzheimer's research more freely available, guarantee overtime pay for home-care workers, and dozens of others. Following up in his 2014 State of the Union address, President Obama called on Congress to raise the minimum wage. He told the legislators, "I'm eager to work with all of you, but America does not stand still—and neither will I. So wherever and whenever I can take steps without legislation to expand opportunity for more American families, that's what I'm going to do."[88] Soon after his address, he signed Executive Order 13658, raising the minimum wage for new federal service contracts.

Addressing this strategy of balancing unilateral command with public persuasion, the *Washington Post*'s Paul Waldman argued, "Obama seems to be creating a new version of the bully pulpit, one that takes executive action as the starting point but depends on Republicans playing their role." He continued, "Obama seized the agenda, saw his initiative dominating the front pages and television news discussions and sent Republicans in Congress scrambling to find some legislative barrier they can throw in his path."[89] The rhetorical and unilateral strategies may be unrelated when presidents pursue some policies in the hope of motivating the public to exert legislative pressure and pursue others without regard to Congress. For instance, in 2013, in the aftermath of a mass shooting at an elementary school in Connecticut, President Obama sought to separately "embrace a comprehensive plan to reduce gun violence that will call for major legislation to expand background checks for gun purchases and lay out 19 separate actions the president could take by invoking the power of his office."[90] Even in this case, though, there were ramifications for public opinion: Obama hoped to promote himself to the public as a strong leader on a key issue in the face of legislative gridlock.

Past presidents have used unilateral power as a means to control the bureaucracy and jump-start public policy. President Obama, by contrast, made broad use of unilateral power as a flashpoint to highlight inaction in Congress and simultaneously to promote his administration's agenda. This tactic marks a significant departure, moving from a sort of shadow policy-making to a public display of political might. The political friction and obstacles to bargaining have accelerated this tactic. President Obama quietly used unilateral power until 2011, when negotiations to raise the debt ceiling and implement a deficit reduction plan collapsed and the country risked defaulting on loans. A shift in tone and temperament altered the administration's course on unilateral power, and the president "proposed a jobs package and gave speeches urging lawmakers to 'pass this bill'—knowing they would not."[91] On foreign policy issues that the president could negotiate (but not finalize) alone, such as the Trans-Pacific Partnership or the deal with Iran to limit its nuclear capacity in return for a gradual lifting of economic sanctions, the president was able to set the table and force Congress to sit down to the meal. Presidents exploit their unilateral first-move advantage to gain policy leverage on Congress, and Obama did this on trade and economic policy.

Hope, Change, or Neither?

President Obama's historic victory in 2008 was replete with challenges and opportunities to lead public opinion and communicate with America in what he called a "post-racial" and "post-partisan" country. Did the White House overestimate its ability to lead public opinion? Edwards calls this phenomenon a classic presidential "overreach" and argues that it occurs when modern presidents propose "policies that lack substantial support in the pubic or Congress, expecting to create opportunities for change by persuading a majority of the public and the Congress to support their policies."[92] This risky behavior may exact a heavy toll on the ability to govern. One political historian concluded that the president's "unifying rhetoric has fallen short of achieving a broad sense of national unity"; in this telling, Obama became just another president who proved unable to bridge the political divide in this partisan era.[93] Indeed, the Obama White House, led by the first president of the social media age, pivoted to his base and spent much of his time speaking narrowly to Democratic supporters. This is a legacy of past recent presidents and a harbinger of future presidential leadership possibilities and limitations (see also chapter 3 in this volume).

Although the president is able to lead mass public opinion only sometimes and only in certain conditions, he can more easily communicate with and mobilize partisans. Indeed, empirical evidence suggests that inactive partisans rally when the president speaks,[94] and partisans are more attentive to the president's messages than to the messages of others,[95] especially in recent administrations.[96] Presidential approval is built on partisan approval,[97] and the stability of partisan approval is enhanced by partisan activity by the president.[98] This is a much narrower and more specific tactic than the broad use of the bully pulpit, but it may be the best recourse presidents have. These viewpoints imply a change in the way presidents lead public opinion and in their tactics to persuade Congress to support legislation. President

Obama found success in communicating to those who liked and trusted him, extending his campaign into the governing arena.

Even partisan leadership has its limits, however. In 2015 the president "went all-out" to convince two dozen House Democrats to vote for the Trans-Pacific Partnership, a trade deal involving twelve Pacific Rim countries to promote economic growth and innovation and to establish labor and environmental protections.[99] The deal was defeated in a 302–126 vote after a financial aid amendment to cushion the blow of unemployment to displaced workers failed to be added to the package. Despite party loyalty, "The president's pitch [was] met with widespread skepticism among Democrats who blame past trade deals for killing jobs and depressing wages for Americans in traditional manufacturing work."[100] It proved to be an enormous challenge to translate mobilization in campaigning into mobilization while governing. This is perhaps one of the enduring legacies of the Obama administration's communication strategies: even with a president who is skilled in various forms of public discourse, a changing media environment and a different context may dramatically limit his reach.

Is a mobilization strategy worth the resources involved, especially if the payoff in congressional support is modest? Several factors suggest that it is. First, presidents can appear to be active agents in the political system, demonstrating that they are responsive and can solve problems while looking presidential. Second, there may be a residual political gain for presidents as they travel around the country, increasing the president's (or his party's) visibility and potential votes in subsequent elections. If presidents can pull "double duty" and merge their political campaign activities with their legislative bargaining strategies, no presidential trip is wasted.[101] Third, bargaining one-on-one with legislators may not produce consistent results, as presidents' success may be dictated by their personal relationships and interpersonal skills. President Obama was reluctant to engage in this activity, but that may have been because it is often ineffective. Observers have suggested that the "Green Lantern" theory of presidential heroism—that is, to accomplish great things just by thinking them—is historically incorrect and grossly overstates presidents' ability to accomplish their goals.[102] Clearly, this use of presidential time is a trade-off between competing options. Such visits can backfire and anger wavering legislators.[103] Nevertheless, if presidents can move reluctant members of Congress, however modestly, with a partisan mobilization strategy, having this option in their toolbox can be a net positive. After all, in a closely divided nation, outcomes may rest on persuading those on the margins.

Likewise, digital technology may not be a savior of presidential leadership, but social media can be a "powerful tool for burnishing the president's image with a sometimes-fickle public." One of the most viewed White House YouTube videos showed Obama taking an unscheduled stroll near the White House, meeting some shocked tourists, and claiming, "The bear is loose." Communications director Dan

Pfeiffer argued that this appearance broke up the narrative of a besieged White House, noting, "Here we had this glimpse of the president as we all wished people could see him."[104] This narrowcasting also had the president giving more interviews to online-only organizations in each consecutive year of his presidency. "Our consideration is these platforms just reach so many people, we can't not play in that space," observed the White House deputy communications director.[105] Those "many people," however, may already be inclined to follow the president and his policies. Because of the shrinking middle, the rising number of inattentive citizens, and the robust influence of partisans in both parties, presidents tend to cater to their party base when it comes to messaging and policy-making. President Obama was not alone in this approach—President Bush before him and President Trump after him used the White House's communications apparatus to rev up partisan flair. This is a reasonable, but not inclusive, strategy when the electorate is divided. True independents are less likely to vote, but partisans always participate. Technology and partisanship have combined to influence presidential communication more than in any period since the rise of cable television.

The use of social media and appearances on popular shows may create a double-edged sword for any administration. What the White House gains in communication, it may lose in credibility. And the erosion of credibility may compromise the president's ability to make factual claims about the need for certain policies. The question is: is credibility moot in an era in which partisanship colors all politicians of the opposition party as "crooks and liars" and viewers discount every statement made by a president from the opposition party?[106] Command of media attention (credible or not) may be a salient factor in communicating as president—Donald Trump's media share allowed him and his issues to dominate the 2016 presidential election landscape, even though the coverage from some outlets was less positive than others.[107] These efforts may too narrowly target potential supporters in a way that alienates a broader segment of Americans, especially those who are not likely to agree with the president. Trump followed this traffic lane to the White House—the Republican base rallied around him to elect a Republican. As president, Trump has commanded little public goodwill and virtually no support among opposition Democrats. But while a complete conversion of negative opinion may be impossible, engendering less anger against the administration's policies may suffice for success in a partisan world.

Notes

1. Transcript: Barack Obama, November 7, 2008, http://edition.cnn.com/2008/POLI TICS/11/04/obama.transcript/.
2. George C. Edwards III, *Predicting the Presidency: The Potential of Persuasive Leadership* (Princeton, NJ: Princeton University Press, 2016), 16.

3. Kevin Liptak, "Six Times Obama Blamed the Message, not the Policy," December 21, 2015, http://www.cnn.com/2015/12/21/politics/obama-communications-strategy/index.html.

4. George C. Edwards III, *Overreach: Leadership in the Obama Presidency* (Princeton, NJ: Princeton University Press, 2012), 42.

5. Ibid., 184.

6. Edwards, *Predicting the Presidency*, 17.

7. Richard E. Neustadt, *Presidential Power and the Modern Presidents: The Politics of Leadership from Roosevelt to Reagan* (New York: Free Press, 1990), 89.

8. Samuel Kernell, *Going Public*, 4th ed. (Washington, DC: CQ Press, 2006).

9. George C. Edwards III, *On Deaf Ears: The Limits of the Bully Pulpit* (New Haven, CT: Yale University Press, 2006).

10. Brandice Canes-Wrone, *Who Leads Whom? Presidents, Policy and the Public* (Chicago: University of Chicago Press, 2006).

11. Brandon Rottinghaus, *The Provisional Pulpit: Modern Presidential Leadership of Public Opinion* (College Station: Texas A&M University Press, 2010). See also Matthew Eshbaugh-Soha and Jeffrey S. Peake, *Breaking through the Noise: Presidential Leadership, Public Opinion and the News Media* (Palo Alto, CA: Stanford University Press, 2011).

12. Jeffrey E. Cohen, *Going Local: Presidential Leadership in the Post-Broadcast Age* (New York: Cambridge University Press, 2010), 3.

13. B. Dan Wood, *The Myth of Presidential Representation* (New York: Cambridge University Press, 2009).

14. Matthew A. Baum and Samuel Kernell, "Has Cable Ended the Golden Age of Presidential Television?" *American Political Science Review* 93, 1 (1999): 99–114; Samuel Kernell and Laurie L. Rice, "Cable and the Partisan Polarization of the President's Audience," *Presidential Studies Quarterly* 41, 4 (2011): 693–711.

15. Stephen J. Farnsworth and S. Robert Lichter, *The Mediated Presidency: Television News and Presidential Governance* (Lanham, MD: Rowman & Littlefield, 2006).

16. Jeffrey E. Cohen, *The Presidency in the Era of 24-Hour News* (Princeton, NJ: Princeton University Press, 2008).

17. Ibid.

18. Pew Research Center, "Labor Unions Seen as Good for Workers, not U.S. Competitiveness," February 17, 2011, http://www.people-press.org/2016/06/22/partisanship-and-political-animosity-in-2016/l; Marc J. Hetherington, "Resurgent Mass Partisanship: The Role of Elite Polarization," *American Political Science Review* 95, 3 (2001): 619–631.

19. Dan Balz, "Red, Blue States Move in Opposite Directions in a New Era of Single-Party Control," *Washington Post*, December 28, 2014.

20. Edwards, *Predicting the Presidency*.

21. James Crugnale, "Obama and Zach Galifianakis' Full Transcript of 'Between Two Ferns,'" March 11, 2014, http://www.thewrap.com/read-obama-zach-galifianakis-full-transcript-two-ferns-interview/.

22. Karissah Thompson, "Obama Dropped the Mic. And Made the Pop Culture World See Politics as Cool," *Washington Post*, September 2, 2016.

23. Donald F. Kettl, "Obama's Stealth Revolution: Quietly Reshaping the Way Government Works," *Public Manager* 4, 1 (2009): 39–42.

24. Bruce Bimber, "Digital Media in the Obama Campaigns of 2008 and 2012: Adaptation to the Personalized Political Communication Environment," *Journal of Information Technology and Politics* 11, 20 (2014): 130–150.

25. Thompson, "Obama Dropped the Mic."

26. Jelesa M. Jones, "10 Times President Obama Did Pop Culture Right," *USA Today*, August 4, 2016.

27. "7 Reasons Why Vice President Biden Thinks You Should Get Covered by March 31," March 27, 2014, https://www.buzzfeed.com/thewhitehouse/7-reasons-why-vice-president-biden-thinks-you-shou-negi.

28. Spencer Kornhaber, "Obama's Last Slow Jam," *Atlantic*, June 10, 2016.

29. Kenneth Olmstead, March Jurkowitz, Amy Mitchell, and Jodi Enda, "How Americans Get TV News at Home," October 11, 2013, http://www.journalism.org/2013/10/11/how-americans-get-tv-news-at-home/.

30. Jeffrey Gottfried and Elisa Shearer, "News Use across Social Media Platforms 2016," May 26, 2016, http://www.journalism.org/2016/05/26/news-use-across-social-media-platforms-2016/.

31. Edwards, *Predicting the Presidency*, 168.

32. Ibid., 176.

33. Barry A. Hollander, "Late-Night Learning: Do Entertainment Programs Increase Political Campaign Knowledge for Young Viewers?" *Journal of Broadcasting and Electronic Media* 49, 1 (2006): 402–415.

34. Ibid.

35. Matthew A. Baum, "Sex, Lies and War: How Soft News Brings Foreign Policy to the Inattentive Public," *American Political Science Review* 96, 1 (2002): 91–109.

36. Hollander, "Late-Night Learning."

37. Jack M. McLeod, Zhongshi Guo, Katie Daily, Catherine A. Steele, Huiping Huang, Edward Horowitz, and Huailin Chen, "The Impact of Traditional and Nontraditional Media Forms in the 1992 Presidential Election," *Journalism and Mass Communication Quarterly* 73, 2 (1996): 401–416.

38. Matthew Rozsa, "How Obama Is Using Pop Culture to Transform the Oval Office," *Daily Dot*, January 3, 2016, http://www.dailydot.com/via/how-obama-pop-culture-change-oval-office/.

39. Juliet Eilperin, "Here's How the First President of the Social Media Age Has Chosen to Connect with Americans," *Washington Post*, May 26, 2015.

40. Callum Borchers, "Obama Is Right about a 'Balkanized' Media Problem," *Washington Post*, March 28, 2016.

41. Michael Grossman and Martha Joynt Kumar, *Portraying the President* (Baltimore: Johns Hopkins University Press, 1981).

42. Steven E. Clayman and John Heritage, "Questioning Presidents: Journalistic Deference and Adversarialness in the Press Conferences of U.S. Presidents Eisenhower and Reagan," *Journal of Communication* 52, 4 (2002): 749–776; Steven E. Clayman, Marc N. Elliott, John Heritage, and Laurie I. McDonald, "Historical Trends in Questioning Presidents, 1953–2000," *Presidential Studies Quarterly* 36, 4 (2006): 561–583.

43. Jackie Calmes, "Live from the Oval Office," *New York Times*, July 9, 2013.

44. John King, "Pre–State of the Union Coverage," transcript, CNN live event, February 12, 2013.

45. Lauren French, "Obama Rallies House Democrats with Fiery Partisan Speech," *Politico*, January 28, 2016, http://www.politico.com/story/2016/01/obama-speech-218369.
46. Ibid.
47. Alan Abramowitz and Kyle L. Saunders, "Ideological Realignment in the American Electorate," *Journal of Politics* 60, 4 (1998): 634–652; Joseph Baufumi and Robert Y. Shapiro, "A New Partisan Voter," *Journal of Politics* 71, 1 (2009): 1–24.
48. Edwards, *Overreach*.
49. Richard Skinner, "George W. Bush and the Partisan Presidency," *Political Science Quarterly* 123, 4 (2009): 605–622.
50. Frances E. Lee, *Beyond Ideology: Politics, Principles and Partisanship in the U.S. Senate* (Chicago: University of Chicago, 2009); David Rohde and Meredith Barthelemy, "The President and Congressional Parties in an Era of Polarization," in *The Oxford Handbook and the American Presidency*, ed. George C. Edwards III and William G. Howell (New York: Oxford University Press, 2010).
51. Edwards, *On Deaf Ears*.
52. Abramowitz and Saunders, "Ideological Realignment."
53. Baufumi and Shapiro, "New Partisan Voter," 1.
54. Carl Hulse and Jeff Zeleny, "Obama Continues Policy Outreach to Republicans," *New York Times*, February 3, 2010.
55. Barack Obama, "Remarks by the President at the GOP House Issues Conference," Baltimore, MD, January 29, 2010.
56. Ibid.
57. Peter Baker and Carl Hulse, "Off Script, Obama and the GOP Vent Politely," *New York Times*, January 30, 2010.
58. Paul Kane and Perry Bacon Jr., "Obama Goes to GOP's House for a Wide Open Exchange," *Washington Post*, January 30, 2010.
59. Sam Stein, "Obama's Post-Partisan Promise Mellows amid First Term Gridlock," *Huffington Post*, January 22, 2013, http://www.huffingtonpost.com/2013/01/21/obama-post-partisan-promise_n_2490700.html.
60. George C. Edwards III, *The Strategic Presidency: Persuasion and Opportunity in Presidential Leadership* (Princeton, NJ: Princeton University Press, 2009).
61. Jeffrey E. Cohen and Ken Collier, "Public Opinion: Reconceptualizing Going Public," in *Presidential Policymaking*, ed. Steven A. Shull (Armonk, NY: M. E. Sharpe, 1999), 121.
62. Edwards, *On Deaf Ears*, 287.
63. Reed L. Welch, "Was Reagan Really a Great Communicator? The Influence of Televised Addresses on Public Opinion," *Presidential Studies Quarterly* 33, 4 (2003): 853–876.
64. Kent Tedin, Brandon Rottinghaus, and Harrell Rodgers, "When the President Goes Public: The Consequences of Communication Mode for Opinion Change across Issue Types and Groups," *Political Research Quarterly* 64, 4 (2010): 506–519.
65. Amnon Cavari, "The Short-Term Effect of Going Public," *Political Research Quarterly* 66, 2 (2012): 336–351.
66. Cohen, *Presidency in the Era of 24-Hour News*; Cohen, *Going Local*; Matthew Eshbaugh-Soha, "Local Newspaper Coverage of the Presidency," *International Journal of Politics/Press* 13, 1 (2008): 103–119.

67. Cohen, *Going Local.*
68. Edwards, *On Deaf Ears*, 176.
69. Cary Covington, J. M. Wrighton, and R. Kinney, "A 'Presidency-Augmented' Model of Presidential Success on House Roll Call Votes," *American Journal of Political Science* 39, 4 (1995): 1001–1024.
70. Rohde and Barthelemy, "President and Congressional Parties."
71. Lee, *Beyond Ideology.*
72. Andrew Gelman and Gary King, "Why Are American Presidential Election Campaign Polls so Variable When Votes Are so Predictable?" *British Journal of Political Science* 23, 4 (1993): 409–451.
73. George C. Edwards III, *Governing by Campaigning: The Politics of the Bush Presidency* (New York: Pearson, 2007).
74. Ibid., 30.
75. Brendan J. Doherty, *The Rise of the Permanent Campaign* (Lawrence: University Press of Kansas, 2012).
76. Cohen, *Going Local*, 3.
77. Eshbaugh-Soha, "Local Newspaper Coverage of the Presidency"; Eshbaugh-Soha and Peake, *Breaking through the Noise.*
78. Jeffery E. Cohen and Richard J. Powell, "Building Public Support from the Grassroots Up: The Impact of Presidential Travel on State-Level Approval," *Presidential Studies Quarterly* 35, 1 (2006): 11–27.
79. Andrew W. Barrett and Jeffrey S. Peake, "When the President Comes to Town: Examining Local Newspaper Coverage of Domestic Presidential Travel," *American Politics Research* 35, 1 (2007): 3–31.
80. Cohen, *Going Local.*
81. Edwards, *Predicting the Presidency*, 59.
82. Jason Linkins, "Apparently It's Weird that the White House Asks Local Media to Inform Local People about Obamacare," *Huffington Post*, December 4, 2013, http://www.huffingtonpost.com/2013/11/26/obamacare-local-media_n_4345973.html.
83. Difference of means tests (assuming equal variance) between election years and non-election years reveal that the difference of means of visits for each population between election years is statistically different from 0 (−4.39, p>.001).
84. Kernell and Rice, "Cable and Partisan Polarization."
85. Matt Gouras, "Obama Visit Puts Focus on Senator for Rural State," *Seattle Times*, August 15, 2009.
86. Ibid.
87. Barack Obama, "Remarks by the President on the Economy and Housing," October 24, 2011.
88. Barack Obama, "President Barack Obama's State of the Union Address," January 28, 2014.
89. Paul Waldman, "Is President Obama Reinventing the Bully Pulpit?" *Washington Post*, December 22, 2014, https://www.washingtonpost.com/blogs/plum-line/wp/2014/12/22/is-president-obama-reinventing-the-bully-pulpit/?utm_term=.ade0a368d9a3.
90. Michael D. Shear and Jennifer Steinhauer, "Obama Willing to Use Executive Orders on Guns," *New York Times*, January 14, 2013.
91. Charlie Savage, "Shift on Executive Power Lets Obama Bypass Rivals," *New York Times*, April 22, 2012.

92. Edwards, *Overreach*, 2.
93. John Kenneth White, "Obama and Washington: Fallen Hopes and Frustrated Change," in *Debating the Obama Presidency*, ed. Steven E. Schier (Lanham, MD: Rowman & Littlefield, 2016), 45.
94. Tedin et al., "When the President Goes Public."
95. Kernell and Rice, "Cable and Partisan Polarization."
96. Sidney M. Milkis, Jesse H. Rhodes, and Emily J. Charnock, "What Happened to Post-Partisanship? Barack Obama and the New American Party System," *Perspectives on Politics* 10, 1 (2015): 57–76.
97. Daniel Ponder and C. David Moon, "A Tale of Three Variables: Exploring the Impact of Alternative Measures of Presidential Approval on Congressional Voting," *Congress and the Presidency* 23, 3 (2005): 157–169; Brian Newman and Emerson Siegle, "The Polarized Presidency: Depth and Breadth of Public Partisanship," *Presidential Studies Quarterly* 40, 2 (2010): 342–363.
98. Douglas Kriner and Liam Schwartz, "Partisan Dynamics and the Volatility of Presidential Approval," *British Journal of Political Science* 39, 3 (2009): 609–631.
99. Chris Cillizza, "The President's 'Bully Pulpit' Is Way Overrated," *Washington Post*, July 12, 2015.
100. Ibid.
101. Doherty, *Rise of the Permanent Campaign*.
102. Greg Sargent, "Why the Green Lantern Theory of Presidential Power Persists," *Washington Post*, April 30, 2013, https://www.washingtonpost.com/blogs/plum-line/wp/2013/04/30/why-the-green-lantern-theory-of-presidential-power-persists/?utm_term=.f1d4b6343441.
103. Kernell, *Going Public*.
104. Julie Hirschfeld Davis, "A Digital Team Is Helping Obama Find His Voice Online," *New York Times*, November 8, 2015.
105. Eilperin, "Here's How the First President of the Social Media Age Has Chosen to Connect."
106. Matthew Baum and Samuel Kernell, "Has Cable Ended the Golden Age of Presidential Television?" *American Political Science Review* 93, 1 (1999): 99–114.
107. John Sides, "Is the Media Bias towards Clinton or Trump?" *Washington Post*, September 20, 2016, https://www.washingtonpost.com/news/monkey-cage/wp/2016/09/20/is-the-media-biased-toward-clinton-or-trump-heres-some-actual-hard-data/?utm_term=.a065ed6fc1f0.

CHAPTER THREE

Party Foul

How Obama Made Partisan, Not Party, Politics in a Polarized Environment

Julia R. Azari

The 2016 election rendered an unexpected and crushing verdict on Barack Obama's party legacy. His chosen presidential successor, Hillary Clinton, was widely predicted to be the winner, and although she won the popular vote, she lost in the Electoral College to Republican Donald Trump. Clinton lost several states that Obama had won comfortably in 2012: Wisconsin, Pennsylvania, and Michigan. Her campaign failed to replicate Democratic gains in the South, and she lost the so-called swing states: Ohio, Iowa, North Carolina, and Florida. An expected Electoral College landslide turned out to be an Electoral College loss. Democrats also fell short of their goal to win control of either chamber of Congress, and they emerged from the election shut out of government in a majority of the states as well.

Perhaps this state of affairs should have been easier to anticipate. In 2006 and 2008 the Democrats made significant congressional gains but lost them—along with nearly 1,000 state legislative seats—to Republicans during Obama's eight years in the White House.[1] This is all the more striking because nothing seemed to be particularly dire, at least according to the usual metrics. The economy maintained a steady, if modest, performance.[2] Obama was substantially more popular than George W. Bush had been at the end of his term, and unlike Bill Clinton, he had not been derailed by a major scandal.[3] In 2016, despite a devastating overall result for the party, Democrats won more votes nationally than Republicans in both the presidential race and the overall vote for the Senate.

In light of 2016's twist of an ending, reminiscent of the film *The Sixth Sense*, how can we understand Obama's impact on the Democratic Party and its standing in American politics? Despite Obama's two majority victories, were the Democrats dead all along?[4]

Understanding Obama's party legacy requires us to understand *party* and *par-*

tisanship as conceptually and analytically distinct. Obama's legacy as the leader of the Democratic Party as an organization is different from his maneuvers in relation to the Democratic Party as an idea and a source of partisan identification. Obama inherited a situation in which party and partisanship had already meaningfully diverged. Within the American party context, presidents are both empowered and constrained. For Democratic presidents, this has often meant balancing a complex coalition of voters, from the classic New Deal coalition to newer groups of socially liberal activists that have become part of the party's modern base. Presidents' actions can have profound and disruptive repercussions resulting from their efforts to maintain existing structures. For twenty-first-century presidents, what presidency scholars have termed "executive-centered party building," with its emphasis on rhetoric, can give way to partisan rhetoric that highlights conflict without building up party strength.[5]

This chapter examines presidents' unique and in many ways constrained role in shaping party and partisanship. It begins with a puzzle about Barack Obama's presidency that I call the transformation paradox, whereby Obama was simultaneously blamed for radically altering the polity and for not changing it enough. I then outline what it means for presidents to make party and partisan politics and why these two realms are distinct. Subsequent sections explore the ramifications of the nationalization of politics for presidential leadership and compare Obama's party leadership to that of Bill Clinton and George W. Bush.

The Transformation Paradox

Obama's 2008 campaign seemed to have all the signs of a transformative project. His campaign rhetoric referred to founding values; he spoke about systemic change; and, at least superficially, the moment seemed right for a significant shift. The outgoing Republican president, George W. Bush, had record-low approval ratings. The economy appeared to be in free fall. Once the election returns were in, Obama became the first Democratic presidential candidate to win a majority of the popular vote since 1976 and the first to win more than 51 percent since 1964. Obama's victories in Virginia and North Carolina raised questions of whether the Democrats might even be able to expand their electoral map into the solid-Republican South.

It was not long after Obama took office, though, that his presidency began to disappoint and divide erstwhile supporters. The new economic stimulus package was large enough to anger conservatives but not large enough to satisfy liberal economists like Joseph Stiglitz and Paul Krugman.[6] Despite efforts to broaden the coalition, the stimulus bill passed by a highly partisan vote in Congress and received no Republican votes in the House of Representatives.[7] Obama's limited capacity to change the partisan divisions in Washington was evident early on. His presidency was almost immediately on track to be among the most polarized in modern history.

Why was Obama's transformation effort stillborn? Presidential scholars point to the simple fact that transformative presidential leadership happens rarely. George Edwards, building on his argument that presidential leadership changes congressional behavior mostly at the margins, identifies Obama's presidency as an instance of "overreach," in which the president's capacity to rally public support failed to match the scope of his promises.[8] Bert Rockman argues that Obama's main challenges were structural; the forty-fourth president had to lead in an environment of "virile hostility" and an institutional structure that was not amenable to sweeping presidential agendas.[9] The Affordable Care Act, for instance, was characterized as "socialized medicine." As Daniel Béland, Philip Rocco, and Alex Waddan point out, "from spring 2010 onward, conservatives waged a very public campaign denouncing the law as wasteful and bad for the economy, which 'legitimized' their strategy of denouncing opposition."[10] The Affordable Care Act was among the focal points of the Tea Party's constitutional objections to Obama's presidency.[11]

Harsh criticisms were also directed at the president himself, questioning his patriotism and even his citizenship and his right to hold office. While opponents on the right were accusing Obama of subverting the foundations of American political life, his decisions provoked challenges from the left that his policies did not go far enough. Obama's early presidency was legislatively productive, but as Lawrence Jacobs and Desmond King point out, a number of structural barriers "slowed and watered down reforms or stopped them in their tracks."[12] Early on, the appointment of officials with deep Wall Street ties prompted anger from progressives.[13] Later, the Affordable Care Act also moved toward the center, eliminating the "public option" from the legislation and gaining approval from key interest groups, including the American Medical Association and the insurance industry. Despite these concessions, the legislation proved to be one of the most politically divisive policies of the modern era, prompting efforts in 2017 to "repeal and replace" the law and the successful elimination of its individual mandate for insurance coverage.

The transformation paradox is also evident in the racial symbolism of Obama's presidency, which both challenged and affirmed the existing racial order. A major theme of his early presidency was caution when approaching "black issues" and his often critical tone when addressing African American groups.[14] Yet, despite rhetoric that has been widely identified with moderation, caution, and transcending rather than engaging racial issues, the impact of Obama's presidency has been one of racial division. As Michael Tesler observes, "Mass politics was indeed more polarized by and over race during Barack Obama's presidency than it was before his 2008 presidential campaign."[15] Tesler finds a "racial spillover effect" whereby issues associated with Obama were also affected by racial attitudes. Other scholars have noted the likelihood that racism depressed Obama's 2008 vote share, and they have established empirical linkages between the Obama presidency, racially conservative attitudes, and the emergence of the Tea Party.[16]

Obama's critics have accused him, in other words, of both seeking to fundamentally alter American politics—including the racial hierarchy—and taking a cautious or even milquetoast approach. This paradox prompts questions about Obama's impact on party and partisan politics. How could Obama's rhetoric and policies be so incremental and yet so disruptive? In part, the answer can be found in the partisan context of Obama's presidency; essentially all his efforts to change and frame policy were received in partisan terms and were taken as attempts to elevate one contested vision of America over another. Attempts to "transcend" everyday party politics did little to assuage this perception and may have even exacerbated it. Obama inherited a situation in which parties were weakened as organizations and were viewed with some suspicion by voters.[17] This state of affairs was accompanied by strong partisanship at the elite level and among the electorate.

How Presidents Affect Politics

Scholars of American political development argue that politics consists of multiple "orders" or systems of political ideas and institutional relationships that operate at the same time and do not always line up neatly. Writing about James K. Polk, for example, Stephen Skowronek describes how the president "made" three distinct types of politics: constitutional politics, party politics, and Jacksonian politics.[18] Polk's decisions with regard to interpreting the Constitution, interacting with party structures, and carrying out the Jacksonian policy legacy all influenced the political legacy of his administration. These different kinds of politics combined the individual judgment and agency of a specific president with the received political conditions of his time in office. The changes that resulted from Polk's presidency also happened more or less simultaneously, during the course of his single four-year term.

This framework is useful for understanding Obama's impact on the party politics situation he inherited from his predecessor, George W. Bush. Like Polk, Obama's actions can be largely understood in the context of received political realities rather than his capacity to remake them. In contrast with Polk, Obama bears the characteristics of a preemptive, "opposition president" in the political time framework, charged even more delicately with responsibility for maintaining dominant priorities and structures.

All presidents—but especially those who come to office before full-throated demands for change have been established—are limited in their capacity to reformulate politics. For Obama, expectations about his ability to reshape politics, paired with opponents' criticism that he was too radical, made this an especially challenging leadership problem. Although presidents nearly always fall short of major transformation, their decisions are nevertheless consequential.

Making Party Politics (or Not)

It is tempting to conclude that because party polarization is strong in the early twenty-first century, parties themselves must be strong as well. However, parties and partisanship are distinct.[19] This distinction is key to understanding Obama's party legacy: He did a great deal to sharpen and clarify the Democratic Party's stances and to bolster its reputation with core Democratic groups. But his efforts to build the party—to elect officials at the state level and to strengthen the Democratic National Committee (DNC)—did not match his rhetorical accomplishments.

Scholars have long noted the tension between party organizations and the modern presidency. Sidney Milkis traces this tension back to the New Deal and the Great Society. Presidents have used their administrative capacity to undermine and supplant party organizations. As Milkis describes, "the development of the modern presidency clearly weakened party organization."[20] Describing how Lyndon Johnson followed Franklin Roosevelt's lead in working around party, Milkis writes, "he took strong action to de-emphasize the role of the formal party organization," noting that Johnson significantly decreased the DNC budget and cut important programs such as voter registration.[21]

Daniel Galvin identifies a pattern in what he terms "presidential party-building": Republicans build up their party organizations, while Democrats are "party predators." Galvin focuses on formal party organizations, noting how presidents can build up durable capacity to fund campaigns, mobilize voters, and recruit candidates and party staff.[22] Among contemporary presidents, this difference across parties has remained. As Sidney Milkis and Jesse Rhodes observe, "[George W.] Bush has surpassed Reagan with his dramatic and unprecedented efforts to build up his party at the congressional, grassroots, and organizational levels."[23]

In weaving these strands of scholarship together, we gain a clearer picture of presidents' mixed incentives to build up party organizations. Party organizations can constrain and force presidents to negotiate with other formidable political actors. However, they can also serve as a durable source of political support, creating the conditions for later party victories. Debate remains about the role played by other types of vehicles, including advocacy organizations and political action committees. A substantial body of research shows that these groups have important similarities to parties;[24] nevertheless, the functions performed by party organizations may be distinct.

Whether presidents build up formal organizational capacity is a significant aspect of how they make party politics and is one facet we must consider. However, making party politics is not just about capacity; it is also about legitimacy. In considering how Obama made party politics, the following analysis takes into account how he approached the legitimacy of the DNC and existing formal and informal structures of party hierarchy. There is a third facet of party politics, too: the cultivation of a "farm team" of rising stars. This includes not only ascendant governors and other state-level politicians but also the politicians elevated to national-level prominence in the administration.

Presidential decisions about how to build party organization have implications for the party's ideological direction. Eisenhower's party-building efforts were aimed at making a moderate, "modern" party, while later party-building activities by Republicans were part of the party's rightward turn.[25] From the vantage point of 2018, these party efforts were highly consequential. Two years after Obama left office, it remains somewhat unclear what it means to be an Obama Democrat (versus what it means to be an Eisenhower, or Reagan, Republican). The steep congressional losses suffered by the Democrats also make it unclear who might carry on this legacy, although the 2018 midterm elections gave momentum to both moderate and left-wing visions for the party's future.

Making Partisan Politics

Scholars have observed the phenomenon of the "partisan presidency" for nearly a decade. Richard Skinner coined the term in a 2008 article about the differences between the era starting with Reagan and the earlier modern presidency. Partisan-era presidents, Skinner argues, are dependent on support from their parties because support across party lines is increasingly rare.[26] As Galvin explains, "Recent presidents are said to have presented more partisan images of themselves to the public, campaigned more vigorously for fellow partisans, used more combative rhetoric toward the opposition party, worked harder to strengthen their party organization and mobilize their base, pushed for policies that unabashedly 'delivered the goods' to their parties' core constituencies, and/or adopted administrative strategies that openly seek to serve their parties' interests."[27] Here, it is important to distinguish between making partisan politics and making party politics.

In the study of public opinion and partisan polarization, the twenty-first-century presidency has emerged as an important focal point. Alan Abramowitz observes that "the effects of both party identification and ideological identification on Bush evaluations increased dramatically between 2000 and 2004."[28] Gary Jacobson finds that both Bush and Obama inspired national "referenda" on their presidencies, turning congressional contests into full-blown national affairs.[29] This characterization stands in contrast to earlier understandings of congressional elections, in which local factors overshadowed national narratives.[30] American politics has become highly nationalized, despite a highly localized electoral system. Journalists identified national factors as especially significant in the 2014 and 2016 Senate elections.[31] Gallup polls consistently reveal that Bush and Obama were the most "polarized" modern presidents, with the largest gaps in approval between partisans and party opponents since the 1950s. Gallup's Jeffrey Jones reported in 2015 that "each of Obama's six years in office ranks among the ten most polarized."[32] Each year of Obama's presidency was more polarized, by this measure, than the one before. While this fact has blended into the larger landscape of polarized partisan politics, its implications warrant further scrutiny in the context of a presidency that made partisan politics.

Presidents regularly confront dilemmas about whether to appeal to the "party base" or to take a more centrist stance.[33] Partisan polarization reshapes this dilemma, making a base-oriented strategy more appealing, as we saw in the presidency of George W. Bush.[34] However, the politics of the 2016 election calls this formulation into question. Does navigating party politics still mean balancing between centrist swing voters and an ideologically motivated core of party supporters? The candidacies of Bernie Sanders and Donald Trump challenged these ideas. While debates still rage about the true drivers of support for these two candidates, their campaign appeals clearly pointed to critiques of elites and the political system. Building up party and partisanship by shoring up the "base" may prove more complicated than it was in the past.

Defining what it means for a president to "make partisan politics" in a highly polarized environment is challenging. The operational definition in what follows rests on two areas of presidential action. The first follows conventional definitions of presidential partisanship: the elevation of the "partisan base" over other rhetorical and political strategies. This can mean consolidating support among sympathetic constituencies. It can also mean amplifying loyal partisan voices in the creation of policy. A second, less familiar but critical aspect of this definition is the treatment of ideas as the central mechanism of party politics. In attempting to understand Obama's partisan politics, I explore how he used policy positions and ideas to bind a broad coalition, and how this effort fell short of what was necessary to ensure a party legacy.

Two key features of making partisan politics warrant clarification. First, although shoring up the partisan base with targeted visits and rhetoric is part of making partisan politics, it is not the whole story. Making partisan politics is also about constructing an abstract party brand that serves as the "glue" holding the partisan electorate together. This process, of course, can include actual policymaking as well as slogans and issue positions.

Second, an analysis of the way Obama made partisan politics is not meant to imply that he had many other options, given that he was forced to operate in a highly partisan environment. Much of that partisan situation was in place before he took office in January 2009, and there were no magic words he could have spoken or tours he could have taken to alter these basic contours. Numerous studies have highlighted the degree of Republican obstruction and hostility toward Obama. The Tea Party emerged as a core Republican constituency focused in part on the idea that Obama's agenda was incompatible with the Constitution and national values.[35] In their extensive account of congressional politics, Thomas Mann and Norman Ornstein describe the extent to which the partisan rancor focused on Obama became dominant: "Mitch McConnell continued to be astonishingly candid about his view that the permanent campaign had trumped policy."[36] Obama's capacity to alter these dynamics was, of course, limited. At the same time, his operation within the politics of the day shaped partisan politics in America.

Conventional wisdom, scholarly and otherwise, about presidents and parties tends to err in multiple directions. Popular narratives often cast the president as the central character whose words and actions can make the difference between bipartisan harmony and partisan rancor. Political scientists, in contrast, are quick to dismiss this formulation and suggest instead that presidents are subject to strong structural forces that limit their power. Even though Obama came into office during a time of high polarization, presidents enjoy considerable capacity to build institutions and set the tone for politics. As a result, Obama's choices were consequential, even if other actors, such as Republican congressional leaders, shared the responsibility for deepening the partisan strife.

How Personal Celebrity Can Transcend Party Politics

Obama's efforts to use his own personal celebrity and image to transcend party politics illustrate how presidents can subvert the idea of party while contributing to partisan, symbolic ways of understanding the presidency. As the previous section notes, it is difficult for presidents to transcend partisan politics when they take office under polarized conditions. The usual path for this transcendence follows an individualistic trajectory. Indeed, one of the defining characteristics of the modern presidency is independence from parties and the ability to communicate directly with the electorate. The idea that the president can lead by personal character, rising above party squabbles, is not a strictly modern one, however. Ralph Ketcham describes the origins of this idea in the American founding and the British political thought that informed it, especially the idea of a "patriot king."[37] Applying this idea to George Washington's precedent-setting presidency, Ketcham writes, "Washington's attention, as he took office, to pomp and etiquette, which in retrospect has seemed ridiculous and misguided in a republic, was in fact another manifestation of his deliberate intention to *lead* the nation not only in a formal, political sense but also in 'tone-setting,' moral ways."[38]

For Washington, as for modern presidents, denial of a partisan undercurrent was a fantasy. By the time Washington left office, two distinct sides were emerging, even within his own administration. Modern presidents' efforts to rise above partisan politics, through the trappings of the office and their own personal reputations, have been similarly caught up in ongoing partisan conflict.

Obama ran for office on the promise of such transcendence, yet the personal image he crafted became the subject of deep partisanship. Jeffrey Alexander points out that Republican reaction to Obama's "celebrity" image began during the 2008 campaign, after Obama traveled to Europe: "The mainstream liberal press admires Obama's foreign adventure, and European crowds love him, but for conservatives who see him in terms of darker, anti-civil qualities, and moderates who might still be convinced to do so, this adulation seems patently undeserved."[39]

Obama's personal popularity often outpaced his job approval,[40] so his reliance on personal image and celebrity did not convert entirely into partisan tension. Nevertheless, many of the traits emphasized in Obama's personal brand—his global experiences, his calm demeanor, his family background—also mapped onto existing cultural and social debates. Furthermore, the emphasis on presidential personality and personal traits illustrates the tension between the modern presidency and the collective enterprise of party politics.

Obama's Political Background and the 2008 Nomination

It is not novel to suggest that presidents do not always get along with their parties. Some of FDR's most vocal opponents were fellow Democrats, from former ally Al Smith to former vice president John Nance Garner. Jimmy Carter's inability to lead his party helped bring down his presidency. And even when George W. Bush led an ideologically unified Republican majority in 2005, he was unable to persuade his party to accept some of his key policy priorities. But Barack Obama entered office in 2009 as perhaps the least party-dependent of the modern presidents to date. (He held that record only until 2017, of course.) Obama's brief political career had been one of challenging the party hierarchy and seniority, including his successful pursuit of the presidential nomination in 2008.

The 2008 presidential contest was the biggest platform on which Obama used his biography and charisma to advance his political goals. However, this brand of personal politics had played a role in his rise up the ranks in Illinois. Obama won his Illinois senate seat by challenging long-term incumbent Alice Palmer, along with three other Democrats. Although Obama's speaking style had yet to develop, David Remnick notes that he was able to secure the endorsement of the "most important anti-machine group to emerge in Chicago after the Second World War"— the Independent Voters of Illinois–Independent Precinct Organization—securing his primary victory over more seasoned opponents.[41] Less successful was Obama's attempt to challenge Bobby Rush for a US House seat, but this effort was representative of his overall approach to politics. As Remnick writes, "Obama's unseating of Palmer planted some bitter seeds. He discovered that when, in Springfield, he joined the Black Caucus and again, to greater distress in 2000 when he challenged the former Black Panther Bobby Rush for his seat in Congress."[42] This trajectory is relevant not only to Obama's evolution in Chicago politics but also to broader party politics. Obama's political instincts seemed to direct him to transcend party politics with a mix of idealism and pragmatism. This tendency was still evident during his presidency; as Galvin points out, Obama neglected both state-level party building and "deeper issues" within the DNC.[43]

Obama's taste for challenging party hierarchy was also evident in his 2008 presidential bid. Although this was hardly the first contested Democratic presidential primary in modern history, the dynamics of 2008 offer some lessons about Obama's approach to party politics and to the party whose politics he inherited when he became president. In 2007 Hillary Clinton was the favorite for the Democratic nomination; Obama did not even show up on a *Washington Post* list of key potential rivals, which included former senator John Edwards, Connecticut senator Christopher Dodd, and former Iowa governor Tom Vilsack.[44] Obama's "insider endorsements" were dwarfed by those received not only by Clinton but also by former senator and 2004 vice-presidential candidate John Edwards.[45] Although Obama ultimately demonstrated that he was acceptable to major factions within the party, including its office-holding "insiders" and national organization officials, he continued to make appeals based on his fresh outsider persona.[46]

With this background in place and these distinctions in mind, we can turn to Obama's specific activities as president—his *party* politics, and then his *partisan* politics.

Obama's Party Politics

Party-Building Activities

Presidents are in a unique position to build up the capacities of their parties. But while Republican presidents generally take advantage of this opportunity, Democratic presidents tend to take more from their parties than they give back.[47] Obama's presidency fits this pattern reasonably well. As Lara Brown observes, from the logo to the location, Obama for America (later Organizing for America, but abbreviated OFA in either case) was moved from party control to the president's control.[48] The presidential focus of the Obama movement was evident early on. According to Barbara Trish, "in 2008, there was very little coordination [between state and local campaigns and the presidential campaign], even in theory, let alone in practice. In fact, it was either the Obama forces *going it alone*, dominating the coordination fully, *or* the state party in effect running a shadow coordination effort."[49] Writing after the 2016 presidential election, Galvin argues that OFA's decision to keep important data to itself rather than share with the DNC led to an "awkward division of informational assets."[50]

Choosing Successors

Although party building tends to focus on organizational capacity, it also involves cultivating candidates for future presidential bids. Again, Obama's actions in this regard were complex, often constrained by existing political conditions. The absence of a deep Democratic "farm team," a circumstance driven heavily by the party's weakness at the state level, has consistently been criticized.[51] However, Obama's choice of close advisers also reflected this problem. In short, his selection of Hillary Clinton for secretary of state and Joe Biden for vice president elevated two politicians who already had strong political profiles. The impetus for these choices in 2008 and 2009 was clear enough. Biden's experience in Congress augmented Obama's relative lack of it. Clinton, as a major primary rival and an important figure in the Democratic Party, also made sense as an appointee to a high cabinet position. Although the political logic of these selections was evident, they were also missed opportunities to elevate new members of the party. Obama's other cabinet selections contributed to the prominence of politicians such as Texas congressman–turned–HUD secretary Julian Castro, believed by some to be a rising star. Further, Obama helped cultivate a few Senate candidates with the potential for national prominence, including Elizabeth Warren of Massachusetts and Kamala Harris of California. The cultivation of national-level Democratic politicians in competitive and red states was limited by the partisan dynamics of Obama's presidency, however. Due to the nature of nationally polarized politics, Obama was unpopular with Republicans and lost red states by wide margins.[52] Senators such as West Virginia's Joe Manchin and North Dakota's Heidi Heitkamp depended on their ability to distance themselves from the administration—in Manchin's case, sometimes boasting about his opposition to it.[53] Partisanship and party building can create a self-reinforcing cycle, whereby the president can promote congressional candidates only in areas where he is already popular, thus ensuring that Democratic gains will be concentrated in states like Massachusetts and California and weaker in the Midwest.

Legitimacy and the DNC

Obama's relationship with the DNC was famously fraught with tension. The path of this relationship illustrates not only Obama's own choices and approach to party politics but also the structural barriers facing a twenty-first-century Democratic president who is inclined to make stronger party politics. Obama's disagreements with DNC chair Debbie Wasserman Schultz were public, yet she remained in the position, signaling the president's indifference toward the national party committee.[54] Although Obama formally declared his support for Wasserman Schultz when her chairmanship ended abruptly amid scandal, rumors had circulated for years about their frosty relationship. Some of this tension was reputedly due to the DNC chair's criticism of the Obama administration. Complete party discipline is unrealistic and probably undesirable, and it is beyond the capacity of any president to impose. However, Obama's disengagement with Wasserman Schultz over these criticisms undermined the legitimacy of the DNC, possibly more so than if he had responded to her more forcefully. Instead, he treated the party organization as an afterthought. The purpose of a national party committee is not entirely clear in popular political discourse, and Obama did little to address these questions. In late 2015 the DNC clashed with Bernie Sanders when his campaign accessed voter information belonging to the Clinton campaign and the DNC cut off access to the data platform to investigate.[55] In the summer of 2016 the website Wikileaks released thousands of internal emails from the DNC. Among the revelations that *Washington Post* writer Aaron Blake identified as "most damaging" were emails in which a Clinton lawyer advised the DNC how to address the Sanders challenge and in which Wasserman Schultz complained that Sanders had "no understanding" of the party.[56] These revelations led to Wasserman Schultz's resignation and a major decline in the DNC's reputation. An *Economist*/YouGov poll showed that, among Democrats, 60 percent thought the DNC had been "biased toward Clinton." Only 15 percent thought the party organization had remained neutral. Among Clinton supporters, 52 percent perceived a pro-Clinton bias and 25 percent thought the DNC had been neutral. Although Obama defended Wasserman Schultz until her resignation, he did little to substantively defend the DNC or its functions as an organization. Obama's approach appears to have changed somewhat after his presidency; he supported the selection of his former labor secretary, Thomas Perez, to chair the DNC over left-wing favorite Keith Ellison.[57]

It is difficult to know what Obama could have done differently in the realm of making party politics. His own political ascent did not offer much affirmation of the role of parties, seniority, or hierarchy. Furthermore, the presidency offers limited tools to address the depth and scope of public skepticism about parties. In this regard, making party politics—or not—reflects structural limitations as well as presidential choices.

Obama's Partisan Politics

Presidential Travel

The practice was once so controversial that it inspired one of the articles of impeachment against Andrew Johnson in 1868, but presidential travel has become a standard part of governing and communicating with the public (see also chapter 2 in this volume). According to Brendan Doherty, presidents can take public tours "to advance their own reelection interests; to raise funds; to support their fellow party members; to promote their policy agenda or achievements in a setting outside the nation's capital; to attend ceremonial events; to respond to natural disasters or other crises; to influence public opinion; or simply to get out of Washington."[58] Because of these multifaceted purposes, it is important to interpret travel patterns carefully. However, Obama's travel tells us something about the partisan implications of his political strategy.

Investigation of Obama's travel reveals some differences between the work of

Table 3.1. Obama's Travel, January–June 2009

	Lost	Close Victory	Large Victory	Total
Visits	3	23	29	55
States	2	7	10	27

governing and the work of campaigning. During his first six months in office in 2009, Obama traveled almost exclusively to states where he had won, and especially to states where he had won by a margin of 10 percentage points or more (see table 3.1). Visiting "safe" states to promote policy and conduct listening sessions with voters is consistent with making partisan politics. This strategy may have had some benefits, but it also represented a missed opportunity to incorporate competitive states and Republican states into his governing strategy, as well as to distinguish between the politics of campaigning and the politics of promoting policy. Instead, Obama's governing strategy was tilted heavily toward states where his ideas were already popular. He delivered speeches to presumably receptive audiences in Chicago, Philadelphia, and Los Angeles. These choices demonstrate a particular kind of logic that reflects the perception of modern parties; rather than building broad-ranging organizations, the top priorities seem to be fund-raising and shoring up the party base.

Not surprisingly, Obama did substantially more traveling in 2012 during his reelection campaign, and his travel schedule for that year had a qualitatively different pattern (see table 3.2). More than half the president's stops were in states that had been competitive in 2008. On its own, this does not defy expectations. However, it contradicts a central premise of "permanent campaigns": that presidents engage in campaign-like behavior even when they are not formally campaigning for office. These divergent patterns suggest that when a president has just concluded a campaign and is traveling to promote policy, it is a qualitatively different campaign. At least in Obama's case, he aimed this type of campaign primarily at areas of strong partisan support.

Obama's travel patterns also suggest a self-reinforcing cycle of partisan politics. While it is possible to imagine a more extensive effort to promote policy in swing states, it is hard to conceive of a successful tour through much of the South, outside

Table 3.2. Obama's Travel, 2012

	Lost	Close Victory	Large Victory	Total
Visits	15	102	80	197
States	5	7	16	27

of urban areas, or in conservative states like Idaho or Oklahoma. When the rigid geography of partisanship limits presidential strategy, presidents tend to limit their outreach efforts to places where they already enjoy support.[59]

Building a Brand

Obama's making of partisan politics also included building up a Democratic Party brand. As Boris Heersink argues, party brands are an important vector by which parties become nationally integrated organizations.[60] In the context of Obama's party legacy, however, we observe an effort to build up the party's reputation around two popular issues: gun control and gay rights. Both these issues distinguish Republicans from Democrats. As Graham Dodds writes, "perhaps no issue has so inflamed the culture wars over the years as gay rights."[61] Milkis and Heersink outline the development of Obama's "evolving" relationship with the LGBT movement, arguing that "forging an alliance with LGBT advocacy groups" can be understood in terms of the idea that parties are an aggregation of groups.[62] When it was politically advantageous, the Obama administration reached out to these groups as part of the Democratic coalition. In this theoretical context, we can understand the administration's LGBT outreach as a group-oriented party-building effort.[63]

However, in his second term, after Obama had publicly announced his support for same-sex marriage (not just civil unions), and after the DNC's adoption of a plank in support of marriage equality in the 2012 platform, LGBT rights also became a branding strategy. For example, twenty-four of Obama's speeches and written communications between 2009 and 2012 mentioned "LGBT" (see table 3.3). Most of these were remarks or memoranda pertaining directly to antidiscrimination policy or addresses to LGBT advocacy groups, such as the Human Rights Campaign (on October 10, 2009). Four were fund-raisers—three for the Obama Victory Fund in 2012, and one for the Democratic Party. Between 2013 and 2016, seventy-six communications included this acronym; ten of these were party fund-raisers (DNC or Democratic Congressional Campaign Committee).[64] There are a number of possible explanations for this increase, including that marriage equality became more popular during this period, crossing the threshold to

Table 3.3. Obama's Party-Branding Rhetoric on New Issues

	LGBT		Gun Control		Inequality	
	Mentions	Fund- raisers	Mentions	Fund- raisers	Mentions	Fund- raisers
2009–2012	24	4	5	0	41	4
2013–2016	76	10	17	0	133	7

majority support during the 2012 election.[65] Gay rights enjoyed especially strong support among younger Americans.[66]

The substantive significance of these shifts, from both the administration and the Democratic Party, should not be downplayed. Obama was the first sitting president to publicly advocate for marriage equality. Until the Obama years, the Democratic Party had been tepid on gay rights; during Obama's presidency, it embraced them as a key aspect of civil rights. Robert Samuels notes in the *Washington Post* that Hillary Clinton was uniquely poised to "make gay rights history" by advocating for same-sex marriage in 2008, but she did not.[67] Although Democrats were generally more sympathetic to gay rights issues, party leaders—such as 2000 presidential candidate Al Gore—did not support marriage equality, and the party had sought a middle ground on contentious cultural issues.[68]

In terms of Obama's party legacy, however, this shift is also an example of making partisan politics. As a party leader, Obama drew on a popular cultural issue to reshape the party brand and excite the base. These efforts to appeal to the party's base may have been strategically wise,[69] as far higher numbers of Democrats supported marriage equality.

Two other major issues stand out as part of Obama's legacy for the party brand. During his second term, economic inequality and gun control achieved greater prominence on the national agenda. Like gay rights, both were compatible with the party's previously held positions. Although they did not represent a significant qualitative shift, they brought to the fore policy questions that Democratic presidential candidates had downplayed in the past as too controversial or too far left of center.

The politics of gun control remained a source of tension throughout Obama's second term. Shortly after his reelection in 2012, a mass shooting in Newtown, Connecticut, killed twenty-eight people, many of them young children, and spurred a push for new gun control legislation. Proposed gun control legislation failed in the Senate on April 17, 2013, when it could not attain the 60-vote majority needed to close debate. In any case, gun control was broadly stymied by the Republican majority in the House of Representatives and later in the Senate as well. Throughout Obama's last four years in office, however, mass shootings continued to occur. Although gun control did not become a dominant theme in Obama's rhetoric, it was a more consistent theme (see table 3.3), and the president delivered several emotional speeches after mass shooting events.

Finally, with the 2008 economic collapse in the past and an economic recovery, however soft, under way, Obama was able to highlight the broader issue of economic inequality in his second term. Similar to gun control and LGBT rights, this topic came up about three times as often in the second term as in the first (see table 3.3). And like the other two topics, fund-raisers did not account for this difference; this rhetoric was targeted at voters as well as party donors. Like the other issues, reducing income inequality was relatively popular with the American public in a diffuse and widespread way. For example, Obama included this description in a weekly address in 2013: "Trends that have been eroding middle class security for decades—technology that makes some jobs obsolete, global competition that makes others moveable, growing inequality and the policies that perpetuate it—all those things still exist, and in some ways, the recession made them worse."[70] This was not a major departure from populist themes that had appeared in Democratic rhetoric before;[71] however, Obama's continued emphasis on the economic recovery's disparate effects on Americans at different income levels challenged conventional ways of understanding the economy as either strong or weak. These themes also pointed to structural problems that, presumably, had structural solutions, rather than simply touting hard work or upward mobility as the remedy for poor economic circumstances.

These three issues were not the only ones Obama emphasized in his second term. But the three of them together constituted a powerful party rebranding. Obama's decision to put the weight of the presidency behind these issues resulted in an overall party identity that was compatible with inherited principles yet also broke new ground. In this sense, it is likely that Obama's leadership had the positive effect of updating the party's issue stances. However, we can also identify the pitfalls in relying primarily on a rhetorical embrace of new issues as a party-building strategy. This is making partisan politics, not party politics. Although the issues that Obama identified were broadly popular, they also engaged long-standing and explosive cultural debates. Rather than exploiting divisions in the existing Republican coalition, these issues, particularly gun control and LGBT rights, reignited old conflicts with well-organized adversaries. Because these issues generally enjoyed majority support, they were assumed to contribute to the so-called blue wall of moderate suburban voters who were likely to reject Republican presidential candidates.[72]

Organizing the party around a brand and an ideological agenda also made the Democrats vulnerable to some of the same challenges faced by the more ideological Republicans.[73] We can observe this in the contest between Bernie Sanders and Hillary Clinton in the 2016 Democratic primary: just as Republicans faced a dynamic in which ideological purity became the basis for challenging experienced figures within the party, Sanders offered a similar challenge to Clinton. To be sure, such debates are not wholly undesirable; they allow parties to engage their most deeply held principles, and the Sanders candidacy in particular offered a perspective that was clearly welcome among a large segment of the Democratic electorate.

However, the general practice of purity politics has proved difficult for both parties, and perhaps especially for the Republicans. In 2016 a fractious primary contest over true conservatism left the party vulnerable to an insurgent candidate; his victory did not resolve the party's struggle to define its agenda and coordinate among its different factions. In the American system, parties are bound to be large and varied coalitions, and compromise is a critical part of policy-making. Ideological purity as the main vector of party cohesion is a very challenging strategy.

Implications

Three political conditions shape how Obama's party legacy has been, and will continue to be, received in American politics: the competing pressures of recalibration and realignment, the phenomenon of nationalized elections, and the growing importance of race in American politics.

Recalibration and Realignment

The long campaign season of 2016 revealed—and perhaps exacerbated—a restless politics. Insurgent candidates shook up both parties. As the campaigns wore on, questions arose about whether the election might offer an "electoral realignment"—a fundamental shake-up of what the parties stood for and which groups they represented. Commentators suggested that the parties might "realign" around issues such as trade. At the time of this writing, the long-term impact of the 2016 election remains unknown. What happened in 2016, however, can be better characterized as recalibration than realignment.[74] It is difficult to argue that politics has been unchanged by the tumultuous campaign. Nevertheless, the basic alignments of politics remain in place. Republicans retain support from the National Rifle Association, antiabortion groups, and business. Despite early signs that Trump's unusual candidacy might alienate some organized constituencies that normally support Republicans, the coalition eventually came together.[75]

Similarly, the Democrats drew support from familiar organized interests—labor, pro-choice groups, and environmentalists. As a party, the Democrats had a difficult time figuring out how to respond to the Black Lives Matter (BLM) movement. A memo from the Democratic Congressional Campaign Committee encouraged officeholders and candidates to meet with BLM supporters but to keep the meetings small and to avoid specific policy promises.[76] At the same time, the party eventually perceived the need to at least appear to be responsive to the movement. While BLM activists initially expressed a desire to remain independent from partisan involvement, the movement had a significant presence at the DNC, highlighted by stories from women whose children had been killed by police officers—the "Mothers of the Movement."

Politics also engaged new issues in 2016. Democrats spoke about racial justice and criminal justice reform in ways that departed from their rhetoric in the 1990s. Republicans responded to these themes, emphasizing law and order and the importance of taking a tough stance on terrorism and immigration. For Republicans, these themes were mixed with other familiar ones about taxes and opposition to abortion. Yet the tone of the Republican National Convention was like no other in recent history, evoking cultural issues and the deaths at the US embassy in Benghazi in 2012. Texas senator Ted Cruz gave a speech that never mentioned the party's nominee, whom Cruz would not endorse until a later date.

In sum, the axes of conflict have remained more or less unchanged, but the central issues and rhetorical tone have shifted. Indicators suggest that voters are experiencing some fatigue with the two major parties and are eager for alternatives. At the same time, elite-level alignments among parties and organized interests seem unlikely to transform.

All Politics Is National

Obama's party legacy also confronts a highly nationalized party system. The symbolism and ideology associated with political parties have long been influenced by presidents.[77] In more recent years, presidents have consolidated this symbolic leadership of their parties. It is relatively straightforward for presidents to alter the terms of the national conversation; it is more challenging for them to alter national policy or the subnational building blocks of the parties. Midterm elections have become largely understood as referenda on presidential performance, a development that was especially consequential during Obama's presidency. The narrative that emerged from the 2010 midterms was that voters were responding angrily to Obama's first two years in office (which was true for a segment of voters). In 2014 the president himself offered up the referendum framework, telling the electorate, "I may not be on the ballot, but my policies are."[78] This presidential focus makes it difficult for presidents *not* to make partisan politics through their decisions and words.

All Politics Is Racial

Race defines the contours of conflict between the two parties, reflecting elements of both the nationalization and the stubborn cleavages of party politics in the early twenty-first century. In Obama's case, this turned the presidency into a racial symbol, a phenomenon that has seemingly extended to his successor, Donald Trump. Race is central to the transformation paradox, whereby Obama was criticized for both doing too much (and being "divisive") and doing too little to alter the status quo for black Americans (see also chapter 4 in this volume). The legacy of racial politics in the Democratic Party was evident at the end of Obama's presidency as well. Primary support for Clinton and Sanders was divided along racial lines, with Sanders having a much whiter base of support. Clinton's record on race, reaching back to her years as first lady in the 1990s, included some statements that angered racial justice activists.[79] Obama's legacy of partisan politics without party building also lands in a context in which race is both a national dividing line between the two parties and a source of internecine conflict among Democrats.

Comparisons with Clinton and Bush

How did Obama's practice of partisan politics without party politics compare with other recent presidents? The conventional wisdom points to a fairly simple explanation: Clinton neglected party politics just as Obama did (if not more), but his "third way" approach, combined with a different context, meant that his presidency was less starkly polarized and polarizing.

A closer look at Clinton's party leadership reveals that he took a very different approach from Obama. Although he drew on his "outsider" status as a governor, Clinton lacked Obama's antiparty career path and message. Part of the reason for this was Clinton's organizational backing from the "New Democrats" movement, which had been picking up steam for more than a decade before Clinton's election in 1992.[80] This movement, more formally called the Democratic Leadership Council (DLC), drew on elements of both party and partisan politics. The DLC helped centrist Democrats develop national profiles, and inherent in its mission was to preserve the careers of Democratic politicians in parts of the country—namely, the South—where the national party platform had become a liability.[81] Although the DLC was a means of resisting a liberal, and cultural, national party brand, Clinton's presidency made this distinction more complicated. Almost by definition, presidents alter what their parties stand for. But Clinton's political identity was consistently focused on individual rather than party, and he remained defiantly tough to pin down.[82] In contrast with Obama's strategy, Clinton pressed at cultural issues, tackling the issue of gay and lesbian persons serving in the military early in his first term. These were hardly party branding opportunities, however. Not surprisingly, Clinton was unable to single-handedly shift public opinion on cultural questions; he was forced to accept unsatisfying compromises that pleased almost no one and left the party's—and the president's—position on issues undefined.[83] In sum, although Clinton's presidency was often characterized by clashes with congressional Republicans, making partisan politics was not Clinton's precise project.

On party politics, Clinton largely fit the pattern Galvin identified for Democratic presidents, who draw on their party's resources without working to replenish them. But Galvin also observed in Clinton an effort—not wholly successful—to "reverse course."[84] Importantly, in contrast with Obama, Clinton did not delegitimize the party organization. His efforts to revitalize it were incomplete, however, limited by the politics of his impeachment scandal.[85] Yet by the end of his presidency, Clinton's close friend and political ally Terry McAuliffe (later the governor of Virginia) became the organization's chair. Clinton's presidency was hardly a major party-building success, but he did not watch the DNC fall into disrepair and disrepute.

The record suggests that George W. Bush made both party and partisan politics a priority. As Galvin observes, Bush—with the help of key aide Karl Rove—fit the Republican party-building pattern, supporting a number of key initiatives to shore up a conservative base and build the capacity of the Republican National Committee during his term. From a somewhat different vantage on party building, Milkis and Rhodes note Bush's "dominance" over the party, especially in the wake of the 2004 election.[86] Some of what they observe is what I call making partisan politics—defining the party's message, engaging in partisan rhetoric, and extending "rhetorical leadership" to new issues such as faith-based charities and education reform.

Even Bush, though, had a mixed party legacy. Like Obama, Bush chose many high-level advisers who already had national profiles in Republican politics, including Vice President Richard Cheney, Secretary of Defense Donald Rumsfeld, and Secretary of State Colin Powell. By the end of Bush's presidency, his low approval rating had become a political liability. GOP nominee John McCain was ostensibly Bush's party successor, but his affiliation with the administration was tenuous. Furthermore, few political careers in the Republican Party were launched as a result of Bush's tenure, and the Republican establishment has fared poorly in the years since he left office. A central but underappreciated facet of party building is bolstering the legitimacy of the party and its organization; the Bush years instead inspired a long-standing party rebellion, from the "maverick" McCain-Palin ticket to the Tea Party to the insurgent candidacy of Donald Trump. Bush's brother Jeb was decisively rejected by presidential primary voters in 2016.

Finally, if we use presidential travel as a metric of making partisan politics, Bush offers a surprising contrast with Obama. On the heels of the "base" strategy for winning the 2004 election, Bush traveled to promote Social Security reform in early 2005. In contrast with Obama's focus (at a different point in his presidency) on visiting states where he had been successful, Bush's tour involved a number of states where he had won by narrow margins—Ohio, Iowa, and New Mexico—as well as some he had lost in 2004, including New Hampshire, New Jersey, and Pennsylvania.

Comparison with Clinton and Bush illustrates two central points. First, Obama's specific legacy of spirited partisan politics and neglected party politics stands apart. Second, while it is widely appreciated that political conditions offer incentives for presidents to make partisan politics, the obstacles to making effective party politics are the result of equally powerful structures. While presidents vary in their attention to building up party organizations, elevating possible successors and bolstering the legitimacy of party politics have proved to be much more challenging tasks.

Conclusion

Hillary Clinton's unexpected Electoral College loss in 2016, along with the Democratic Party's losses at other levels, leaves a weakened legacy. Commentators will likely spend years debating what went wrong for the Democrats, and Obama's party leadership will be part of that story. Obama's legacy is one of neglecting key aspects of party building, both concrete and abstract. He built support for his policy agenda in friendly states but did so less vigorously in more competitive ones. He attempted to rebrand the party around popular issues and around his own dynamic personality, but this proved to be an insufficient substitute for organization building.

Structural conditions were conducive to Obama's combination of partisan politics without party politics. Simply put, it is easy for presidents to make partisan politics. The modern presidency is well situated for making public statements about the party's values and for reading diffuse national opinion on major issues. These things can help shape the party brand but not the party itself. Contemporary partisan politics also means that presidents enjoy resilient popularity with their supporters and have very little chance of winning over partisan opponents. When these dynamics influence what presidents say and where they say it, presidential partisan politics becomes a cycle that is hard to break. In contrast, it is difficult for presidents to make party politics. This seems to be especially true of Democratic presidents, who lead an unwieldy coalition that is perhaps predisposed to be suspicious of centralized power.[87]

Obama's postpresidential actions indicate that he is poised to take a new direction, though it remains somewhat unclear what that direction will be. With Obama's support, former attorney general Eric Holder has begun working to counterbalance the Republican redistricting efforts of the 2010s. Obama has remained a leading figure in the Democratic Party, although his conflicted internal negotiations about what that means are evident. He endorsed eighty-one congressional and down-ballot general election candidates on August 1, 2018. Notably, this list did not include New York's Alexandria Ocasio-Cortez, whose sudden rise to star status within the party contains elements of Obama's own rapid ascent. Ocasio-Cortez did not face a competitive general election in 2018, perhaps accounting for the absence of an early Obama endorsement, which did not arrive until October 1. Alternatively, this may have been an instance of the party's established leadership distancing itself from the socialist label adopted by some of the new candidates who have emerged since Obama took office.

In any case, ideological caution is consistent with Obama's party leadership style. This mix of caution and, to use a classic word from the Obama years, audacity was on display in a speech he delivered at the University of Illinois on September 7, 2018. The former president threaded a delicate needle, criticizing Donald Trump and the political forces that brought him to power, while maintaining that "none of this is conservative."[88] He used the speech to promote Democratic candidates and priorities, while simultaneously reassuring his audience of the values, ideas, and history that can ultimately transcend partisan concerns.

The distinct conditions that structure how presidents make partisan and party politics help us understand the transformation paradox of Obama's presidency. He adhered closely to existing political orders, found most of his legislative agenda thwarted, and abandoned promises of serious change. Nevertheless, his presidency left behind a profoundly disrupted political landscape. The distinction between partisan and party politics helps explain the depth and expanse of the opposition to Obama's presidency. It also helps explain the emergent divisions within the Democratic Party and the party's lack of organizational resources to address these splits. It seems unlikely that the Democratic Party will address its circumstances by reinvigorating the national party organization. Although Republican presidents have been more vigorous in their party building, Donald Trump seems a likely candidate to make partisan politics without accompanying party strength. Partisanship without parties has great potential to result in superficial and divisive politics and presidencies that are disruptive without transformation.

Notes

1. Katie Sanders, "Have Democrats Lost 900 Seats in State Legislatures since Obama Became President?" Politifact.com, January 25, 2015, http://www.politifact.com/punditfact/statements/2015/jan/25/cokie-roberts/have-democrats-lost-900-seats-state-legislatures-o/.
2. Matthew Winkler, "Ranking the Obama Economy," Bloomberg.com, January 19, 2017, https://www.bloomberg.com/view/articles/2017-01-19/ranking-the-obama-economy.
3. Gallup Daily, Obama Job Approval, http://www.gallup.com/poll/113980/gallup-daily-obama-job-approval.aspx.
4. In the 1999 film *The Sixth Sense*, a child who sees spirits of the dead receives help from a child psychologist played by Bruce Willis. At the end of the film, we learn that Willis's character is also a ghost.
5. Sidney Milkis, Jesse Rhodes, and Emily Charnock, "What Happened to Post-Partisanship? Barack Obama and the New American Party System," *Perspectives on Politics* 10 (2012): 57–76.
6. Jackie Calmes and Michael Cooper, "New Consensus Sees Stimulus Package as Worthy Step," *New York Times*, November 20, 2009; Paul Krugman, "Failure to Rise," *New York Times*, February 12, 2009.
7. Jackie Calmes, "House Passes Stimulus Plan with No GOP Votes," *New York Times*, January 28, 2009.
8. George C. Edwards III, *Overreach: Leadership in the Obama Presidency* (Princeton, NJ: Princeton University Press, 2015).
9. Bert Rockman, "The Obama Presidency: Hope, Change, and Reality," *Social Science Quarterly* 93 (2012): 1065–1080.
10. Daniel Béland, Philip Rocco, and Alex Waddan, *Obamacare Wars: Federalism, State Politics, and the Affordable Care Act* (Lawrence: University Press of Kansas, 2016), 53–54.

11. Kate Zernike, *Boiling Mad: Behind the Lines in Tea Party America* (New York: Macmillan, 2010).

12. Lawrence R. Jacobs and Desmond S. King, "Varieties of Obamaism: Structure, Agency, and the Obama Presidency," *Perspectives on Politics* 8 (2010): 793–802.

13. See, e.g., the critique by journalist Matt Taibbi, "Obama's Big Sell Out: The President Has Packed His Economic Team with Wall Street Insiders," CommonDreams.org, December 13, 2009, http://www.commondreams.org/news/2009/12/13/obamas-big-sellout-president-has-packed-his-economic-team-wall-street-insiders.

14. Melanye Price, *The Race Whisperer: Barack Obama and the Political Uses of Race* (New York: NYU Press, 2016); Fredrick Harris, *The Price of the Ticket: Barack Obama and the Rise and Decline of Black Politics* (New York: Oxford University Press, 2014).

15. Michael Tesler, *Post-Racial or Most Racial: Race and Politics in the Obama Era* (Chicago: University of Chicago Press, 2016), 5.

16. Michael Lewis-Beck, Charles Tien, and Richard Nadeau, "Obama's Missed Landslide: A Racial Cost?" *PS: Political Science and Politics* 43 (2010): 69–76.

17. Howard J. Gold, "American's Attitudes toward the Parties and the Party System," *Public Opinion Quarterly* 79 (2015): 803–819.

18. Stephen Skowronek, *The Politics Presidents Make* (Cambridge, MA: Harvard University Press, 1993), 155–176.

19. Daniel Schlozman and Sam Rosenfeld, "The Hollow Parties," in *Can America Govern Itself?* ed. Frances Lee and Nolan McCarty (Cambridge: Cambridge University Press, forthcoming).

20. Sidney Milkis, *The President and the Parties: The Transformation of the American Party System since the New Deal* (New York: Oxford University Press, 1995), 11.

21. Sidney Milkis, "The Presidency and the Political Parties," in *The Presidency in the Political System*, ed. Michael Nelson (Los Angeles: Sage/CQ Press, 2014), 311.

22. Daniel J. Galvin, *Presidential Party-building: Dwight Eisenhower to George W. Bush* (Princeton, NJ: Princeton University Press, 2009), 5.

23. Sidney M. Milkis and Jesse H. Rhodes, "George W. Bush, the Republican Party, and the 'New' American Party System," *Perspectives on Politics* 5 (2007): 468.

24. Gregory Koger, Seth Masket, and Hans Noel, "Cooperative Party Factions in American Politics," *British Journal of Political Science* 38 (2010): 33–53.

25. Galvin, *Presidential Party-building*, 43; Milkis and Rhodes, "Bush, the Republican Party, and the 'New' American Party System."

26. Richard M. Skinner, "George W. Bush and the Partisan Presidency," *Political Science Quarterly* 123 (2008): 605–622.

27. Daniel J. Galvin, "Presidential Partisanship Reconsidered: Nixon, Ford, and the Rise of Polarized Politics," *Political Research Quarterly* 66 (2012): 46.

28. Alan Abramowitz, *The Disappearing Center: Engaged Citizens, Polarization, and American Democracy* (New Haven, CT: Yale University Press, 2011), 29.

29. Gary C. Jacobson, "Obama and Nationalized Electoral Politics in the 2014 Midterm," *Political Science Quarterly* 130 (2015): 1–25.

30. See, e.g., Richard Fenno, *Homestyle: House Members in Their Districts* (Boston: Little, Brown, 1978); David Mayhew, *Congress: The Electoral Connection* (New Haven, CT: Yale University Press, 2005).

31. Harry Enten and Dhrumil Mehta, "The 2014 Elections Were the Most Nationalized

in Decades," FiveThirtyEight.com, December 2, 2014; Harry Enten, "There Were No Purple* States on Tuesday," FiveThirtyEight.com, November 10, 2016.

32. Jeffrey M. Jones, "Obama Ratings Still Historically Polarized," Gallup.com, February 6, 2016.

33. Julia R. Azari, Lara M. Brown, and Zim G. Nwokora, eds., *The Presidential Leadership Dilemma: Between the Constitution and a Political Party* (Albany, NY: SUNY Press, 2013).

34. James Campbell, "Presidential Politics in a Polarized Nation: The Reelection of George W. Bush," in *The George W. Bush Legacy*, ed. Colin Campbell, Bert A. Rockman, and Andrew Rudalevige (Washington, DC: CQ Press, 2008).

35. Christopher Parker and Matt Barreto, *Change They Can't Believe In: The Tea Party and Reactionary Politics in America* (Princeton, NJ: Princeton University Press, 2013); Theda Skocpol, Vanessa Williamson, and John Coggin, "The Tea Party and the Remaking of American Conservatism," *Perspectives on Politics* 9 (2011): 25–43.

36. Thomas E. Mann and Norman J. Ornstein, *It's Even Worse than It Was: How the American Constitutional System Collided with the New Politics of Extremism*, 2nd ed. (New York: Basic Books, 2016), 25. Their analysis precedes the ultimate example of McConnell's commitment to this tenet: the year-long refusal to fill the Supreme Court vacancy created by the death of Justice Antonin Scalia in early 2016.

37. Ralph Ketcham, *Presidents above Party: The First American Presidency, 1789–1829* (Chapel Hill: University of North Carolina Press, 1987).

38. Ibid., 91.

39. Jeffrey Alexander, "Barack Obama Meets Celebrity Metaphor," *Society* 47 (2010): 412.

40. Stuart Rothenberg, "Obama: Mr. Popularity," WashingtonPost.com, June 23, 2016.

41. David Remnick, *The Bridge: The Life and Rise of Barack Obama* (New York: Alfred A. Knopf, 2010), 293.

42. Ibid., 295.

43. Daniel J. Galvin, "Obama Built a Policy Legacy. But He Didn't Do Enough to Build the Democratic Party," *Monkey Cage* (blog), WashingtonPost.com, November 16, 2016.

44. Dan Balz, "Hillary Clinton Opens Presidential Bid," *Washington Post*, January 21, 2007.

45. Kathleen Bawn, Martin Cohen, David Karol, and Seth Masket, "A Theory of Political Parties: Groups, Policy Demands, and Nominations in American Politics," *Perspectives on Politics* 10 (2012): 571–597.

46. Melvin J. Hinich, Daron R. Shaw, and Taofang Huang, "Insiders, Outsiders, and Voters in the 2008 US Presidential Election," *Presidential Studies Quarterly* 40 (2010): 264–285.

47. Galvin, *Presidential Party-building*.

48. Lara Brown, "Obama Really Didn't Build That," USNews.com, November 10, 2014.

49. Barbara Trish, "Organizing for America," in *The State of the Parties*, ed. John C. Green and Daniel J. Coffey (Lanham, MD: Rowman & Littlefield, 2011), 164 (emphasis in original).

50. Galvin, "Obama Built a Policy Legacy."

51. Matthew Yglesias, "The Democrats Are in Denial. Their Party Is Actually in Deep

Trouble," Vox.com, October 19, 2015; Jamelle Bouie, "Down and Out," Slate.com, December 11, 2014.

52. Obama won only about 32 percent of the vote in Idaho in 2012 and about 33 percent in Oklahoma. The American Presidency Project, www.presidency.ucsb.edu.

53. See, e.g., Paul Steinhauser, "Dem Senator Breaks with His Party and Obama, Again," CNN.com, March 21, 2011.

54. Perhaps the most dramatic of these clashes was Wasserman Schultz's criticism of Obama's immigration policy in 2014. This violated expectations that the party chair will support the president's agenda. Edward-Isaac Dovere, "DWS, O'Malley Agree on Border Kids," Politico.com, August 20, 2014. Wasserman Schultz was repeatedly criticized for her hapless comments as party spokesperson, such as her suggestion that the Wisconsin governor had "given women the back of his hand." Stephanie Akin, "Five Times Debbie Wasserman Schultz Angered Her Own Party," Roll Call, May 25, 2016. Deeper problems at the DNC also plagued her tenure as its leader. The role of the national party committee remained unclear, as the party's ability to weigh in on its presidential nominee was blocked by rules demanding neutrality. The party's discipline and capacity were frequently called into question. Dan Balz, "Leaked Emails Aside, DNC Problems Festered for Years," Washington Post, July 26, 2016.

55. See Michelle Hackman, "The Feud between Bernie Sanders and the DNC, Explained," Vox.com, December 18, 2015.

56. Aaron Blake, "Here Are the Latest, Most Damaging Things in the DNC's Leaked Emails," Washington Post, July 25, 2016.

57. Don Gonyea, "Labor Secretary Tom Perez, an Obama Favorite, Running for DNC Chair," NPR.org, December 15, 2016.

58. Brendan Doherty, The Rise of the President's Permanent Campaign (Lawrence: University Press of Kansas, 2012), 90–91.

59. Existing research also suggests that travel patterns may be complex. One study found that prior to Clinton, presidents traveled to a fairly even mix of competitive and uncompetitive states (margin within 3 percentage points). Emily Charnock, James McCann, and Kathryn Dunn Tenpas, "Presidential Travel from Eisenhower to George W. Bush: An 'Electoral College' Story," Political Science Quarterly 124 (2009): 323–339.

60. Boris Heersink, "Beyond Service: National Party Organizations and Party Brands in American Politics" (unpublished dissertation).

61. Graham Dodds, "The Culture Wars in the 2012 Election," in Culture, Rhetoric, and Voting: The Presidential Election of 2012, ed. Douglas M. Brattebo, Tom Lansford, Jack Covarrubias, and Robert J. Pauly Jr. (Akron, OH: University of Akron Press, 2016), 76.

62. Sidney M. Milkis and Boris Heersink, "Through Seneca Falls, and Selma, and Stonewall: Barack Obama and the Gay Rights Movement" (working paper). See also Bawn et al., "Theory of Political Parties."

63. Milkis and Heersink, "Through Seneca Falls."

64. The American Presidency Project.

65. Frank Newport, "Half of Americans Support Legal Gay Marriage," Gallup.com, May 8, 2012.

66. Hunter Schwarz, "How Gay Marriage Became a Major Issue for a Generation Uninterested in Marriage," Washington Post, June 23, 2015.

67. Robert Samuels, "Hillary Clinton Had the Chance to Make Gay Rights History. She Refused," *Washington Post*, August 29, 2016. See also Amy Sherman, "Hillary Clinton's Changing Position on Same-Sex Marriage," Politifact.com, June 17, 2015.
68. In a presidential debate with George W. Bush on October 11, 2000, Al Gore reaffirmed his opposition to legalized same-sex marriage. The American Presidency Project.
69. Pew Research Center, "Public Opinion on Same-Sex Marriage," May 12, 2016.
70. Barack Obama, "President's Weekly Address: A Better Bargain for the Middle Class," July 27, 2013.
71. See, e.g., Terri Bimes and Quinn Mulroy, "The Rise and Decline of Presidential Populism," *Studies in American Political Development* 18 (2004): 136–150; John Gerring, *Party Ideologies in America, 1828–1996* (New York: Cambridge University Press, 1998).
72. Daniel Bush, "Have Republicans Lost the Suburbs?" *PBS News Hour*, November 1, 2016; Katie Glueck, "The County that's Ground Zero for Trump's Suburban Woes," Politico.com, October 16, 2016.
73. Matt Grossmann and David A. Hopkins, *Asymmetric Politics: Ideological Republicans and Group Interest Democrats* (New York: Oxford University Press, 2016).
74. Julia Azari, "Trump May Bring a Republican Recalibration, Not a Realignment," FiveThirtyEight.com, September 7, 2016.
75. Julia R. Azari and Marc J. Hetherington, "Back to the Future? What the Politics of the Late 19th Century Can Tell Us about the 2016 Election," *Annals of the American Academy of Political and Social Science* 67 (2016): 92–109; Andrew Rudalevige, "The Meaning of the Election," in *The Elections of 2016*, ed. Michael Nelson (Washington, DC: CQ Press, 2017).
76. Julia Craven, "Leaked 2015 Memo Told Dems: 'Don't Offer Support' for Black Lives Matter Policy Positions," *Huffington Post*, August 31, 2016.
77. Daniel Klinghard, "Grover Cleveland, William McKinley, and the Emergence of the President as Party Leader," *Presidential Studies Quarterly* 35 (2005): 736–760.
78. Daniel Halper, "Obama: 'My Policies Are on the Ballot. Every Single One of Them," WeeklyStandard.com, October 2, 2014.
79. Kirsten West Savali, "For the Record: 'Superpredators Is Absolutely a Racist Term," TheRoot.com, September 30, 2016.
80. Jon F. Hale, "The Making of the New Democrats," *Political Research Quarterly* 110 (1995): 207–232.
81. Ibid., 214.
82. See Stephen Skowronek, *Presidential Leadership in Political Time*, 2nd ed. (Lawrence: University Press of Kansas, 2011).
83. Jason L. Mast, *The Performative Presidency: Crisis and Resurrection during the Clinton Years* (New York: Cambridge University Press, 2013), 71.
84. Daniel J. Galvin, "Changing Course: Reversing the Trajectory of the Democratic Party from Bill Clinton to Barack Obama," *Forum* 6 (2008): 1–21.
85. Galvin, *Presidential Party-building*, 236.
86. Milkis and Rhodes, "Bush, the Republican Party, and the 'New' American Party System."
87. The 2008 Democratic platform, for example, highlighted the need to curb executive power. The impulse toward internal democracy has a long history in the Democratic

Party, dating back to some of the nation's earliest presidential primaries. Julia R. Azari and Seth Masket, "The Mandate of the People: The 2016 Sanders Campaign in Context," in *The State of the Parties: The Changing Role of Contemporary American Parties*, ed. John C. Green, Daniel J. Coffey, and David B. Cohen (New York: Rowman & Littlefield, 2018).

88. Libby Nelson, "Read the Full Transcript of Barack Obama's Fiery Anti-Trump Speech," Vox.com, September 7, 2018.

CHAPTER FOUR
Obama's Legacy for Race Relations

Alvin B. Tillery Jr.

Although it is rarely discussed in presidential studies, every chief executive since George Washington has left a legacy in the field of race relations. This is due to the fact that the United States was founded on the twin brutalities of settler colonialism and African slavery.[1] Moreover, from the founding of the republic to the passage of the Voting Rights Act in 1965, the United States was a *Herrenvolk* (master race) democracy maintained through a violent racial caste system.[2] In other words, only whites could participate fully in America's democratic institutions. As political scientists Hanes Walton and Robert Smith have argued, the majority of the men who occupied the White House left both rhetorical and policy legacies that reinforced these systems of racial oppression or fomented greater levels of inequality.[3] As the first known multiracial American (and self-identified African American) to occupy the White House in the 240-year history of the United States,[4] it seemed likely that President Barack Obama would cut a different path than most of his predecessors. This chapter gauges how well Obama promoted racial equality in the United States and answers the question: did having a president of color make a difference for Americans of color?

This question has been hotly debated among scholars of race, ethnicity, and politics since Obama won the White House on November 4, 2008. At present, there is a growing consensus that although Obama often genuflected to the civil rights movement during his campaigns, promoting racial equality was never a centerpiece of his domestic policy agenda, to the disappointment of many liberal activists.[5] It is hard to disagree with this assessment. Indeed, during his eight years in office, President Obama frequently presented the neoliberal view that African Americans had to draw on their own resources and initiatives to complete the work of the civil rights movement and guarantee full racial equality.[6]

Even though activists frequently attacked Obama in the media for not doing enough to advance racial equality,[7] he maintained high approval ratings in communities of color throughout his two terms in office.[8] Indeed, Obama had the highest approval ratings among minority voters of any president in the post–civil rights era. Moreover, a recent ranking of modern presidents based on editorial content in African American newspapers placed Obama seventh out of nineteen for his handling of race relations.[9] I argue that this unwavering support from minority voters and media outlets was a key resource that allowed him to deflect the criticism of those who were disappointed that he was not the second coming of Martin Luther King Jr.

Some analysts have suggested that Obama's high approval ratings were a function of minority communities valuing symbolic representation over substantive representation. There is no doubt that minority voters attached a high degree of symbolic significance to Obama's presidency. At the same time, the suggestion that this was the main reason why communities of color supported him obscures his record. While it is true that President Obama—like the other seven presidents who have governed in the post–civil rights era—approached racial issues in a cautious and reactive way compared with those who served during the civil rights era, he distinguished himself from his cohorts on the traditional metrics of appointments, policy initiatives, and rhetorical engagement. In short, I argue that Obama's leadership on issues related to diversity and racial equality places him at the top of the class of post–civil rights era presidents.

Finally, it is important to note that Obama's path to productivity in the field of race relations was fraught with the weight of being the first nonwhite president. From the first day of his presidency, he became an avatar upon which the nation projected its hopes and anxieties about race relations. Just days after his election, for example, the Gallup organization reported that a large majority of Americans believed that Obama's election was among the three most important advances for African Americans "in the past 100 years."[10] A few short months into his first term, however, it became apparent that his election had also generated a racist backlash in some quarters of the electorate.[11] Some have even argued that racism was a motivating factor in the staunch partisan opposition he faced from the Republican Party during his eight years in office.[12] For the most part, President Obama managed to stay above the fray and quietly pursue a modest yet consequential agenda promoting racial equality.

The remainder of this chapter traces the various elements of that assessment, starting with the people Obama appointed to his administration, then turning to his policy initiatives, and finally analyzing his rhetoric on racial issues.

Appointments: The Most Diverse Cabinet in History

The appointments clause of Article II of the US Constitution gives the president broad powers to appoint ambassadors, judges, and cabinet-level officials.[13] Presidents have historically made appointments for a variety of strategic, organizational, and idiosyncratic reasons.[14] Moreover, there is broad consensus within the literature that a president's high-level appointments symbolize the administration in the minds of the American people.[15]

The color bar on high-level federal appointments ended in 1869, when President Ulysses Grant began the practice of appointing African American leaders to diplomatic posts in Haiti and Liberia.[16] In 1877 President Rutherford B. Hayes appointed Frederick Douglass to serve as US marshal for the District of Columbia. Douglass was the first person of color nominated and confirmed by the US Senate to a civil service position within the federal government.[17] These milestones were widely celebrated within the African American community. Moreover, a president's willingness to appoint members of the African American elite to these and other patronage positions was seen as an indicator of his broader support for civil rights; this became an article of faith in African American political culture in the Reconstruction and counter-Reconstruction periods.[18]

This view persisted into the twentieth century. The African American community lavished President Franklin Roosevelt with praise in 1937 when he nominated William Hastie to serve as the first African American federal judge in US history.[19] President Dwight Eisenhower was lauded by the African American community when he integrated the White House staff with the appointment of E. Frederic Morrow, a prominent civil rights activist and World War II veteran, as administrative officer for special projects.[20] There was a similar reaction when President Lyndon Johnson broke the color bars at the US Supreme Court and at the cabinet level of the executive branch with his nominations of Thurgood Marshall and Robert C. Weaver, respectively.[21]

The number of minority appointments is an imperfect measure of a president's commitment to equalitarian ideals in the fields of race relations and civil rights. Indeed, as African American elites have consistently fretted since Douglass's appointment in 1877, these appointments can actually undermine racial equality if they merely represent tokenism. Flawed as it may be, the diversity of presidential appointments remains a much-discussed metric in the literature on presidential leadership.[22]

President Obama's performance on this score is one of the strongest dimensions of his record. Indeed, when compared with the six presidents preceding him, Obama ranks first in terms of the ethnic and racial diversity of his cabinet-level appointments (see table 4.1). Moreover, he and George W. Bush share the distinction of being the only presidents to appoint multiple Asian Americans to their cabinets. Obama appointed Gary Locke (Commerce), Steven Chu (Energy), and Eric Shinseki (Veterans Affairs) in his first term.

President Obama also has a strong record of ethnically and racially diverse appointments to the federal judiciary. His decision to elevate Sonia Sotomayor from the US Court of Appeals for the Second Circuit to the US Supreme Court made her the first person of Hispanic heritage and woman of color to serve on the highest

Table 4.1. Diverse Cabinet Appointments, Ford through Obama

Minority Group	Ford	Carter	Reagan	Bush (41)	Clinton	Bush (43)	Obama
African American	1	2	1	1	7	4	5
Asian American	0	0	0	0	1	3	3
Hispanic/Latino	0	0	1	1	2	2	4
Total	1	2	2	2	10	9	12

court in the land. Although the Sotomayor appointment was obviously the crown jewel in Obama's record of promoting diversity on the federal bench, it was not his only achievement. In fact, Obama appointed more minority jurists to the two lower tiers of the federal court than any of his predecessors (see also chapter 8 in this volume).[23]

Policy Initiatives: Active but Not an Activist

The negative power of the veto player is the president's main domestic policy-making role prescribed by Article II of the US Constitution. In the modern era, presidents have expanded their roles in this arena in two ways. First, they have used their unparalleled ability to communicate with the American people to recommend policies to Congress and then persuade legislators to act.[24] Second, modern presidents have increasingly used executive orders to legislate from the White House.[25] Numerous studies in political science, sociology, and history have shown that these dimensions of presidential activism were crucial to winning the long struggle for African American civil rights in the middle decades of the twentieth century.[26]

The racial gaps that exist between people of color and their white co-nationals in the United States touch virtually every facet of modern American life.[27] In light of this reality, presidents taking office in the post–civil rights era have had the opportunity to pursue an activist policy agenda on many fronts. Yet most of them have taken precisely the opposite tack. Fears of white backlash have encouraged presidents in the post–civil rights era to develop discursive strategies aimed at making race relations and the racial inequalities that continue to plague US society invisible on their watches. This means that, as a group, the presidents who assumed office after 1968 tended to be more reactive than proactive on these issues. Consider, for example, that the five presidents who governed in the era of the civil rights movement wrote eleven landmark executive orders aimed at advancing racial equality in the United States. By contrast, the eight presidents who have served since passage of the Voting Rights Act in 1965 have issued only two landmark executive orders promoting racial equality.

Much to the chagrin of some of his critics in the African American community,[28] Obama followed this well-worn pattern established by his cohorts. In other words, neither candidate Obama nor president Obama made solving America's race problems a top priority. Political scientist Andrew Rudalevige has demonstrated that presidents are very strategic about the issues they recommend to Congress for action because they realize they cannot get everything they want.[29] Some media accounts suggested that Obama wanted to do more on race early in his first term but was worried that it would jeopardize his ability to pass the Affordable Care Act.[30] When he chose to enter the fray, it was on issues—such as the problem of mass incarceration—that engendered a burgeoning elite consensus that something *had* to be done. At other times, the centrality of people of color to Obama's coalition forced him to act on more controversial issues—such as police reform and immigration—or risk alienating his base. This section examines Obama's successes and failures at moving the ball forward on race relations and racial inequality once he became active on those issues.

The strongest dimension of Obama's record on race was in the area of criminal justice. Over the past thirty years, the United States has become a society marred by the "mass incarceration" of its citizens.[31] Indeed, only China, an authoritarian regime with four times the population of the United States, incarcerates more of its citizens. Moreover, there is such a pronounced racial gap in the levels of incarceration that legal scholar Michelle Alexander has argued that the American criminal justice system is the fount of a "new Jim Crow" order.[32] In 2016, for example, the Sentencing Project, a nonprofit group that analyzes data from the Bureau of Justice Statistics and various state-level departments of correction, concluded that African Americans are incarcerated at 5.1 times the rate of their white counterparts. The same report found that Latinos are incarcerated at 1.4 times the rate of whites.[33]

Obama was a law professor before he entered politics, so he was well aware of the racial inequalities in our criminal justice system when he took office. From the beginning of his first term, Obama used his power to pardon and commute federal sentences to chip away at those inequalities. Indeed, he issued more pardons and commutations than any other president in the sixty-four years since Harry Truman was in office. During his two terms, Obama offered clemency to 1,927 individuals. That was only slightly lower than the 2,044 persons to whom Truman granted clemency and substantially higher than the 1,187 grants of clemency ordered by Lyndon Johnson (who ranked second to Obama on this score).[34] It is also important to note that Obama explicitly targeted persons of color who had been convicted of drug crimes and imprisoned under sentencing guidelines with racially disparate impacts.[35]

Obama also instructed his Department of Justice (DOJ) to take an active role in undoing these sentencing guidelines and other policies that led to an explosion of the African American, Latino, and indigenous prison populations over the past three decades.[36] For example, early in Obama's first term, Attorney General Eric Holder issued a memo instructing federal prosecutors to file charges in drug cases to avoid mandatory minimum sentences whenever possible.[37] The work the DOJ did on this issue was consolidated when the president signed the Fair Sentencing Act of 2010 into law.[38]

The DOJ was the main agency Obama leaned on to respond to demands for police reform from communities of color. Since the summer of 2014, the deaths of unarmed African American men in encounters with white police officers have sparked urban unrest in several American cities, as well as a national protest movement called Black Lives Matter.[39] This social movement has cast a spotlight on the racial disparities in policing in the United States. Obama responded by instructing the DOJ to use its oversight authority to review the practices of police forces in several cities that experienced unrest. In Ferguson, Missouri, and Baltimore, Maryland, DOJ investigations led to scathing rebukes of racially discriminatory police practices. Both cities entered consent decrees with the federal government to end these practices in 2016.

Although the consent decrees in Ferguson and Baltimore were certainly victories for the police reform movement in those cities, their broader significance for the nation—where unarmed men of color are twice as likely to be killed by the police as their white counterparts—is unclear. The reactive, case-by-case nature of the DOJ approach left no blueprint for national reform, and even that approach has not been continued under the Trump administration, which ran against police reform in the 2016 presidential election.[40]

President Obama attempted to leave a broader template for national reform with the report issued in May 2015 by his Task Force on 21st Century Policing. The report has had a minimal impact on reform efforts, however, because of the decentralized nature of policing under our federal system of government, which gives the 18,000 police departments in the nation ample opportunity to ignore any calls for reform.[41] Given the Trump administration's actions on this issue, advocates for police accountability can only hope that the report will serve as a guide for a future Democratic administration. Ultimately, sweeping legislative action will likely be needed to achieve the kinds of change desired by Obama and the national movement for police reform. This route became untenable when the Republicans in Congress adopted obstruction of Obama's domestic initiatives as their main political strategy during his second term (see also chapters 6 and 9 in this volume).

The fragile fate of these administrative efforts under President Trump highlights how crucial Obama's first two years in office were for establishing a strong domestic policy agenda for racial equality. During the 111th Congress, Obama's party had large majorities in both chambers, putting the Democrats in a strong position to enact progressive legislation. The 111th Congress partnered with President Obama to fulfill this vision, becoming the most productive legislative session since the 89th Congress (1965–1967) enacted President Johnson's Great Society programs.[42]

The signature piece of legislation emerging from the 111th Congress was the Patient Protection and Affordable Care Act (soon dubbed "Obamacare") of 2010.[43] Beyond this measure, which was passed through the budget reconciliation process, Congress focused like a laser on jump-starting the economy and strengthening regulations against the kinds of financial malfeasance that had caused the Great Recession.[44] Congress also partnered with the president to pass the Lilly Ledbetter Fair Pay Act of 2009. This landmark legislation changed the statute of limitations on pay discrimination lawsuits based on gender bias, with an eye toward closing the infamous gender pay gap.[45] The Ledbetter Act was long overdue. Both gender discrimination and the gender pay gap had been persistent problems in the American workplace for decades.[46] The racial pay gap was also a significant public policy problem; in fact, at the time President Obama signed the Ledbetter Act into law, the black-white wage gap was larger than the gap between white men and women.[47] Even so, Obama did not urge Congress to extend the same protections to people of color that the Ledbetter Act proffered to women. Given the labor market's role in fomenting racial inequalities in American society,[48] the failure to extend those protections was an important missed opportunity for the administration, particularly because economic data showed that the Great Recession hit people of color harder than their white counterparts in terms of job losses, foreclosures, and reductions in wealth.[49]

It is impossible to know whether President Obama was aware of the Great Recession's disparate impact on people of color at the start of his tenure in the White House. Certainly, government agencies were already reporting that the unemployment rate for African Americans was at 15 percent—6 points higher than the rate for their white counterparts—when the Obama administration and the 111th Congress passed the American Recovery and Reinvestment Act in 2009. The lack of targeted relief for minority communities in the stimulus measures crafted by the Democratic-controlled Congress was a missed opportunity to address the racial gaps stemming from decades of outsourcing and disinvestment in those communities.

This is not to say that minority communities failed to benefit from the stimulus measures and from the president's overall stewardship of the economy. Indeed, as Obama prepared to leave office, the Bureau of Labor Statistics reported that the unemployment rate for African Americans was hovering at around 9 percent. And Obama stated that getting the African American unemployment rate back to where it had been before the recession was an accomplishment that brought him satisfaction. The problem is that a 9 percent unemployment rate was still twice the national average for white Americans. In other words, Obama's leadership on jobs did absolutely nothing to reduce the racial gap in employment opportunities that had persisted for a generation.

What is even more troubling is that the president's economic stimulus package had a racially disparate impact. Unemployment rates calculated by the Bureau of Labor Statistics beginning in 2008 illustrate that white Americans saw immediate relief after implementation of the stimulus measures. By contrast, the unemployment rate for African Americans actually increased in the two years after passage of the American Recovery and Reinvestment Act. In this context, and with his party controlling both houses of Congress, it would have been easy for Obama to request an amendment to the stimulus package that added targeted relief—in the form of training programs, strong affirmative action mandates, and the like—for the African American community. He chose not to do this. Moreover, when the leaders of the nation's civil rights organizations told him that such measures were warranted, he rebuffed them, saying that he believed race-neutral legislation would provide sufficient assistance to the African American community.[50]

The problem with President Obama's position was that the racial gaps in society had been created largely through racial exclusions in the putatively race-neutral New Deal programs.[51] Ira Katznelson describes how racial bias was built into the foundations of the American social insurance state: "By not including the occupations in which African Americans worked, and by organizing racist patterns of administration, New Deal policies for Social Security, social welfare, and labor market programs restricted black prospects while providing positive economic reinforcement for the great majority of white citizens."[52] In light of this history, Obama's faith in race-neutral programs was unwarranted. Indeed, the decision not to level the playing field in the middle of the Great Recession will likely reverberate through communities of color for a generation. This is particularly problematic, given that these economic inequalities are the basis for inequalities in education, criminal justice, and housing.

Rhetoric: The Racial Insider

President Obama's language, and the intent behind his words, has been dissected since he first burst onto the stage at the Democratic National Convention in 2004 with his famous speech imploring Americans to find commonalities with one another. Many of the early studies of Obama's rhetoric argued that his language about race and racial inequality was designed to "deracialize" himself or to "avoid" association with African Americans.[53] Using web-scraping and computer-assisted content analyses of presidential rhetoric on racial inequality from FDR to Obama, political scientist Daniel Gillion found that Obama talked less about racial inequality than the other presidents in this group.[54] Melanye Price, an African American studies and political science scholar, examined Obama's few major speeches on the

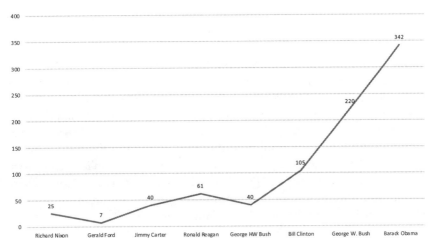

Fig. 4.1. Public Mentions of African Americans, Nixon through Obama

issue and concluded that he always found a way to stake out a position as an avatar for multiple ethnic and racial groups and multiple perspectives on race relations.[55] Consider, for example, Obama's "A More Perfect Union" speech during the 2008 campaign. In that speech, Obama presented himself as equally sympathetic to the hardships African Americans faced due to the legacies of "legalized discrimination" and the "resentments of white Americans" that sprang from their "legitimate concerns" about welfare and affirmative action.[56]

There is significant validity in all these perspectives on Obama's rhetoric about race and race relations. What has been missing from the discussion thus far is an acknowledgment of his frequent use of positive language about African Americans and their contributions to the United States to genuflect to his base in the African American community. Indeed, as figure 4.1 illustrates, President Obama referred to African Americans more than any other president in the post–civil rights era.

At this stage of history, it is impossible to know how strategic these invocations of minority groups were for Obama; however, it is clear that he leaned on rhetorical flourishes when he lacked the power to move the ball forward in the policy-making arena. The two most noteworthy examples of this behavior occurred in Obama's second term. The first was the statement he made on July 19, 2013, in reaction to the acquittal of George Zimmerman in the shooting death of Trayvon Martin, an unarmed African American teenager. The second example was his rhetorical response to the fiftieth anniversary of the Voting Rights Act—parts of which had been struck down as unconstitutional in a 5–4 decision of the US Supreme Court two years earlier.

The shooting death of Trayvon Martin in Sanford, Florida, on February 26,

2012, was a watershed moment in American race relations. Martin, who was unarmed, was fatally shot by George Zimmerman after a brief physical confrontation. Zimmerman, a volunteer for his gated community's (unregistered) neighborhood watch program, had profiled and followed Martin as the teenager left a local convenience store. Zimmerman claimed he shot Martin in self-defense. The case became a lightning rod for national controversy when Sanford authorities refused to charge Zimmerman, based on the assumption that Florida's "stand your ground" statute applied in his case. The law, which then-governor Jeb Bush had signed in 2005, gives individuals the right to use lethal force if they believe their lives are threatened, even when retreat is an option.[57] In response to intense public pressure, Rick Scott, the Republican governor of Florida, appointed a special prosecutor to examine the case. After a six-week investigation, the prosecutor charged Zimmerman with second-degree murder—only to see him acquitted of all charges after sixteen hours of jury deliberation.[58] It was in the wake of this verdict that President Obama gave his memorable speech on race relations.

On July 19, 2013, President Obama entered the White House Press Room with handwritten notes.[59] As the national networks interrupted their scheduled programs to broadcast his remarks, Obama opened by telling the White House press corps that his statement would be brief and he would take no questions afterward. He then shocked the room and the nation with his candor. "When Trayvon Martin was first shot I said that this could have been my son," the president said. "Another way of saying that is Trayvon Martin could have been me 35 years ago." Obama then became the first chief executive in the history of the United States to give a prolonged account of how his own life had been marred by the kind of racial profiling that led to the conflict between Martin and Zimmerman.[60]

Melanye Price points out two troubling elements in Obama's rhetorical style when discussing race relations. The first is his tendency to position himself as a "racial interlocutor" between groups, even when there is no real middle position.[61] The second is his tendency to "point to stereotypes based in beliefs about African American cultural pathology."[62] She is absolutely correct that both these troubling elements were present even in his July 2013 statement, which could be considered his most successful speech on race from the standpoint of African Americans. Indeed, he closed the speech by referencing black-on-black crime as being just as pernicious a threat to African American youths as the sad fate that befell Trayvon Martin.

Even so, the context in which President Obama offered his remarks about Trayvon Martin clearly demonstrated his desire to humanize and defend people of color at a crucial moment in American race relations. After all, public opinion about the Zimmerman verdict was racially polarized: 85 percent of African Americans were dissatisfied with Zimmerman's acquittal, but only 30 percent of whites disagreed with the outcome of the case.[63] Thus, just by giving this speech, President Obama demonstrated that he was not a "deracialized" politician. Moreover, by speaking so poignantly about his own experiences with racism, he provided the nation with an important counterpoint to the view that the case was not about race—a view that dominated white public opinion. No other president in the post–civil rights era has spoken so directly about the existence of racism.

Perhaps Obama's commentary on the Zimmerman trial was so direct because rhetoric was the only tool he had in his arsenal at that point. Ultimately, whether Zimmerman would be held accountable for Martin's death was beyond even the awesome power of the presidency. Whether the state of Florida would strike its "stand your ground" law from the books was also out of his hands. When faced with such limitations, the only recourse presidents have is their "power of persuasion."[64] In this speech, President Obama took the bold step of using his own narrative to persuade white Americans that racism is real and that it shapes the lives of people of color in profound ways.

Another extraordinary example of Obama's attempt to use his bully pulpit to tip the scale in favor of racial justice came in the aftermath of the Supreme Court's 5–4 decision in *Shelby County v. Holder* (2013). At issue was the constitutionality of section 4(b) and section 5 of the Voting Rights Act of 1965 (VRA). Passed at the height of the civil rights movement, the VRA was designed to end the many discriminatory practices that had denied African Americans the ability to exercise their Fifteenth Amendment rights in the southern United States.[65] Section 4(b) explicitly stated which jurisdictions were covered by the law. Section 5, known as the preclearance clause, required any jurisdiction covered by the law to gain the approval of the US attorney general or the US District Court for the District of Columbia before implementing any changes in its voting laws.[66] The preclearance clause aimed to ensure that state and local jurisdictions with histories of discrimination against African American voters would not be able to continue these practices.

The VRA worked exceedingly well in protecting the rights of African American and other minority voters.[67] Moreover, the law had widespread bipartisan support in Congress for four decades. Indeed, the VRA was reauthorized or amended to strengthen its provisions in 1970, 1975, 1982, 1992, and 2006.[68] In all five cases, the new version of the VRA was signed into law by Republican presidents. The 2006 reauthorization of the VRA, which extended the law for twenty-five years, sailed through a Republican-controlled Congress by votes of 390–33 in the House of Representatives and 98–0 in the Senate. Although some Republicans in Congress objected to the VRA's coverage formula during the debates over reauthorization,[69] the majority rejected these concerns and kept the coverage formula in place.

Given this recent legislative history, the Roberts Court's ruling in *Shelby County v. Holder* was unexpected but perhaps foreseeable, given the ideological leanings of the majority.[70] While the Supreme Court maintained that section 5 of the VRA was constitutional, it struck down section 4(b) on the grounds that the coverage maps had not been updated since 1975.[71] At the state level, Republican-controlled legislatures in the coverage area quickly moved to implement new policies that would make it harder for minority voters to get to the polls.[72] In Alabama, the Republican-controlled legislature drew a new apportionment map that diluted African American voting strength in the state.[73] Several states implemented tough new voter identification laws.[74] Although the social science evidence about the impact of these laws was mixed,[75] the operative assumption among politicians and civil rights advocates was that they would make it harder for people of color to vote in all these jurisdictions. High-ranking officials in the Obama administration seemed to share these sentiments in public statements issued after the *Shelby County v. Holder* decision.

With a more conservative Republican Party now in control of Congress (compared with the one that had reauthorized the VRA in 2006), Obama knew it would be impossible to get a new coverage formula for section 4(b) on the books. Thus, the president went public with his views. On August 12, 2015, as the nation prepared to celebrate the VRA's fiftieth anniversary, he published a powerful call for Congress to renew the Voting Rights Act in the form of a letter to the editor of the *New York Times*.[76] President Obama began by referencing the VRA's importance to his own place in history. "I am where I am today," he wrote, "because men and women like Rosanell Eaton [a 94-year-old civil rights activist in North Carolina] refused to accept anything less than a full measure of equality." This comment marked the first time in American history that a US president attributed his electoral success to the reforms brought about by the civil rights movement. Obama even went so far as to suggest that his presidency was part of the embodiment of his generation—the so-called Joshua generation—picking up the mantle and continuing the work of the civil rights movement.[77] This was a watershed moment for race relations, given that the two previous Democratic presidents, who had also gained office as a result of the enhanced voting power of minorities, had shied away from making such explicit claims.

The letter was noteworthy because Obama minced no words about his belief that the laws passed to restrict ballot access in the wake of *Shelby County v. Holder* were designed to suppress minority voters. "From the moment the ink [on the VRA] was dry," he wrote, "there has been a concentrated effort to undermine this historic law and turn back the clock on its progress." Indeed, he continued, "the recent push to restrict Americans' voting rights . . . are not a sign that we have moved past the shameful history that led to the Voting Rights Act. Too often, they are rooted in that history."[78] This statement, shaming the opposition party for engaging in voter suppression, will undoubtedly be remembered as one of the most powerful deployments of the bully pulpit in the post–civil rights era. It was cemented when Obama and his family marched across the Edmund Pettus Bridge in Selma, Alabama, a multigenerational affirmation of the past and future of equal rights.

Conclusion

President Obama left office on January 20, 2017, with an average approval rating of 59 percent. During his eight years in office, Obama's approval ratings among nonwhite voters were always substantially higher than his overall ratings. The highest approval rating he achieved among white voters was 57 percent in 2009. By contrast, his average approval ratings among African Americans (88 percent) and Latinos (63 percent) were much higher.[79] For some scholars, this reality is somewhat paradoxical, given that Obama did not implement any major policies aimed at closing the massive gaps in the material conditions of white and nonwhite Americans.[80] On the contrary, Obama presided at a time when these gaps became even more crystallized in American society.[81] Moreover, the "age of Obama" was also the age of retrenchment in civil rights policies aimed at protecting ethnic and racial minorities in the United States. During Obama's tenure in the White House, the conservative majority on the US Supreme Court voted to overturn key legal precedents that had stood for decades as major tools for the promotion of racial equality.[82] Obama was slow to use his bully pulpit or administrative actions to challenge the rolling back of these laws.[83]

This chapter has examined the Obama paradox in minority public opinion, focusing on the three dimensions of presidential leadership—rhetoric, policy activism, and appointments—that have figured prominently in scholarly discussions of modern presidents' role in race relations. While it is true that President Obama did not make addressing racial inequality a central part of his domestic program, he had some notable achievements in this area. He sent a clear message to the nation by appointing the most racially and ethnically diverse cabinet in US history. And he used his power to pardon while working through the Department of Justice to address racial inequalities in the criminal justice system.

As we have seen, President Obama's rhetoric on race relations has drawn considerable criticism from both progressive activists and scholars for reinforcing narratives about the pathologies of people of color. There is no doubt that much of this criticism is justified. At the same time, Obama deserves credit for the consistent symbolic representation he provided ethnic and racial minorities in his speeches. No president in history talked as frequently or as positively about the contributions made by people of color to the United States. Obama's commitment to discussing the corrosive effects of racism in American life from his perspective as a racial insider was a monumental contribution to race relations.

Notes

1. Anthony W. Marx, *Making Race and Nation: A Comparison of South Africa, the United States, and Brazil* (New York: Cambridge University Press, 1998); Gary B. Nash, *Red, White, and Black: The Peoples of Early North America* (Upper Saddle River, NJ: Pren-

tice Hall, 1974); Audrey Smedley, *Race in North America: Origin and Evolution of a Worldview* (Boulder, CO: Westview Press, 2007).

2. Allen W. Trelease, *The Ku Klux Klan Conspiracy and Southern Reconstruction* (Westport, CT: Greenwood Press, 1979); Philip Dray, *At the Hands of Persons Unknown: The Lynching of Black America* (New York: Modern Library, 2007); Michael Omi and Howard Winant, *Racial Formation in the United States: From the 1960s to the 1990s* (New York: Routledge, 1994).

3. Hanes Walton and Robert C. Smith, *American Politics and the African American Quest for Universal Freedom* (New York: Longman, 2011).

4. I describe Obama as the first president with a *known* multiracial ancestry because it is possible that earlier presidents had non-European ancestors in their family trees. Moreover, during the *Herrenvolk* phase of American history, it was not uncommon for politicians to be accused of mixed-race ancestry by opponents looking to appeal to racist white voters. This tactic was deployed so often against President Warren G. Harding during his 1920 campaign against James Cox that it became accepted folklore among some in the African American community and the source of debate among Harding biographers. The issue was finally resolved in the negative through a DNA test of Harding's descendants. See Peter Baker, "DNA Shows Warren Harding Wasn't America's First Black President," *New York Times*, August 18, 2015.

5. Fredrick C. Harris, *The Price of the Ticket: Barack Obama and the Rise and Fall of Black Politics* (New York: Oxford University Press, 2012); Robert C. Smith Jr., *John F. Kennedy, Barack Obama and the Politics of Ethnic Incorporation and Avoidance* (New York: SUNY Press, 2013).

6. Thomas Sugrue, *Not Even Past: Barack Obama and the Burden of Race* (New York: Princeton University Press, 2010); Smith, *Kennedy, Obama and the Politics of Ethnic Incorporation*; Melanye Price, *The Race Whisperer: Barack Obama and the Political Uses of Race* (New York: NYU Press, 2016).

7. Krissah Thompson, "Cornel West's Criticism of Barack Obama Sparks Debate among African Americans," *Washington Post*, May 18, 2011.

8. For analyses of Obama's high approval ratings among African Americans, see Marissa Abrajano and Craig M. Burnett, "Polls and Elections: Do Blacks and Whites See Obama through Race-Tinted Glasses? A Comparison of Obama's and Clinton's Approval Ratings," *Presidential Studies Quarterly* 42, 2 (2012): 363–375; Don Kinder and Allison Dale-Riddle, *The End of Race? Obama, 2008, and Racial Politics in America* (New Haven, CT: Yale University Press, 2012). For Obama's approval ratings among Latinos, see Mark Hugo Lopez and Ana Gonzalez-Barrera, "Latino Voters Support Obama by 3–1 Ratio, but Are Less Certain than Others about Voting" (Pew Hispanic Center Report, Washington, DC, 2012).

9. Alvin B. Tillery Jr. and Hanes Walton Jr., "Presidential Greatness in the Black Press: Ranking the Modern Presidents on Civil Rights Policy and Race Relations, 1900–2016," in *Politics, Groups, and Identities* (2017), http://dx.doi.org/10.1080/2156550 3.2017.1318760.

10. "Americans See Obama Election as Race Relations Milestone," in *The Gallup Poll* (Washington, DC, 2008).

11. Vincent L. Hutchings, "Change or More of the Same? Evaluating Racial Attitudes in the Obama Era," *Public Opinion Quarterly* 73, 5 (2009): 917–942; Michael Tesler and David Sears, *Obama's Race* (Chicago: University of Chicago Press, 2010); Mi-

chael Tesler, "The Spillover of Racialization into Healthcare: How President Obama Polarized Public Opinion by Racial Attitudes and Race," *American Journal of Political Science* 56, 3 (2012): 690–704; Kinder and Dale-Riddle, *End of Race?*

12. Smith, *Kennedy, Obama and the Politics of Ethnic Incorporation*; Christopher S. Parker and Matt A. Barreto, *Change They Can't Believe In: The Tea Party and Reactionary Politics in America* (Princeton, NJ: Princeton University Press, 2014).

13. G. Calvin Mackenzie, *The Politics of Presidential Appointments* (New York: Free Press, 1981); Michael J. Gerhart, *The Federal Appointments Process: A Constitutional and Historical Analysis* (Durham, NC: Duke University, 2000), 14–31.

14. James W. Riddlesperger and James D. King, "Presidential Appointments to the Cabinet, Executive Office, and White House Staff," *Presidential Studies Quarterly* 16, 4 (1986): 691–699; David E. Lewis, "Presidential Appointments and Personnel," *Annual Review of Political Science* 14 (2011): 47–66.

15. Richard E. Neustadt, *Presidential Power and the Modern Presidents: The Politics of Leadership from Roosevelt to Reagan* (New York: Free Press, 1990); James J. Best, "Presidential Cabinet Appointments: 1953–1976," *Presidential Studies Quarterly* 11, 1 (1981): 62–66; James D. King and James W. Riddlesperger, "Presidential Cabinet Appointments: The Partisan Factor," *Presidential Studies Quarterly* 14 (1984): 231–237.

16. James A. Padget, "Ministers to Liberia and Their Diplomacy," *Journal of Negro History* 22 (1): 50–92; Elliot Skinner, *African Americans and US Policy toward Africa* (Washington, DC: Howard University Press, 1992), 68–80; Alvin B. Tillery Jr., *Between Homeland and Motherland: Africa, US Foreign Policy, and Black Leadership in America* (Ithaca, NY: Cornell University Press, 2011).

17. William S. McFeely, *Frederick Douglass* (New York: W. W. Norton, 1991), 289–293.

18. Nell Irvin Painter, *Exodusters: Black Migration to Kansas after Reconstruction* (New York: W. W. Norton, 1977); Thomas Holt, *Black over White: Negro Political Leadership in South Carolina during the Reconstruction* (Urbana: University of Illinois Press, 1979).

19. J. William Snorgrass, "The Baltimore *Afro-American* and the Election Campaigns of FDR," *American Journalism* 1, 2 (1984): 35–50; William E. Leuchtenburg, *The White House Looks South: Franklin D. Roosevelt, Harry S. Truman, Lyndon B. Johnson* (Baton Rouge: LSU Press, 2005).

20. Karen Hult and Charles Walcott, *Governing the White House: From Hoover through LBJ* (Lawrence: University Press of Kansas, 1995), 124–125.

21. John Hope Franklin, *From Slavery to Freedom: A History of Negro Americans* (New York: Vintage Books, 1969); Barbara Perry, *A "Representative" Supreme Court? The Impact of Race, Religion and Gender on Appointments* (Westport, CT: Greenwood Press, 1991); Wendell E. Pritchett, *Robert C. Weaver and the American City: The Life and Times of an Urban Reformer* (Chicago: University of Chicago Press, 2010).

22. Robert C. Smith Jr., "Black Appointed Officials: A Neglected Area of Research in Black Political Participation," *Journal of Black Studies* 14, 3 (1981): 369–388; Smith, *Kennedy, Obama and the Politics of Ethnic Incorporation*.

23. Carl Tobias, "Diversity and the Federal Bench," *Washington University Law Review* 87 (2010): 1197–1211; Smith, *Kennedy, Obama and the Politics of Ethnic Incorporation*.

24. Neustadt, *Presidential Power*; Samuel Kernell, *Going Public: New Strategies for Presidential Leadership* (Washington, DC: CQ Press, 1986); Jeffrey E. Cohen, "Presidential Rhetoric and the Public Agenda," *American Journal of Political Science* 39, 1 (1995): 87–107.

25. Kenneth R. Mayer, *With the Stroke of a Pen: Executive Orders and Presidential Power* (Princeton, NJ: Princeton University Press, 2002); William Howell, *Power without Persuasion: The Politics of Direct Presidential Action* (Princeton, NJ: Princeton University Press, 2003).

26. Harold C. Fleming, "The Federal Executive and Civil Rights: 1961–1965," *Daedalus* (1965): 921–948; Harvard Sitkoff, "Harry Truman and the Election of 1948: The Coming of Age of Civil Rights in American Politics," *Journal of Southern History* 37, 4 (2009): 597–616; Hugh Davis Graham, *Civil Rights and the Presidency: Race and Gender in American Politics, 1960–1972* (New York: Oxford University Press, 1992).

27. David Card and Alan B. Krueger, "Trends in Relative Black-White Earnings Revisited," *American Economic Review* 83, 2 (1993): 85–91; Melvin L. Oliver and Thomas M. Shapiro, *Black Wealth/White Wealth: A New Perspective on Racial Inequality* (New York: Routledge, 1995); Robert Barsky, John Bound, Kerwin Ko Charles, and Joseph P. Lupton, "Accounting for the Black-White Wealth Gap: A Nonparametric Approach," *Journal of the American Statistical Association* 97, 459 (2002): 663–673.

28. Ricky L. Jones, *What's Wrong with Obamamania? Black America, Black Leadership, and the Death of Political Imagination* (Albany, NY: SUNY Press, 2008); Ben Pitcher, "Obama and the Politics of Blackness: Antiracism in the 'Post-Black' Conjuncture," *Souls* 12, 4 (2010): 313–322; Roy L. Brooks, *Racial Justice in the Age of Obama* (Princeton, NJ: Princeton University Press, 2009).

29. Andrew Rudalevige, *Managing the President's Program: Presidential Leadership and Legislative Policy Formulation* (Princeton, NJ: Princeton University Press, 2002).

30. Michael D. Shear and Yamiche Alcindor, "Jolted by Deaths, Obama Found His Voice on Race," *New York Times*, January 14, 2017.

31. Dorothy E. Roberts, "The Social and Moral Cost of Mass Incarceration in African American Communities," *Stanford Law Review* (2004): 1271–1305; Marie Gottschalk, *The Prison and the Gallows: The Politics of Mass Incarceration in America* (New York: Cambridge University Press, 2006); Todd R. Clear, *Imprisoning Communities: How Mass Incarceration Makes Disadvantaged Neighborhoods Worse* (New York: Oxford University Press, 2009); Michelle Alexander, *The New Jim Crow: Mass Incarceration in the Age of Colorblindness* (New York: New Press, 2012).

32. Alexander, *New Jim Crow.*

33. Ashley Nellis, *The Color of Justice: Racial and Ethnic Disparity in State Prisons* (Washington, DC: Sentencing Project, 2016).

34. John Gramlich and Kristen Bialik, "Obama Used Clemency Power More Often than Any President since Truman," in *Fact Tank* (Washington, DC: Pew Research Center, 2017).

35. Douglas A. Berman, "Turning Hope-and-Change Talk into Clemency Action for Nonviolent Drug Offenders," *New England Journal on Criminal and Civil Confinement* 36 (2010): 59–73.

36. Lanny A. Breuer, "The Attorney General's Sentencing and Corrections Working Group: A Progress Report," *Federal Sentencing Reporter* 23, 2 (2010): 110–114; Marie Gottschalk, "The Past, Present, and Future of Mass Incarceration in the United States," *Criminology and Public Policy* 10, 3 (2006): 483–504; Michael Tonry, "Remodeling American Sentencing: A Ten-Step Blueprint for Moving Past Mass Incarceration," *Criminology and Public Policy* 13, 4 (2014): 503–533.

37. Rachel E. Barkow, "Clemency and Presidential Administration of Criminal Law," *NYU Law Review* 90 (2015): 802.
38. Scott Wilson, "Obama Signs Fair Sentencing Act," *Washington Post*, August 3, 2010; Sarah Hyser, "Two Steps Forward, One Step Back: How Federal Courts Took the Fair out of the Fair Sentencing Act of 2010," *Penn State Law Review* 117 (2012): 503.
39. Alicia Garza, "A Herstory of the #blacklivesmatter Movement," in *Are All the Women Still White? Rethinking Race, Expanding Feminisms*, ed. Janell Hobson (New York: SUNY, 2014); Barbara Ransby, "The Class Politics of Black Lives Matter," *Dissent* 62, 4 (2015): 31–34; Jennifer Chernega, "Black Lives Matter: Racialised Policing in the United States," *Comparative American Studies: An International Journal* (2016): 1–12.
40. Yamiche Alcindor, "Minorities Worry What a 'Law and Order' Trump Presidency Will Mean," *New York Times*, November 11, 2016.
41. Maya Rhodan, "Why President Obama's Police Reform Is a Work in Progress," *Time*, July 9, 2016.
42. Sidney M. Milkis and Jerome M. Mileur, *The Great Society and the High Tide of Liberalism* (Boston: University of Massachusetts Press, 2005); Julian E. Zelizer, *The Fierce Urgency of Now: Lyndon Johnson, Congress, and the Battle for the Great Society* (New York: Penguin, 2015).
43. Jill Quadagno, "Right-Wing Conspiracy? Socialist Plot? The Origins of the Patient Protection and Affordable Care Act," *Journal of Health Politics, Policy and Law* 39, 1 (2014): 35–56.
44. Christina Romer, "The Case for Fiscal Stimulus: The Likely Effects of the American Recovery and Reinvestment Act" (remarks presented at the University of Chicago, 2009); Stephen W. Stathis, *Landmark Legislation 1774–2012: Major US Acts and Treaties* (Washington, DC: CQ Press, 2014).
45. Vicky Lovell, "Evaluating Policy Solutions to Sex-Based Pay Discrimination: Women Workers, Lawmakers, and Cultural Change," *University of Maryland Law Journal of Race, Religion, Gender and Class* 9, 1 (2009): 45–61; Charles A. Sullivan, "Raising the Dead: The Lilly Ledbetter Fair Pay Act," *Tulsa Law Review* 84, 3 (2009): 499–565; Carolyn E. Sorock, "Closing the Gap Legislatively: Consequences of the Lilly Ledbetter Fair Pay Act," *Chicago-Kent Law Review* 85, 3 (2010): 1199–1215.
46. Barbara R. Bergmann, "Occupational Segregation, Wages and Profits When Employers Discriminate by Race or Sex," *Eastern Economic Journal* 1 (1974): 103–110; Sara M. Evans and Barbara J. Nelson, *Wage Justice: Comparable Worth and the Paradox of Technical Reform* (Chicago: University of Chicago Press, 1991); Francine D. Blau and Lawrence M. Kahn, "The Gender Earnings Gap: Learning from International Comparisons," *American Economic Review* 82, 2 (1992): 533–538; Francine D. Blau and Lawrence M. Kahn, "Swimming Upstream: Trends in the Gender Wage Differential in the 1980s," *Journal of Labor Economics* 15, 1 (1997): 1–42.
47. The observed aggregate racial wage gap has been larger than the aggregate gender gap since the phenomenon became a major subject of interest for the social sciences in the 1970s. Moreover, the gap exists at all levels of educational and skills attainment and has grown wider over the past forty years. For excellent studies and reporting on the racial wage gap, see James D. Gwartney and James E. Long, "The Relative Wage Earnings of Black and Other Minorities," *Industrialized Labor Relations Review* 31, 3 (1978): 336–346; William A. Darity Jr., "The Human Capital Approach to Black-White Earnings Inequality: Some Unsettled Questions," *Journal of Human Resources*

17, 1 (1982): 72–93; Kenneth Couch and Mary C. Daly, "Black-White Inequality in the 1990s: A Decade of Progress," *Economic Inquiry* 40, 1 (2002): 31–41; Tanzina Vega, "Wage Gap between Blacks and Whites Is Worst in Nearly 40 Years," CNN, September 20, 2016.

48. Cordelia W. Reimers, "Labor Market Discrimination against Hispanic and Black Men," *Review of Economics and Statistics* (1983): 570–579; Kenneth J. Arrow, "What Has Economics to Say about Racial Discrimination?" *Journal of Economic Perspectives* 12, 2 (1998): 91–100; Devah Pager and Hana Shepherd, "The Sociology of Discrimination: Racial Discrimination in Employment, Housing, Credit, and Consumer Markets," *Annual Review of Sociology* 34 (2008): 181–209; Devah Pager, Bruce Western, and Bart Bonikowski, "Discrimination in a Low-Wage Labor Market: A Field Experiment," *American Sociological Review* 74, 5 (2008): 777–799.

49. Hilary Hoynes, Douglas L. Miller, and Jessamyn Schaller, "Who Suffers during Recessions?" *Journal of Economic Perspectives* 26, 3 (2012): 27–47; Fabian T. Pfeffer, Sheldon Danziger, and Robert F. Schoeni, "Wealth Disparities before and after the Great Recession," *Annals of the American Academy of Political and Social Science* 650, 1 (2013): 98–123; Rakesh Kochar and Richard Fry, "Wealth Inequality Has Widened along Racial, Ethnic Lines since the End of the Great Recession" (Pew Research Center Report, Washington, DC, 2014).

50. Associated Press, "Black Leaders Meet with Obama on Economy," February 10, 2010.

51. Robert C. Lieberman, *Shifting the Color Line: Race and the American Welfare State* (Cambridge, MA: Harvard University Press, 2001); Ira Katznelson, *When Affirmative Action Was White: An Untold History of Racial Inequality in Twentieth-Century America* (New York: W. W. Norton, 2005); Linda Faye Williams, *Constraint of Race: Legacies of White Skin Privilege in America* (State College: Penn State Press, 2010).

52. Katznelson, *When Affirmative Action Was White*, 29.

53. Smith, *Kennedy, Obama and the Politics of Ethnic Incorporation*.

54. Daniel Q. Gillion, *Governing with Words: The Political Dialogue on Race, Public Policy, and Inequality in America* (New York: Cambridge University Press, 2016).

55. Price, *Race Whisperer*.

56. Barack Obama, "A More Perfect Union," speech at the National Constitution Center, Philadelphia, March 18, 2008.

57. Zachary L. Weaver, "Florida's Stand Your Ground Law: The Actual Effects and the Need for Clarification," *University of Miami Law Review* 63 (2008): 395; T. R. Lave, "Shoot to Kill: A Critical Look at Stand Your Ground Laws," *University of Miami Law Review* 67, 1 (2012): 827–860.

58. Lizette Alvarez and Cara Buckley, "Zimmerman Is Acquitted in Killing of Trayvon Martin," *New York Times*, July 13, 2013.

59. Mark Landler and Michael D. Shear, "President Offers a Personal Take on Race in U.S.," *New York Times*, July 19, 2013.

60. Barack Obama, "Remarks by the President on Trayvon Martin," July 19, 2013, https://obamawhitehouse.archives.gov/the-press-office/2013/07/19/remarks-president-trayvon-martin.

61. Price, *Race Whisperer*, 138–139.

62. Ibid., 139.

63. Krissah Thompson and Jon Cohen, "Trayvon Martin Case: Poll Finds Stark Racial Divide," *Washington Post*, April 10, 2012; Michael Dawson, "Racial Tragedies, Polit-

ical Hope, and the Tasks of American Political Science," *Perspectives on Politics* 10, 3 (2012): 669–673.

64. Neustadt, *Presidential Power*, 29–50.

65. David J. Garrow, *Protest at Selma: Martin Luther King, Jr., and the Voting Rights Act of 1965* (New Haven, CT: Yale University Press, 1978); Chandler Davidson, *Quiet Revolution in the South: The Impact of the Voting Rights Act, 1965–1990* (Princeton, NJ: Princeton University Press, 1994).

66. John P. MacCoon, "Enforcement of the Preclearance Requirement of Section 5 of the Voting Rights Act of 1965," *Catholic University Law Review* 29, 1 (1979): 107–127.

67. Mark E. Haddad, "Getting Results under Section 5 of the Voting Rights Act," *Yale Law Journal* 94, 1 (1984): 139–162; Samuel Issacharoff, "Is Section 5 of the Voting Rights Act a Victim of Its Own Success?" *Columbia Law Review* 104, 6 (2004): 1710–1731.

68. Mark A. Posner, "Time Is Still on Its Side: Why Congressional Reauthorization of Section 5 of the Voting Rights Act Represents a Congruent and Proportional Response to Our Nation's History of Discrimination in Voting," *New York University Journal of Legislation and Public Policy* 10, 1 (2006): 51–133; J. Morgan Kousser, "The Strange, Ironic Career of Section 5 of the Voting Rights Act, 1965–2007," *Texas Law Review* 86, 4 (2007): 667–777.

69. Rick Lyman, "Extension of Voting Rights Act Is Likely Despite Criticism," *New York Times*, March 29, 2006.

70. James Thomas Tucker, "Politics of Persuasion: Passage of the Voting Rights Act Reauthorization Act of 2006," *Journal of Legislation* 33 (2006): 205–268.

71. Adam Liptak, "Supreme Court Invalidates Key Part of Voting Rights Act," *New York Times*, June 25, 2013; Ellen D. Katz, "Dismissing Deterrence," *Harvard Law Review Forum* 127 (2013): 248–253; James Blacksher and Lani Guinier, "Free at Last: Rejecting Equal Sovereignty and Restoring the Constitutional Right to Vote; *Shelby County v. Holder*," *Harvard Law and Policy Review* 8, 1 (2014): 39–71.

72. Richard L. Hasen, "Race or Party: How Courts Should Think about Republican Efforts to Make It Harder to Vote in North Carolina and Elsewhere," *Harvard Law Review Forum* 127 (2013): 58–75.

73. Robert Barnes, "Supreme Court Hands Win to Opponents of Alabama Redistricting Plan," *Washington Post*, March 25, 2015.

74. Michael C. Herron and Daniel A. Smith, "Race, Shelby County, and the Voter Information Verification Act in North Carolina," *Florida State University Law Review* 43 (2015): 465–507.

75. Shelley De Alth, "ID at the Polls: Assessing the Impact of Recent State Voter ID Laws on Voter Turnout," *Harvard Law and Policy Review* 3 (2009): 185–203; Rene R. Rocha and Tetsuya Matsubayashi, "The Politics of Race and Voter ID Laws in the States: The Return of Jim Crow?" *Political Research Quarterly* 67, 3 (2014): 666–679.

76. Barack Obama, letter to the editor, *New York Times*, April 12, 2015.

77. Barack Obama, "Remarks at the Selma Voting Rights March Commemoration in Selma, Alabama," March 4, 2007.

78. Obama, letter to the editor.

79. "Gallup Daily: Obama Job Approval" (Washington, DC, 2017).

80. Harris, *Price of the Ticket*; Smith, *Kennedy, Obama and the Politics of Ethnic Incorporation*.

81. Brooks, *Racial Justice in the Age of Obama*; Harris, *Price of the Ticket*; Kochar and Fry, "Wealth Inequality Has Widened."

82. Richard L. Engstrom, "*Shelby County v. Holder* and the Gutting of Federal Preclearance of Election Law Changes," *Politics, Groups, Identities* 2, 3 (2014): 530–548.

83. Joel William Friedman, "The Impact of the Obama Presidency on Civil Rights Enforcement in the United States," *Indiana Law Journal* 87 (2012): 349–367.

CHAPTER FIVE

Obama's Latino Legacy
From Unknown to Never Forgotten

Angela Gutierrez, Angela X. Ocampo, and Matt A. Barreto

On February 10, 2007, the junior senator from Illinois, Barack Obama, announced that he was running for president. At the time, Obama was a political unknown in the Latino community. The first polls in 2007 indicated that 44 percent of Latino voters had never heard of or had no opinion about the senator.[1] Fast-forward to 2017, when President Obama left the White House with an approval rating among Latinos that was close to 80 percent,[2] compared with 56 percent among the general public.[3] How did Obama go from being a political unknown to a trusted and well-liked figure among Latinos? Gaining their support took serious efforts on the campaign trail as well as in the White House. In this chapter, we detail how Obama's voter outreach while campaigning, his appointment of Sonia Sotomayor to the Supreme Court, his passage of the Affordable Care Act, his executive action on immigration, and his efforts to change US policy toward Cuba all worked to construct Obama's Latino legacy.

One result is that Obama forged an extensive liaison between Latinos and the Democratic Party, constituting another important legacy. Obama left office on the verge of fully realigning the Latino community from a moderately Democratic constituency in the 2004 election (which John Kerry lost) to a historically strong Democratic constituency in 2012 and 2016. This was crucial to the Democrats because the Latino vote was growing rapidly. In 2016 Latinos accounted for about 17 percent of the national population and 11 percent of voters.[4] In comparison, Latinos made up less than 4 percent of the electorate in 1992. Obama won large majorities of the Latino vote, precisely as Latino voters were growing in number and influence. Obama may have fallen short in his efforts at state-level party building, but he helped define the Democratic Party's position on a number of key policy areas that were important to Latino voters. In so doing, he reversed Democratic losses in the Latino-influenced states of Florida, New Mexico, Colorado, Nevada, and Virginia from 2004 to 2008 and held those states in 2012, even in a much closer election. While Latinos often have low turnout rates, models controlling for income and education indicate that reported voter participation by Latinos trails that of non-Hispanic whites by only 4 percent,[5] a phenomenon Obama surely contributed to through his dedicated Latino voter outreach. In 2016 Latinos continued to vote overwhelmingly for Democrat Hillary Clinton, who received a record high 79 percent of the Latino vote, compared with Donald Trump's 18 percent. This gap was the largest ever recorded by a Latino Decisions election eve poll,[6] surpassing Obama's share of the Latino vote in 2012. Although Obama's legacy contributed to the creation of a staunch Democratic constituency, in 2016 Latinos were strongly motivated to vote against Trump's anti-immigrant and anti-Latino agenda. Obama's executive orders creating both Deferred Action for Childhood Arrivals (DACA) and Deferred Action for Parents of Americans (DAPA) signaled to Latino voters that the Democratic Party was on their side at a time when they felt under attack. Even if indirectly, through policies, appointments, and mobilization of Latino voters, among other actions, Obama forged a strong relationship between the Latino community and the Democratic Party. As Julia Azari argues (in chapter 3 of this volume), he achieved results in the realm of partisan politics even though he could not build and strengthen the party's organizational structure.

An important question remains. Can Democratic candidates now count on the strong support Obama earned? Obama worked hard to establish and sustain the affinity between Latino voters and the Democratic Party. However, there is no guarantee that any new Democratic candidate will enjoy overwhelming Latino support. Maintaining and strengthening that support is critical for the party, since the growth rate of the Latino population is driven heavily by young US-born Latinos. According to demographers Rob Griffin, William Frey, and Ruy Teixeira, Latinos will account for 18 percent of the eligible US voting population by 2032, and by then, twelve states will have minority majorities.[7] What's more, the Latino vote is gaining importance in newly emerging battleground states such as Arizona and Georgia. The Obama years made it clear that Latinos are a pivotal voting bloc for any Democratic candidate hoping to win the White House, a trend that will surely continue. Barack Obama's outreach to and advocacy on behalf of the Latino community may serve as a blueprint for how candidates, and then presidents, can strengthen their relationship with Latino voters.

The 2008 Election: *Quien es Barack Obama?*

The parties determine the order in which the states vote during primary season. In 2008 the Democratic Party deliberately placed diversely populated states near the beginning of the primary calendar. In keeping with tradition, Iowa was still the first caucus to vote and New Hampshire was still the first primary, but Nevada moved up to the fourth spot; its election was held on January 19, 2008, just sixteen days into the primary season. As a result, there was an unprecedented focus on Latino voters from the very start of the presidential campaign. As the news media descended on the Silver State, it was clear that Barack Obama was relatively unknown to the average Latino voter, whereas Hillary Clinton was highly regarded and well liked in the Latino community. This was best depicted in a Spanish-language news report from the Nevada caucuses, where some Latino voters were unclear as to who was running against Clinton. "They were looking for an Omega, not an Obama."[8]

During the primary, Obama faced a tough battle for the Latino vote. He needed to make a big splash in Iowa if he was going to gain momentum, and the 2008 Iowa caucuses featured virtually no Latino outreach. While Obama was busy campaigning heavily in the Hawkeye State, Clinton focused on a broad strategy that included early Latino outreach in some of the other states with early primaries, including Nevada and the Super Tuesday states of California, Colorado, Illinois, Arizona, New Jersey, New York, and New Mexico. Clinton received high-profile Latino endorsements in every one of those states, while Obama had relatively few Latino supporters early on. Former Denver mayor Federico Peña and Congressman Luis Gutierrez (a fellow Chicagoan) both endorsed Obama early in the primary season, but that was about it. Bill Richardson, the Hispanic former governor of New Mexico, was also in the running and received numerous endorsements from Latino politicians, but not as many as Clinton. That left Obama with few Latino surrogates to make his case and little choice but to spend much of his time campaigning in Iowa, where he needed an upset to establish his viability. Although Obama did score that upset in Iowa and gained considerable momentum, Clinton's strong support in the Latino community and the long list of Latino-rich states voting on Super Tuesday meant that Obama's path to the Democratic nomination would be a long and difficult one.

The Nevada caucus highlighted the difficulty of making inroads with Latino voters. Obama had a good showing, garnering 45.2 percent of the vote, but Clinton won the caucus with 50.7 percent of the overall vote and was supported by roughly two-thirds of Latino voters in the state.[9] However, Obama came out ahead in the delegate count due to Nevada's allocation system.[10] (Obama's campaign would prove much more adept than Clinton's in understanding the workings of delegate allocation.)

Obama recognized the importance of bringing Latino voters into his campaign, and both he and Clinton incorporated Latino outreach into their game plans. Both campaigns hired high-profile Latino campaign staffers and consultants and sought endorsements from Hispanic elected officials and public figures.[11] The campaigns aired ads in Spanish and English targeted at Latino audiences and established field offices in locales that would maximize Latino outreach.[12]

Obama's position as a Washington outsider who was ready to change the status quo was part of his ultimate appeal, but initially, that outsider image was a hurdle he had to overcome. The media raised doubts that Latinos would vote for Obama, but he and his campaign knew he could gain their support; it would just take some time to establish himself. The concern that Latinos would not support Obama was based primarily on racial prejudice. Research indicated that due to their similar economic standing, blacks and Latinos viewed themselves as in competition with each other.[13] Many thought Latinos would not vote for a black candidate because of their animosity and prejudice toward blacks.[14]

But prior experience from his campaign in Chicago suggested that these concerns about racial prejudice were overstated and that Obama's race would not be a problem in courting the Latino vote. In 2004, when Obama ran for the US Senate in Illinois, more Latinos voted for him than for his Hispanic challenger Gerry Chico in the Democratic primary, and he received 84 percent of the Latino vote in the general election. In Chicago, Obama was well liked among Latinos. The concern was not that Latinos would not like Obama but that, elsewhere in the nation, they had no idea who he was. Indeed, after Obama announced the launch of his campaign in February 2007, the share of Latinos with no opinion of Obama actually increased from 35 to 44 percent during that year. As the election cycle continued, however, the share of Latinos with no opinion dropped sharply, and Obama's favorability rose from 41.3 percent in August 2007 to 66.2 percent in February 2008.

As Obama continued to win caucuses and primaries, Latino voters (and voters overall) became more familiar with him. Although Obama was making gains among Latinos, Hillary Clinton's reputation, as well as her husband's legacy, kept her in the lead in that regard. According to a Latino Decisions poll, 76 percent of Latino Democratic primary voters had a favorable view of Clinton, and 48 percent had a *very* favorable view of her. In contrast, about 50 percent of Latino voters had a favorable impression of Obama, but only 19 percent had a *very* favorable view of him.[15] The Obama campaign realized that if it wanted to win the Latino vote in the general election, the candidate would have to establish himself among the Latino community. Obama and the Democratic National Committee invested $20 million in Latino outreach to increase support in key swing states such as Colorado, Florida, Nevada, and New Mexico.[16] But hardly anyone expected Obama to win nearly three-quarters of the Latino vote in the 2008 general election.[17] Back in 2004, George W. Bush had received about 40 percent of the Latino vote to John Kerry's 57 percent.[18] This seventeen-point gap more than doubled in 2008, when John McCain received about 25 percent of the Latino vote to Obama's 72 percent—a forty-seven-point difference. So how did Obama manage to make such large gains among Latino voters in just four years?

McCain, like Bush, was from the Southwest and advocated immigration reform, but McCain's relationship with the Latino community was not as strong as Bush's. And because Obama also supported immigration reform, there was no contrast between the two candidates on this issue. But immigration was not Latino voters' main concern in 2008; they were more concerned about unemployment and economic stability, as well as the war in Iraq.[19] This created an opening for Obama, since he was not a member of the incumbent president's party and was vigorously opposed to Bush's economic policies as well as the war in Iraq. In particular, Obama staked out a strong position against that war that resonated with many Latinos, whose attitudes on Iraq were directly related to their votes in 2008. For example, a November 2008 Latino Decisions poll found that 74 percent of those who believed the current policy in Iraq was working and should be continued cast a ballot for McCain. In contrast, among those who favored an immediate withdrawal of US forces, 83 percent voted for Obama. Of course, Latino voters were overwhelmingly in the latter camp. In the months prior to the 2008 election, Latino Decisions conducted polls in four battleground states: Colorado, Florida, Nevada, and New Mexico.[20] In those four states (all of which switched from the GOP to the Democrats that November), Latino opposition to the Iraq war was palpable. In Florida, 61 percent of Latino registered voters said the war was not worth fighting; in the other three states, that number ranged from 74.7 percent to 78.1 percent. In terms of policy preference, 76.4 percent in Florida favored either a reduction in troop levels or immediate withdrawal. In the other three states, the number exceeded 80 percent.

Obama highlighted his opposition to the war, as well as his domestic policy positions, in positive-toned Spanish-language ads highlighting how he would help Latinos achieve the American dream through access to health care and college assistance.[21] Furthermore, by eliminating tax cuts for the wealthy and implementing a tax cut of up to $500 per person for working families, Obama claimed he would better serve middle-class America.[22] Ultimately, McCain's pro–immigration reform stance was not enough to retain Latino support when Obama was offering the same kind of reform and much more—economic relief, access to health care, and strong opposition to Bush's policies in Iraq. When Barack Obama was sworn in on January 20, 2009, the millions of Latinos who had voted for him now looked to the new president to deliver on his promises.

The Appointment of Sonia Sotomayor

The retirement of Justice David Souter in early 2009 paved the way for what would be one of Obama's key legacies in the judiciary and beyond, as well as a milestone for the Latino community. As the vacancy on the bench made headlines, liberal groups pressured the president to nominate a woman—the Supreme Court had only one female justice at the time. Those on the short list included Solicitor General Elena Kagan; Dianne Wood, a judge for the US Court of Appeals for the Seventh Circuit; Secretary of Homeland Security Janet Napolitano;

and Sonia Sotomayor, who was serving on the US Court of Appeals for the Second Circuit.[23]

The nomination of a Latino Supreme Court justice had been on the agenda of Latino advocacy organizations and civil rights groups such as the Mexican American Legal Defense and Education Fund and the Hispanic National Bar Association for decades. These organizations heavily lobbied Presidents Bill Clinton and George W. Bush to appoint a Hispanic, but during those administrations, other political and ideological factors took precedence.[24] Thus, there was an opportunity for Obama to make history in 2009.

Immediately following the announcement of Souter's retirement, leaders of the Congressional Hispanic Caucus actively encouraged President Obama to appoint a Latino justice.[25] After interviewing those on his short list, Obama was impressed with Sotomayor's extensive experience. She had worked as both a corporate litigator and a prosecutor, and she had spent more time on the bench than any of the other Supreme Court justices at the time of their appointments.[26] On May 26, 2009, President Obama made his choice official: Sotomayor became the first Hispanic nominated to the US Supreme Court.[27] She promised to be a different type of justice: as White House officials underscored, she was from the "real world"—a *Boricua* (Puerto Rican) from the Bronx who had been diagnosed with diabetes at 8 years old, grew up in public housing, and was raised by a single mother after her father, a factory worker, died.[28] Yet Sotomayor had graduated summa cum laude from Princeton University and received her law degree from Yale. As Obama himself put it, what Sotomayor would "bring to the court then [was] not only the knowledge and experience acquired over a course of a brilliant legal career but the wisdom accumulated from an inspiring life's journey."[29]

Sotomayor's confirmation hearings during the summer of 2009 featured strong criticism from Republicans about her affiliation with liberal groups, her past remarks about her Latina identity, and some of her previous rulings. Sotomayor was critiqued for her involvement in an appeals panel that had dismissed a challenge to a decision by the city of New Haven, Connecticut, to scrap a promotion test for firefighters because too few minorities qualified. She was interrogated about remarks in a speech at the University of California–Berkeley, where she had suggested that, as a "wise Latina," she might reach better conclusions than a white male counterpart. Sotomayor's leadership role on the board of the Puerto Rican Legal Deference and Education Fund (now known as LatinoJustice PRLDEF) from 1980 to 2002 also led to questioning by Senate Republicans. Throughout the confirmation hearings, Sotomayor reemphasized her objectivity and proclaimed that she did not base her judgments on her personal experiences, feelings, or biases.[30] Ultimately, with a united Democratic caucus and support from eight Republican senators, Sotomayor was confirmed by a vote of 68–31.

According to research by Sylvia Manzano and Joseph Ura, the Sotomayor nomination was popular among Latinos across national origin groups.[31] Not just Puerto Ricans on the East Coast but also Mexican Americans in the Southwest, Central Americans, South Americans, and others were excited by the elevation of the first Hispanic to the US Supreme Court. This important moment further solidified Obama's approval in the Latino community.

In addition, President Obama was responsible for a record number of appointments of Latinos to other federal offices (see also chapter 8 in this volume). Within his first year in office, thirty-five of Obama's forty-eight Latino senior federal appointees had been confirmed by the Senate (compared with thirty Latino appointees by Bill Clinton and thirty-four by George W. Bush).[32] During Obama's eight years in office, he appointed 324 judges—half of them racial and ethnic minorities. Obama appointed thirty-one Latino federal judges, more than any other US president.[33] Without a doubt, Latinos made significant strides during Obama's presidency in terms of representation through judicial and federal appointments.

The Affordable Care Act

From the campaign trail well into his first term, President Obama made it clear that health care reform would be one of his top priorities. In February 2009 Obama reiterated his desire to work with Congress on this issue, and in November of that year the House of Representatives passed a version of a health insurance bill. Amid much controversy, claims of unconstitutionality, and growing opposition from the nascent Tea Party and other conservative groups, in December 2009—with the support of only Democrats and two independents—the Senate approved its own version of what would become the Patient Protection and Affordable Care Act (ACA). After a long process of reconciliation, President Obama signed the health care bill into law in March 2010.

Even prior to its enactment, the ACA (aka "Obamacare") was poised to greatly benefit the Latino community. Latinos are generally younger and less likely to have health insurance than the US population as a whole; as such, they were expected to be prime beneficiaries of the ACA. In fact, the Latino population is the least likely demographic group to have health insurance: in 2010, the National Health Interview Survey found that more than 40 percent of Latinos were not insured, compared with 11 percent of non-Hispanic whites.[34] This was due to Latinos' lack of access to employer-based insurance, access that has been in decline in recent years in comparison to other minority groups.[35] Latinos are more likely to be employed in industries that do not provide health care benefits, such as agriculture, service, mining, domestic work, and construction.[36] As a result, the Affordable Care Act represented a critical turning point that would tremendously benefit the Latino community.

Latinos also promised to be a pivotal group with regard to the ACA's implementation. The disproportionate rates of uninsured Latinos, in combination with the youth of the overall Latino population, made the ACA heavily dependent on Latino support and enrollment. For the law to succeed, young, healthy Americans had to sign up to balance the makeup of enrollees and bring down overall costs. This put Latinos at the forefront of health care reform and its success.

Prior to the ACA's final passage, Latino Decisions had been tracking Latinos' attitudes on the issue. A November 2009 survey found that most Latinos (61 percent) believed the federal government should guarantee that all people have health insurance, even if that meant increasing taxes.[37] Latinos also supported two significant policy changes that did not make it into the final law passed by Congress: the public option and the inclusion of undocumented immigrants as beneficiaries of reform. By March 2010, surveys showed that health care reform was the top issue for Latino registered voters (32 percent), followed by the economy and jobs (29 percent) and immigration reform (17 percent).

Despite the historic victory by Obama and his fellow Democrats in Congress, the passage of health care reform prompted substantial pushback in the political arena. Republican candidates rode the wave of voter frustration and won a majority in the US House in the 2010 midterm elections. Nonetheless, Latino support for the ACA remained much higher than that of the general public. According to results from an ImpreMedia and Latino Decisions poll in 2010, most Latinos still supported the ACA, and in general, Latinos' attitudes toward the ACA remained quite stable over time, and their clear preference for health care reform was largely unchanged. In October 2011, for example, 50 percent of the Latino electorate believed the law should remain in place, and only 29 percent believed it should be repealed. Despite skepticism among Latinos about changes in the quality of health care, they remained largely positive about the ACA and, if anything, believed the law did not go far enough and needed to be expanded and improved.

In the 2012 presidential campaign, Mitt Romney vowed to repeal Obamacare on day one of his presidency. Given that, on the eve of the election, 61 percent of Latinos still supported Obamacare,[38] health care reform was one of a series of issues—as discussed in more detail below—that propelled 75 percent of Latinos to support Obama's reelection in 2012. Only 23 percent of Latinos cast their votes for Romney. Indeed, later polls found that Latino support for the ACA endured into Obama's second term. One 2013 poll sponsored by the Robert Wood Johnson Foundation showed that 75 percent believed the ACA was good for Latinos in the United States.[39] In 2014 the W. K. Kellogg Foundation State of the Latino Family Poll found that 47 percent of Latinos believed access to health care was improving, while only 29 percent thought it was getting worse.[40] In another poll taken before the 2014 midterm elections, health care continued to be one of the top issues for Latino voters, in addition to the economy and immigration, and Latinos strongly favored Medicaid expansion (77 percent).[41]

In 2015 the Robert Wood Johnson Foundation's Center for Health Policy at the University of New Mexico designed (and Latino Decisions implemented) the most comprehensive survey to date on Latinos and the impact of the ACA. The findings revealed that implementation of the ACA had decreased the percentage of Latinos who lacked insurance from 27 to 17 percent—representing the largest drop in uninsured after the ACA.[42] Another study conducted by the Centers for Disease Control gave different figures but indicated a very similar impact. The number of uninsured among non-Hispanic whites fell by about 10 percentage points between 2010 and 2016, but the rate of Latino uninsured fell from more than 40 percent to 24.5 percent in the same period—the largest drop occurring between 2013 and the first three months of 2016.[43]

The Affordable Care Act was a significant turning point for Latino health and well-being. Even as Obama left office, a National Council of La Raza (NCLR) National Health Care Survey found that a majority of Latinos (55 percent) believed that the ACA was mostly working well, that it should remain in place, and that it should be improved by reducing out-of-pocket costs.[44] Moreover, Latinos continued to show very strong support for specific provisions of the ACA. Ninety percent agreed that people should not be denied coverage due to preexisting conditions, and 83 percent supported the provision that allowed young adults to be covered by their parents' insurance until age 26.

Despite the work that still remains to ensure that all Latinos have equal access to affordable and quality health care, Obama's monumental health care reform had an extraordinary impact on members of the Latino community. Thus, it is not surprising that they continued to support this policy—and Obama himself.

DACA: From "Deporter in Chief" to No. 1 Supporter of DREAMers

Passing comprehensive immigration reform was an oft-repeated policy goal of Barack Obama's campaign in 2008. In an interview with Univision anchor Jorge Ramos, Obama promised to promote an immigration bill within the first year of his presidency. However, *La Promesa de Obama* did not happen. Instead, Latinos witnessed record levels of immigration enforcement in the first few years of Obama's presidency. He believed he needed to be tough on immigration enforcement if he wanted to win congressional Republicans' support on a compromise immigration bill. Among these enforcement measures were memoranda of understanding between local governments and the Department of Homeland Security (DHS) to act as immigration enforcement agents and the Secure Communities program, a deportation initiative that relied on a partnership among local, state, and federal law enforcement agencies.[45] Building on these programs, the administration and the DHS, headed by Secretary Janet Napolitano, pursued an aggressive immigration enforcement strategy. Deportations climbed to 400,000 per year by 2012, and by 2014, Obama had deported more than 2 million undocumented people—more than any other president in US history.

These statistics pushed Obama's approval rating to a low point among Latinos. From their perspective, he had failed to establish an active agenda on immigration in his first two years in office and had not delivered on his promises. Latino enthusiasm for Obama and his administration was further depressed by the Senate's failure to move forward on the Development, Relief, and Education for Alien Minors (DREAM) Act in September 2010, despite its large Democratic majority. By 2011, the Latino community was deeply disappointed by the government's inaction on immigration and the administration's claims that it had no choice but to aggressively enforce the law. Immigration activists called for Obama to act against the devastating impact of deportations, which were nearing a total of 1.2 million since January 2009.[46] In June 2011 a poll of Latino registered voters showed that about 41 percent believed Obama was talking about immigration reform only because the election was approaching, and only 49 percent said they would vote for him in 2012 (recall that he had received close to 70 percent of the Latino vote in 2008). It was clear that the president did not have the Latino support he once enjoyed.[47]

The administration claimed it could do nothing to relieve the strain of its aggressive deportation policies. However, this claim was met with harsh criticism and pushback from immigration activists and DREAMers—the population of young people who had been brought to the United States as children. After Obama's speech at the 2011 National Council of La Raza convention, DREAMers rose from the audience wearing T-shirts that read, "Obama Deports DREAMers." As the president tried to argue that he did not have the power to halt deportations, given federal law, the crowd chanted, "Yes you can"—a sarcastic repurposing of Obama's 2008 campaign slogan. Leading up to the 2012 election, repeated actions by young undocumented activists sent the administration a message: they were disappointed, and something had to be done. For instance, DREAMers went on a hunger strike in Obama's Colorado reelection office. The Latino media also harshly criticized Obama. No journalist was harsher than Jorge Ramos, who pointedly asked Obama why he had not kept his promises, why he had deported so many Latinos and split up so many families. Overall, Latino enthusiasm for Obama reached an all-time low by the end of his first term, at which point only 43 percent of Latinos said they would support his reelection.[48]

But on June 15, 2012, two days after the end of the hunger strike in Colorado, Obama announced his executive action on DACA, which allowed undocumented youths who had come to the United States before age 16 and met certain eligibility criteria (such as a clean criminal record and a history of educational attainment or military service) to be exempt from deportation and to obtain temporary work permits. Immediately after the announcement of DACA, polls showed a dramatic increase in Latinos' enthusiasm and support for the president. Prior to June 2012, a Univision/Latino Decisions poll indicated that 53 percent of Latino voters were less enthusiastic about Obama in 2012 than they had been in 2009, and only 22 percent were more enthusiastic (a net enthusiasm deficit of –19 points). However, after the president announced DACA, 49 percent of Latino voters said they were more enthusiastic about Obama, compared with 14 percent who were less enthusiastic (a net enthusiasm advantage of +35 points).[49]

DACA was a clear and immediate win for Obama's campaign, as his support grew rapidly among Latinos. The executive action also forced Mitt Romney to take a position on the program, and he eventually stated that his administration would not participate in it; instead, he would ask Congress to take a permanent position on immigration issues. During a Republican presidential candidates' debate, Romney also offered his infamous "self-deportation" proposal, whereby life circumstances in the United States would become so dire for undocumented immigrants that they would have no choice but to go back to their home countries. These stances by Romney further solidified Latino support for Obama and other Democratic candidates. In the 2012 Latino Decisions election eve poll, DACA emerged as an important win for Obama; it was a significant contributor to both the high turnout among Latinos and Obama's historic Democratic vote share (75 percent). The executive action allowed Obama to shift his reputation from being DREAMers' "deporter in chief" to being their primary political supporter.

The 2012 Reelection Campaign

In the 2012 election, the Latino vote would prove critical to Barack Obama's success. Whether Latinos would be willing to turn out for Obama again, given the struggling economy and the lack of progress on broader immigration reform, was a serious question for the Democrats. Many Latinos saw themselves as the group that had suffered the most from the financial crisis;[50] certainly the overall process of economic recovery had been very slow. The high levels of unemployment in Latino communities could hurt Obama, given the role of retrospective voting in electoral decision-making: Latinos were not necessarily better off than they had been four years before.[51] Indeed, many Latinos had lost their jobs and faced home-ownership insecurity because of the mortgage crisis. By 2009, Latinos had sustained greater asset losses than both whites and blacks and were experiencing record levels of poverty, especially among children.[52] It is no surprise that from 2011 to 2012 the economy was consistently the most important issue among Latino Decisions survey respondents. In August 2007 the Latino unemployment rate had been 5.5 percent; in 2009, in the midst of the recession, Latino unemployment was 13 percent. By 2012, when the campaign was in full swing, Latino unemployment had improved but was nowhere close to its pre-recession level. In fact, Latino unemployment was still hovering at around 10 percent in the summer and fall of 2012.[53]

It seemed as if the economy would be the defining issue of the 2012 election, and Romney hoped to capitalize on this. So why didn't Latino voters punish Obama for the slow economic recovery? Part of the reason was that Latinos trusted Democrats over Republicans when it came to securing their economic interests. In 2011, even though Obama had been in office for three years, Latinos still blamed George W. Bush for the state of the economy, and they had more faith in Democratic leadership to pull them out of the recession.[54]

Many thought the economy would overshadow other policy issues, but immigration was the topic that resonated with Latino voters. On the campaign trail, Obama was able to market himself as the candidate who best served Latino interests, which led to a strong Latino turnout. Many vote choice models focus on pocketbook voting, but among the Latino electorate, the candidate who can best tap into the minority voters' identity and give the impression that the candidate is "on their side" often performs best. Additionally, by 2012, Obama had recovered from much of the damage done to his political standing by his early immigration policy. Obama's and Romney's contrasting views on immigration worked in Obama's favor when reaching out to Latino voters.

Also important was the *Ya Es Hora* campaign, put together by a number of grassroots groups to encourage Latinos to register to vote and take part in the 2012 election. Both presidential candidates invested significant resources in Latino outreach, with Obama spending nearly $20 million and Romney $10 million to target voters in key battleground states such as Florida, Nevada, Colorado, and Virginia. However, the campaigns were not created equal in this regard, and the messages to Latino voters were hardly "by the book." Immigration reform had been a nonissue in 2008, but in 2012 the rhetoric from the Republican Party was so pronounced that the Latino community often felt like it was under attack.

Unlike the 2008 election, in which the Republican and Democratic candidates both supported a path toward legalization for the undocumented,[55] the Republican candidates running in the 2012 primaries aligned further to the right on this issue. As noted earlier, one of the most notable comments on immigration came from Mitt Romney. He proposed instituting a series of laws cracking down on unauthorized immigrants in an effort to make it impossible for them to find work and make ends meet. Ultimately, their lives in the United States would become so difficult that they would have no choice but to "self-deport."

Additionally, because DACA went into effect before the election, Republican candidates were pressured to state that they would repeal the executive order. Romney doubled down on his anti-immigrant message; he not only vowed to repeal DACA but also appointed Kris Kobach as his principal adviser on immigration. While Kansas secretary of state, Kobach had served as a consultant of sorts to other elected officials seeking to take draconian action against immigration; he was the architect of the Arizona SB 1070 anti-immigrant legislation and had a hand in copycat legislation in Alabama. SB 1070 was widely decried by immigrant rights groups and the American Civil Liberties Union as discriminatory due to a key provision that required members of state and local law enforcement to attempt to determine an individual's legal status when making a lawful stop, detention, or arrest. SB 1070 also allowed officers to arrest individuals who were suspected of being in the United States illegally.[56] During a primary debate in Arizona, Romney called SB 1070 a model for the nation and said he approved of the mandatory use of "e-verify," a federal electronic database designed to crack down on the hiring of undocumented immigrants.

Obama spoke out firmly against SB 1070. When the Supreme Court struck down three-quarters of the law in June 2012 (in *Arizona v. United States*), Obama praised the decision and vowed that the Department of Justice would keep fighting to overturn the fourth provision as well, which allowed police to ask for proof of citizenship. Romney's reaction to the court's decision was to issue a statement saying that he opposed the federal government's interference in states' rights and that Arizona should be free to enact its own laws.

Given the clear contrast between the two candidates on this issue, Obama's failure to convince Congress to pass a comprehensive immigration bill paled in comparison to Romney's stated interests and values. Additionally, Latinos trusted Obama with the economy—they blamed Bush, not Obama, for its problems—and believed their situation was more likely to improve under Democratic leadership. Romney invested financially in Latino outreach, but his rhetoric was not what Latino voters wanted to hear. President Obama was not disappointed by the Latino turnout in 2012. Latinos accounted for one out of ten votes cast nationwide in the presidential election, and Obama received a full three-quarters of those votes.

From DACA to DAPA

With the 2012 election behind him, Obama called for Congress to finally pass comprehensive immigration reform. A Republican National Committee "autopsy" of the 2012 results bolstered his, and Latinos', hopes: "It does not matter what we say about education, jobs or the economy; if Hispanics think we do not want them here, they will close their ears to our policies. Among the steps Republicans take in the Hispanic community and beyond, we must embrace and champion comprehensive immigration reform."[57] But this did not happen. The Senate passed a sweeping bipartisan bill in June 2013—winning 68 votes for a package that included guest worker provisions, greater border security, and a path to citizenship for currently undocumented residents.[58] But the House, pressured by its Tea Party–aligned "Freedom Caucus," refused to even consider the measure.

Following the 2014 midterm elections—in which Democrats lost their Senate majority—President Obama decided to take immigration policy into his own hands. On November 20, 2014, he announced the Deferred Action for Parents of Americans and Lawful Permanent Residents (DAPA), which also expanded the DACA program. DAPA sought to temporarily defer action against parents of US citizens or lawful permanent residents. The DACA modification eliminated the age ceiling and expanded eligibility to individuals who had resided in the United States on or before January 1, 2010. DAPA, in combination with DACA, would have suspended the deportations of slightly less than half of the 11 million undocumented individuals in the United States.[59] However, it was not long before these programs were challenged in federal court by the state of Texas and twenty-five others. Stymied by judicial injunctions, they never took effect (see also chapters 9 and 10 in this volume).

Like the original DACA, the announcement of DAPA came at a time when both Congress and the White House had failed to make any sustained progress on immigration reform, and the Obama administration's approval rating among Latinos had dipped again. But both DAPA and the expanded DACA were met with great enthusiasm from the Latino community. A 2014 poll found that 89 percent of Latinos supported both executive actions, and 80 percent of Latinos would oppose efforts to repeal or block these actions.[60] DAPA was particularly important because it focused on keeping families together, responding to the pleas of many in the immigrant community.

Obama strongly defended DACA and DAPA to the end of his administration. After a split decision from the Supreme Court in June 2016 upheld the temporary injunction from a lower court, Obama argued that continuing to block the programs "doesn't just set the system back even further, it takes us further back from what our country aspires to be."[61] Even though he was unsuccessful in expanding DACA and implementing DAPA—and the Trump administration expressed no interest in arguing the merits of the executive actions—it was evident to Latinos that President Obama had taken critical steps on their behalf. Obama had failed to keep his original promise—immigration reform within his first year in office—but by the end of his term, he had shown that he was committed to the Latino community and was willing to take action to delay deportations and keep Latino families together.

Cuba

In December 2014 President Obama announced the restoration of diplomatic relations with Cuba. After more than fifty years, since Fidel Castro's rise to power, the United States was going to reopen its embassy in Havana. Recognizing that isolation had not succeeded in ending Castro's regime, Obama opted for a new strategy in dealing with the Cuban government. After normalizing relations with

Cuba, Obama sought to ease restrictions on travel to the island.[62] He eliminated the requirement that American visitors must spend their time in Cuba with US tour operators who were forced to use government tour buses and stay in state-run hotels. This increased tourism on the island, despite the ongoing restrictions on certain types of travel. Additionally, as a sign of goodwill toward the Cuban government, Obama called on Congress to lift the embargo on Americans traveling to and doing business in Cuba, which would have allowed all types of travel to the island. However, Congress opted not do so. Although the changes in US policy did not completely remove the restrictions put in place during the Cold War, one of the most significant changes was to end the "wet foot/dry foot" policy, which had allowed Cubans trying to reach the United States by sea to apply for legal permanent residency as long as they made it onto American soil.[63]

Obama's push to open trade with Cuba was likewise historic, as well as beneficial to the Democratic Party's evolving relationship with Cuban Americans. Although a majority of Latino voters are Democratic, especially those of Puerto Rican and Mexican origin, Latinos of Cuban descent have historically voted Republican in US elections.[64] This is largely due to the United States' strained relationship with the Castro regime and Republican support for the Cuban embargo. Cuban Americans make up just a small portion of the Latino population in the United States—roughly 3.5 percent—but they are heavily concentrated in one state, Florida, where they account for a very large portion of the Latino population. Florida has a long history of close elections, which increases the importance of the Cuban population, especially in presidential races.

Cuban allegiance to the Republican Party goes back to the rise of the Castro regime at the end of the 1950s. Those who fled Cuba in the early 1960s were against the communist regime, and a majority of these refugees settled in the Miami area. The Cuban population in Florida was drawn to the Republicans' militant anticommunist position and quickly established themselves within Miami's Republican Party.[65] Although Cubans who immigrated prior to 1980 were strongly anti-Castro and largely identified as Republican, a public opinion survey from 2008 found that two-thirds of Cubans who immigrated to the South Florida area after 1980 opposed the embargo.[66] The decline of the early immigrant population and the differing views of new immigrants created an antiembargo shift among Florida's Cuban population.[67] Studies of Cuban voters have found that younger Cubans are considerably less conservative than both their parents and grandparents and the Republican Party.[68]

Obama's election in 2008 coincided with this shift: for the first time, a majority of Cubans in South Florida did not support the embargo. At the same time, Republican Party registration among Cuban Americans slowed, while Democratic and independent identification increased.[69] This change in Cuban American ideology indicated a challenge to the anti-Castro policy—and an opportunity for Democratic gains.

This trend was only amplified during Obama's second term. An October 2014 *New York Times* poll found that respondents favored reestablishing relations with Cuba by a nearly two-to-one margin.[70] Notably, Cuban American opinion was not much different from that of the American public overall. A poll from Florida International University (reported in the *Miami Herald*) found that more than two-thirds of Cuban Americans favored reestablishing diplomatic relations and easing the travel ban, and a 52 percent majority favored an end to the economic embargo.[71] Additionally, leadership on the island was changing. Ninety-year-old Fidel Castro had transferred political leadership to his brother Raul (who would himself retire in April 2018). The Castro regime's control over Cuba was coming to an end, and so were the old ways of the Cold War. So when President Obama announced a renewal of relations between Cuba and the United States in December 2014, this seemed like a move most Americans would support. Although there was some outcry in Miami, only about 250 people rallied to protest the change in US-Cuba relations. Highlighting this shift, Obama himself visited the island in March 2016, the first president to do so in nearly a century. "*¿Que bolá Cuba?*" he tweeted as he arrived. "Just touched down here, looking forward to meeting and hearing directly from the Cuban people."[72]

Traditionally, Cuban Americans have not been a target group for Democrats, but Obama's easing trade and travel restrictions on Cuba paved the way for improving the Democratic Party's relationship with Cuban Americans. Given the decline of Republican registrants and the shift on Cuba, with some effort, Democrats may be able to increase their support among Cuban Americans and further solidify the Democratic hold on the Latino vote.

Obama, Latinos, and 2016

Starting in early July 2016, Barack Obama made history by becoming the first president in 100 years to campaign so strongly for his successor.[73] To ensure that his legacy was in good hands, Obama appealed to crowds in swing states, touting Hillary Clinton's preparedness and condemning Republican nominee Donald Trump. "We cannot afford, suddenly, to treat this like a reality show," the president warned. "We can't afford to act as if there's some equivalence here."[74] For Obama, the 2016 election was about more than electing a Democrat. It was about preserving his legacy and ensuring that the policies passed and executive actions taken by his administration were safe for years to come.[75]

Throughout the campaign, Latinos were adamantly against the Republican nominee, who had, after all, notoriously launched his campaign by stating, "I will build a great, great wall on our southern border. And I will have Mexico pay for that wall."[76] Trump went on to claim that immigrants from Mexico were "criminals and rapists." The rhetoric was outlandish, and the policies Trump campaigned for would undermine Obama's executive orders and ensure that they never became law. Latino voters recognized this and were quick to respond.

Donald Trump's run for the presidency was viewed as a threat by many Latinos, not only those of Mexican origin. Given his proclaimed policies—notably, to reduce immigration from Latin America and remove undocumented people living in the United States—Trump's candidacy undermined the likelihood of Latino support for the Republican Party. In fact, voting among Latinos increased in Florida, Nevada, Texas, and other states, in seeming repudiation of Trump's campaign.[77] Obama was a trusted voice in the Latino community, and he served as a strong surrogate to reinforce the importance of voting for Clinton on Election Day.

Barack Obama spent every day of the week before the election stumping for Hillary Clinton. White House press secretary Josh Earnest stated that the Clinton campaign considered Obama an effective messenger in making the case for Clinton.[78] Although Obama campaigned in Florida and North Carolina, his main efforts involved getting out the African American vote, which had displayed weaker early voter turnout than in previous years. Latino voters were voting early, and their enthusiasm indicated that Obama and Clinton had made great strides in consolidating Latino support for the Democratic Party.

In the end, Clinton won 79 percent of the Latino vote.[79] She won the popular vote by about 3 million votes but lost the Electoral College. Trump took office, still promising to "build the wall," in January 2017. Hanging in the balance were more than 728,000 people registered for DACA, 20 million people newly insured under Obamacare, and open relations with Cuba.

Lasting Legacy?

Obama made great strides to secure a strong legacy among Latino voters. But whether that will translate to a lasting policy legacy on their behalf is now uncertain. On some fronts, such as health care and judicial appointments, Obama's legacy will have a lasting impact. But when it comes to immigration and relations with Cuba, it seems less likely that the changes implemented under the Obama administration will have longevity.

Donald Trump prioritized the repeal and replacement of Obamacare even before he formally took office. Within the first few months of his mandate, Trump and members of his administration made frequent remarks that the repeal and replacement of the ACA would happen and that this would translate into "insurance for everybody," "no cuts to Medicare," and "everybody would be taken care of," among other blanket statements.[80] In March 2017 Republicans in the House released the American Health Care Act, a plan to repeal and replace parts of the ACA. In the coming months, Republicans in the House and Senate engaged in markups, revisions, and additional drafts in an attempt to appease GOP conservatives and moderates alike. Trump's support of multiple versions of the bill in both chambers, as well as his steady belief that Obamacare would "explode" and "crash and burn," characterized his stance during the GOP's failed attempts to garner the necessary votes to repeal and replace Obama's signature health care policy.[81] In late September 2017 Obama's legacy on health care withstood its last challenge in the Senate, ensuring that millions of Latinos would remain covered. Evidence suggests that Latinos continue to rely on the ACA, given the increase in the share of Latino consumers of Obamacare from 10 percent in 2017 to 12 percent in 2018.[82]

Obama's legacy seems less certain in the area of immigration. Starting his campaign with a call to stop immigration on the southern border, the Trump administration seemed intent on not only reversing policies such as DACA but also reducing legal immigration and making it more difficult for those already in the United States to obtain citizenship.[83] For instance, Trump has proposed denying citizenship to any person who has used government services such as Obamacare, Social Security, or other programs by classifying such an individual as a "public charge." Trump has also sought to terminate DACA, but as of this writing, these efforts have been blocked by the courts, where the program's fate currently rests.[84] Efforts by Democrats to forge a deal with the Trump administration—enacting DACA by statute in exchange for partial funding to construct the president's promised border wall—had failed as of the end of 2018.

Trump's approach to immigration policy has upset many Americans. In 2018 the public protested the Trump administration's policy of separating families at the US-Mexico border—taking children, including babies, from their parents and sending them to child detention centers that were ill equipped to care for them.[85] And even when the administration was ordered by the courts to reunite these families, the lack of information collected by border officials meant that reunification was easier said than done. At the same time, there were significant changes to the temporary protected status given to migrants fleeing war or natural disaster. The Trump administration is seeking to phase out this program, and many people who have been living and working legally in the United States for decades have been given eighteen months to leave the country. This has disproportionately affected thousands of Hondurans, Nicaraguans, and Salvadorans.[86]

In the area of political diplomacy, the new administration seems intent on undoing Obama's efforts to normalize relations with Cuba.[87] Since Trump's inauguration, there has been a reduction in personnel at the US embassy in Cuba,[88] and in November 2017 new travel and trade policies were enacted that closed many of the doors opened during Obama's presidency. These policy changes not only limit trade but also restrict travel by individuals, who can no longer apply for individual travel visas.[89] A US-based tour group that engages in US-approved activities must once again accompany Americans hoping to travel to Cuba.

Donald Trump's actions and attitudes toward Latinos serve as a constant reminder of how much better the Latino community fared when a Democrat was in office. Whereas Obama increased Latino outreach, Trump and his policies directly harmed this community. This was vividly demonstrated by his response when Hurricane Maria struck Puerto Rico in 2017.

During his tenure as president, Obama publicly vowed on multiple occasions to support Puerto Ricans as they plotted their own future.[90] Obama visited the island in 2011, making the first official trip of a sitting American president since 1961. He praised Puerto Ricans for their contributions in "writ[ing] the American story" and promised to stand with them as they decided on the island's political status. Nonetheless, as Puerto Rico's debt troubles deepened, Obama signed the bipartisan Puerto Rico Oversight, Management, and Economic Stability Act (PROMESA) into law. PROMESA was critiqued by many, including Senators Bob Menéndez and Bernie Sanders, for imposing "colonial" control on the island and exacerbating its troubles by allowing debt restructuring at greater cost through an unelected financial control board. Some of its supporters, such as Puerto Rican representative Nydia Velázquez (D-NY), argued that although the bill had shortcomings, there was no viable alternative.[91] This sentiment was shared by Obama, who was determined to help Puerto Rico out of its financial crisis, even if it meant signing a less-than-perfect bill.

Obama's positions did not always align with Puerto Ricans' view of what was best for the island, but they were certainly better than the Trump administration's actions in the aftermath of Hurricane Maria, which devastated Puerto Rico in late September 2017 and resulted in some 3,000 deaths.[92] Trump's response has been characterized as neglectful and inadequate, given the magnitude of the destruction caused by the hurricane. The enduring visual from Trump's visit to the island was the president tossing paper towels into a crowd at a relief center, a gesture Puerto Ricans considered disgraceful and lacking in empathy for people who had no food, clean water, or electricity. Trump was soon feuding with San Juan mayor Carmen Yulín Cruz and claiming that his administration did a "fantastic job" in handling the recovery process.[93] In fact, the administration's response was shockingly poor, particularly when compared with the faster reaction and greater aid received by the Texas cities hit by Hurricane Harvey just a few weeks earlier.

Observers have long wondered whether Latinos' natural affinity ought to be with the Republican Party.[94] Yet, given Obama's strong outreach efforts toward the Latino community and Trump's seeming determination to drive it away, it seems unlikely that Latino support will shift toward the Republicans any time soon. Obama's efforts to improve policy in areas that matter to Latinos, coupled with Trump's hostile policy toward immigrants, lead us to believe that we can put the conservative Latino theory to bed once and for all. That in itself may be an important and lasting legacy of the Obama era.

Notes

1. Results are from a survey of 400 Latino voters conducted in Nevada in July 2007.
2. Results are from NALEO/Telemundo/Latino Decisions 2016 weekly tracking poll, http://www.latinodecisions.com/files/1514/7839/2130/Wk8_Full_Tracker.pdf.
3. Based on a Gallup poll conducted in December 2016.
4. Estimates were calculated using the Latino Decisions (LD) Turnout Predict tool and the total number of ballots cast.
5. Shaun Bowler and Gary Segura, *The Future Is Ours: Minority Politics, Political Behavior, and the Multiracial Era of American Politics* (Thousand Oaks, CA: Sage, 2011).
6. Matt A. Barreto and Gabriel Sanchez, "In Record Numbers, Latinos Voted Overwhelmingly against Trump. We Did the Research," *Monkey Cage* (blog), *Washington Post,* November 11, 2016.
7. *States of Change: The Demographic Evolution of the American Electorate, 1980–2060,* February 24, 2015, https://www.americanprogress.org/issues/democracy/news/2015/02/24/107166/interactive-the-demographic-evolution-of-the-american-electorate-1980-2060/.
8. James Rainey, "Clinton Gets Warm Welcome from Latinos," *Los Angeles Times,* January 23, 2008, http://articles.latimes.com/2008/jan/23/nation/na-hillary23.
9. Shailagh Murray and Anne E. Kornblut, "Women, Latinos Propel Clinton to First Place," *Washington Post,* January 19, 2008, http://www.washingtonpost.com/wp-dy/content/article/2008/01/19/AR2008011902598.html.
10. Real Clear Politics, "Elections 2008, Nevada Democratic Caucus," http://www.realclearpolitics.com/epolls/2008/president/nv/nevada_democratic_cau cus-236.html.
11. Monica Langley, "Clinton's Right-Hand Woman Scrambles for a Win in Iowa," *Wall Street Journal,* December 26, 2007; Jeff Zelney, "Richardson Endorses Obama," *New York Times,* March 21, 2008.
12. Ira Teinowitz, "Hispanic Spending in Texas to Surpass $2 Million," *AdAge,* February 25, 2008.
13. Paula D. McClain et al., "Black Americans and Latino Immigrants in a Southern City: Friendly Neighbors or Economic Competitors?" *Du Bois Review* 41, 1 (2007): 97–117.
14. Adam Nagourney and Jennifer Steinhauer, "In Obama's Pursuit of Latinos, Race Plays Role," *New York Times,* January 15, 2008; Amy Goldstein, "Democrats' Votes Display Racial Divide," *Washington Post,* February 6, 2008; John B. Judis, "Hillary Clinton's Firewall," *New Republic,* December 18, 2007.
15. Latino Decisions primary surveys 2007, 2008. For complete tables and survey findings, see Matt Barreto and Gary Segura, *Latino in America* (New York: PublicAffairs, 2014), 87–89.
16. Lindsay Daniels, "Engaging the Latino Electorate," National Council of La Raza, March 3, 2011, http://publications.unidosus.org/bitstream/handle/123456789/1139/latinovotereportfinal.pdf?sequence=1&isAllowed=y; Arian Campo-Flores, "Obama's Latino Edge," *Newsweek,* November 4, 2008.
17. Estimates are from http://www.latinodecisions.com/blog/2008/11/19/record-latino-voter-turnout-in-2008-helps-obama-win-key-battleground-states/.
18. Gary M. Segura, "Latino Public Opinion and Realigning the American Electorate," *Daedalus* 141 (2012): 98–113.

19. Freddy Balsera, "How Obama Closed the Deal with Hispanics," *PR Newswire*, November 4, 2008.

20. "New Poll Suggests Latino Voters May Make the Difference in Four Key States," Latino Decisions, October 10, 2008, http://web.archive.org/web/20160218094055 /http://www.latinodecisions.com/blog/2008/10/07/new-poll-suggests-latino-voters -may-make-the-difference-in-four-key-states/.

21. Balsera, "How Obama Closed the Deal."

22. Barack Obama's Plan, "Provide Middle Class Americans Tax Relief," https://web .archive.org/web/20080102201307/http://www.barackobama.com/issues/economy /#tax-relief.

23. Nina Totenberg, "Supreme Court Justice Souter to Retire," NPR, April 30, 2009; Karen Tumulty, "Why Obama Picked Her," *Time*, May 26, 2009.

24. Tony Mauro, "Pressure Is on Obama to Name First Hispanic Supreme Court Justice," *Legal Times*, December 1, 2008.

25. Jeremy Jacobs, "Hispanic Caucus Ramps up SCOTUS Pressure on Obama," *The Hill*, May 1, 2009.

26. Robert Barnes and Michael A. Fletcher, "Sotomayor Embodies Obama's Criteria for Supreme Court," *Washington Post*, May 27, 2009.

27. Robyn Kurland and Corrine Yu, "First Hispanic Justice Confirmed to U.S. Supreme Court," in *Civil Rights Monitor*, ed. William L. Taylor (Leadership Conference Education Fund, 2010), 22–23, http://civilrightsdocs.info/pdf/monitor/cr-monitor-2010 .pdf.

28. Lauren Collins, "Number Nine," *New Yorker*, January 11, 2010.

29. Transcript of Obama's announcement, May 26, 2009, http://www.cnn.com/2009 /POLITICS/05/26/obama.sotomayor.transcript/index.html?iref=24hours.

30. Amy Goldstein, Robert Barnes, and Paul Kane, "Sotomayor Emphasizes Objectivity, Explains 'Wise Latina' Remark," *Washington Post*, July 15, 2009.

31. Sylvia Manzano and Joseph D. Ura, "Desperately Seeking Sonia? Latino Heterogeneity and Geographic Variation in Web Searches for Judge Sonia Sotomayor," *Political Communication* 30, 1 (2013): 81–99.

32. Laura Wides-Munoz, "Obama Naming Hispanics to Top Posts at Record Pace," *San Diego Union-Tribune*, December 21, 2009, http://www.san diegouniontribune .com/sdut-obama-naming-hispanics-to-top-posts-at-record-pace-2009dec21-story .html.

33. John Gramlich, "Trump Has Appointed a Larger Share of Female Judges than Other GOP Presidents, but Lags Obama," Pew Research Center, October 2, 2018, http:// www.pewresearch.org/fact-tank/2018/03/20/trumps-appointed-judges-are-a-less-di verse-group-than-obamas/.

34. This study was carried out by the National Health for Center Statistics, the Centers for Disease Control and Prevention, and the US Department of Health and Human Services. The full report can be found at https://www.cdc.gov/nchs/data/series/sr_10 /sr10_251.pdf.

35. Philip Cooper and Barbara Steinberg Schone, "More Offers, Fewer Takers for Employment-Based Health Insurance: 1987 and 1996," *Health Affairs* 16, 6 (1997): 142–149; Gabriel R. Sanchez, Amy Sue Goodin, Amelia A. Rouse, and Richard Santos, "The Impact of Ethnicity on Attitudes toward Health Care Reform in New Mexico," *Social Science Journal* 47, 2 (2010): 326–343.

36. Emilio J. Carrillo, Fernando M. Trevino, Joseph R. Betancourt, and Alberto Coustasse, "Latino Access to Health Care: The Role of Insurance, Managed Care, and Institutional Barriers," in *Health Issues in the Latino Community*, ed. Marilyn Aguirre-Molina, Carlos W. Molina, and Ruth Enid Zambrana (San Francisco: Jossey-Bass, 2001), 55–73.

37. Latino Decisions poll, November 2009, http://www.latinodecisions.com/files/3813 /7718/8199/RWJ_AARP_LD_Health_Care_Toplines_Nov_2009.pdf.

38. ImpreMedia–Latino Decisions election eve poll, 2012, http://www.latinodecisions .com/files/9313/5233/8455/Latino_Election_Eve_Poll_-_Crosstabs.pdf.

39. The poll, which surveyed 800 Latinos nationally, was sponsored by the Robert Wood Johnson Foundation's Center for Health Policy at the University of New Mexico and by ImpreMedia; it was administered by Latino Decisions.

40. W. K. Kellogg Foundation State of the Latino Family Poll, 2014, http://www.docu mentcloud.org/documents/1357155-wkkf-state-of-latino-family-2014.html. This poll surveyed Latino adults on a variety of topics, including health and well-being.

41. Latino Decisions election eve poll, 2014, http://www.latinodecisions.com/files/6414 /1520/9800/Election_Eve_2014_-_NATIONAL_TOPLINES.pdf. This poll surveyed 4,200 Latino voters in ten states.

42. "Data Shows Affordable Care Act Coverage Greatly Improves Latinos' Access to Health Care," http://familiesusa.org/blog/2015/10/data-show-affordable-care-act-cover age-greatly-improves-latinos-access-health-care.

43. For the full report, see https://www.cdc.gov/nchs/data/nhis/earlyrelease/insur201609 .pdf.

44. This poll was conducted in October 2016. See http://www.latinodecisions.com /files/3514/7758/0047/NCLR_Policy_Deck_Oct_2016.pdf.

45. Tanya Golash-Boza, *Immigration Nation: Raids, Detentions, and Deportations in Post-9/11 America* (London: Paradigm Publishers, 2012).

46. Muzaffar Chishti, Sarah Pierce, and Jessica Bolter, "The Obama Record on Deportations: Deporter in Chief or Not?" Migration Policy Institute, January 26, 2017.

47. "Latinos Divided on Obama and Immigration," http://www.latinodecisions.com/blog /2011/06/13/latinos-divided-on-obama-and-immigration/.

48. Pilar Marrero, "70 Percent of Latinos Approve of Obama—But Only 43 percent Are Certain to Vote for Obama in 2012," February 11, 2011, http://www.latinodecisions .com/blog/2011/02/14/70-of-latinos-approve-of-obama/.

49. For more details, see http://www.latinodecisions.com/blog/2012/06/17/new-poll -latino-voters-enthusiastic-about-obama-dream-announcement-oppose-romney-pol icy-of-self-deport/.

50. Paul Taylor, Mark Hugo Lopez, Gabriel Velasco, and Seth Motel, "Hispanics Say They Have the Worst of a Bad Economy," Pew Research Center, January 26, 2012, http://www.pewhispanic.org/2012/01/26/hispanics-say-they-have-the-worst-of-a -bad-economy.

51. Morris Fiorina, "Economic Retrospective Voting in American National Elections: A Micro-analysis," *American Journal of Political Science* 22 (May 1978): 426–443.

52. Rakesh Kochhar, Richard Fry, and Paul Taylor, *Wealth Gaps Rise to Record Highs between Whites, Blacks, Hispanics*, Executive Summary (Pew Research Center, 2011); Mark Hugo Lopez and Gabriel Velasco, *The Toll of the Great Recession: Childhood*

Poverty among Hispanics Sets Records, Leads Nation (Pew Hispanic Center, 2011); Robin A. Cohen and Michael E. Martinez, *Health Insurance Coverage: Early Release of Estimates from the National Health Interview Survey, 2008* (Hyattsville, MD: National Center for Health Statistics, CDC, 2009).

53. US Bureau of Labor Statistics, Labor Force Statistics from the Current Population Survey, https://data.bls.gov/timeseries/LNS14000009.

54. Univision News–LD El Voto Latino poll, November 8, 2011, http://www.latinodeci sions.com/files/6013/4697/4877/Univision_Nov_2011.pdf.

55. *New York Times* election profile, http://elections.nytimes.com/2008/president/issues /immigration.html.

56. Ballotpedia, Arizona SB 1070, https://ballotpedia.org/Arizona_SB_1070.

57. Garance Franke-Ruta, "What You Need to Read in the RNC Election Autopsy Report," *Atlantic*, March 18, 2013, https://www.theatlantic.com/politics/archive/2013 /03/what-you-need-to-read-in-the-rnc-election-autopsy-report/274112/.

58. Ashley Parker and Jonathan Martin, "Senate, 68 to 32, Passes Overhaul for Immigration," *New York Times*, June 28, 2013, http://www.nytimes.com/2013/06/28/us /politics/immigration-bill-clears-final-hurdle-to-senate-approval.html.

59. Haeyoun Park and Alicia Parlapiano, "Supreme Court's Decision on Immigration Case Affects Millions of Unauthorized Immigrants," *New York Times*, June 23, 2016, http://www.nytimes.com/interactive/2016/06/22/us/who-is-affected-by-supreme -court-decision-on-immigration.html?_r=0.

60. "National Poll Finds Overwhelming Support For Executive Action on Immigration," *Latino Decisions*, November 24, 2014, http://www.latinodecisions.com/blog /2014/11/24/new-poll-results-national-poll-finds-overwhelming-support-for-execu tive-action-on-immigration/.

61. Amanda Sakuma, "Immigration: The Legacy Battle Obama May Never Win," NBC News, June 23, 2016, http://www.nbcnews.com/news/us-news/immigration-legacy -battle-obama-may-never-win-n597886.

62. Peter Baker, "U.S. to Restore Full Relations with Cuba, Erasing a Last Trace of Cold War Hostility," *New York Times*, December 17, 2014.

63. Julie Hirschfeld Davis and Frances Robles, "Obama Ends Exemption for Cubans Who Arrive without Visas," *New York Times*, January 12, 2017.

64. Michael Alvarez and Lisa Garcia Bedolla, "The Foundations of Latino Voter Partisanship: Evidence from the 2000 Election," *Journal of Political Science* 65, 1 (2003): 31–49.

65. Carole J. Uhlaner and Chris F. Garcia, *Foundations of Latino Party Identification: Learning, Ethnicity and Demographic Factors among Mexicans, Puerto Ricans, Cubans and Anglos in the United States* (Irvine: University of California Irvine, Center for the Study of Democracy, 1998).

66. Institute for Public Opinion Research at Florida International University, panel study of Cubans in Miami-Dade County, 2008; Chris Girard, Guillermo J Grenier, and Hugh Gladwin, "The Declining Symbolic Significance of the Embargo for South Florida's Cuban Americans," *Latino Studies* 8, 1 (2010): 4–22.

67. Benjamin G. Bishin and Casey A. Klofstad, "The Political Incorporation of Cuban Americans: Why Won't Little Havana Turn Blue?" *Political Research Quarterly* 65, 3 (2012): 586–599.

68. Chris Girard, Guillermo J. Grenier, and Hugh Gladwin, "Exile Politics and Republi-

can Party Affiliation: The Case of Cuban Americans in Miami," *Social Science Quarterly* 93, 1 (2012): 42–57.

69. Ibid.

70. *New York Times* poll, 2014, https://www.nytimes.com/interactive/2014/12/17/world/americas/17first-draft-polling.html?module=inline.

71. Marc Caputo and Juan O. Tamayo, "Of Demographics and Drift: 'The Re-Cubanization of Miami' and Waning Support for the Embargo," *Miami Herald*, June 17, 2014, https://www.miamiherald.com/news/nation-world/world/americas/article1966831.html.

72. Obama's question translates to "What's up, Cuba?" See Dan Roberts, "Obama Lands in Cuba as First US President to Visit in Nearly a Century," *Guardian*, March 21, 2016, https://www.theguardian.com/world/2016/mar/20/barack-obama-cuba-visit-us-politics-shift-public-opinion-diplomacy. More generally, see Ben Rhodes, *The World as It Is* (New York: Random House, 2018).

73. Scott Horsley, "Obama Makes 2016 Campaign Debut: 'I'm Ready to Pass the Baton,'" NPR, July 5, 2016.

74. For the full transcript, see http://www.npr.org/2016/09/13/493801062/obama-stumps-for-clinton-in-battleground-state-of-pennsylvania.

75. Kevin Liptack, "Obama's Last Campaign," *CNN Politics*, November 7, 2016.

76. For the full transcript, see http://time.com/3923128/donald-trump-announcement-speech/.

77. Lisa Mascaro, "Latino Support for Clinton Set to Hit Record High for a Presidential Candidate—and for Trump, a New Low," *Los Angeles Times*, November 6, 2016.

78. Jordyn Phelps, "Why President Obama's Campaign Blitz for Hillary Clinton Is Historic," *ABC News*, November 2, 2016.

79. The national exit poll estimated a lower percentage of Latino voters who favored Clinton (69 percent–29 percent). These estimates should be regarded with skepticism. Latino Decisions' estimates came from its election eve poll, which was a bilingual national poll (n = 5,600) that included a randomized statewide sample and a representative sample of Latino voters. The national exit poll was carried out by Edison Media Research, which compiles exit polls based on small and not very representative samples of a handful of precincts. In the recent past, Edison Media Research suggested that its sampling "is not designed to yield very reliable estimates of the characteristics of small, geographically clustered demographic groups." The results of the Latino Decisions election eve poll were very similar to those obtained by other high-quality, large-sample bilingual polls conducted by other groups. For example, Latino support for Trump was estimated at 19 percent by the Univision/*Washington Post* poll, 17 percent by NBC/*Telemundo*, 14 percent by NALEO/*Telemundo*, and 13 percent by FIU/New Latino Voice. Additionally, a wealth of research from other political scientists who rely on actual precinct turnout data and use ecological inference to estimate the turnout of Latinos in heavily Latino precincts found that the Latino Decisions estimates were much closer to these statistical estimates. See Stephen Nuño and Bryan Wilcox-Archuleta, "Why Exit Polls Are Wrong about Latino Voters in Arizona," *Arizona Republic*, November 26, 2016; Ali Valenzuela and Tyler Reny, "Trump Fared Worse than Romney in Florida Hispanic Vote," *The Hill*, December 12, 2016, http://thehill.com/blogs/pundits-blog/presidential-campaign/310760-study-finds-trump-faired-worse-than-romney-with.

80. Henry C. Jackson, "6 Promises Trump Has Made About Health Care," *Politico*, March 13, 2017, https://www.politico.com/story/2017/03/trump-obamacare-promises-236 021; Robert Costa and Amy Goldstein, "Trump Vows 'Insurance for Everybody' in Obamacare Replacement Plan," *Washington Post*, January 15, 2017, https://www .washingtonpost.com/politics/trump-vows-insurance-for-everybody-in-obamacare -replacement-plan/2017/01/15/5f2b1e18-db5d-11e6-ad42-f3375f271c9c_story.ht ml?utm_term=.193c4e478f9f.

81. David A. Graham, "'As I Have Always Said': Trump's Ever-Changing Positions on Health Care," *Atlantic*, July 28, 2017, https://www.theatlantic.com/politics/archive /2017/07/as-i-have-always-said-trumps-ever-changing-position-on-health-care /535293/.

82. Centers for Medicare and Medicaid Services, "Health Insurance Marketplaces 2017 Open Enrollment Period Final Enrollment Report: November 1, 2016–January 31, 2017," March 15, 2017, https://www.cms.gov/newsroom/fact-sheets/health-insurance -marketplaces-2017-open-enrollment-period-final-enrollment-report-november-1 -2016; Centers for Medicare and Medicaid Services, "Health Insurance Exchanges: 2018 Open Enrollment Period Final Report," April 3, 2018, https://www.cms.gov /newsroom/fact-sheets/health-insurance-exchanges-2018-open-enrollment-period -final-report.

83. Julia Ainsley, "Now the Trump Administration Wants to Limit Citizenship for Legal Immigrants," NBC News, August 7, 2018.

84. Editorial Board, "Even This Ultra-Conservative Judge Rejects Trump's Argument on DACA," *Washington Post*, September 9, 2018.

85. Jessica Kwong, "Trump Immigration Policy: From Separating Families to H-1B Visas, Here Are His Restrictions so Far," *Newsweek*, July 7, 2018.

86. Ibid.

87. Alan Gomez, "Trump Cracks down on U.S. Business and Travel to Cuba. Here's What's Changing," *USA Today*, November 8, 2017.

88. Karen DeYoung, "White House Implements New Cuba Policy Restricting Travel and Trade," *Washington Post*, November 8, 2017.

89. Ibid.

90. "Obama Vows to Help Puerto Ricans 'Build Their Own Future,'" BBC, June 14, 2011, https://www.bbc.com/news/av/world-us-canada-13768422/obama-vows-to-help -puerto-ricans-build-their-own-future.

91. Patricia Guadalupe, "Here's How PROMESA Aims to Tackle Puerto Rico's Debt," NBC News, June 30, 2016, https://www.nbcnews.com/news/latino/here-s-how-pro mesa-aims-tackle-puerto-ri co-s-debt-n601741.

92. David Nakamura, "'We Did a Fantastic Job in Puerto Rico': Trump Defends Response Despite Spike in Deaths after Hurricane Maria," *Washington Post*, August 29, 2018, https://www.washingtonpost.com/news/post-politics/wp/2018/08/29/we-did -a-fantastic-job-in-puerto-rico-trump-defends-response-despite-spike-in-deaths-af ter-hurricane-maria/?utm_term=.2b3e4affae95.

93. Ibid. See also Matthew Choi and Emily Goldberg, "Trump Reignites Hurricane Feud with Puerto Rican Officials," *Politico*, September 12, 2018, https://www.politico .com/story/2018/09/12/donald-trump-puerto-rico-a-plus-job-815801.

94. Rodolfo de la Garza and Jeronimo Cortina, "Are Latinos Republicans but Just Don't Know It?" *American Politics Research* 35 (2007): 202–223.

CHAPTER SIX

Obama and Congress

Molly E. Reynolds

When Barack Obama took the oath of office on January 20, 2009, he became the first former senator since Richard Nixon, and the first sitting senator since John F. Kennedy, to be sworn in as president. Though Obama's Senate tenure was short (just three years), he, unlike three of his four immediate predecessors, had actually walked the halls of Capitol Hill as a legislator. (President George H. W. Bush had served in the House in the early 1970s.) Vice President Joe Biden, meanwhile, was fresh off a thirty-five-year Senate career.

As Obama's time in the White House unfolded, however, it became clear that while knowledge of the ins and outs of Capitol Hill may have benefited the administration at the margins in certain situations, the major factors affecting its relationship with Congress were structural. Factors like partisanship and polarization mattered much more than personality, helping to create a legislative environment dominated by obstruction and brinkmanship. In this chapter, I begin by describing how the president approaches his dealings with Congress and why we should expect contextual factors to be the primary drivers of that relationship. Next, I explore how several of these dynamics played out during the Obama administration at the aggregate level before diving into one particular issue area—fiscal policy—that was especially prominent. Because the relationship between Congress and the president is about more than legislation, I also examine the politics of advice and consent during the Obama years. In each of these areas, we see that polarization and partisan politics dictated the contours of President Obama's relationship with Congress.

The Importance of Context in Executive-Congressional Relations

Before examining President Obama's experience with the elected representatives at the other end of Pennsylvania Avenue, let us first set the stage. An extensive political science literature explores *how* presidents work with Congress and suggests that a chief executive has a range of strategies available to try to achieve the policy and political goals articulated upon arrival in office. First, presidents can prioritize some issues over others for legislative action, often referred to as the "president's program." Congress, after all, does not have unlimited time to devote to legislating, and the president does not have unlimited resources to deploy in pursuit of legislative achievement; choices, then, must be made. We expect the president, with help from his advisers, to be strategic in making these choices. He is likely to factor in the composition of Congress, knowing that, based on its partisan and ideological makeup, some of his preferred policies are more likely to be adopted than others.[1] He also may incorporate information about the nation's fiscal situation, emphasizing different issues depending on whether the budgetary environment is rosy or dark.[2] Other important considerations may play a role as well. Presidents know that Congress has its own set of priorities, consisting largely of expiring programs and therefore somewhat predictable. In addition, presidents may prioritize issues that are salient with the public; when voters are concerned about a particular issue, especially one that has arisen due to unanticipated events in the world, prioritizing that issue may pay political dividends.[3]

Once presidents have selected a set of issues to prioritize, they formulate legislative proposals, which vary in their specificity. The degree to which these proposals are developed centrally in the White House versus in a more decentralized manner has varied over time,[4] but once they are sent to Congress, the legislative branch generally responds to them in some way.[5] Presidentially initiated agenda items often constitute a significant share of the legislation on which Congress works; previous estimates have pegged the portion at around one-third.[6] Not surprisingly, given his informational advantage in the area, the president appears to be most successful in getting foreign policy issues on the congressional calendar but also plays a role in structuring congressional consideration of a range of domestic policy issues, including health care and the environment.[7]

If Congress chooses to take up an issue on which the president has offered a proposal, important lobbying may occur at the beginning of the process. The president may need to persuade leaders in his own party to take up his particular proposal rather than a different one addressing the same issue. In addition, he may find it useful to try to deter members who are likely to oppose the bill to avoid difficult battles on the floor later on; these legislators may be members of the president's own party or the opposite one. Of course, during the bill's active consideration on the floor, the president may find himself trying to persuade legislators to vote in line with his position as well.[8]

Finally, when Congress chooses to act on an issue not advocated by the president, we do not expect the president to sit idly by. Indeed, the president takes positions on a wide range of items under consideration by Congress. Again, we expect this behavior to be strategic, with the president anticipating Congress's likely reaction. In some situations, in an effort to avoid legislative embarrassment, the president may be reluctant to take a stand. He may be more likely to take a position on those issues where he expects to win.[9] In other instances, however, the president may engage in "strategic disagreement"—that is, he may purposely articulate a position counter to the one he expects Congress, especially members in the opposite party, to take.[10] Doing so may strengthen his bargaining position or allow him to achieve political goals by sending a clear signal to voters about where he stands. This behavior may be especially prevalent in the context of veto threats, which represent a key way for the president to indicate his preferences to Congress.[11]

Importantly, there is reason to believe that presidential position-taking not only indicates to Congress where the executive stands but also affects legislators' own behavior. The president, after all, is the most visible member of his party, and when he takes a position on an issue, any successful future action on that issue may be positively associated with his party. Conversely, failure or an unpopular policy action may reflect negatively on the president and his co-partisans among voters. As a result, when the president takes a position on an issue, members of his own party are more likely to support it, while legislators in the opposite party are less so, even controlling for the content of the policy in question.[12]

Of course, presidents deploy each of these strategies for a reason: they do so because they have policy and political goals they want to achieve by prioritizing, proposing, persuading, and position-taking. An equally extensive literature has explored how *successful* presidents are in getting their way with Congress. First, interbranch partisanship appears to play a major role in determining the president's success in the legislative arena. When the presidency and a house of Congress are controlled by the same party, presidents should expect greater success in that chamber. Given the advantages enjoyed by the majority party in both the House and the Senate in terms of getting issues related to its policy and political goals on the agenda,[13] the president should find that the congressional calendar contains more issues on which he and his congressional allies favor action during periods of shared party control. Once a measure actually comes up for a vote, the numerical advantage of congressional party majorities kicks in. Importantly, although it appears that presidents enjoy an advantage in times of unified government, this effect varies across the chambers. It is notably larger in the House than in the Senate, largely thanks to the Senate filibuster.[14] In the contemporary Senate, the need to garner 60 votes to invoke cloture on most significant measures (and, in the absence of a formal cloture process, the increasing use of negotiated agreements that include 60-vote thresholds) means that unless the president's party enjoys an exceptionally large majority in the chamber, or unless he can persuade his fellow party members to use unorthodox tactics to change the rules, he will have to win the votes of at least a small number of senators from the other party.

If we move beyond considering how frequently members of Congress vote with the president and think about gridlock—or the degree to which Congress and the president are limited in their ability to adopt policy change—the effects of unified party control are less clear. In his influential work *Divided We Govern*, David Mayhew suggests that legislative outcomes have not been substantially different under unified versus divided government, while Keith Krehbiel's *Pivotal Politics* explains why we may observe inaction even in the presence of unified party control.[15] Subsequent research by Sarah Binder examined not just legislative achievements but also the share of issues on the national agenda that Congress was able to address. An analysis of the years 1947 to 2000 identified higher levels of gridlock under divided party control,[16] but a more recent update incorporating the George W. Bush presidency and the first term of the Obama administration suggests that unified party control may no longer have the wheel-greasing effect it once did.[17]

While interbranch partisan dynamics matter a great deal in influencing executive-congressional relations, the partisan forces *within* Congress also affect the president's ability to be successful in the legislative arena. Since the 1980s, congressional parties have become consistently more polarized; the average Democratic member is now more different from the typical Republican member. In addition, the Democratic Party has become more homogeneous, mainly because of the decline of the party's fortunes in the South, which was formerly a bastion of more conservative Democratic members. Although there are also fewer northern Republicans, the level of homogeneity in the Republican Party has remained fairly constant; however, the entire party has moved rightward, as more moderate members have been replaced by more extreme ones.[18]

Recent work on the role of polarization in presidential legislative success suggests that its primary effect occurs in interaction with interbranch partisanship and varies between the chambers. Some research has found that when polarization is high—as it is in the contemporary period—presidents who enjoy shared partisan control with the House are substantially more successful than presidents whose party does not control the House. In the Senate, however, the reverse appears to be true. High levels of polarization result in less legislatively successful presidents, regardless of whether the chamber is controlled by the same party as the White House.[19] Other research has found that polarization suppresses presidential success under divided government in both chambers.[20] Polarization also increases gridlock more generally, making it less likely that significant policy changes will be adopted.[21]

Polarization, however, may not be the only partisan dynamic in Congress that can affect the success of the president's legislative agenda. Intraparty dynamics, including between the chambers, may play an important role. When one or both chambers of Congress are controlled by the opposite party from the president and bipartisan negotiations are a necessary condition for legislative achievement, the institutional strength of party leaders can affect those discussions. Senate party leaders, for example, are more likely to bargain with an opposite-party president when they are institutionally strong. Put differently, "the opposition party's numbers and/ or ideological congruence facilitate bipartisan contact, but the relative importance of each remains unsettled."[22] In addition, work on legislative gridlock suggests that a divergence in preferences between the House and the Senate, even when they are controlled by the same party, is a significant predictor of whether Congress will be successful at tackling the issues on its agenda.[23]

An additional factor that may influence presidential success in Congress is the president's popularity. Why might a popular president be more successful in getting Congress to follow his lead? The principal account of how approval affects support for the president's legislative program emphasizes that members of Congress, concerned about their own reelection prospects, may be less likely to vote against the position of a popular president. Conversely, if the president is unpopular, any legislator who is inclined to disagree with him has more latitude to do so.[24] Empirical work on the consequences of supporting the president suggests that legislators are not wrong to consider the electoral repercussions, as voters appear to punish representatives who are thought to be too supportive of the president's positions.[25]

The empirical evidence on whether presidential approval affects legislative success is mixed. Some work finds a limited relationship between public approval of the president and his success in advancing his legislative goals, suggesting that it matters only at the margins and that its effects have faded in recent years.[26] Other research suggests that more popular presidents are more productive in the congressional arena,[27] especially when the substance of the legislation, rather than a binary success-failure outcome, is examined.[28] Yet other work finds that approval can affect legislative success, but only in some cases, and depending on other factors. The president's approval rating among voters of his own party, for example, appears to have more influence on his success with Congress than the support he receives from members of the other party or independents, perhaps because strong support from his own party members may make legislators especially nervous about rejecting the president's preferred policy.[29] Presidential popularity also has a greater effect on legislative success when congressional voting behavior is less partisan because members may be relying on other cues, external to the chamber, to make their decisions.[30] The content of the specific issue appears to matter as well, with presidential popularity mattering more for legislative action on complex *and* salient issues. This particular combination leads legislators to respond to presidential approval as an indicator of public preferences; in this case, voters are unlikely to have clear opinions about the issue itself because it is difficult to understand, but they are also likely to care about the issue because it is heavily covered in the media.[31]

Partisanship, Polarization, and Popularity

How did partisanship—both between the branches and within Congress—and popularity affect Obama's relationship with Congress? Let us begin by examining the role of divided government. To anyone who paid even moderate attention to Congress during the Obama years, it would not be surprising to learn that the president was less successful in the six years of his presidency when Republicans controlled one or both houses of Congress (2011–2016) than in the first two years (2009–2010), when both chambers were controlled by Democrats, including a short-lived filibuster-proof majority in the Senate. To illustrate the magnitude of this difference, figure 6.1 displays *Congressional Quarterly's* presidential success scores, or the share of votes on which Congress supported the president's position on issues for which he made his stance known.[32] The solid bars represent periods of unified government (House, Senate, and White House all controlled by the same party), and the hollow bars indicate divided government.

As we see in figure 6.1, Obama was quite successful in Congress during his first two years in office. In 2009 Congress supported him on 96.7 percent of the votes on which he took a position—a historic high. The following year, his success rate of 85.8 percent was lower, but still high by historical standards (in fact, the tenth highest on record).[33] Indeed, many of the major legislative achievements of the Obama administration—the economic stimulus package, the Affordable Care Act (ACA), the Dodd-Frank financial reform law, the repeal of the military's "Don't Ask, Don't Tell" policy, and student loan reform, to name a few—were signed into law during those two years. Once Republicans assumed control of the House after the 2010 elections, however, Obama's success rate declined notably. What's more, the post-2010 high point, a 68.7 percent success rate in 2014, was driven largely by the number of appointee confirmations following a 2013 change in the Senate's procedures for considering nominations (this change is discussed in greater detail below). If we consider only legislation in 2014, Obama's success rate falls to 24.4 percent.

As discussed earlier, however, party control often interacts with partisan polarization in important ways to affect the president's legislative success. As Jon Bond, Richard Fleisher, and Jeffrey Cohen have shown, even when Democrats controlled the Senate during the first six years of the Obama administration, increasing levels of polarization lessened the partisan advantage Obama enjoyed.[34] The distance between the average Democrat and the average Republican in the Senate was at a post–World War II high during Obama's first Congress (111th), and it only grew over time. In addition, for the duration of Obama's two terms, all Senate Democrats were to the left of all Senate Republicans.[35] This made building the necessary bipartisan coalitions to move legislation through the Senate more difficult. From a purely ideological standpoint, the fact that the most moderate Republican and

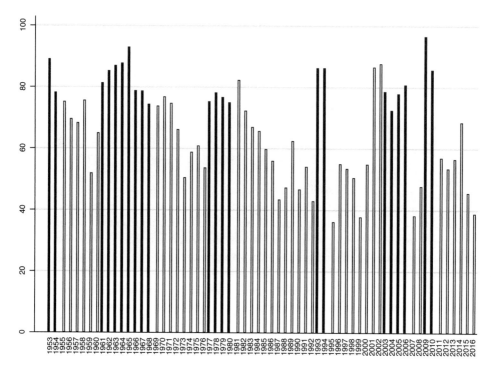

Fig. 6.1. *Congressional Quarterly's* Presidential Success Scores, 1953–2016

the most moderate Democrat in each successive Congress of the Obama administration were at least as far apart as they had been in the previous session meant
that the policy concessions necessary to bring members of the other party on board
were larger.[36]

The complicated role of party control becomes clear when we extend our consideration beyond presidential success on roll-call votes and consider gridlock.
While the president's success on votes in Congress is a frequent and useful metric
for judging the president's relationship with Congress, it tells us little about the
ultimate policy outcomes they are able to achieve. Measures of gridlock, or what
the branches are *not* able to do, are useful for capturing this dynamic, and indeed,
we see that deadlock was at a near all-time high in the 112th and 113th Congresses
(2011–2014). In those two sessions (as well as in the last two years of the Clinton administration), "lawmakers and the president deadlocked on almost three-
quarters of the most salient issues on the agenda."[37]

Unified party control is no longer reliably associated with lower levels of gridlock. Rather, polarization and, to a lesser degree, differences between the chambers
produce frequent stalemates between Congress and the president. Congressional
parties are more polarized than ever, and importantly, the movement resulting in

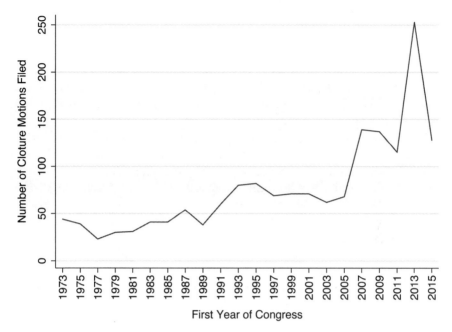

Fig. 6.2. Cloture Motions in the Senate, 1973–2015

today's level of division has been asymmetric; Republicans have moved farther to the right than Democrats have shifted to the left.[38] During the Obama adminis-tration, polarization, especially the extreme position of congressional Republicans in the House, made compromise more difficult and created major leadership chal-lenges, including the ousting of the Speaker of the House. This trend has been particularly acute on major fiscal issues (discussed in more detail below), but it has surfaced in other policy areas as well. Emergency spending bills addressing disas-ters such as Hurricane Sandy and the Zika outbreak got bogged down in debate over whether the money spent had to be offset by cuts elsewhere.[39] Even histori-cally popular issues among business-minded Republicans, such as trade and the Export-Import Bank, struggled in the face of a growing conservative faction within the congressional Republican Party.[40]

In addition to the levels of polarization present during the Obama era, Bind-er's explanation of *why* unified party control may matter less than it once did in alleviating gridlock is key to understanding the relationship between Obama and Congress. The "rising proclivity of opposition party senators to insist on sixty votes for adoption of most amendments and measures," she argues, "has undermined the legislative power of majority parties in periods of unified party control."[41] From the earliest days of the Obama administration, Republicans in the Senate were a largely unified front against his policy initiatives.[42] In the words of then-senator

George Voinovich (R-OH), "'if he was for it, we had to be against it.'"[43] Although the number of cloture motions is an imperfect measure of the level of obstruction in the chamber,[44] figure 6.2 suggests that Senate minorities—first the Republicans through 2014, and then the Democrats in 2015 and 2016—routinely made use of this particular procedural right. (The large spike in the 113th Congress is related to the November 2013 change related to the consideration of nominations, discussed later in the chapter.)

Certainly, Obama was not the first president who had to contend with routine Senate obstruction or whose major legislative proposals were affected by the filibuster.[45] In addition, once Republicans regained control of the House after the 2010 elections, they represented the biggest roadblock for many of Obama's legislative priorities. Even if there were sufficient votes to end a filibuster on legislation favored by the Democrats in the Senate, building a coalition for passage in the House was a challenge. Several key fiscal battles, including the one that contributed to the Speaker's resignation in 2015, can be characterized this way (these are discussed in more detail in the next section). The failure of comprehensive immigration reform in 2013 also followed this trajectory. A bipartisan group of senators, with White House input, developed an immigration bill.[46] It cleared the Senate with 68 votes in June,[47] only to have the House Republican leadership refuse weeks later to even consider the Senate's measure or anything like it.[48]

At the same time, examples from the Obama administration illustrate how the frequent use of the Senate filibuster shaped consideration of his preferred policies, even in times of unified government. The ACA was finally shepherded across the finish line with help from the budget reconciliation process, which protects certain budgetary legislation from the possibility of a Senate filibuster; however, the law's initial development was profoundly shaped by the need to garner 60 votes from the Democratic caucus. In September 2009, for example, when asked whether the health care bill would include a so-called public option,[49] Senate Finance Committee chairman Max Baucus (D-MT) said, "'no one has been able to show me how we can count up to 60 votes with a public option. I want a bill that can become law.'"[50] By November, two senators—Democrat Ben Nelson of Nebraska and Joe Lieberman of Connecticut, an independent who caucused with the Democrats—had formally threatened to side with Republicans on the matter of ending a filibuster if the public option was not removed from the proposal.[51] The ACA ultimately passed, but other legislative priorities were unsuccessful under unified party control, hindered by the need to "get to 60." After Speaker of the House Nancy Pelosi (D-CA) lobbied wavering House Democrats to adopt an environmental cap-and-trade bill in 2010, for example, it ultimately failed in the Senate, in part because of insufficient support among Democrats.[52]

What about popularity? As noted earlier, the results of analyses of the relationship between presidential approval and legislative success are mixed. Although I

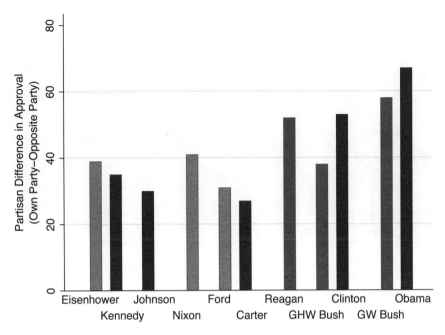

Fig. 6.3. Differences in Presidential Approval by Party, Eisenhower through Obama

do not specifically evaluate that relationship here, there is reason to believe that it did not help Obama significantly, especially during the last six years of divided government. Recall that the mechanism by which approval might be expected to improve the president's legislative prospects is an electoral one. When legislators are concerned about their own reelection prospects, they may be less likely to oppose a popular president. Conversely, if the president is unpopular, representatives who are inclined to disagree with him may feel freer to do so. In addition, some members who might otherwise support the president's position may see his unpopularity as a sign that their constituents prefer someone who has distanced himself or herself from the executive.

When we examine the public's attitude toward President Obama, we see that people were highly—indeed, historically—polarized by party, complicating this electoral story. Figure 6.3 displays the average difference in approval between members of the president's own party and members of the other party for each administration since Eisenhower's. During the Obama administration, the average difference in approval between Democrats and Republicans was 67 percentage points—a full 9 points higher than for George W. Bush, the president with the next highest difference.

Obama's approval was more polarized by party than that of any other president

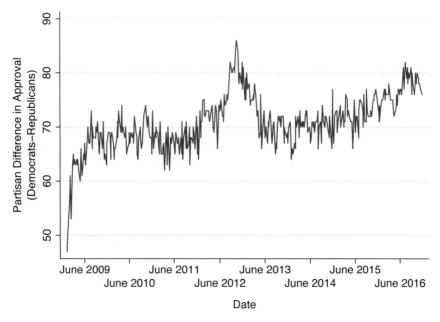

Fig. 6.4. Obama's Weekly Gallup Approval Rating among Democrats and Republicans, June 2009–June 2016

since Eisenhower, and the gap grew steadily over his eight years in office. Figure 6.4 demonstrates this trend, displaying the difference in Obama's weekly Gallup approval rating among Democrats and Republicans. During Obama's first term, his popularity gap grew steadily from an average of 65 percent in the first year to an average of 75 percent in the fourth year. Notably, the gap did not reset significantly in the first year of Obama's second term; instead, it fell slightly to 72 percent before rising again to 77 percent in his final year in office.

These trends have important implications for our understanding of the potential role of presidential approval in Obama's legislative success. Although the president's approval rating fluctuated over time, he was deeply unpopular among Republicans for most of his presidency. Notably, after 2009, Obama's approval rating among Republicans topped 20 percent only once: in May 2011, the week after US forces killed Osama bin Laden in Pakistan. If any positive relationship between popularity and legislative success works through an electoral mechanism, Obama likely reaped limited benefits, even when he was more popular. To the extent that a principal obstacle to legislative achievement after 2010 was the difficulty of garnering the necessary Republican votes, a marginally more popular president likely did little to bring them on board, since he was deeply unpopular with the party's base voters.

Finally, let us consider another dynamic identified in the literature that affected

Obama's relationship with Congress: whenever the president takes a position on an issue, it makes that issue more partisan, regardless of its content. Frances Lee examines this relationship in the Senate during an earlier period (1981–2004),[53] but there is evidence of a similar pattern in the House during the Obama years. I follow Lee's method for examining party cohesion, which measures the degree to which the president's party was more or less cohesive on a given vote than the chamber as a whole.[54] A simple difference-of-means test reveals that, in the House between 2009 and 2014, the president's party was more cohesive when he took a position (an average value of 0.50) than when he did not (0.43); these averages are statistically different ($p = 0.001$).

This is consistent with former senator Voinovich's assessment that if Obama was for something, the Republicans were against it. An example involving the Trade Promotion Authority (TPA) and the Trans-Pacific Partnership (TPP) illustrates how presidential involvement heightened the partisanship of an issue during the Obama years. Dating to the early 1970s, the TPA authorizes the president to negotiate trade agreements with other nations, and it grants those deals certain procedural protections from amendment and obstruction when they come before Congress for approval. President Obama favored renewing the TPA; he mentioned it in his 2014 State of the Union address, only to draw sharp rebukes from members of his own party, many of whom opposed free-trade pacts like the TPP.[55] When Republicans—traditionally more supportive of trade deals—won a majority in the Senate after the 2014 elections, Obama sensed a new opportunity. He mentioned the TPA again in his 2015 State of the Union address, instructing Congress to "give [him] Trade Promotion Authority to protect American workers."[56] Republican leaders, including then–House Ways and Means chairman Paul Ryan (R-WI), whose committee had jurisdiction over trade issues, bristled at that rhetoric. As one account of the TPA's passage describes it: "Shortly after, Ryan's staff reached out to Katie Fallon, the administration's director of legislative affairs, and urged Obama to stop asking Congress to 'give' him anything. Ryan didn't want Republicans to think they were granting Obama any special authority. After that call, Republicans said they noticed a change in rhetoric."[57] The president was apparently such a polarizing figure among Republicans that emphasizing his role in a policy area in which many (but certainly not all) of them shared his position was a source of concern for the legislation's prospects.

"A Hostage That's Worth Ransoming": The Role of Brinkmanship

If we examine only the outcomes of Obama's interactions with Congress, we get more or less the picture we would expect: some successes, largely concentrated early in his term when contextual factors, especially unified Democratic control of the

House, the Senate, and the White House, favored legislative success.[58] To limit our focus to the final product of the legislative process, however, misses an important part of the story: *how* those relations played out. The details of how negotiations were carried out can help us better understand how those outcomes came to be, and they can shed light on how future interactions between presidents and congressional leaders of the opposite party are likely to take shape. Recent work in political science illustrates that the policy-making environment in which members of Congress are socialized plays an important role in their future behavior.[59]

If we were to characterize executive-legislative interactions during the Obama administration—especially after Republicans assumed control of the House of Representatives after the 2010 elections—with a single word, it would be *brinkmanship*: "'governing by threat, high stakes, and cliffhangers. You wait until the last minute.'"[60] Certainly, the notion that Congress relies on deadlines to force its hand is not new. Legislators recognize the need to create mechanisms to compel future action, and they often choose, voluntarily, to design policies in such a way that they must revisit them.[61] Under the right circumstances, these kinds of "penalty defaults" can facilitate congressional and interbranch negotiation and can yield electoral benefits to the members who work on the issue each time it appears on the congressional agenda.[62]

Under Obama, this executive-legislative brinkmanship was perhaps most prominently displayed in the fiscal policy arena, which is no stranger to high-stakes, deadline-based deal-making.[63] Between 1976 and 2016, there were eighteen "funding gaps" (colloquially referred to as "partial government shutdowns") because Congress and the president could not reach a deal on one or more appropriations measures, and 177 continuing resolutions were adopted to ensure that funding was available in the absence of a regular appropriations bill.[64] Similarly, members of the opposite party from the president have often used the debt limit to force members of his party to go on record with a potentially unpopular vote, especially since 1980.[65]

During the last six years of the Obama administration, however, negotiations over nearly every fiscal policy choice were pushed to the brink.[66] High-stakes bargaining between Obama and key legislative leaders, including Speakers of the House John Boehner (R-OH) and, beginning in 2015, Paul Ryan; House minority leader Nancy Pelosi; and Senate leaders Mitch McConnell (R-KY) and Harry Reid (D-NV), ensued. (As a headline in the satirical website *The Onion* put it in February 2013, just days before compulsory budget cuts were set to take effect, "Obama, Congress Must Reach Deal on Budget by March 1, and Then April 1, and Then April 20, and Then April 28, and Then May 1, and Then Twice a Week for Next Four Years."[67])

In the opening weeks of the 112th Congress in 2011, the newly elected House Republican majority attempted to extract major funding cuts in exchange for their support of a measure to keep the government running, foreshadowing the hard-line position they would take into that summer's showdown over the debt limit. After failed attempts to reach a "grand bargain," Congress and the president managed to agree to a deal that was passed just hours before the deadline. The Budget Control Act of 2011 (BCA) raised the debt ceiling, but only in exchange for caps on discretionary federal spending for the next ten years and the creation of the Joint Select Committee on Deficit Reduction. This so-called supercommittee was tasked with identifying $1.5 trillion in cuts, and if it failed to do so, automatic reductions (known as sequestration) would result.

When the supercommittee failed to fulfill its mandate in late 2011, that helped set the stage for another major multipronged showdown in late 2012. One component involved whether to allow the automatic spending cuts to go into effect. A second component concerned a set of tax cuts, originally passed under President George W. Bush and extended in 2010, that, if allowed to expire, would cause large tax increases for many Americans. A third aspect involved the need to prevent (as Congress had repeatedly done since 2003) payment cuts to doctors under Medicare (the so-called doc fix).[68] A deal on these interconnected issues was reached as the clock approached midnight on December 31.

Three months later, Congress managed to prevent a partial government shutdown a full week before the March 27 deadline—a mark of "success" that was quickly forgotten in October, when Republicans, led by Senator Ted Cruz (R-TX), engineered a partial government shutdown after the Democrat-controlled Senate and President Obama refused to repeal or significantly delay implementation of the ACA. The measure ending the shutdown, which lasted sixteen days and affected approximately 40 percent of the civilian federal workforce, resolved the budgetary conflict only temporarily; Congress gave itself until January to come up with a plan to fund the government for the rest of the fiscal year and ultimately needed an additional short-term extension to complete its work.

The following year (2014) was no different. After delaying the completion of appropriations bills until December (after the midterm elections), Congress and the president toiled until the deadline and then some, requiring two short stopgap measures. Thanks to a conflict over funding for the implementation of President Obama's executive actions on immigration, another shutdown was threatened but narrowly avoided. After Republicans assumed control of the Senate in January 2015, Senate Democrats refused to consider any appropriations bills unless their colleagues across the aisle would agree to relax the BCA's spending caps for both defense and nondefense discretionary programs. This budgetary stalemate continued into September, when it collided with demands from some congressional Republicans to defund Planned Parenthood and a growing general restiveness among the conservative House Freedom Caucus and its allies that produced the resignation of Speaker Boehner and the elevation of Ryan to the Speaker's chair. A two-month stopgap measure—adopted on the September 30 deadline—took Congress until December. After two additional short-term bills, the House and Senate approved, and the president signed, legislation funding the government for the rest of the fiscal year. And, as was fitting, the Obama administration ended 2016 with a late September short-term bill, followed by a December measure, signed in the early hours of the morning after the previous measure had expired at midnight, to keep government programs running into 2017.

Brinkmanship was clearly the dominant feature of fiscal policy-making in the period of divided government during the Obama administration. Why were congressional Republicans repeatedly willing to take budget matters hostage, even if they were not always willing to shoot that hostage, while the Democrats, led by President Obama, stood firm across the aisle?[69] One explanation—consistent with the increasing and asymmetric partisan polarization described earlier—involves the notion of "strategic disagreement."[70] Under this logic, both sides are better off, at least initially, disagreeing than compromising. Standing firm allows each party to send clear signals to voters about its position and, ideally, to undercut the collective reputation of its partisan opponents in the process.[71] Survey data from 2007–2013, moreover, demonstrate that Republican identifiers preferred politicians who "stick to their principles" over those who "make compromises" at higher rates than did Democratic respondents.[72] Republican legislators may have perceived greater potential electoral rewards from supporting brinkmanship. Democrats likely hoped that standing firm against Republican hostage-taking would identify their party as more capable of effective governing.

In addition, the size of the Republican majority in the House may have contributed to repeated brinkmanship. After the 2010 elections, the House Republicans' 242-seat majority was the largest the party had held since 1948. Although they lost some seats in 2012, gains in 2014 brought their majority up to 247, the largest since 1931. Larger majorities tend to be less cohesive than their smaller counterparts,[73] leaving them open to the emergence of rump factions, such as the House Freedom Caucus. Because party leaders have more room for error, the cost of an individual legislator's defection is smaller relative to whatever benefits he or she expects to gain through opposition. Once such a group is organized and has made its opposition clear, it may force party leaders to take a more moderate position and try to attract some members of the minority (here, Democratic) party to avoid going over the brink. Meanwhile, the existence of the Senate filibuster already encourages some bipartisan compromise in that chamber, allowing members of the emergent rump faction to claim that they stuck to their principles—a position favored by their constituents—while ultimately avoiding catastrophe.[74]

Fiscal issues were an especially attractive target for Republicans to use to hash out their intraparty conflicts, whether over substance or tactics,[75] during the latter half of the Obama administration. Appropriations bills, budget agreements, and debt ceiling measures were frequently described as "must pass" legislation, given the consequences of inaction. This "must pass" status made them attractive candidates for intraparty battles. Because the issues involved such high stakes, factions within a party—in this case, the Republicans—could use them to draw distinctions between themselves and some of their co-partisans in the same way the two major parties do. The more significant an issue, the more likely it is that voters are paying attention. During the first week of the government shutdown in October 2013, for example, a full 73 percent of respondents in a Pew Research Center poll indicated that they were following the issue "very closely" or "fairly closely." By comparison, only 64 and 57 percent of respondents said the same about reports on the state of the economy and the troubled rollout of the ACA's healthcare.gov, respectively.[76] In addition, if gridlock in Congress has increased,[77] the "must pass" items that are likely to become law in one form or another are especially attractive targets for actions that differentiate one group from the rest of the party. Legislators know these items will appear on the agenda because they must receive attention. Leaders can remove certain bills from the floor temporarily, as Speaker Boehner did with appropriations bills in July 2015,[78] or they can structure the procedures for consideration in a way that minimizes the opportunity for active dissent, but eventually, these bills will return. By comparison, agenda items on which Congress does not *need* to act, such as an antiabortion bill opposed by a number of female Republican legislators in January 2015, can fade away more easily under the threat of intraparty division.[79]

Divisions within the Republican Party may have contributed to brinkmanship in another important way as well. Presidential negotiations with Senate leaders of the opposite party are less frequent when the leader in question is institutionally weak, where strength is measured by the size of the party's majority in the chamber and by how ideologically coherent it is.[80] Strong leaders are believed to have more deal-making credibility, since they will likely be able to deliver the votes necessary to adopt whatever agreement is struck. Although the study demonstrating this relationship focused on the frequency of contact, rather than the outcome, and examined only the Senate, we might expect the logic to extend to the broader bargaining environment—that is, congressional leaders of the opposite party are better negotiating partners for the president when they are institutionally strong.

Indeed, for several of the Obama administration's fiscal fights, there is reason to believe that the weak institutional position of House Republican leaders contributed to the brinkmanship that characterized negotiations. Perhaps the best example was the battle over whether to raise the debt limit in the summer of 2011. Congressional Republicans were divided. Some House Republicans were refusing to support an increase of the debt limit unless it was accompanied by big spending cuts—perhaps as much as dollar for dollar. Others were more inclined to make a deal, as long as it was favorable to their party. Still others believed that defaulting on the debt might not have the calamitous consequences the experts predicted. For their part, Democrats were also divided in important ways. Some members were willing to adopt some spending cuts, but not without accompanying tax increases to lessen the blow, while others were loath to vote for anything that cut popular entitlement programs such as Medicare and Social Security.

Initial talks between Vice President Joe Biden and House majority leader Eric Cantor (R-VA) in June, and then between President Obama and Speaker Boehner in early July, fell apart because both Republican leaders faced resistance from members of their conference over the issue of revenue increases. Larger negotiations over a so-called grand bargain collapsed roughly ten days before the deadline for raising the debt limit. In the words of the *New York Times's* Matt Bai, "Obama managed to persuade his closest allies to sign off on what he wanted them to do, and Boehner didn't, or couldn't."[81] Democrats may have been divided, but the diversity of views within Boehner's conference was simply too large to overcome. The final vote on the BCA, which ultimately resolved the immediate crisis, did not come easily in the House. Republican leaders rescheduled the initial vote once to give them time to whip up enough support for their proposal; it passed with 4 votes to spare before being immediately rejected by the Senate. Finally, on the day before the August 2 deadline, the House cleared the BCA, but Speaker Boehner had to rely on 95 votes from Democratic members to do so.[82] Many Democrats, for their part, were not enthused about the bill or the process by which it was negotiated. Representative Emmanuel Cleaver (D-MO), for instance, called "this deal . . . a sugar-coated Satan sandwich."[83] In this way, the debt ceiling crisis marked the start of an ongoing dynamic whereby House Republican leaders' struggle to hold their conference together on important fiscal matters profoundly shaped negotiations with the Obama White House.

Beyond Legislation: The Politics of Advice and Consent

Bargaining over legislation represents an important interaction between the president and Congress, but it is by no means the only one. Nominations to the judiciary and other executive branch positions subject to Senate confirmation constitute another important dynamic in the executive-legislative relationship. Just as other presidents have faced routine obstruction of their legislative priorities by Senate minorities, Obama was not the first president whose nominees ran into obstacles. In 2005, for example, a confrontation over Democrats' obstruction of several of President George W. Bush's judicial nominees was narrowly defused by a bipartisan group of senators (known as the "Gang of 14") before Senate majority leader Bill Frist (R-TN) could exercise the so-called nuclear option, by which the threshold for cloture on nominations was reduced to a simple majority.[84]

The politics of advice and consent during the Obama administration, however, was notable in several key ways. The first involved the experience of the nominees. The first involved the experience of the nominees. The decision by the Republican-controlled Senate to forgo action on Merrick Garland's nomination to the Supreme Court in 2016 was perhaps the highest-profile example of how the advice and consent function was handled differently under Obama; however, other data support the claim that Obama's nominees had a different experience than their predecessors. According to data collected by Anne Joseph O'Connell, through 2014, Obama's nominations failed at a higher rate (28 percent) than those put forward by Presidents Ronald Reagan (17.5 percent), George H. W. Bush (17 percent), Bill Clinton (22.9 percent), and George W. Bush (26.4 percent). They also took longer to process, averaging 127.2 days from nomination to confirmation—a full month longer than the previous high of 97.4 days under George W. Bush.[85]

The second important development in the politics of advice and consent involved the president's ability to make recess appointments. Under the Constitution, the president can install nominees without the advice and consent of the Senate to "fill vacancies that may happen during the recess of the Senate."[86] Such appointments expire at the end of the next session of Congress. Recess appointments began to increase in the 1980s, and when George W. Bush made heavy use of the tactic, then–Senate majority leader Reid responded by announcing in November 2007 that he would keep the chamber in so-called permanent session to prevent additional recess appointments. Because congressional rules allow the Senate to adjourn for three full days without technically going into recess, under Reid's plan, every few days a senator would gavel the Senate into pro forma session and then immediately gavel it back out.[87]

The political stakes surrounding recess appointments remained high during the Obama administration. In 2011, when Republicans controlled the House but not the Senate, they forced the Senate to remain in session by holding their own pro forma meetings (since the Constitution prevents one chamber from adjourning without the consent of the other).[88] This conflict came to a head in January 2012, when the president made four recess appointments, including three members of the National Labor Relations Board, despite the Senate holding periodic pro forma sessions. In 2014 the Supreme Court ruled this action unconstitutional, holding that the president had to honor the Senate's own judgment on whether it was in recess and that any recess of fewer than ten days was generally too short to trigger the president's power.[89] As a result, Congress could continue to block recess appointments by convening briefly, which it did for the balance of Obama's presidency.[90]

The final—and perhaps most significant—event affecting nomination politics during the Obama administration was the decision by Senate Democrats in November 2013 to do what their Republican predecessors in 2005 had not: "go nuclear" on some nominations. In response to rising frustration among the majority party over filibusters of the president's nominees—including of Chuck Hagel as defense secretary—then–Senate majority leader Reid engineered a new precedent under which all nominations, with the exception of those for the Supreme Court, would require only a simple majority vote.[91] Implementing this new rule in a way that required only a simple majority of senators to agree was complicated procedurally,[92] but it represented a major shift in how the Senate does business.

What were the consequences of the Democrats going nuclear? As we saw in figure 6.2, the Senate considered a larger than normal number of cloture motions in the 113th Congress, and 150 of them involved nominations in the postnuclear period. In the first year after the rule change, judicial nominees were confirmed more frequently and more quickly, but they were not significantly more liberal.[93] Confirmation rates for other, nonjudicial appointments increased in the first year, but nominations took longer to receive attention.[94] (See also chapter 8 in this volume.)

The Consequences of Limited Presidential Influence

This chapter's account of Obama's experience working with Congress emphasizes the role of institutional characteristics in shaping the interbranch negotiating environment. But a notable narrative that emerged in the press during the Obama years tells a different story. This is largely thanks to criticism leveled at the president, often by members of his own party. At various points, congressional Democrats expressed the feeling that "'we're almost being ignored'"[95] and that the administration "'might have learned more by doing more'" congressional outreach.[96] Obama, argued Senator Claire McCaskill (D-MO), sometimes "'sees the world through his eyes and doesn't do, I think, enough work on being empathetic about how other people view things.'"[97] These critiques were buttressed by similar claims in the media, such as when Maureen Dowd of the *New York Times* said of Obama, "it is his job to get them to behave . . . to somehow get this dunderheaded Congress . . . to do the stuff he wants them to do. It's called leadership."[98] Unsurprisingly, Obama's legislative advisers have pushed back aggressively against this narrative. For example, in an interview about the how the White House worked with Congress in the first year of the new administration, Obama's first director of the Office of Legislative Affairs, Phil Schiliro, called the administration's outreach "constant" and said that "a disproportionate amount of his time was with Congress."[99]

My approach here reflects the principal way that political scientists think about the working relationship between Congress and the president: personality matters less than factors such as partisanship and polarization. As a result, when the institutional factors suggest that collaborating with Congress is likely to be difficult, there is only so much that even a president with excellent legislative skills can do. Recent work on Lyndon Johnson—famous for his "will and skill" in relation to Congress—suggests that even he was aided significantly by conditions that favored continued, high-level bipartisan negotiation.[100]

For Obama, one response to these constraints was to turn to executive actions. Although he issued fewer executive orders than any other two-term president since World War II,[101] he used that particular tool to advance important new policies on immigration, gun control, and the minimum wage.[102] He also used executive actions to direct federal agencies, such as when he extended federal benefits to federal workers' same-sex partners via a presidential memorandum in 2010.[103] In the regulatory arena, the *New York Times* called him "one of the most prolific authors of major regulations in presidential history."[104] (See also chapters 7 and 10 on this point.)

The use of executive power allowed Obama to implement new policies in areas where congressional policy-making was difficult, but relying on his pen rather than legislation left many initiatives open to legal challenge. In 2016 alone, major actions on immigration and the environment were halted, at least temporarily, by the courts.[105] The president himself recognized these limits. As he said in an interview with NPR after the election of his successor, "going through the legislative process is always better, in part because it's harder to undo."[106] Indeed, dismantling various executive actions taken by President Obama was a major focus in the early months of the Trump administration.[107]

As illustrated by the foregoing discussion, however, "going through the legislative process" simply would not have achieved the policy changes President Obama and his co-partisans wanted to see during his eight years in office. Although Obama and congressional Democrats achieved major legislative victories on economic recovery, health care, and financial regulation in the first two years of his term, high levels of partisanship and polarization made coalition building challenging, including during the early period of unified party control. (The early experience of President Trump, Speaker Ryan, and Majority Leader McConnell suggests that Republicans were faced with similar challenges, making some of Obama's accomplishments, including the ACA, more durable than initially expected.)

These dynamics led to policy-making that was repeatedly dominated by brinkmanship between Congress and the White House and resulted in a major change in how the Senate considers nominations. President Obama's greatest legislative legacy, then, is not one of accomplishments but one of constraints.

Notes

1. Jeffrey E. Cohen, *The President's Legislative Policy Agenda, 1789–2012* (New York: Cambridge University Press, 2012); Matthew Eshbaugh-Soha, "The Politics of Presidential Agendas," *Political Research Quarterly* 58, 2 (June 2005): 257–268; Andrew Rudalevige, *Managing the President's Program: Presidential Leadership and Legislative Policy Formulation* (Princeton, NJ: Princeton University Press, 2002).
2. Eshbaugh-Soha, "Politics of Presidential Agendas."
3. Jeremy Gelman, Gilad Wilkenfeld, and E. Scott Adler, "The Opportunistic President:

How U.S. Presidents Determine Their Legislative Programs," *Legislative Studies Quarterly* 40, 3 (August 2015): 363–390.

4. Rudalevige, *Managing the President's Program.*

5. Mark Peterson, *Legislating Together: The White House and Capitol Hill from Eisenhower to Reagan* (Cambridge, MA: Harvard University Press, 1990).

6. George C. Edwards and Andrew Barrett, "Presidential Agenda Setting in Congress," in *Polarized Politics: Congress and the President in a Partisan Era*, ed. Jon R. Bond and Richard Fleisher (Washington, DC: CQ Press, 2000), 109–133; Barbara Sinclair, "Hostile Partners: The President, Congress, and Lawmaking in the Partisan 1990s," in ibid., 134–153.

7. Paul E. Rutledge and Heather A. Larsen-Price, "The President as Agenda-Setter in Chief: The Dynamics of Congressional and Presidential Agenda Setting," *Policy Studies Journal* 42, 3 (August 2014): 443–464.

8. Matthew N. Beckmann, *Pushing the Agenda: Presidential Leadership and U.S. Lawmaking, 1953–2004* (New York: Cambridge University Press, 2010).

9. Bryan W. Marshall and Brandon C. Prins, "Strategic Position Taking and Presidential Influence in Congress," *Legislative Studies Quarterly* 32, 2 (May 2007): 257–284.

10. John B. Gilmour, *Strategic Disagreement: Stalemate in American Politics* (Pittsburgh, PA: University of Pittsburgh Press, 1995).

11. Charles E. Cameron, *Veto Bargaining: Presidents and the Politics of Negative Power* (New York: Cambridge University Press, 2000); Tim Groseclose and Nolan McCarty, "The Politics of Blame: Bargaining before an Audience," *American Journal of Political Science* 45, 1 (January 2001): 100–119.

12. Frances E. Lee, *Beyond Ideology: Politics, Principles, and Partisanship in the U.S. Senate* (Chicago: University of Chicago Press, 2009).

13. Gary Cox and Mathew McCubbins, *Setting the Agenda: Responsible Party Government in the U.S. House of Representatives* (New York: Cambridge University Press, 2005); John H. Aldrich and David W. Rohde, "The Consequences of Party Organization in the House: The Role of Majority and Minority Parties in Conditional Party Government," in Bond and Fleisher, *Polarized Politics*, 31–72; Chris Den Hartog and Nathan Monroe, *Agenda Setting in the U.S. Senate: Costly Consideration and Majority Party Advantage* (New York: Cambridge University Press, 2011).

14. Jon R. Bond, Richard Fleisher, and Jeffrey E. Cohen, "Presidential-Congressional Relations in an Era of Polarized Parties and a 60-Vote Senate," in *American Gridlock: The Sources, Character, and Impact of Political Polarization*, ed. James A. Thurber and Antoine Yoshinaka (New York: Cambridge University Press, 2015), 133–151; Jeffrey E. Cohen, Jon R. Bond, and Richard Fleisher, "The Implications of the 2012 Presidential Election for Presidential-Congressional Relations: Change or More of the Same?" in *The 2012 Presidential Election: Forecasts, Outcomes, and Consequences*, ed. Amnon Cavari, Richard J. Powell, and Kenneth R. Mayer (Lanham, MD: Rowman & Littlefield, 2014), 151–172; Jeffrey E. Cohen, Jon R. Bond, and Richard Fleisher, "Placing Presidential-Congressional Relations in Context: A Comparison of Barack Obama and His Predecessors," *Polity* 45, 1 (January 2013): 105–126.

15. David Mayhew, *Divided We Govern* (New Haven, CT: Yale University Press, 2005); Keith Krehbiel, *Pivotal Politics* (Chicago: University of Chicago Press, 1998).

16. Sarah A. Binder, *Stalemate: Causes and Consequences of Legislative Gridlock* (Washington, DC: Brookings Institution Press, 2005).

17. Sarah A. Binder, "Legislating in Polarized Times," in *Congress Reconsidered*, 11th ed., ed. Lawrence C. Dodd and Bruce I. Oppenheimer (Washington, DC: CQ Press, 2016), 189–206.

18. Nolan McCarty, Keith T. Poole, and Howard Rosenthal, *Polarized America: The Dance of Ideology and Unequal Riches*, 2nd ed. (Cambridge, MA: MIT Press, 2016).

19. Bond, Fleisher, and Cohen, "Presidential-Congressional Relations in an Era of Polarized Parties"; Cohen, Bond, and Fleisher, "Placing Presidential-Congressional Relations in Context"; Cohen, Bond, and Fleisher, "Implications of the 2012 Presidential Election."

20. Daniel Paul Franklin and Michael P. Fix, "The Best of Times and the Worst of Times: Polarization and Presidential Success in Congress," *Congress and the Presidency* 43, 3 (August 2016): 377–394.

21. Binder, *Stalemate*; Binder, "Legislating in Polarized Times."

22. Matthew N. Beckmann, "Up the Hill and across the Aisle: Discovering the Path to Bipartisanship in Washington," *Legislative Studies Quarterly* 41, 2 (May 2016): 269–295.

23. Binder, "Legislating in Polarized Times."

24. Richard Neustadt, *Presidential Power* (New York: Wiley, 1960); George C. Edwards, "Presidential Approval as a Source of Influence in Congress," in *The Oxford Handbook of the American Presidency*, ed. George C. Edwards and William Howell (New York: Oxford University Press, 2011), 182–207; Caitlin E. Dwyer and Sarah A. Treul, "Indirect Presidential Influence, State-Level Approval, and Voting in the U.S. Senate," *American Politics Research* 40, 2 (March 2012): 355–379.

25. Paul Gronke, Jeffrey Koch, and J. Matthew Wilson, "Follow the Leader? Presidential Approval, Presidential Support, and Representatives' Electoral Fortunes," *Journal of Politics* 65, 3 (August 2003): 785–808; Barry C. Burden and David C. Kimball, *Why Americans Split Their Tickets: Campaigns, Competition, and Divided Government* (Ann Arbor: University of Michigan Press, 2009).

26. George C. Edwards, *The Strategic President* (Princeton, NJ: Princeton University Press, 2009); Kenneth Collier and Terry Sullivan, "New Evidence Undercutting the Linkage of Approval with Presidential Support and Influence," *Journal of Politics* 57, 1 (1995): 197–209; Richard Fleisher et al., "The Demise of the Two-Presidencies," *American Politics Research* 28, 1 (2000): 3–25; Cohen, Bond, and Fleisher, "Placing Presidential-Congressional Relations in Context."

27. Douglas Rivers and Nancy L. Rose, "Passing the President's Program: Public Opinion and Presidential Influence in Congress," *American Journal of Political Science* 29, 2 (May 1985): 183–196.

28. Andrew W. Barrett and Matthew Eshbaugh-Soha, "Presidential Success on the Substance of Legislation," *Political Research Quarterly* 60, 1 (March 2007): 100–112.

29. Matthew J. Lebo and Andrew J. O'Geen, "The President's Role in the Partisan Congressional Arena," *Journal of Politics* 73, 3 (August 2011): 718–734.

30. Jon R. Bond, Richard Fleisher, and B. Dan Wood, "The Marginal and Time-Varying Effects of Public Approval on Presidential Success in Congress," *Journal of Politics* 65, 1 (February 2003): 92–110.

31. Brandice Canes-Wrone and Scott de Marchi, "Presidential Approval and Legislative Success," *Journal of Politics* 64, 2 (May 2002): 491–509.

32. There are several reasons why other measures of presidential success are preferred by

some scholars. For a discussion of some of these arguments, see Edwards, *Strategic President.*

33. "Legislative Success for Obama Came with Political Challenge," in *CQ Almanac 2010* (Washington, DC: CQ Press, 2011), B-3–B-11.

34. Bond, Fleisher, and Cohen, "Presidential-Congressional Relations in an Era of Polarized Parties."

35. McCarty, Poole, and Rosenthal, *Polarized America.*

36. Calculations of the distance between the most moderate Republican and the most moderate Democrat is based on Poole and Rosenthal's Common Space DW-NOMINATE scores. For the 111th Congress, this value was 0.098; for the 112th, it was 0.121; and for the 113th and 114th, it was 0.17.

37. Binder, "Legislating in Polarized Times," 197.

38. Jacob S. Hacker and Paul S. Pierson, *Off Center: The Republican Revolution and the Erosion of American Democracy* (New Haven, CT: Yale University Press, 2006); Thomas E. Mann and Norman J. Ornstein, *It's Even Worse than It Looks: How the American Constitutional System Collided with the New Politics of Extremism* (New York: Basic Books, 2012).

39. Raymond Hernandez, "Stalling of Storm Aid Makes Northeastern Republicans Furious," *New York Times,* January 2, 2013; Molly E. Reynolds, "What Emergency Zika Funding Tells Us about Congressional Dysfunction," *FixGov,* May 18, 2016, https://www.brookings.edu/blog/fixgov/2016/05/18/what-emergency-zika-funding-tells-us-about-congressional-dysfunction/.

40. Emma Dumain, "Trade Rule Passes Despite Conservative Mutiny," *Roll Call,* June 11, 2015; Matt Fuller, "House Freedom Caucus Lines up Opposition to Export-Import Bank," *Roll Call,* May 19, 2015.

41. Binder, "Legislating in Polarized Times," 202.

42. Robert Draper, *When the Tea Party Came to Town: Inside the U.S. House of Representatives' Most Combative, Dysfunctional, and Infuriating Term in Modern History* (New York: Basic Books, 2012).

43. Quoted in Michael Grunwald, *The New New Deal: The Hidden Story of Change in the Obama Era* (New York: Simon & Schuster, 2012), 19.

44. Sarah Binder, "How We Count Senate Filibusters and Why It Matters," *Monkey Cage* (blog), May 15, 2014, https://www.washingtonpost.com/news/monkey-cage/wp/2014/05/15/how-we-count-senate-filibusters-and-why-it-matters/?utm_term=.ab0612adf358.

45. For a historical perspective, see Sarah A. Binder and Steven S. Smith, *Politics or Principle: Filibustering in the United States Senate* (Washington, DC: Brookings Institution Press, 1997).

46. Ryan Lizza, "Getting to Maybe," *New Yorker,* June 24, 2013.

47. Ashley Parker and Jonathan Martin, "Senate, 68 to 32, Passes Overhaul for Immigration," *New York Times,* June 27, 2013.

48. Ashley Parker and Jonathan Weisman, "Republicans in House Resist Overhaul for Immigration," *New York Times,* July 10, 2013.

49. If enacted, the public option would have involved a federally run health insurance plan available to individuals and small businesses in competition with other privately run plans available for purchase on the health insurance marketplaces (which were also created by the law).

50. Quoted in Paul Starr, *Remedy and Reaction: The Peculiar American Struggle over Health Care Reform* (New Haven, CT: Yale University Press, 2011), 226.

51. Joseph Berger, "Centrist Senators Say They Oppose Health Care Bill," *New York Times,* November 22, 2009.

52. Jonathan Chait, "Who Killed Cap and Trade?" *New Republic,* October 6, 2010. For a perspective that attributes the bill's failure elsewhere, see Ryan Lizza, "As the World Burns," *New Yorker,* October 11, 2010.

53. Lee, *Beyond Ideology.*

54. Formally, Lee's measure of party cohesion is the difference between overall chamber cohesion and cohesion of the president's party. The cohesion of the president's party is calculated by taking the absolute difference between the share of the party voting yea and the share of the party voting nay. Overall cohesion is the absolute difference between the total share of representatives voting yea and the total share voting nay. The measure takes on a value of 0 if the vote is unanimous, values near 1 when the president's party is more cohesive, and values near −1 when the president's party is less cohesive. Data used for this analysis from Michael H. Crespin and David Rohde, Political Institutions and Public Choice Roll-Call Database, 2016, http://www.ou.edu/carlalbertcenter/research/pipc-votes.

55. Eric Bradner and Manu Raju, "Harry Reid Rejects President Obama's Trade Push," *Politico,* January 29, 2014.

56. "Remarks by the President in State of the Union Address," January 20, 2015, https://www.whitehouse.gov/the-press-office/2015/01/20/remarks-president-state-union-address-january-20-2015.

57. Manu Raju and Jake Sherman, "How Obama Joined Hands to Conquer His Party on Trade," *Politico,* June 25, 2015.

58. The characterization of the debt limit as a "hostage that's worth ransoming" comes from then–Senate minority leader Mitch McConnell (R-KY); see David A. Fahrenthold, Lori Montgomery, and Paul Kane, "In Debt Deal, the Triumph of the Old Washington," *Washington Post,* August 3, 2011.

59. Sean M. Theriault, *The Gingrich Senators: The Roots of Partisan Warfare in Congress* (New York: Oxford University Press, 2013); Jordan M. Ragusa, "Partisan Cohorts, Polarization, and the Gingrich Senators," *American Politics Research* 44, 2 (March 2016): 296–325.

60. Julian Zelizer quoted in Mark J. Oleszek and Walter J. Oleszek, "Congress and President Obama," in *Rivals for Power: Presidential-Congressional Relations,* 5th ed., ed. James A. Thurber (Lanham, MD: Rowman & Littlefield, 2013), 259–292, 287.

61. E. Scott Adler and John D. Wilkerson, *Congress and the Politics of Problem Solving* (New York: Cambridge University Press, 2013).

62. Ibid.; Sarah A. Binder and Frances E. Lee, "Making Deals in Congress," in *Political Negotiation: A Handbook,* ed. Jane Mansbridge and Cathie Jo Martin (Washington, DC: Brookings Institution Press, 2015), 91–120.

63. Joseph White, "How Did We Get Here? The Roots of Deficit Brinksmanship," *Scholars Strategy Network,* March 2013, https://www.scholarsstrategynetwork.org/sites/default/files/ssn_basic_facts_white_on_deficit_brinksmanship.pdf.

64. Jessica Tollestrup, "Federal Funding Gaps: A Brief Overview," Congressional Research Service, October 11, 2013; James V. Saturno and Jessica Tollestrup, "Continuing Resolutions: Overview of Components and Recent Practices," Con-

gressional Research Service, January 14, 2016; "Appropriations for Fiscal Year 2017," congress.gov.

65. Frances E. Lee, *Insecure Majorities: Congress and the Perpetual Campaign* (Chicago: University of Chicago Press, 2016).

66. For additional details of these events, see Molly E. Reynolds and Philip A. Wallach, "The Fiscal Fights of the Obama Administration," Brookings Institution, December 8, 2016, https://www.brookings.edu/research/the-fiscal-fights-of-the-obama-administration/.

67. Quoted in Roy T. Meyers, "The Implosion of the Federal Budget Process: Triggers, Commissions, Cliffs, Sequesters, Debt Ceilings, and Shutdowns," *Public Budgeting and Finance* (Winter 2014): 1–23.

68. For a history of the doc fix, see Billy Wynne, "May the Era of Medicare's Doc Fix (1997–2015) Rest in Peace. Now What?" *Health Affairs* (blog), April 14, 2015, http://healthaffairs.org/blog/2015/04/14/may-the-era-of-medicares-doc-fix-1997-2015-rest-in-peace-now-what/.

69. The original use of this rhetoric to describe congressional negotiations is generally attributed to Senator Phil Gramm (R-TX). See Stephen Labaton, "Deal on Bank Bill Was Helped along by Midnight Talks," *New York Times,* October 24, 1999.

70. Gilmour, *Strategic Disagreement.* In the specific context of budget battles, see Roy T. Meyers, "Late Appropriations and Government Shutdowns: Frequency, Causes, and Remedies," *Public Budgeting and Finance* (Fall 1997): 25–38.

71. Lee, *Beyond Ideology.*

72. Matt Grossman and David A. Hopkins, "Ideological Republicans and Group Interest Democrats: The Asymmetry of American Party Politics," *Perspectives on Politics* 13, 1 (March 2015): 119–139.

73. Douglas Dion, *Turning the Legislative Thumbscrew: Minority Rights and Procedural Change in Legislative Politics* (Ann Arbor: University of Michigan Press, 1997).

74. Sarah Binder, "This Is Why Some Republicans Keep Threatening to Take the Government Hostage," *Monkey Cage* (blog), September 16, 2015, https://www.washingtonpost.com/news/monkey-cage/wp/2015/09/16/this-is-why-some-republicans-keep-threatening-to-take-the-government-hostage/?utm_term=.43c44492ccb8.

75. Molly E. Reynolds, "What Is the House Freedom Caucus, and What Do They Want?" *FixGov,* October 8, 2015, https://www.brookings.edu/blog/fixgov/2015/10/08/what-is-the-house-freedom-caucus-and-what-do-they-want/; Ryan Lizza, "A House Divided," *New Yorker,* December 14, 2015.

76. Pew Research Center for the People & the Press Poll, October 2013, USPSRA.100713, Princeton Survey Research Associates International (producer), Roper Center for Public Opinion Research, Cornell University (distributor).

77. Binder, "Legislating in Polarized Times."

78. Cristina Marcos, "House Cancels Vote amid Fight over Confederate Flag," *The Hill,* July 9, 2015.

79. Ed O'Keefe, "Abortion Bill Dropped amid Concerns of Female GOP Lawmakers," *Washington Post,* January 21, 2015.

80. Beckmann, "Up the Hill and across the Aisle."

81. Matt Bai, "Who Killed the Debt Deal?" *New York Times Magazine,* March 28, 2012.

82. Draper, *When the Tea Party Came to Town.* See House votes 677 and 690, 112th Congress, 1st session.

83. Quoted in Draper, *When the Tea Party Came to Town*, 255–256.

84. "'Gang of 14' Averts Judicial Showdown," in *CQ Almanac 2005* (Washington, DC: CQ Press, 2006), 14-8–14-9.

85. Anne Joseph O'Connell, "Shortening Agency and Judicial Vacancies through Filibuster Reform? An Examination of Confirmation Rates and Delays from 1981 to 2014," *Duke Law Journal* 64 (2015): 1645–1715.

86. US Constitution, Article II, section 2.

87. Ryan C. Black, Michael S. Lynch, Anthony J. Madonna, and Ryan J. Owens, "Assessing Congressional Responses to Growing Presidential Powers," *Presidential Studies Quarterly* 41, 3 (September 2011): 570–589.

88. Pete Kasperowicz, "House Forces Pro-Forma Sessions to Avoid Recess Appointments," *The Hill*, August 4, 2011.

89. National Labor Relations Board v. Canning, 573 U.S. __ (2014); Josh Gerstein, "SCOTUS Strikes Appointments," *Politico*, June 26, 2014.

90. See, e.g., Kelsey Snell, "Senate Republicans Don't Plan to Let Obama Replace Scalia over Recess," *Washington Post*, February 23, 2016.

91. Paul Kane, "Reid, Democrats Trigger 'Nuclear' Option; Eliminate Most Filibusters on Nominees," *Washington Post*, November 21, 2013.

92. Valerie Heitshusen, "Majority Cloture for Nominations: Implications and the 'Nuclear' Proceedings," Congressional Research Service, December 6, 2013.

93. Christina L. Boyd, Michael S. Lynch, and Anthony J. Madonna, "Nuclear Fallout: Investigating the Effect of Senate Procedural Reform on Judicial Nominations," *Forum* 13, 4 (December 2015): 623–641.

94. O'Connell, "Shortening Agency and Judicial Vacancies."

95. Mike Lillis, "House Democrats Feel Jilted by the President in Budget, Debt Talks," *The Hill*, June 29, 2011.

96. Manu Raju and Jonathan Martin, "Hill Dems Want More Love from Obama," *Politico*, February 4, 2013.

97. Jordan Fabian, "McCaskill Details Obama's 'Shortcomings' in Working with Congress," *The Hill*, December 10, 2015.

98. Maureen Dowd, "Bottoms up, Lame Duck," *New York Times*, April 30, 2013.

99. "First Year: POTUS 2017, Legislative Affairs Roundtable," transcript, Miller Center, University of Virginia, August 2, 2016, http://web1.millercenter.org/first year2017/2016-0802-LegislativeAffairs-transcript.pdf.

100. Matthew N. Beckmann, Neilan S. Chaturvedi, and Jennifer Rosa Garcia, "Targeting the Treatment: The Strategy behind Lyndon Johnson's Lobbying," *Legislative Studies Quarterly* 42, 2 (May 2017): 211–234.

101. "Executive Orders," American Presidency Project, John T. Woolley and Gerhard Peters, 1999–2017, http://www.presidency.ucsb.edu/data/orders.php.

102. Michael D. Shear, "Obama, Daring Congress, Acts to Overhaul Immigration," *New York Times*, November 20, 2014; David Nakamura and Juliet Eilperin, "Obama Details Executive Action on Gun Restrictions," *Washington Post*, January 4, 2016; Reid J. Epstein, "Obama Signs Minimum Wage Order," *Politico*, February 12, 2014.

103. Darla Cameron, "What President Obama's Executive Actions Mean for President Trump," *Washington Post*, December 6, 2016, https://www.washingtonpost.com /graphics/politics/executive-action/.

104. Binyamin Applebaum and Michael D. Shear, "Once Skeptical of Executive Power, Obama Has Come to Embrace It," *New York Times,* August 13, 2016.

105. Adam Liptak and Michael D. Shear, "Supreme Court Tie Blocks Obama Immigration Plan," *New York Times,* June 23, 2016; Adam Liptak and Coral Davenport, "Supreme Court Deals Blow to Obama's Efforts to Regulate Coal Emissions," *New York Times,* February 9, 2016.

106. Scott Detrow, "Obama Warns Trump against Relying on Executive Power," National Public Radio, December 29, 2016, http://www.npr.org/2016/12/19/505860058 /obama-warns-trump-against-relying-on-executive-power.

107. Juliet Eilperin and Darla Cameron, "How Trump Is Rolling Back Obama's Legacy," *Washington Post,* June 1, 2017, https://www.washingtonpost.com/graphics/politics /trump-rolling-back-obama-rules/?utm_term=.d8b33fb5cded.

CHAPTER SEVEN

The President and the Executive Branch

Sharece Thrower

> I intend to do everything in my power to act on behalf of the American people, with or without Congress . . . we can't wait for an increasingly dysfunctional Congress to do its job. Where they won't act, I will.
>
> —President Barack Obama, October 24, 2011[1]

Following the Senate's refusal to pass the American Jobs Act, President Barack Obama announced his intention to impose these economic reforms through executive action instead, thus beginning his new mantra against a recalcitrant Congress: "We Can't Wait." Although he widely utilized this approach on issues ranging from immigration to infrastructure, Obama was not the first president to use executive branch control as an impetus for policy change.

Despite long-standing attention to their legislative actions, presidents retain a tremendous amount of power under Article II of the Constitution, which stipulates that "the executive Power shall be vested in a President" and requires the president to "take Care that the laws be faithfully executed."[2] The "executive power" is never defined. But as they have evolved in practice across American history, these clauses have given presidents ample authority to implement policy as head of the executive branch, far beyond the limits of the legislative arena.

Furthermore, presidents have used the Constitution to justify even more executive branch control. In his widely influential essay "The Politicized Presidency," Terry Moe argues that the growth of the executive branch, along with mounting public expectations, has incentivized presidents to wield greater authority over bureaucratic institutions to ensure that their actions are congruent with the chief executive's.[3] As such, presidents since Franklin Roosevelt have relied on two main mechanisms of control: politicization and centralization. Politicization is the appointment of loyal, ideologically like-minded individuals to key executive positions, while centralization is the practice of placing agency activities under the coordination, supervision, or direct responsibility of the White House. Presidents have argued that both mechanisms are essential in fulfilling their constitutional duty to faithfully execute the law by ensuring proper policy implementation. While presidents want to gain control over the executive branch, their ability to accomplish that goal may be hindered by a number of political obstacles.[4]

This chapter explores the degree to which President Obama was able to influence the executive branch as a means to pursue his own political goals, largely through politicization and centralization. Additionally, it examines the effectiveness of his unilateral directives. Although presidents can indirectly guide policy by appointing loyalists and overseeing bureaucratic activities, these orders provide agencies with direct, unequivocal instructions on how to implement the law.

This chapter addresses two questions. First, did Obama attempt to exert dominance over the bureaucracy in the same ways pursued by previous presidents? Second, how successful was he in using these control mechanisms to influence the executive branch and, more to the point, to attain his policy goals? I conclude that while Obama endeavored to pursue his goals through bureaucratic control, as his predecessors had done, the effectiveness of these strategies was severely hampered by the difficult political environment—specifically, constraints imposed by an oppositional legislature and judiciary. These limitations may have implications for future presidencies, as discussed in the chapter's final section.

Politicization through Appointments

Although presidents can politicize the bureaucracy in a variety of ways, presidential appointments with Senate confirmation are perhaps the most consequential means of selecting like-minded individuals to steer the direction of agencies.[5] According to the White House, Obama nominated a total of 1,214 individuals for these executive positions, 1,023 of whom were confirmed.[6] A number of vacancies naturally emerged. In a January 2016 article, *Politico* reported 101 vacancies among the 379 Senate-confirmed senior positions at the cabinet and subcabinet levels within agencies in the Obama administration.[7] Occasional administrative openings are common, but their prevalence was particularly troublesome for Obama. Indeed, one study of all nonroutine civilian executive branch nominations considered by the Senate between 1981 and 2016 found that Obama had more failed nominees than any other president. Thirty percent of his nominees were not confirmed, reflecting a trend of increasingly unsuccessful confirmations: 16 percent failed under Ronald Reagan, 16 percent under George H. W. Bush, 21 percent under Bill Clinton, and 25 percent under George W. Bush.[8] Notably, many of these unconfirmed nominees were the result of prolonged filibusters, such as Craig Becker's 2010 nomination to the National Labor Relations Board (NLRB) and Richard Cordray's 2011 nomination as director of the Consumer Financial Protection Bureau (CFPB).[9] Moreover, failure rates are influenced by the inclusion of those nominees who withdrew their names from consideration following threats of Senate opposition, including Dawn Johnsen (nominated to head the Office Legal Counsel in the Justice Department) and Enroll Southers (nominated as administrator of the Transportation Security Administration), both in 2010.

Unsuccessful confirmations can also involve individuals who withdrew themselves from consideration before being formally nominated, owing to fierce political opposition. One example is Susan Rice, considered for secretary of state in 2012. Additionally, nominees can be returned to the president without a vote, essentially killing their candidacy. This happened to Peter Diamond three times in 2010 and 2011, when Senate Republicans on the Banking Committee prevented the Federal Reserve nominee's confirmation from proceeding.

In addition to a high failure rate, Obama's nominees faced the longest confirmation delays, enduring an average of 122 days until being confirmed—a 36 percent increase from his immediate predecessor.[10] Average confirmation times were lower for other presidents, but they have been increasing since the 1980s: 60 days under Reagan, 62 under G. H. W. Bush, 86 under Clinton, and 90 under G. W. Bush. Furthermore, *FiveThirtyEight* reports that Obama's cabinet nominees hold the record for the longest intervals between nomination and confirmation.[11] Loretta Lynch waited a total of 161 days before being confirmed by the Senate as attorney general, the longest since 1977. The other top two record holders, John Bryson (secretary of commerce) and Thomas Perez (secretary of labor), are also from the Obama administration.

Causes and Consequences of Failed Nominations

Of course, prolonged delays and failed nominations lead to critical administrative vacancies, which can cause agency inaction, internal conflict, and a lack of accountability.[12] Beyond institutional dysfunction, vacancies can also undermine politicization. Unappointed career civil servants often fill these vacancies, and although they bring experience to the job, they may be less responsive to presidential commands and thus can impede the executive's political goals.[13]

Many of Obama's confirmation impediments stemmed from Republican fears of politicization. Even when he attempted to nominate conservatives for executive positions, conflict materialized. For example, in February 2009 Republican senator Judd Gregg withdrew his name from consideration just days after being nominated for commerce secretary. He clashed with the Obama administration over his unwillingness to support the economic stimulus package and the impending White House oversight of the 2010 census—in addition to being pressured by his own party.[14] Gregg lamented these control issues in an interview, saying, "For 30 years, I've been my own person in charge of my own views, and I guess I hadn't really

Table 7.1. Obama Cabinet Nominees

Nominee	Cabinet Position	Confirmed	Years Served in Office	Party Affiliation
Tom Vilsack	Secretary of agriculture	Yes	2009–2017	Democrat
Eric Holder	Attorney general	Yes	2009–2015	Democrat
Loretta Lynch	Attorney general	Yes	2015–2016	Democrat
Bill Richardson*	Secretary of commerce	No	—	Democrat
Judd Gregg†	Secretary of commerce	No	—	Republican
Gary Locke	Secretary of commerce	Yes	2009–2011	Democrat
John Bryson	Secretary of commerce	Yes	2011–2012	Democrat
Penny Pritzker	Secretary of commerce	Yes	2013–2017	Democrat
Robert Gates‡	Secretary of defense	Yes	2006–2011	Republican
Leon Panetta	Secretary of defense	Yes	2011–2013	Democrat
Chuck Hagel	Secretary of defense	Yes	2013–2015	Republican
Ashton Carter	Secretary of defense	Yes	2015–2017	Democrat
Arne Duncan	Secretary of education	Yes	2009–2016	Democrat
John King	Secretary of education	Yes	2016–2017	Democrat
Steven Chu	Secretary of energy	Yes	2009–2013	Democrat
Ernest Moniz	Secretary of energy	Yes	2013–2017	Democrat
Tom Daschle	Secretary of health and human services	No	—	Democrat
Kathleen Sebelius	Secretary of health and human services	Yes	2009–2014	Democrat
Sylvia Burwell	Secretary of health and human services	Yes	2014–2017	Democrat
Janet Napolitano	Secretary of homeland security	Yes	2009–2013	Democrat
Jeh Johnson	Secretary of homeland security	Yes	2013–2017	Democrat
Shaun Donovan	Secretary of housing and urban development	Yes	2009–2014	Democrat
Julian Castro	Secretary of housing and urban development	Yes	2014–2017	Democrat

Name	Position	Years		Party
Ken Salazar	Secretary of interior	2009–2013	Yes	Democrat
Sally Jewell	Secretary of interior	2013–2017	Yes	Democrat
Hilda Solis	Secretary of labor	2009–2013	Yes	Democrat
Thomas Perez	Secretary of labor	2013–2017	Yes	Democrat
Hillary Clinton	Secretary of state	2009–2013	Yes	Democrat
John Kerry	Secretary of state	2013–2017	Yes	Democrat
Ray LaHood	Secretary of transportation	2009–2013	Yes	Republican
Anthony Foxx	Secretary of transportation	2013–2017	Yes	Democrat
Timothy Geithner	Secretary of the treasury	2009–2013	Yes	Independent
Jack Lew	Secretary of the treasury	2013–2017	Yes	Democrat

Source: Compiled from "Obama Cabinet Nominations," US Senate, https://www.senate.gov/reference/Obama_cabinet.htm.

* Withdrew his nomination on January 4, 2009.

† Withdrew his nomination on February 12, 2009.

‡ Continued to serve from the George W. Bush administration.

focused on the job of working for somebody else and carrying their views."[15] Despite this setback, Obama remained committed to appointing a cabinet with bipartisan consensus.

As a presidential candidate, Obama had vowed to appoint a "team of rivals" consisting of individuals who were best qualified for the job rather than just loyal, ideological sycophants.[16] Indeed, former primary rivals Joe Biden and Hillary Clinton were selected as vice president and secretary of state, respectively. Furthermore, Obama appointed more cabinet members outside of his party than any other president.[17] As table 7.1 shows, he nominated Republican representative Ray LaHood for secretary of transportation and Tim Geithner, a former Republican turned independent, for treasury secretary. Robert Gates, originally appointed by George W. Bush in 2006, was asked to stay on as secretary of defense; former Republican senator Chuck Hagel accepted the position in 2013. Despite these bipartisan triumphs, Obama politicized the executive branch by appointing more loyalists in his second term, such as Jack Lew as treasury secretary and John Kerry as secretary of state.[18]

However, as previously mentioned, Obama's success in politicizing the executive branch was constrained by delays and failures in the confirmation process. A prolonged selection process, an increased number of positions, and frequent turnover certainly contributed to this difficulty,[19] but perhaps the most important reason was obstruction by Republican senators—particularly when they assumed majority control in 2015. Given that ideological polarization in Congress was at an all-time high and that Democrats mostly failed to maintain a filibuster-proof majority in the Senate during his administration, it is not surprising that Obama faced more vacancies and delays than any previous president, consistent with academic accounts of the debilitating effects of these political phenomena on executive confirmations.[20]

Reforms to the Nomination and Confirmation Process

Given these growing difficulties in the appointment process, several reforms were offered. On August 10, 2012, Obama signed the Presidential Appointment Efficiency and Streamlining Act of 2011, eliminating confirmation requirements for 163 executive positions. Similarly, the Senate passed Senate Resolution 116 on June 29, 2011, allowing nominees for 272 executive positions to bypass formal committee consideration. Although these acts were designed to fill vacancies quickly by easing senators' workload, they did not facilitate greater politicization, given that these positions were mostly administrative, with little or no role in policy-making.[21]

Perhaps most notably, on November 21, 2013, Senate Democrats invoked the "nuclear option" to eliminate the use of the filibuster on executive and non–Supreme Court judicial nominations. The rule change was intended to reduce the number of vacancies and the length of confirmation delays by requiring only a simple majority for cloture, rather than the 60 votes previously needed to end debate. Despite its best intentions, the nuclear option failed to eliminate Senate obstruction. In fact, evidence shows that neither the length of time for executive confirmations nor the overall failure rate decreased after this reform took effect.[22] In lieu of lengthy floor debates, Republican senators found other ways to delay Obama's nominations, such as requiring candidates to answer extensive written questions ahead of a committee vote. Thus, delays and barriers to politicization persisted, even under Democratic control.

One final solution was recess appointments, whereby individuals nominated during Senate breaks can serve temporarily without formal confirmation until the end of the next congressional session. Obama actually made fewer recess appointments than his predecessors. During his first term, Obama made 32 such appointments, while Clinton and George W. Bush made 35 and 106, respectively, by the end of their fourth years in office.[23] One reason for this decrease could be the Senate's regular use of pro forma sessions, beginning in November 2007, in an attempt to obviate recess appointments. Pro forma sessions are brief Senate meetings—often lasting only a few seconds—during regularly scheduled intermissions; their primary purpose is to avoid a recess long enough (usually three days) to allow these surprise presidential appointments. Notwithstanding previous norms, Obama made four recess appointments between pro forma sessions on January 4, 2012: Richard Cordray as CFPB director and Terrence Flynn, Sharon Block, and Richard Griffin to the NLRB.[24] Ultimately, the Supreme Court invalidated the NLRB appointments on June 26, 2014, and limited the president's recess appointment power to breaks of at least ten days, effectively allowing the Senate to continue to use pro forma sessions as impediments to these appointments.[25]

Following this case, Obama made no more recess appointments.[26] Consequently, the courts inhibited the president's ability to bypass the confirmation process and therefore his ability to politicize the executive branch in the face of senatorial obstruction. Moreover, this case leaves the door open for future court decisions that could further limit recess appointments to intersession breaks or vacancies arising at such times, as the DC Circuit previously interpreted.[27]

Like his predecessors, Obama tried to politicize the executive branch. However, he faced political obstacles—from both the Senate and the courts—that seriously limited his ability to do so. Consequently, he faced more Senate rejections, confirmation delays, and administrative vacancies than any previous president. Congressional reform and recess appointments proved an inadequate fix. It is possible that these barriers to politicization could place other constraints on the president. Future presidents may need to spend more time vetting candidates, or qualified candidates may be deterred if they anticipate an obstructionist Senate, further extending the nominating process. In fact, President Donald Trump's cabinet nominees have already faced longer average delays and more filibuster attempts than those of previous presidents.

Yet, when it comes to Obama's legacy with regard to executive branch appointments, all is not lost. According to the *Washington Post*, his administration was the most demographically diverse in history, and he appointed more women and minorities than any other president.[28] Obama also increased the number of LGBT individuals serving in the executive branch, most notably, appointing Eric Fanning as the first openly gay head of a military branch (secretary of the army).

Centralization

Did centralization increase during the Obama administration to counteract deficiencies in politicization, or was it likewise inhibited by a highly conflictual political environment? This section evaluates Obama's overall effectiveness at bureaucratic control through several methods of centralization, including White House staff and agencies, policy czars, and central clearance.

Decision-Making within the White House

One way to gauge centralization is to determine the extent to which presidents rely on their White House staff. These individuals tend to be the most responsive and loyal bureaucrats, given presidents' wide discretion in appointing people to fill these mostly non-Senate-confirmed positions. White House staffers often oversee and coordinate agencies' activities. As such, the more presidents depend on their White House apparatus, the more likely it is that centralization is occurring across the executive branch. Qualitative evidence suggests that Obama was highly dependent on White House staff to centralize decision-making across the executive branch. In his article "Decision Making in the Obama White House," James P. Pfiffner argues that every president has progressively engaged in this kind of centralization, extending through the Obama administration.[29] In fact, former secretary of defense Robert Gates criticized Obama's tight control over the bureaucracy, writing, "his White House was by far the most centralized and controlling in national security of any I had seen since Richard Nixon . . . the controlling nature of the Obama White House and the NSS staff took micromanagement and operational meddling to a new level."[30] Former secretaries of defense and state, Leon Panetta and Hillary Clinton, expressed similar concerns in their own memoirs.[31]

Obama became much more involved in the details of policy than George W. Bush had been. He relied primarily on chief of staff Rahm Emanuel and other close White House advisers for policy advice.[32] Even though Obama often sought opposing views from a "team of rivals," much of this information was filtered through his inner circle, and he maintained ultimate decision-making power.[33] Even when

Obama initially delegated decision-making power over detainee policy to Attorney General Eric Holder—someone more insulated from his control—he eventually shifted that authority back into the hands of White House officials, amidst criticism surrounding the Department of Justice.[34]

Policy Czars

Perhaps most notably, Obama became known for the use of policy czars to exert greater control over the bureaucracy. Despite the lack of consensus on its exact definition, most agree that a czar is an administrative position created by the president, and the person occupying that position is responsible for coordinating the activities of various agencies within the executive branch for a salient policy area.[35] Czar positions are usually solely or jointly located within a White House office and often operate outside of congressional oversight. Some czars are confirmed by the Senate, but many are not. Some view this as problematic, given that czars have "significant authority"[36] over decision-making, budgets, regulations, and binding orders to public and private officials.[37] Consequently, this allows presidents to empower loyal partisans to carry out their will in the absence of congressional interference, further ensuring executive branch compliance.

Despite the widespread criticism of Obama's use of czars, most presidents since Franklin Roosevelt have employed at least one. Yet, according to Mitchell Sollenberger and Mark Rozell, Obama appointed more non-Senate-confirmed czars than any other president; between 2009 and 2012, he appointed twenty-seven—more than Gerald Ford through George W. Bush combined.[38] Even when accounting for media-labeled czars, who are often Senate-confirmed, Obama's czar usage still surpassed that of his predecessors, with fifty-nine.[39] Yet, this appears to be part of a trend toward an increased use of czars: Ronald Reagan and George H. W. Bush each had three media-labeled czars, Bill Clinton had eighteen, and George W. Bush had forty-one.[40] Beyond these numbers, Justin Vaughn and Jose Villalobos argue that Obama used czars in a much more centralized way than previously seen.[41] He often created these positions to head newly minted offices in the Executive Office of the Presidency (EOP), including the "urban affairs czar" (Office of Urban Affairs) and the "health czar" (Office of Health Reform).[42]

Overall, Obama's use of czars advanced his policy agenda in several ways. First, it allowed him to control the bureaucracy by centralizing its activities under an official who was largely outside the purview of congressional control.[43] Second, it aided in politicization by permitting him to appoint key officials without Senate confirmation. Finally, it demonstrated to the public that his administration was actively involved in addressing pressing policy concerns. On the downside, it led to public and political backlash from both sides of the aisle. In addition to negative media attention, legislative attempts to curtail czar usage surfaced under the Obama administration—including public statements, letters, congressional hearings, and failed legislation.[44] If this criticism continues, future presidents may find it difficult to use czars as a tool for centralization. However, it was arguably one of Obama's most effective strategies to achieve bureaucratic control, given the number of positions he created under his direct command to oversee several salient policy areas.

Executive Office of the Presidency

Obama strategically established EOP agencies to house new czar positions, but presidents have long used agency creation as a way to centralize the executive branch, often taking unilateral action to form bureaucratic structures that are less insulated from their control.[45] Given that many of these unilaterally created agencies are located within the EOP, presidents can exert greater authority over their actions. Compared with previous presidents, Obama relied slightly more on unilateral agency creation as a means of centralization. He created an average of seven agencies per year, compared with four under G. W. Bush, six under Clinton, four under G. H. W. Bush, and six under Reagan.[46] Similar to his predecessors, Obama formed new agencies to manage salient issues, such as the President's Economic Recovery Advisory Board in 2009, in the midst of the economic recession.[47] Yet, in contrast to previous presidents, many of his new agencies were not located within the EOP. In fact, only 31 percent of Obama's unilaterally created agencies were placed in the EOP, versus 84 percent under Reagan, 60 percent under G. H. W. Bush, 45 percent under Clinton, and 55 percent under G. W. Bush. Many of Obama's non-EOP agencies were created within a cabinet department, such as the Commission on Enhancing National Cybersecurity, established in the Department of Commerce in 2016.[48] Additionally, Obama relied on interagency task forces, such as the Task Force on Space Industry Workforce and Economic Development and the Task Force on Skills for America's Future, both created through memoranda in 2010.

Central Clearance

Yet another way to centralize executive branch activities is through White House or EOP approval of various agency decisions. An example of this type of central clearance is the management of agency budgets and legislative requests by the Office of Management and Budget (OMB); however, one of the most consequential methods is formal regulatory review. Created by Reagan via Executive Order (EO) 12291 in 1981, this process requires executive agencies to submit all regulations to the Office of Information and Regulatory Affairs (OIRA), a subunit within the OMB, for approval before being finalized and published in the *Federal Register*.[49] By overseeing one of the most important agency activities, OIRA's regulatory review provides presidents with a tremendous ability to centralize and ensure bureaucratic control. Subsequent administrations reformed this process. Clinton imposed the most substantial change by narrowing the scope of OIRA review from all rules to "significant" rules.[50] George W. Bush restored greater centralization by expanding OIRA's review to include guidance documents, such as nonbinding policy statements, and requiring each agency to designate a political appointee as a "regulatory policy officer" responsible for internally overseeing its rule-making activities.[51]

Immediately after taking office, Obama revoked Bush's attempt to expand presidential power and issued EO 13497, essentially restoring the previous process. Likewise, Obama's other executive orders made mostly minor changes to the process rather than substantively advancing centralization. For instance, EO 13563 explicitly reaffirmed the review process delineated in Clinton's EO 12866; similarly, it required agencies to provide online public access to their rule-making dockets and to submit retrospective regulatory reviews. EO 13579 extended this requirement to independent regulatory agencies.

Beyond reforms, Obama did not significantly centralize regulatory activities to pursue his goals. Although the number of reviews decreased following EO 12866, OIRA can audit agency rules and determine which ones are "significant" enough for review. In this way, presidents can target troublesome agencies with greater regulatory oversight. Obama engaged in fewer OIRA reviews than either Clinton or Bush, suggesting less overall involvement in rule-making activities under his administration. OIRA conducted an average of 533 reviews per year under Obama, 648 under Bush, and 588 under Clinton.[52] Furthermore, evidence suggests that Obama did not deliberately target ideologically hostile agencies with OIRA audits, in contrast to Bush, who consistently used this strategy as a form of presidential control.[53]

Still, Obama was sharply criticized for record-long delays in OIRA reviews of controversial agency rules.[54] In fact, under Obama, regulations were under review an average of eighty-three days, far longer than under both Clinton (forty-seven days) and Bush (fifty-five days).[55] Although Obama was accused of using these delays for political purposes—for instance, to push controversial regulations past the 2012 election—they could have been the result of deficiencies within OIRA.[56] For instance, record-high review times under the Obama administration corresponded to record-low staffing levels in OIRA,[57] likely leading to problems in managing the workload. Furthermore, evidence suggests that when OIRA lacks institutional capacity, it inhibits presidents' ability to pursue their ideological goals through targeted delays.[58]

Although Obama was quite limited in his ability to control the bureaucracy through politicization, he was more successful at centralization—to a certain degree. In some ways, Obama made small advances toward centralizing the executive branch. He relied more extensively on White House staff for policy advice and was more directly involved in decision-making details. Perhaps most notably, he used a concentrated strategy of creating czar positions to head new unilaterally created agencies. Thus, he was able to proactively centralize decision-making to advance his policy agenda in new ways.

However, Obama faced some challenges. Fewer of his unilaterally created agencies were within the EOP, perhaps due to the threat of retaliatory legislation or defunding from an ideologically hostile Congress opposed to expansive presidential control.[59] Obama did not make significant changes to the regulatory review process, and in fact, he reversed Bush's attempts to exert more presidential control over it. There is no evidence that Obama utilized OIRA to strategically target ideologically deviant agencies—likely because of its challenges in performing its oversight responsibilities. Of course, Congress largely decides how to invest OIRA's capacity (e.g., staff, budget) and can constrain centralization in this way.

Overall, the fact that Obama was more successful in centralizing the executive branch than politicizing it lends at least modest support to the argument that these two control methods are substitutes for each other.[60] Yet, as the Obama administration demonstrates, many of the barriers to politicization are also serious constraints to centralization, suggesting a complementary relationship. Whether the two are substitutes for or complements to each other may ultimately depend on what metric we use to assess centralization. Nonetheless, we can conclude that Obama's use of czars was one of his most successful centralization strategies. However, such techniques may be tenuous in the future if congressional opposition continues to mount against them.

Unilateral Directives: Executive Orders and Memoranda

Beyond politicization and centralization, presidents can more directly ensure bureaucratic compliance by issuing explicit orders to agencies via unilateral directives. How effective was this strategy under the Obama administration? Did he significantly advance presidential power and his priorities with these directives? Or did he face difficulties in overcoming familiar institutional constraints in utilizing this controversial tool?

In general, unilateral directives are presidential instructions dispensed to executive branch agencies on how to implement or interpret the law. Although there are several different types at the president's disposal, one of the most important is the executive order. Given that EOs are widely viewed by the courts as having the force of law, barring any blatant legal violations, executive orders provide presidents with a tangible way to influence policy through agency implementation, often bypassing legislative processes.

Despite media claims that Obama issued many more executive orders than his predecessors, he actually issued fewer than any president since Grover Cleveland. He issued an average of thirty-five orders per year, compared with thirty-six by

G. W. Bush, forty-six by Clinton, forty-two by G. H. W. Bush, and forty-eight by Reagan. Notably, the trend toward fewer orders over time corresponds to the increasing frequency of divided government, consistent with prevalent scholarly findings.[61]

Obama issued orders for traditional purposes such as agency creation, coordination, economic sanctions, and government efficiency. And like his predecessors, Obama issued important orders during his first year in office to rescind previous administration policies.[62] In his first 100 days, he revoked nine executive orders issued by George W. Bush related to presidential records, lawful interrogation, stem cell research, labor standards, and regulatory review. Obama used other orders to implement policies on texting and driving, energy and environmental performance, biological attacks, and veterans' employment.

Obama actually increased his reliance on another unilateral tool: presidential memoranda. Although his average of forty-one memoranda per year was more than the average number issued by Reagan (seventeen), G. H. W. Bush (twenty-one), and G. W. Bush (twenty-six), he issued slightly fewer than Clinton (forty-three).[63]

Much like other unilateral directives, memoranda are used to direct agency implementation of the law and are often issued contemporaneously with executive orders to guide their execution. For instance, in response to executive orders concerning regulatory review issued on January 30, 2009, and July 11, 2011,[64] Obama also issued memoranda requesting agencies to review procedures and recommend plans for their implementation.[65] Similar memos were issued related to detainee policy, stem cell research, and security classification.

On the whole, memoranda can be a relatively quick and discreet alternative to executive orders, since they do not require publication in the *Federal Register*. Yet they did not provide Obama with a solution to interbranch constraints, for a number of reasons. First, memoranda add to existing policy rather than creating policy itself. Many are used to reinforce or elaborate simultaneously issued executive orders. Moreover, many memoranda directly respond to or delegate authority given in legislation. Additionally, they are commonly used as symbolic devices to publicly show presidential attention to an issue without actually committing new resources.[66]

Second, although the courts have clearly stated that executive orders are legally valid policy tools equivalent to the law, the legal status of memoranda remains ambiguous. Presidents generally view memoranda as legally equivalent to executive orders, but the courts have yet to agree.[67] Following administrative procedures, agencies must rely on clear sources of authority, which can include unilateral directives, when engaging in rule-making activities. This authority is likely stronger when based on directives that are clearly viewed as having the force of law. Thus, although memoranda can be useful tools for presidents, they are not necessarily significant or enduring substitutes for executive orders. Finally, recent research suggests that presidents are constrained in the use of memoranda, much like executive orders, and they issue fewer under a divided government.[68]

Overall, Obama was limited in the use of unilateral directives to influence policy implementation. He issued fewer executive orders than previous presidents, likely due to threats of congressional and judicial reprimands. Though memoranda were seemingly a viable alternative to orders, Obama issued these judiciously as well, for similar reasons. Furthermore, questions remain over the memorandum's value as a policy device, given its legally dubious status. In light of these constraints, Obama did not make large advances in presidential power and bureaucratic control via unilateral directives.[69]

As such, unilateral directives are unlikely to be the most useful tool for making advancements for future presidencies. As interbranch conflict continues to increase, presidents will likely find it even more difficult to effectively exercise unilateral power, remarkably similar to the challenges associated with politicization and centralization. Furthermore, because they can be easily revoked by subsequent presidents, unilateral actions may not be the most effective way to permanently impact the bureaucracy.

What these devices do offer is a way to initiate and guide the current rule-making processes. For example, many agency regulations were issued in direct response to Obama's unilateral directives related to nondiscriminatory employment requirements for federal contractors, gun control, and the minimum wage. Yet these and other regulations run the risk of being overturned by the courts, even more so than unilateral actions, given that they are covered by judicial review standards articulated in the Administrative Procedures Act.[70] Legal challenges to Obama-era Environmental Protection Agency rules on carbon emissions of coal power plants provide just one example.[71] In addition to court challenges, regulations can be altered by subsequent administrations and Congresses alike. Thus, Obama's legacy (and that of future presidents) in shaping policy through bureaucratic control with executive actions is likely tenuous (see also chapter 10 in this volume).

Conclusion

With each year, the size of government has grown, reaching record highs at the end of the Obama administration. In 2015 alone, the government spent more than $3.2 trillion—an appreciable increase over the $734 billion spent just thirty years before.[72] Rising public demands, unforeseen natural disasters, as well as debilitating economic and international crises have led to the creation of new programs spawned by both legislative and executive action—the Affordable Care Act, Dodd-Frank, the American Recovery and Reinvestment Act, and the Deferred Action for

Childhood Arrivals, to name a few—administered by a growing executive branch with more responsibilities. To manage expanding bureaucratic activities and to implement his policy preferences, Obama made efforts to exert greater control over the bureaucracy—as modern presidents had commonly done before. He attempted to politicize the executive branch through appointments and centralize its activity through an increased reliance on White House staff, new agencies, and czars. He issued unilateral directives to agencies to implement policies salient to his agenda. Yet Obama's ability to extend presidential control over the bureaucracy was severely hampered by interbranch constraints imposed by ideological opponents in the legislature and judiciary.

Of these three control mechanisms, Obama had the most difficulty with politicization. In particular, he confronted more administrative vacancies, unconfirmed nominees, and confirmation delays than any other president—despite various reforms to expedite this process under his administration. In addition to congressional constraints, the courts undermined his attempts to politicize through recess appointments. Likewise, increased vetting and candidate deterrence ahead of confirmation battles delayed the nomination process, further inhibiting politicization.

When it comes to centralization, Obama experienced mixed success in controlling the bureaucracy, depending on how this concept is measured. In general, he relied greatly on White House associates and his own personal involvement in decision-making. Most notably, he advanced the use of czars in ways previously unseen, employing more of them to coordinate policy across the executive branch in conjunction with newly created agencies. Yet Obama failed to promote centralization in other ways. He did not significantly reform the regulatory review process to increase control over agency actions, and he actually reversed Bush-era advancements in presidential oversight. Relatedly, Obama did not aggressively target the activities of deviant agencies to induce compliance. Finally, a number of his unilaterally created agencies were not exclusively located within the EOP, unlike those created by his predecessors.

Some of Obama's difficulties in centralization can be attributed to deficiencies in critical coordinating agencies, such as OIRA, which failed to properly perform their duties and pursue presidential goals. Notably, even though the size of the White House staff increased slightly over time, OIRA staff steadily decreased. Yet, as in the case of politicization, these difficulties can also be attributed to interbranch conflicts. For instance, Congress controls the allocation of resources to these coordinating agencies, thus indirectly influencing presidential oversight. Furthermore, the threat of legislative retaliation could have deterred Obama from creating less insulated agencies. Even his most successful means of centralizing the executive branch, the use of policy czars, may be in jeopardy for future presidents, given the mounting bipartisan congressional opposition to them.

Finally, despite heavy criticism of his use of unilateral directives, Obama did not significantly advance presidential power with this tool. In fact, he issued fewer executive orders than his predecessors. Although he relied more heavily on memoranda, he mostly acted within his statutory authority. Fears of congressional and judicial retaliation likely decreased the frequency and extremity of Obama's unilateral directives to shape policy.

Many of Obama's difficulties in controlling the executive branch were part of larger trends across presidencies related to stalled policy-making. At the same time, polarization has continued to increase, and divided government has become a common fixture in American politics. Though the desire to rely on these bureaucratic control mechanisms may be constant, the degree to which presidents can do so is limited by the separation-of-powers context and the constraints imposed by the other branches of government.

Greater interbranch cooperation is needed if future presidents are to have any chance of achieving bureaucratic control. Congress would have to permit the president to make executive appointments, create agencies, and issue unilateral directives. It would also have to devote greater resources to sustaining the capacity of important coordinating agencies to allow the president to effectively centralize bureaucratic activities. Judicial nominees would have to be readily confirmed by the Senate so that presidents could select judges who are likely to uphold their executive actions. Of course, all this is contingent on Congress being willing to cooperate with the president. Given the trajectory of partisanship and interbranch conflict, future presidents are likely to face an uphill battle in trying to control the executive branch. Furthermore, a president's impact on the bureaucracy is likely transitory, given that successors can easily reverse previous presidential actions. President Donald Trump, for instance, threatened to overturn many of Obama's actions long before he ever set foot in the Oval Office. In fact, within six months of assuming office, Trump had already issued fifteen executive actions and thirty-three agency actions, with several others in the works, canceling sixty-three regulations and many other Obama-era policy changes related to health care, the environment, civil rights, education, and labor.[73] In short, Obama's executive branch legacy remains in jeopardy.

Notes

1. Barack Obama, "Remarks in Las Vegas," October 24, 2011, American Presidency Project, Gerhard Peters and John T. Woolley, http://www.presidency.ucsb.edu/ws/index.php?pid=96941&st=we+can%5C%27t+wait&st1=.
2. US Constitution, Article II, sections 1 and 3.
3. Terry Moe, "The Politicized Presidency," in *The New Direction in American Politics*, ed. John E. Chubb and Paul E. Peterson (Washington, DC: Brookings Institution, 1985), 235–271.
4. See, e.g., David Lewis, *The Politics of Political Appointments: Political Control and Bu-

reaucratic Performance (Princeton, NJ: Princeton University Press, 2008); Andrew Rudalevige, *Managing the President's Program: Presidential Leadership and Legislative Policy Formulation* (Princeton, NJ: Princeton University Press, 2002).

5. Politicization can also include Senior Executive Service and Schedule C appointments.

6. The White House, "Nominations and Appointments," accessed October 2016, https://www.whitehouse.gov/briefing-room/nominations-and-appointments.

7. Darren Samuelshohn, "Obama's Vanishing Administration," *Politico*, January 5, 2016, http://www.politico.com/story/2016/01/obamas-vanishing-administration-217344.

8. Anne Joseph O'Connell, "Staffing Federal Agencies: Lessons from 1981–2016," Brookings, 2017, https://www.brookings.edu/research/staffing-federal-agencies-lessons-from-1981-2016/; Anne Joseph O'Connell, "Shortening Agency and Judicial Vacancies through Filibuster Reform? An Examination of Confirmation Rates and Delays from 1981 and 2014," *Duke Law Journal* 64 (2005): 1645–1715. O'Connell defines a failed nominee as one voted down by the Senate, withdrawn, or returned to the president.

9. Cordray's initial nomination was blocked on December 8, 2011, but confirmed on July 16, 2013, following a recess appointment.

10. See O'Connell, "Staffing Federal Agencies"; Anne Joseph O'Connell, "Waiting for Leadership: President Obama's Record in Staffing Key Agency Positions and How to Improve the Appointments Process" (Center for American Progress, 2010).

11. Harry Enten, "Obama Has Waited Longer for Cabinet Confirmations than Any Other Recent President," *FiveThirtyEight*, April 23, 2015, http://fivethirtyeight.com/datalab/obama-has-waited-longer-for-cabinet-confirmations-than-any-other-recent-president/.

12. See Anne Joseph O'Connell, "Let's Get It Started: What President-elect Obama Can Learn from Previous Administrations in Making Political Appointments" (Center for American Progress, January 2009); O'Connell, "Waiting for Leadership."

13. James P. Pfiffner, "Presidential Appointments and Managing the Executive Branch," Political Appointee Project, accessed November 1, 2016, http://politicalappointee project.org/presidential-appointments-and-managing-the-executive-branch.html. Moreover, some suggest that Obama had a strained relationship with careerists in the executive branch. See William Resh, *Rethinking the Administrative Presidency* (Baltimore: Johns Hopkins University Press, 2015).

14. See Jeff Zeleny, "Gregg Ends Bid for Commerce Job," *New York Times*, February 12, 2009, http://www.nytimes.com/2009/02/13/us/politics/13gregg.html.

15. Associated Press, "Gregg Withdraws as Nominee for Commerce," NBC News, February 12, 2009, http://www.nbcnews.com/id/29166218/#.WAUdlpMrJR4.

16. Todd Purdum, "Team of Mascots," *Vanity Fair*, July 2012, http://www.vanityfair.com/news/2012/07/obama-cabinet-team-rivals-lincoln.

17. Robert Farley, "Three Cabinet Appointees from Opposing Party Is Unmatched," February 10, 2009, http://www.politifact.com/truth-o-meter/statements/2009/feb/10/barack-obama/Three-Republicans-Cabinet-Most/.

18. See David J. Rothkopf, "Obama's Cabinet: From a Team of Rivals to the Usual Suspects," *Washington Post*, January 11, 2013, https://www.washingtonpost.com/opinions/obamas-cabinet-from-a-team-of-rivals-to-the-usual-suspects/2013/01/11/bbc8 3f78-59cc-11e2-beee-6e38f5215402_story.html?utm_term=.15fa38eb5af6. See also

Andrew Rudalevige, "Rivals, or a Team? Staffing and Issue Management in the Obama Administration," in *The Presidency of Barack Obama: Appraisals and Prospects*, ed. Bert A. Rockman, Andrew Rudalevige, and Colin Campbell (Washington, DC: CQ/Sage, 2012).

19. See O'Connell, "Let's Get It Started"; O'Connell, "Waiting for Leadership"; Pfiffner, "Presidential Appointments and Managing the Executive Branch."

20. See Nolan McCarty and Rose Razighan, "Advice and Consent: Senate Response to Executive Branch Nominations, 1885–1996," *American Journal of Political Science* 43, 3 (1999): 1122–1143.

21. See Maeve P. Carey, "Presidential Appointments, the Senate's Confirmation Process, and Changes Made in the 112th Congress" (Congressional Research Service Report R41872, 2012).

22. See O'Connell, "Staffing Federal Agencies."

23. See Henry B. Hogue, "Recess Appointments Made by President Barack Obama" (Congressional Research Service Report R42329, 2015).

24. Although Democrats controlled the Senate, the Republican House still had the constitutional power to force the Senate into a pro forma session by holding one of its own. See Michelle Cottle, "How the Senate Foils Obama Even When It's in Recess," *Atlantic*, March 23, 2016, https://www.theatlantic.com/politics/archive/2016/03/pro-forma-senate/474930/.

25. See National Labor Relations Board v. Noel Canning, 134 S. Ct. 22550 (2014).

26. See Hogue, "Recess Appointments."

27. See Noel Canning v. National Labor Relations Board, D.C. Cir. 2013, No. 12-1115.

28. See Juliet Eilperin, "Obama Has Vastly Changed the Face of the Federal Bureaucracy," *Washington Post*, September 20, 2015, https://www.washingtonpost.com/politics/obama-has-vastly-changed-the-face-of-the-federal-bureaucracy/2015/09/20/73ef803a-5631-11e5-abe9-27d53f250b11_story.html.

29. James P. Pfiffner, "Decision Making in the Obama White House," *Presidential Studies Quarterly* 41, 2 (2011): 244–262. More generally, see Rudalevige, *Managing the President's Program.*

30. Robert M. Gates, *Duty: Memoirs of a Secretary at War* (New York: Vintage Books, 2014), 585–587.

31. Leon Panetta, *Worthy Fights: A Memoir of Leadership in War and Peace* (New York: Penguin Books, 2014); Hillary Rodham Clinton, *Hard Choices* (New York: Simon & Schuster, 2014).

32. See Pfiffner, "Decision Making."

33. See Rudalevige, "Rivals, or a Team?"

34. See Pfiffner, "Decision Making."

35. See Barbara L. Schwemle, Todd Garvey, Vivian S. Chu, and Henry B. Hogue, "The Debate over Selected Presidential Assistants and Advisors: Appointment, Accountability, and Congressional Oversight" (Congressional Research Service Report R40856, 2014); William G. Howell, *Thinking about the Presidency: The Primacy of Power* (Princeton, NJ: Princeton University Press, 2013); Justin S. Vaughn and Jose D. Villalobos, *Czars in the White House: The Rise of Policy Czars as Presidential Management Tools* (Ann Arbor: University of Michigan Press, 2015); Mitchell A. Sollenberger and Mark J. Rozell, *The President's Czars: Undermining Congress and the Constitution* (Lawrence: University Press of Kansas, 2012).

36. See Buckley v. Valeo, 424 U.S. 1 (1976).

37. See Sollenberger and Rozell, *President's Czars.*

38. Ford, 0; Carter, 0; Reagan, 3; G. H. W. Bush, 2; Clinton, 4; G. W. Bush, 10. See Sollenberger and Rozell, *President's Czars.*

39. See Sollenberger and Rozell, *President's Czars.*

40. Ibid.

41. Vaughn and Villalobos, *Czars in the White House.*

42. See Executive Orders 13503 and 13507.

43. Tom Daschle was originally intended to be both the secretary of health and human services and a health czar, further demonstrating Obama's efforts to centralize power. See Rudalevige, "Rivals, or a Team?"

44. See, e.g., the Czar Accountability and Reform Act of 2009 and the Czar Accountability Act of 2010; see also Sollenberger and Rozell, *President's Czars.*

45. David Lewis, *Presidents and the Politics of Agency Design: Political Insulation in the United States Government Bureaucracy, 1946–1997* (Stanford, CA: Stanford University Press, 2003).

46. These data were collected by counting the number of agencies created by executive order and memorandum, ascertained from searches of databases maintained by the American Presidency Project.

47. See Executive Order 13501.

48. See Executive Order 13718.

49. This order also required agencies to submit cost-benefit analyses on major rules.

50. See Executive Order 12866. According to this executive order, a "significant regulatory action" is one that has a $100 million impact on the economy (or an adverse effect), interferes with another agency, has significant budgetary impacts, or "raises novel legal or policy issues."

51. See Executive Order 13422.

52. These numbers are for regulations between 1994 and 2015; see Maeve P. Carey, "Counting Regulations: An Overview of Rulemaking, Types of Federal Regulations, and Pages in the Federal Register" (Congressional Research Service Report R43056, 2016).

53. See Alex Acs and Charles Cameron, "Regulatory Auditing at the Office of Information and Regulatory Affairs" (working paper, 2014).

54. See Juliet Eilperin, "White House Delayed Enacting Rules Ahead of 2012 Election to Avoid Controversy," *Washington Post*, December 14, 2013, https://www.washing tonpost.com/politics/white-house-delayed-enacting-rules-ahead-of-2012-election -to-avoid-controversy/2013/12/14/7885a494-561a-11e3-ba82-16ed03681809_story .html.

55. See Carey, "Counting Regulations."

56. See Alexander Bolton, Rachel Potter, and Sharece Thrower, "Organizational Capacity, Regulatory Review, and the Limits of Political Control," *Journal of Law, Economics, and Organization* 32, 2 (2016): 242–271.

57. Average OMB staff sizes: Reagan, 597; G. H. W. Bush, 566; Clinton, 521; G. W. Bush, 492; Obama, 512. Staff decreased throughout Obama's term, reaching an all-time low in 2013 with 456 employees. See Harold W. Stanley and Richard G. Niemi, *Vital Statistics on American Politics, 2015–2016* (Washington, DC: CQ Press, 2015).

58. See Bolton, Potter, and Thrower, "Organizational Capacity."

59. See William G. Howell, *Power without Persuasion* (Princeton, NJ: Princeton University Press, 2003); Lewis, *Presidents and the Politics of Agency Design.*

60. See, e.g., Andrew Rudalevige and David E. Lewis, "Parsing the Politicized Presidency: Centralization and Politicization as Presidential Strategies for Bureaucratic Control" (working paper, 2015).

61. See Howell, *Power without Persuasion*

62. See ibid.; Kenneth Mayer, *With the Stroke of a Pen: Executive Orders and Presidential Power* (Princeton, NJ: Princeton University Press, 2001).

63. Data were collected from the *Public Papers of the President.* Similar to previous studies, presidential determinations are not included. See Kenneth Lowande, "After the Orders: Presidential Memoranda and Unilateral Action," *Presidential Studies Quarterly* 44, 4 (2014): 724–741. However, memoranda both published and not published in the *Federal Register* are included, given that no clear distinction exists. See Phillip J. Cooper, *By Order of the President: The Use and Abuse of Executive Direct Action* (Lawrence: University Press of Kansas, 2014).

64. See Executive Orders 13497 and 13579.

65. See "Memorandum on Regulatory Review," January 30, 2009; "Memorandum on Regulation and Independent Regulatory Agencies," July 11, 2011.

66. Cooper, *By Order of the President.*

67. Ibid.

68. See Lowande, "After the Orders."

69. While presidents have a variety of other unilateral directives at their disposal, these two have the most relevant implications for executive policy-making in both domestic and foreign policy.

70. See Sharece Thrower, "The President, the Court, and Policy Implementation," *Presidential Studies Quarterly* 41, 1 (2017): 122–145.

71. See Valerie Volcovici, "Obama Power Plant Rules Face Key Test in Court," Reuters, September 27, 2016, http://www.reuters.com/article/us-usa-climatechange-lawsuit-idUSKCN11X0Z9.

72. See Office of Management and Budget, "Historical Tables," accessed October 1, 2016, https://www.whitehouse.gov/omb/budget/Historicals.

73. See Juliet Eilperin and Darla Cameron, "How Trump Is Rolling Back Obama's Legacy," *Washington Post*, June 19, 2017, https://www.washingtonpost.com/graphic/politics/trump-rolling-back-obama-rules/?utm_term=.d7470d02316e.

CHAPTER EIGHT

Obama and the Courts

Judicial Policy-Making as a Last Resort

David A. Yalof

On the morning of June 28, 2012, President Barack Obama's signature legislative achievement was in serious trouble. He would need the US Supreme Court, led by its conservative majority, to rescue the Affordable Care Act (ACA—aka "Obamacare") from being rendered null and void before it ever got off the ground. Suddenly the Obama administration faced desperate times before the high court.

It was never supposed to come to this. As a Harvard-trained lawyer and one-time instructor of constitutional law at the University of Chicago, Obama surely knew that a band of five determined justices could set aside high court precedents and, in the process, reshape the constitutional landscape. Yet he was equally confident that some past rulings were so enmeshed in the fabric of American jurisprudence as to place them beyond the reach of even the most activist justices. Included among these sacred precedents were *Marbury v. Madison*,[1] *New York Times v. Sullivan*,[2] and a handful of New Deal cases that had effectively created an economic order befitting a modern national economy.[3] Since the 1930s, the Supreme Court had accepted the premise that Congress enjoys a near limitless capacity to regulate the economy. The modern welfare state rests on this constitutional understanding; accordingly, Obama and his aides were confident that although the ACA was politically controversial, it was immune from any serious constitutional attack.

Yet the president's confidence was misplaced. By the time the Supreme Court agreed to hear the case of *NFIB v. Sebelius* in late 2011, the health care law was in dire constitutional straits. During the previous eighteen months, a handful of lower courts had overturned the so-called individual mandate, the ACA's central requirement that all individuals without proof of health insurance must either sign up for such insurance by January 1, 2014, or pay a financial penalty. With five conservative justices sitting on the high bench, experienced court watchers were predicting that the law would be struck down in some fashion. Moreover, even if the legislative scheme as a whole was spared, the Court could still strike down the individual mandate. The justices might take that bold step even if it meant tearing up numerous 80-year-old precedents in the process.

Thus, Obama had cause for concern as the Supreme Court prepared to hand down its ruling on that fateful Thursday morning in June. Yet, as it turned out, the Court actually pulled the law back from the precipice, handing the administration an unexpected victory in *NFIB v. Sebelius*.[4] Even the individual mandate enjoyed a reprieve, as Chief Justice John Roberts voted with the liberals to uphold that controversial provision. By one account, Roberts shifted his vote in the final weeks after initially siding with the four other conservatives.[5] The chief justice agreed with them that Congress's power to regulate interstate commerce did *not* extend to the regulation of economic inactivity, such as the refusal to purchase insurance; yet he also recognized that Congress had the power to impose a tax on those without insurance, and on that basis, he provided the crucial fifth vote to validate the legislation. Only the provision threatening to withhold all federal Medicaid funding from states that refused to comply with the ACA's Medicaid expansion provisions failed to garner the Court's support; seven of the nine justices deemed that threat unconstitutionally coercive.[6]

Of course, elections have consequences, and just four years later, the outcome of the 2016 election determined that Obamacare would continue on a bumpy road, even after the Supreme Court had its say. Indeed, President Donald Trump and the Republican congressional majorities spent the first half of 2017 actively plotting the law's demise. (Their efforts narrowly failed, although the individual mandate was repealed as part of tax reform legislation passed later that same year.) Still, a central question remains with regard to President Barack Obama's legal defense of Obamacare in the years following its 2010 passage: how did the fate of his administration's most important domestic accomplishment come to hang so precariously in the balance? Not since the New Deal had a US president been forced to stand by helplessly as the high court determined the fate of his prized legislative agenda. And unlike Franklin Roosevelt, Obama's reelection chances seemed to be hanging in the balance as well.

In fact, a larger theme may have been at work. Did President Obama naïvely disregard the role of judicial policy-making, and if so, was he unprepared for the role the courts ultimately played in determining his political fate? *New Yorker* reporter Jeffrey Toobin believed that President Obama's general approach to courts and the judiciary was marked by apathy and neglect—the Obamacare case was simply another example of the president's refusal to take the judicial challenge more seriously.[7] Justin Driver of the *New Republic* went a step further, positing that Obama's lethargy with regard to judicial appointments and other court-focused initiatives reflected his more general rejection of a liberal activist judging philosophy.[8] While the definition of *judicial activism* is itself a subject of considerable disagreement, the most prevalent modern interpretation of the term encompasses a willingness on the part of courts to strike down legislation and executive acts as part of an "overall flexing of judicial power" at the expense of the other branches of government.[9] For many liberals, the Warren Court's willingness to confront the political branches in the 1950s and 1960s represented some of the finest moments in the high court's long and storied history.

President Obama subscribed to an alternative principle: judges should stay out of the way so progressive policy-makers can have their say.[10] As early as 2006, when he was first preparing to run for the White House, Obama wrote in *The Audacity of Hope* that the Left of the 1960s would have been better off winning battles in the Electoral College instead of relying on the courts to vindicate important rights.[11] Given this view, one might expect Obama to exert limited efforts to cultivate the judiciary and (where possible) exploit it for political gain. Rejecting the courtroom as a primary venue to wage policy battles, Obama preferred to fight on the political battlefield.

This conviction distinguishes Obama from other modern Democratic presidents, many of whom counted heavily on the judiciary's help to advance progressive causes during the middle and late twentieth century. Beginning in the 1960s, the relationship between the Supreme Court and the Democratic Party shifted dramatically. A Republican president (Eisenhower) appointed five straight justices during the 1950s, yet two of those appointees (Earl Warren and William Brennan) emerged as heroes to the Left because of their willingness to assert judicial authority in support of political equality, defendants' rights, and other social causes. For much of the 1960s, the Warren Court exercised a heroic conception of the law that "went hand in hand with a heroic role for the courts."[12] As Professor Steven Teles of Johns Hopkins University explains, "satisfying legal liberals' aspirations for the law was the powerful moral status of 'rights' produced by the civil rights struggle and the image of a Warren court that was substantively humane."[13] The political implications of this new alliance between the Supreme Court and crucial elements of the Democratic Party continued into the 1970s and beyond. According to Mark Silverstein, the "principal beneficiaries of the expanded access to the federal courts [were] groups and interests generally aligned with the Democratic party; upper-middle class Democratic interests, including environmentalists, consumers and feminists . . . considered the open-door policy of the federal judiciary to be of extraordinary benefit."[14] Like Obama, President Bill Clinton hoped that his administration would win its share of political battles in the 1990s; yet once the Republicans seized control of Congress following the November 1994 elections, Clinton's legislative agenda quickly ground to a halt, and yet another Democratic president found himself relying on the Supreme Court to preserve hard-won victories in the social wars.

Toobin, Driver, and others believe that President Obama's reluctance to rely on judicial policy-making marked a fundamental shift in tenor from other Democratic presidents. This does not mean that his administration failed to place its stamp on the long-term makeup of the judiciary, as Obama appointed two Supreme Court justices and 329 Article III lower court judges during his two terms in office. It does suggest, however, that Obama invested less capital and fewer resources than his predecessors in strategizing and winning judicial battles. Certainly, the Obama White House emphasized numerous other issues first and foremost: legislative initiatives (including the ACA), foreign policy agreements (including the Paris climate agreement and the Iranian nuclear deal), and the war on terrorism in Afghanistan. Second-guessing by key Democratic constituencies for whom social issues were a chief priority was perhaps inevitable. Consider that although the Obama administration won high-profile court battles over Obamacare, same-sex marriage, and abortion rights, the president won just 47 percent of the Supreme Court cases in which he or his administration was a party. That figure makes him the least successful president on this score since Harry Truman.[15] How many more victories would the Obama administration have won if the chief executive had spent more time and resources on judicial matters, whether by proactively framing legal issues at the outset or by nominating greater numbers of lower court judges early on, when the Democrats' huge margin in the Senate rendered the Republican minority helpless to resist?

Obama's Supreme Court Appointments: Late Failure Overshadows Early Success

Democratic hopes for reshaping the US Supreme Court were understandably high when President Obama took office in January 2009. To be sure, Bill Clinton had reduced the conservatives' advantage on the high court with his own two appointments; although Stephen Breyer's succession to the seat held by Harry Blackmun barely moved the needle, the appointment of Ruth Bader Ginsburg to the seat previously held by Byron White shifted the ideological makeup of the court leftward. Still, a majority of the remaining justices were solid conservatives, with the balance of the Court resting in the hands of Reagan appointees Anthony Kennedy and Sandra Day O'Connor (President George W. Bush replaced the latter with the even more conservative Samuel Alito in 2005). Depending on who retired, three Supreme Court appointments by Obama would likely create a majority of Democratic-appointed justices on the high court for the first time since the early 1970s. Aided by a Democratic-controlled Senate that enjoyed an eighteen-seat advantage in January 2009 and a filibuster-proof majority of sixty by the end of the year, Obama would enjoy numerous advantages in staffing the high court.

How did President Obama ultimately fare in the selection of Supreme Court nominees? The Obama White House addressed the first two Supreme Court vacancies it faced in relatively short order. Approximately six weeks passed between

Justice David Souter's decision to retire in mid-April 2009 and President Obama's nomination of 54-year-old Sonia Sotomayor, a judge on the US Court of Appeals for the Second Circuit, to fill Souter's seat on May 26, 2009. Even less time passed between Justice John Paul Stevens's notice of his intent to retire (sent to the White House on April 9, 2010) and the decision to name Solicitor General Elena Kagan as his successor on May 10, 2010. These short selection windows were not much longer than the time taken by George W. Bush to select John Roberts (eighteen days until nominated) and his second nominee to replace O'Connor, legal counsel Harriet Miers (thirty days). In contrast, Obama's selections offered models of efficiency compared with Clinton's appointments of Ginsburg (eighty-eight days) and Breyer (thirty-seven days).

If the success of a vetting process is measured by its capacity to reveal and address all potential pitfalls in advance, Obama's vetting process must receive high ratings. Soon after Judge Sotomayor's nomination went public, two potential threats to a smooth confirmation emerged: her claim in a 2001 lecture that, as a "wise Latina," she might reach better conclusion than other judges;[16] and her recent vote in *Ricci v. DeStefano*,[17] an affirmative action case in which Judge Sotomayor elected not to rehear a claim by white firefighters in New Haven that their rights had been violated. No other threats to Sotomayor's confirmation arose, and she managed to navigate past both controversies to the satisfaction of all but her most heated detractors. Sotomayor's seventeen years of experience made her an especially difficult nominee to target. (The Senate confirmed her appointment on August 6, 2009, by a 68–31 vote, with as many as nine Republicans offering their support.)

The same relatively carefree confirmation process unfolded a year later when Obama nominated his solicitor general, Elena Kagan, to the high court. The only objection raised against the 50-year-old Kagan was her lack of judicial experience compared with other current justices. In fact, the former Harvard Law School dean would become the first justice who lacked prior judicial service to be appointed in nearly four decades. Though criticized for her evasiveness during the Senate confirmation hearings, Kagan was ultimately confirmed by a vote of 63–37 on August 5, 2010, with five Republicans joining all but one Democratic senator in supporting her appointment. If President Obama's primary goal was to keep the confirmation process "uneventful" and "boring," his two appointments would have to be rated a success.

The effectiveness of Obama's Supreme Court appointment process must also be measured in raw political terms. As neither of the two nominees garnered significant negative attention, the White House expended few unnecessary resources on their behalf. Sotomayor began the appointment process with broad support from the electorate; according to a *USA Today*/Gallup poll, she enjoyed a 54 percent favorability rating in early June 2009 and had lost little support two months later.[18] The same occurred with Kagan: she began the process with a 46 percent public approval rating (versus 32 percent disapproval) in May 2010, and that number had barely budged by her confirmation hearings at the end of July.[19]

The final judgment on Obama's Supreme Court appointments relies on an examination of actual judicial votes. The three highest profile cases decided during Obama's first term in office were *Citizens United v. Federal Election Commission* (2010), *Arizona v. United States* (2012), and *NFIB v. Sebelius* (2012). Justice Kagan participated only in *Sebelius*, and she voted with Breyer and Ginsburg to uphold the bulk of the ACA. Justice Sotomayor voted with Breyer and Ginsburg in all three cases. During Obama's second term, five cases consumed the bulk of the White House's attention: two same-sex marriage cases with national implications (*United States v. Windsor* [2013] and *Obergefell v. Hodges* [2015]), the second Obamacare case (*King v. Burwell* [2015]), a high-profile affirmative action case (*Fisher v. Texas* [2016]), and a case involving Obama's executive orders on immigration (*United States v. Texas* [2016]). Because of her earlier participation as solicitor general, Justice Kagan recused herself in the *Fisher* case (Justice Sotomayor joined the 4–3 majority allowing the use of race in admissions decisions). In the other four cases, both of Obama's appointees voted in the direction clearly and publicly favored by the administration. Based on this limited sample, Justices Kagan and Sotomayor consistently cast votes that met rather than undermined their appointing president's expectations.

Of course, a full reckoning of President Obama's success in appointing like-minded Supreme Court justices must take into account the bitter disappointment of failing to fill the seat left vacant by the death of Justice Antonin Scalia on February 13, 2016. Just twenty-seven days passed between Scalia's death and Obama's public announcement of the nomination of 63-year-old Merrick Garland, chief judge of the US Court of Appeals for the DC Circuit. Sensitive to the need for compromise during an especially bruising election year, Obama clearly intended Garland to be an olive branch to the Republicans; he had more federal judicial experience than any nominee in history, and he was the oldest Supreme Court nominee since 64-year-old Lewis Powell had been tapped in 1971. At the time of Kagan's nomination six years earlier, Senator Orrin Hatch (R-UT) had called Garland a "consensus nominee," predicting that he would have won Senate confirmation with bipartisan support. Hatch's analysis may have been accurate in 2010, but it no longer applied in 2016. Smelling blood, and rolling the dice on the results of the upcoming presidential election, Senate majority leader Mitch McConnell (R-KY) and his fellow Republicans quickly united around the position that only the "next president" should choose Scalia's successor, and they vowed to hold no hearings for Garland in 2016.

In the modern era, the Senate's refusal to hold hearings for Garland was unprecedented. Certainly, presidents have faced stern opposition to Supreme Court nominees in presidential election years, especially when a lame-duck chief executive seeks to appoint one last justice before the clock strikes midnight on his presidency. In the fall of 1968 Lyndon Johnson was forced to abandon his efforts to promote Justice Abe Fortas to chief justice when he realized that Senate Democrats would be unable to end a filibuster. Still, given Democratic control of that chamber, Fortas had received a full hearing from the Senate earlier that fall. More recently, presidents facing a Senate controlled by the opposition in a presidential election year have rushed compromise nominees through the chamber as quickly as possible. Thus, on November 28, 1975, President Gerald Ford nominated John Paul Stevens to replace William O. Douglas on the Supreme Court; after a quick three days of hearings, Stevens was confirmed on December 19 by a 98–0 vote. Nearly as quick was the confirmation process for Anthony Kennedy, President Reagan's third choice to fill the seat vacated by Lewis Powell.[20] Nominated on November 11, 1987, Kennedy glided through his hearings, culminating in yet another unanimous Senate confirmation vote (97–0) on February 3, 1988.

Unlike Stevens and Kennedy, Garland's formal nomination occurred in the presidential election year itself. The last time a successful Supreme Court candidate was nominated during the appointing president's final year in office was February 15, 1932, when President Herbert Hoover nominated Benjamin Cardozo of the New York State Court of Appeals. Cardozo epitomized the "consensus candidate" in every sense of the word. The *New York Times* wrote, "seldom, if ever, in the history of the Court has an appointment been so universally commended."[21] By nominating Cardozo, a Democrat, the Republican president was able to defuse partisan tensions that might have blown up any of Hoover's nominations that year. President Eisenhower borrowed from that playbook twenty-four years later when he nominated William Brennan, a Democrat, as a recess appointment just three weeks before he faced the voters for reelection in 1956. (Brennan was confirmed for a permanent seat on the high court by the Democratic-controlled Senate the following year.)

In hindsight, it is hard to blame President Obama for his failed nomination of Garland. The Senate strategy to refuse hearings would have been applied just as fiercely to a nominee with a more liberal voting record. If President Obama had named an African American or Hispanic American candidate, would the progressive interest groups' campaign to confirm Obama's nominee maintained its momentum throughout the summer months? More likely, with Hillary Clinton leading in the polls, those groups would have engaged in what turned out to be a failed waiting game. Regardless, Obama's efforts at compromise proved futile, and his Republican successor had an immediate Supreme Court vacancy to fill. And while there is no basis for concluding that Garland's selection amounted to evidence of the president's apathy toward the courts, nothing in the previous seven years of his presidency positioned him to pull a rabbit out of a hat when dealing with a hostile Senate majority.

Obama's Lower Court Appointments: "Diversity Now, Diversity Tomorrow"

With a strong Democratic Senate majority in place at the outset of the 111th Congress, President Obama possessed a golden opportunity to staff the courts with judges who could push beyond the edge of the so-called mainstream. Eight years later, the forty-fourth president of the United States had transformed the federal judiciary in some dramatic ways. That said, the fiercest liberals in the coalition that had elected Obama twice were left wondering whether a chief executive with qualms about activist judicial policy-making had squandered an opportunity to transform the constitutional landscape in a decidedly more liberal direction. This much is clear: during his two terms in office, President Obama placed the need for a diverse and broadly representative judiciary over the need to appoint the most ideologically liberal judges.

To be sure, the White House had to overcome several obstacles to put its firm ideological stamp on the judiciary. First, it faced the harsh reality that hyperpartisanship had become the new norm in judicial appointment politics. Consider that between 1939 and 1977, just one court of appeals nomination and six district court nominations received negative votes from the Senate Judiciary Committee. By contrast, recent modifications in the so-called blue-slip system (the process by which a senator can issue an opinion on a federal judicial nominee who resides in that senator's state) have taken their toll on the judicial appointment process. Whereas blue slips began as a means of communication between individual senators and the Judiciary Committee chairperson, today they have become a check on presidential power: individual senators can determine the fate of a nomination even after it has been reported to the Senate floor by using blue slips as a "silent, unaccountable veto."[22] Thus, from the outset of Obama's presidency, he faced the reality that Republican senators in Florida, Pennsylvania, and elsewhere were prepared to unilaterally block his nominees without any explanation whatsoever. By contrast, during the Trump presidency, the Republican majority in the Senate (led by Judiciary Committee chair Charles Grassley of Iowa) often ignored Democratic senators' objections to judicial nominees from their states.

Even more troubling from Obama's perspective was the proliferation of the filibuster to prevent votes on judicial nominees who otherwise would have enjoyed the support of a majority of senators. Even though Democrats controlled the Senate throughout Obama's first term as president, Republicans in the 111th Congress broke the record for the number of filibusters in a session, surviving 100 cloture votes in all. In 2011 Senate Democrats raised the possibility of the "nuclear option"—ending the use of filibusters against executive or judicial appointments by a simple majority vote. Yet for the entirety of President Obama's first term—and for most of 2013 as well—Democrats could not rally the 51 votes they needed to take that extreme measure. Accordingly, Obama's lower court appointments faced a gauntlet of minority opposition tactics—including the all-powerful filibuster—throughout this period.

Nor did the Obama White House help matters by its occasional foot-dragging on lower court appointments. In 2012 the *New York Times* reported that Obama had been "lagging on filling seats in the judiciary," noting that he was set to end his first term "with dozens fewer lower-court appointments" than past presidents had achieved during their first four years.[23] Obama did not nominate his eleventh judge until November 2009, and he waited more than eighteen months to submit a candidate for one of the two highly prized vacancies on the DC Circuit.

Even so, Senate Republicans bear considerable responsibility for what amounts to a broken judicial appointment process. One scholar found that the hurdles placed before lower court appointments reached unprecedented levels under Obama, as Senate Republicans often refused to let nominees proceed in the Judiciary Committee or on the Senate floor.[24] A handful of extremely conservative Tea Party senators in particular used the blue-slip system to force an extended review of even some moderate nominees and an outright halting of others. The Obama administration was especially stymied in getting its nominees to the federal trial courts confirmed. The Senate confirmed just 68.8 percent of his district court nominations, compared with an 87.5 percent success rate for George W. Bush.[25] This evidence bears out claims by Obama's supporters that he was the victim of a strategically manufactured "judicial vacancies crisis"[26] caused by "unprecedented" stalling tactics.[27]

Did President Obama lack the determination to name more liberal ideologues? At the time, legal analyst Jeffrey Toobin openly questioned whether Obama's choice of judges during his first year as president reflected traditional legal liberalism or, rather, a movement away from those old categories in favor of more restraint and less activism.[28] The slowness of Obama's first-term nominations may have overshadowed "a lack of judicial nominees who seem inclined to engage in the hard work of combating the conservative constitutional agenda."[29] The liberal Alliance for Justice would have preferred nominees from beyond the ideological safety zone—individuals who could be "counters to the Posners, the Easterbrooks."[30] By contrast, Obama's most liberal nominee, California state justice Goodwin Liu, saw his nomination to the Ninth Circuit filibustered in 2010 and then withdrawn the following year. Rather than fighting such long-shot battles to the end, President Obama was betting that even his more moderate nominees would have a sizable impact if confirmed. As one Obama aide explained it, some of the most progressive groups "want bleeding heart liberal judges . . . but you don't need bleeding heart liberals to get the kind of justice we need."[31]

While Obama was slow out of the gates with judicial appointments in 2009 and 2010, he picked up speed during the 112th Congress in 2011–2012 and then gained considerable steam following his reelection victory. By the end of 2014, his administration's raw numbers began to approach those of his predecessors, even as the Democrats' margin in the Senate fell substantially. Two Senate reforms in the year after Obama's reelection were responsible for this resurgence. The first change in the Senate rules was not controversial. Passed at the start of the 113th Congress, this new rule required that if cloture was invoked on a district court nominee, the required post-cloture debate time would be reduced from thirty hours to two hours.[32] This led to a marked rise in the number of district court judges confirmed in 2013, though it did little to break the logjam on circuit court nominees. Efforts to address that larger concern began to take shape in May 2013, after Senate Republicans filibustered three consecutive DC Circuit nominees. With Republicans digging in so early in the president's second term, Senate majority leader Harry Reid readied plans to finally invoke the "nuclear option," prohibiting filibusters for all district and circuit court nominees. Even Senator Patrick Leahy (D-VT), a longtime defender of the filibuster, shifted his views in response to the Republicans' intransigence.[33] Once the Senate majority pushed through the rule change on November 20, 2013, it fundamentally altered the way the Senate had been operating for decades.[34] Going nuclear broke the logjam for many long-stalled nominees, who immediately received party-line votes in the months that followed. Between December 12, 2013, and April 30, 2014, the Senate confirmed thirty-five federal judges, including the three circuit court judges who had faced heavy opposition from Senate Republicans.

Once the 2014 midterm elections shifted Senate control back to the Republicans, the process of confirming Obama's lower court nominations ground to a halt once again. The Senate confirmed just twenty-two judicial nominees during the 114th Congress of 2015–2016, by far the lowest number in the past thirty years.[35] That did not prevent Obama from amassing a solid record on the judicial appointments front. In all, he made 331 lifetime appointments to the bench, amounting to more than one-third of the entire federal judiciary. While that falls short of the final tallies credited to Reagan (384) and Clinton (379), it matches George W. Bush's 330 appointments. The first two years of Obama's second term proved most critical to this success, as twenty of twenty-two appeals court nominees were confirmed during the 113th Congress. As a final measure of success, when President Obama first took office, Republican appointees controlled ten of the thirteen circuit courts of appeals; in a complete turnaround, Democratic appointees constituted a majority on nine of the thirteen circuits when Obama left office.

Where Obama clearly surpassed most of his predecessors was on the issue of diversity. President Jimmy Carter is rightly credited as being the first president to implement a far-reaching appointment strategy with diversity as its cornerstone. By the end of his sole term in office, Carter had appointed forty-one women (15.7 percent of all Carter appointees), thirty-seven African Americans (14.2 percent),

Table 8.1. Number and Percentage of Female and Minority Article III Federal Judges Confirmed, Clinton through Obama

Confirmed Judges	Clinton (1993–2001)	G. W. Bush (2001–2009)	Obama (2009–2016)
Female	106 (29%)	71 (22%)	138 (41%)
African American	61 (16%)	24 (7%)	58 (16%)
Hispanic	23 (7%)	23 (9%)	37 (13%)
Asian American and Pacific Island	1 (1%)	1 (1%)	19 (8%)

Sources: whitehouse.gov; "How Obama Reshaped the Federal Courts," ALM Network of Legal Publications, law.com.

and sixteen Hispanics (6.1 percent). Because the federal bench was still so heavily dominated by white males, even a handful of appointments of women and minorities was seen as progress at the time. Thus, decades later, racial, ethnic, and gender imbalance continue to plague the federal courts.[36]

In an interview conducted in 2014, President Obama stated that diversification of the bench would be "an important component of the legacy of his administration."[37] His legacy in that regard is now evident (see table 8.1). Obama appointed more women and Hispanics to federal judgeships than any president in history, and he appointed more Asian Americans (nineteen) to the bench than all his predecessors combined.[38] In raw percentages, 41 percent of Obama's judges were female, and 37 percent were racial or ethnic minorities. For the first time ever, white male judges constituted a minority on the US Courts of Appeals. President Obama also appointed ten openly gay judges to the federal bench. If this hyperfocus on diversity came at the expense of appointing tried-and-true liberal extremists, it was a price the White House was willing to pay. Consider the case of Carlton Reeves: As a janitor, he had once cleaned the office of Mississippi's first African American federal judge. Reeves later became the second African American federal jurist to serve in Mississippi when Obama appointed him to the district court in 2010. Reeves's background as a private lawyer and as an officer in the US attorney's office offered few assurances that he would be an extremely liberal judge.

Like the Garland nomination, questions remain about the fifty-three judicial nominees Obama left on the battlefield during his final two years as president. On the day he was inaugurated in 2017, President Donald Trump was presented with approximately a hundred judicial vacancies to fill immediately, as well as the high-stakes Supreme Court vacancy. If a far more diverse judiciary represents President Obama's proudest legacy, those many unfilled vacancies (and the extreme partisanship that contributed to them) must be considered part of his legacy as well. Of course, it is impossible to know whether Obama could have done anything (short of caving in to Republican demands that he appoint only moderates) to reduce that high level of partisanship.

The Obama Administration Goes to Court: A Reluctant Approach to Judicial Policy-Making

If Barack Obama's skeptical view of judicial activism manifested itself in the appointment of less activist judges and justices, it also may have influenced the discretion exercised by his Justice Department and other executive branch entities in litigation matters. As noted earlier, traditional Democratic interest groups, including environmentalists, consumers, feminists, and others, had long benefited from judicial activism facilitated by greater court access. Would the Obama administration expend its limited resources to go to court and vindicate those rights once again?

A brief review of the Obama administration's litigation practices in a handful of policy contexts reveals a reluctance to place the courts front and center in its overall approach to public policy. In some cases, there was evident tension between President Obama's commitment to little *d* democratic values and what might be considered more traditional Democratic Party values.

Civil Rights

Perhaps the one area in which Obama administration lawyers aggressively and enthusiastically utilized a court-centered strategy to make nationwide policy was civil rights. There, the administration trod on ground tilled by other Democratic presidents in the modern era. Yet the administration's aggressive approach to protecting and defending innovative new civil rights claims was notable, in that it did not cease even when local governments asserted their own interests in the case. During the Reagan and Bush administrations, the federal government typically waded into state or local cases only when the outcome affected a clear federal interest, such as national security or diplomacy. By contrast, the Justice Department under Attorneys General Eric Holder and Loretta Lynch directly interceded in cases involving legal aid in New York, transgender students in Michigan, juvenile prisoners in California, and people who took videos of police officers in Baltimore.[39] Refusing to defer to state interests even in high-profile legal battles, Justice Department lawyers filed a lawsuit in 2016 to strike down North Carolina's controversial gender-identity bathroom law; in multiple other states the department backed the legal claims of transgender students fighting for the right to use the restroom that matched their gender identity.[40]

The Justice Department also prosecuted a record number of hate crimes under Obama's watch.[41] To do that, the administration capitalized on passage of the 2009

Shepard-Byrd Hate Crimes Prevention Act, which expanded the definition of hate crimes to include bias-motivated crimes based on a victim's actual or perceived sexual orientation, gender, or gender identity. Subsequent to the law's enactment, US attorney's offices across the country established dedicated units of prosecutors to pursue such violations. The Justice Department's Civil Rights Division also established a dedicated Fair Lending Unit to stop discriminatory lending practices against minorities.

Critics of the administration's approach to civil rights violations note that hate crimes in the last two years of Obama's presidency actually increased slightly over previous years. Of course, such claims rely on the accurate tracking and reporting of hate crimes, which remain spotty three decades after Congress first directed the Justice Department to collect such data. Thus, an increase in reports of hate crimes may not correlate with an increase in actual crimes at all. Regardless, the Justice Department under Obama must be credited with shining a greater light on the problem, thanks to its aggressive pursuit of such matters in the courts.

State-sponsored initiatives that posed obstacles to voting offered a final challenge for Obama's Justice Department and its stated commitment to fight potential voter suppression. Voter ID laws in numerous states restricted access to the ballot box, especially among poorer voters, who were less likely to carry state-authorized drivers' licenses. In 2016 federal appeals courts struck down strict voter ID laws in Texas and North Carolina, citing intent to discriminate against minority voting populations. In each of the two cases, the Justice Department aggressively supported the court challenges. The Obama administration also joined plaintiffs throughout the country in opposing states' requests for delays while they rewrote the voter ID laws to meet more exacting standards.

Health Care

The Supreme Court's decision to uphold the Affordable Care Act in *NFIB v. Sebelius* (2012) may have saved a key item of the Obama administration's agenda, but it did little to undercut political opposition that threatened its long-term survival. Still, the ruling injected new life into a scared White House and offered a critical talking point in the president's looming reelection campaign. How did the administration's political fate end up in the hands of a judicial body that was, in most respects, a conservative stronghold? Ironically, it was the decision to borrow from earlier Republican proposals and build health care reform around the controversial individual mandate that set into motion the furious litigation efforts that followed.

Several critical features of the legislation suggest that its drafters were barely thinking about court approval. First, the law did not include a standard provision for expedited judicial review, which would have reduced or eliminated opportunities for hostile lower courts to provide momentum for the opposition.[42] Second, many crucial provisions of the law (including the individual mandate) would not be implemented until 2014, which allowed critics to target the law before even one person was reaping its benefits. Other aspects of the law, such as the provisions for state waivers, would not go into effect until 2017.[43] If White House lawyers were concerned about challenges to the law's constitutionality, these provisions only increased the risk that court review would hang over the process for years to come.

In strictly legal terms, White House confidence that the ACA would pass constitutional muster was well grounded. To secure every possible vote in Congress, the White House accepted the argument that the individual mandate—though enforced via tax filings—was not a tax but a "penalty" imposed under Congress's power to regulate interstate commerce.[44] White House officials, including the president's chief economic adviser Lawrence Summers, budget director Peter Orszag, and Nancy-Ann DeParle, the president's chief adviser on health care, received assurances from lawyers within and outside the administration that both the interstate commerce clause and the tax and spending power offered more than enough constitutional grounding. No less a conservative authority than Charles Fried, solicitor general during the Reagan administration, admitted that, "like most students of constitutional law," he found "the argument that [the individual mandate] violated the Constitution bordered on the frivolous."[45] Accordingly, the power of Congress to enact the individual mandate could be questioned only by returning to a pre-1937 understanding of the Constitution.[46] The power to lay and collect taxes was especially broad, as the Supreme Court has interpreted the clause to confer on Congress a plenary power to impose taxes and to spend money for the general welfare.

If that were not enough, some recent high court decisions offered positive signs as well. In *United States v. Comstock* (2010),[47] decided by the Supreme Court less than two months after the ACA was signed into law, the justices had held by a vote of 7–2 that a federal law authorizing courts to order the civil commitment of sexually dangerous prisoners who had already served their criminal sentences was a valid exercise of the necessary and proper clause. Chief Justice Roberts had joined the majority to uphold the law (Alito and Kennedy had concurred on other grounds). Following the logic of *Comstock*, the individual mandate could be considered "a necessary and proper means of accomplishing the comprehensive market reforms in the law, and those reforms clearly fell within Congress's enumerated power to regulate."[48] At a minimum, *Comstock* suggested that Roberts might be open to the government's necessary and proper clause argument in the health care cases.

Hope could also be found in Justice Scalia's concurrence in *Gonzales v. Raich* (2005).[49] In *Raich*, by a 6–3 vote, the Court had upheld the Controlled Substances Act, banning the use of marijuana even if states had approved its use for narrow medicinal purposes. (In 2009 the Justice Department issued new guidelines declaring that it would no longer enforce the ban in such cases.) Scalia's concurrence argued that his own understanding of the necessary and proper clause allowed him to uphold the commerce clause application in this instance because it was "neces-sary to make the interstate regulation effective." If Scalia remained faithful to that theory, the White House lawyers reasoned, "he might seriously entertain the argu-ment that the individual mandate was an integral part of a comprehensive scheme of economic regulation."[50]

Five days before the health care law was actually signed, Neil Katyal, the dep-uty solicitor general, warned Attorney General Eric Holder that legal complaints against the ACA "were clearly written to be filed right away," and the administration needed to be prepared to go to court without delay.[51] Almost immediately, Holder asked Robert Weiner of the law firm Arnold & Porter to oversee the defense of the health care law. Weiner quickly agreed and noted that it was his "view from the beginning that if the courts applied the law as it stood we would win . . . whether courts would apply the law at each level was not as clear."[52] Katyal's information was correct: exactly seven minutes after Obama signed the ACA into law and put down his pen, a lawyer in the office of Florida's Republican attorney general filed the first lawsuit challenging its constitutionality. By the close of business that day, three additional challenges had been lodged in federal district courts in Richmond, Lynchburg, and Detroit.[53]

Twenty-eight states in all filed lawsuits challenging the constitutionality of the individual mandate within six months of the ACA's passage. Some courts were more prepared than others to take on the various precedents buttressing the ad-ministration's optimism. On January 31, 2012, district court judge Roger Vinson of Tallahassee, a Reagan appointee with nearly three decades of judicial service, ruled that the individual mandate, which imposed a "shared responsibility penalty" on Americans who failed to purchase health insurance, lay outside the power of Congress.[54] Equally alarming from the administration's perspective, Judge Vinson held that the mandate could not be severed from the rest of the ACA, so he struck down the entire act as unconstitutional. Vinson's ruling offered a blueprint for a returning to the pre-1937 approach to constitutional law. In all, five federal district courts and three US appeals courts weighed in on the act before the US Supreme Court took its turn. Survival of the Obama administration's signature legislation was now in the hands of the Supreme Court, for better or worse.

In the final analysis, President Obama and his top aides ignored several funda-mental truths about litigation. First, by taking the constitutionality of the law al-most for granted, the White House ceded the litigation playing field to opponents with nothing to lose. Even if the ACA was ultimately validated, the questions hang-ing over it in the interim encouraged critics to continue the fight and weakened the law politically. Second, the challengers' ability to forum shop in search of activist conservative judges ensured some split decisions in the appeals courts. So armed, the law's opponents were able to sell their attacks as mainstream arguments to be taken seriously.[55]

President Obama could ill afford to ignore the role of the courts in crafting bold new policy. That much was clear after the health care reform saga of 2010–2012, and it was confirmed in the aftermath of *NFIB v. Sebelius.* Opponents filed subsequent lawsuits against the ACA. One suit maintained that the original bill had been improperly introduced in the Senate rather than in the House, where all revenue bills are supposed to be generated.[56] Another claimed that the formal text of the act appeared to authorize the establishment of health care exchanges only by the states. This latter claim—which would have eliminated the federal exchanges in many states—made its way all the way to the Supreme Court in *King v. Burwell* (2015).[57] An adverse ruling in *Burwell* would not have invalidated the legislation per se, but it would have unraveled the law's financial machinery to such a degree that it might have been impossible to save. Once again, the Supreme Court interpreted the law in the administration's favor, this time by a slightly more comfortable 6–3 vote.

A final lawsuit caught the Obama administration off guard during the president's final months in office. One provision of the ACA aimed to reimburse insurers for providing cost-sharing subsidies to low-income customers who purchased exchange coverage. Yet when Congress passed the subsidy program, it never actually provided for such money in the form of federal appropriations; accordingly, several Republican members of the House of Representatives brought suit, claiming that the Obama administration had improperly funded the provision through the use of refundable tax credits. On May 12, 2016, a federal judge ruled that these subsidies were illegal, absent express congressional appropriations to support them. The administration appealed, and the lawsuit remained unresolved when President Obama left office in early 2017. Yet another aspect of Obamacare funding was thus left in the hands of his Republican successor.

Immigration

During his 2008 campaign for the White House, Obama emphasized the need for a tough immigration policy. To that end, he laid out several new initiatives, including creating more secure borders, cracking down on employers that hired illegal immigrants, and fixing the dysfunctional immigration bureaucracy. As president, however, he immediately sought to qualify these initiatives with a policy of selective enforcement. Obama thus distinguished himself from past Democratic presidents by explicitly embracing "nonenforcement powers," which he planned to deploy in innovative ways. For decades, liberals had been sounding the alarm about Republican administrations' underenforcement of "laws governing consumer safety, the environment and a range of business practices."[58] In the context of immigration, however, the tables were now turned, as Republicans complained that the president had failed in his duty to "faithfully execute the laws."

With Congress refusing to pass immigration reform, Obama championed efforts to bring undocumented aliens out of the shadows by offering a form of "back-door amnesty": pay a fine, learn English, and go to the back of the line for the opportunity to become a citizen. He also emphasized better relations with Mexico and sought alternatives to deportation for those who qualified under legislative initiatives such as the "DREAM Act," which failed in Congress. To be sure, the Obama administration walked a political tightrope in this policy area: On the one hand, any efforts to accommodate the nation's 12 million illegal immigrants risked angering citizens in border states. On the other hand, his administration was reaching out to a population of Hispanic Americans whose political power was growing exponentially. Yet if state government officials were likely to challenge the president's enforcement policies at every turn, how would the courts fit into the administration's overall strategy?

Enacted on April 23, 2010, Arizona's SB 1070 represented the first effort by a state to step up enforcement on its own: it authorized local police (at their discretion) to check the immigration status of every person stopped. Critics of the law focused on the possibility of bias, as Hispanic Americans and legal residents might be mistaken for illegal immigrants due to racial profiling. The federal government's interest was spurred by more than concerns for federalism: regardless of whether the federal government was authorized to make such stops, Arizona was assuming federal regulatory powers that would undermine consistent and fair enforcement of the law. It also threatened to disrupt US relations with Mexico, Ecuador, and other Latin American states.

After wavering for more than two months, the Justice Department finally took action, filing suit against the state of Arizona on July 6, 2010.[59] The federal government's brief argued that "the Constitution and the federal immigration laws do not permit the development of a patchwork of state and local immigration policies throughout the country." This argument had not enjoyed much success before the high court: since the early 1990s, it had voted to sustain the exercise of state authority in all but two cases. Thus, the administration's primary considerations were political rather than legal. Five lawsuits had already been filed by civil rights groups and others, and the government's failure to participate might be viewed as a show of apathy toward issues of great importance to a core constituency of the Democratic Party. Of greater concern, laws such as Arizona's SB 1070 were starting to proliferate: at the time the Justice Department filed its lawsuit, legislators in five other states (South Carolina, Pennsylvania, Minnesota, Rhode Island, and Michigan) had already proposed bills similar to Arizona's, requiring police to check the immigration status of people they had lawfully stopped if they suspected such individuals were in the country illegally. Two other states passed laws simply affirming their support for SB 1070.[60] The bottom line? Federal inaction on SB 1070 had invited frustrated state lawmakers to take matters into their own hands.

The Obama administration won a significant early victory in the high court. In

Arizona v. United States (2012), the justices voted 5–3 to nullify three provisions of the law that (1) made it a crime to be in Arizona without legal papers, (2) forbade aliens to apply for or obtain jobs in the state, and (3) allowed police to arrest individuals (without a warrant) on a simple showing of probable cause so long as there was some basis for their removal from the United States. But the Court left intact the controversial provision requiring police to arrest and hold anyone they believed had committed a crime and was thought to be in the country illegally, at least until his or her immigration status could be checked.[61]

This early victory over immigration policy was soon followed by defeat. Two weeks after the 2014 midterm elections, the White House announced unilateral action on federal immigration policy that emphasized two elements: (1) a legal reprieve (thus removing the threat of deportation) for the undocumented parents of US citizens and permanent residents who had resided in the country for at least five years, and (2) expansion of the 2012 Deferred Action for Childhood Arrivals (DACA) program to allow immigrants older than 30 (who had entered the United States before age 16) and more recent arrivals (those who had entered the country between 2007 and 2010) to apply for deportation deferral as well. These actions were challenged in district court by twenty-six states, resulting in a preliminary injunction against their implementation pending a full and comprehensive judicial review. A shorthanded Supreme Court split 4–4 in *United States v. Texas* (2016),[62] leaving the preliminary injunction in place and effectively denying Obama the power to implement his orders.

Same-Sex Marriage

During his 2008 presidential campaign, Obama took a tempered approach to the issue of same-sex marriage. Just four years earlier, voters had rejected gay marriage initiatives in all eleven states where they were on that ballot. That included such Democratic strongholds as Michigan and Oregon, where President George W. Bush had been soundly defeated. That same year, a national Pew Research Center poll found that 60 percent of respondents opposed same-sex marriage, compared with just 31 percent who favored it.[63]

As a US Senate candidate in Illinois in 2004, Barack Obama had opposed same-sex marriage, and he planned to stand by that declaration during his run for the presidency. Much had changed in the interim, however. By 2008, only a bare majority (51 percent) said they opposed same-sex marriage. And although the 2008 Democratic Party platform stopped short of supporting the institution, it did include language opposing the Defense of Marriage Act (DOMA), the federal law signed by Democrat Bill Clinton that defined marriage for federal purposes as the union of one man and one woman.[64] According to the polls, steadily increasing numbers of Americans were now prepared to endorse same-sex marriage outright.

The issue of same-sex marriage remained a thorny one for President Obama. A broad Supreme Court ruling protecting same-sex marriage in all fifty states would take him off the hook and seemingly end the matter once and for all. Yet there was no guarantee that the Supreme Court would issue such a ruling during his presidency. It was just as likely that the Court would leave the decision to the states. The Obama administration thus took its first step toward resolving the issue on February 23, 2011, when the Justice Department declared that it would no longer defend section 3 of DOMA. Though consistent with the language of the Democratic Party platform three years earlier, this represented a dramatic shift from Justice Department policy at the outset of the administration.

The administration's willingness to halt the enforcement of DOMA received an assist from the high court two years later. On June 26, 2013, the Supreme Court held that section 3 of DOMA, which restricted the interpretation of marriage to only opposite-sex unions under federal law, violated the due process clause of the Fifth Amendment.[65] President Obama hailed the ruling as a victory for democracy, and it meant that he would no longer have to defend his administration's strategic refusal to enforce DOMA. When the Supreme Court subsequently held same-sex marriage to be a constitutionally protected right in *Obergefell v. Hodges* (2015),[66] Obama experienced a new phenomenon in his relationship with the third branch. Rather than placing the president at the center of a brewing storm, the Court essentially shouldered the burden itself and took the Obama administration off the proverbial hot seat.

Some Final Thoughts

Narratives play an especially useful role in educating the masses about complicated political events. Average citizens are more likely to care about political affairs when they are recast as simple stories of good versus evil, forces of progress versus forces of tradition, and so forth. In reporting on Washington, DC, and the battles waged by the president against his political opposition, seasoned observers often search for a simpler way to understand and frame these events. In the case of Obama and the courts, what often emerged was the narrative of a young and inexperienced chief executive who was far more comfortable engaging in grassroots politics and legislative battles than he was waging battles in the courtroom.

Was such a narrative consistent with the facts? Even before he was inaugurated as the nation's forty-fourth president, Barack Obama complained that Democrats had been overly reliant on judges to compensate for their losses at the polls; rejecting that approach, he urged his party to view the political system itself as the more appropriate venue for pursuing political change.[67] This rhetoric was not merely contrived in pursuit of the presidency; it was a common view among the community organizers he worked with in Chicago and among scholars at the University of Chicago, where he once taught constitutional law.[68]

As president, Obama continued to de-emphasize the courts as a panacea to America's problems, and this may have impacted his appointment of judges. White House chief of staff Rahm Emmanuel made it clear that he did not want to waste "precious political capital on polarizing judges while trying to pass a stimulus bill, Obamacare and new Wall Street rules."[69] President Obama himself frustrated many of his own supporters by viewing political change as best achieved incrementally, rather than through sweeping pronouncements from the courts and elsewhere. The president put it this way in an interview with podcaster Marc Maron in 2014:

> Sometimes the task of government is to make incremental improvements or try to steer the ocean liner two degrees north or south so that ten years from now, suddenly, we're in a very different place than we were. At the moment people may feel like we need a fifty degree turn . . . that we don't need a two-degree turn. And you say back, "well if I turn 50 degrees, the whole ship turns over."[70]

Here, President Obama sounded like a politician wary of activist judicial policy-making, such as that which occurred in *Roe v. Wade* or *Citizens United v. FEC*. Yet he might also appreciate the role of the courts in enacting this incremental, two-degree change, if only by subsequent validation or affirmation.

Presidential legacies are often shaped by grand and decisive moments in the life of an administration—the signing of landmark legislation, a successful military operation, the appointment of a Supreme Court justice. In the case of Barack Obama, that was certainly the case. Historians seeking to understand how the forty-fourth president shaped the future will no doubt focus on those types of moments: the passage of the Affordable Care Act, the capture and killing of Osama bin Laden, and the appointment of the first Latin American justice, among others. Yet a president's legacy is also built on more subtle exercises of executive power, such as prosecutorial discretion. Lawyers in the Obama Justice Department exercised their discretion to more aggressively pursue civil rights violators, yet in other areas, they were far more reluctant to use the courts to press their advantage, and in the case of DOMA, they sought to undercut the legal process through outright defiance. President Obama's reluctance to rely heavily on the courts for solutions was clearly reflected in how his administration exercised these forms of discretion.

Shep Melnick, a leading judicial scholar, wrote that, "in the end, the most important factor influencing relations between the President and the judiciary is . . . the extent to which the ideas that guide the incumbent administration . . . are also dominant within the judicial branch."[71] Perhaps if Barack Obama had been president during the Warren Court era, the former community organizer and the progressive Supreme Court would have forged an alliance for the ages. Even without such an alliance, the Roberts Court left Obama's domestic agenda mostly intact, and it provided the Democratic coalition with some major victories it would not have won otherwise. That may not be the legacy Obama sought, but—for better or worse—it is the one he achieved.

Notes

1. Marbury v. Madison, 5 U.S. (1 Cranch) 137 (1803).
2. New York Times v. Sullivan, 376 U.S. 254 (1964).
3. See, e.g., U.S. v. Darby Lumber Co., 312 U.S. 100 (1941); Wickard v. Filburn, 317 U.S. 311 (1942).
4. NFIB v. Sebelius, 567 U.S. 519 (2012).
5. See Jan Crawford, "Roberts Switched Views to Uphold Health Care Law," CBSnews .com, July 2, 2012, http://www.cbsnews.com/news/roberts-switched-views-to-uphold -health-care-law/.
6. This final issue would later have disruptive consequences as the Obama administration sought to implement the Medicaid expansion provisions during the president's second term. Yet at the time of the Supreme Court decision in June 2012, that issue was mostly overshadowed by the decision to save the bulk of Obamacare, including the controversial individual mandate.
7. Jeffrey Toobin, "Obama's Unfinished Judicial Legacy," *New Yorker*, July 31, 2012, http://www.newyorker.com/online/blogs/comment/2012/07/why-judges-matter .html. See also Jeffrey Toobin, *The Oath: The Obama White House and the Supreme Court* (New York: Doubleday, 2012).
8. Justin Driver, "Obama's Law," *New Republic*, June 30, 2011, 11.
9. Craig Green, "An Intellectual History of Judicial Activism," *Emory Law Journal* 58, 5 (2009): 1195, 1217.
10. Driver, "Obama's Law," 11.
11. Barack Obama, *The Audacity of Hope* (New York: Crown, 2006), 83.
12. Steven M. Teles, *The Rise of the Conservative Legal Movement* (Princeton, NJ: Princeton University Press, 2008), 45–46.
13. Ibid.
14. Mark Silverstein, *Judicious Choices* (New York: W. W. Norton, 1994), 139.
15. Peter Baker, "Obama's Tangled History with Supreme Court Sets Stage for Nominee Fight," *New York Times*, February 28, 2016, 1, http://nyti.ms/21tJ3jC.
16. The controversial line, which Sotomayor repeated in several speeches, including a 2001 Berkeley law lecture, was as follows: "I would hope that a wise Latina woman with the richness of her experiences would more often than not reach a better conclusion than a white male who hasn't lived that life."
17. Ricci v. DeStefano, 530 F.3d 87 (2d Cir. 2008).
18. *USA Today*/Gallup poll; N = 1,006 adults nationwide; margin of error ±4: "Now, turning to the U.S. Supreme Court: As you may know, Sonia Sotomayor is the federal judge nominated to serve on the Supreme Court. Would you like to see the Senate vote in favor of Sotomayor serving on the Supreme Court, or not?"
19. *USA Today*/Gallup poll; N = 1,208 adults nationwide; margin of error ±3: "As you may know, Solicitor General Elena Kagan is the person nominated to serve on the Supreme Court. Would you like to see the Senate vote in favor of Kagan serving on the Supreme Court, or not?"

20. Reagan's first nominee, Robert Bork, failed to win Senate confirmation after extraordinarily contentious hearings and floor debate; his second, Douglas Ginsburg, withdrew from consideration after reports of drug use surfaced.

21. "Cardozo Is Named to Supreme Court; Nomination Hailed; Hoover Sends Appointment to Senate and Confirmation at Once Is Expected," *New York Times*, February 16, 1932, 1.

22. Sahil Kapur, "How Republicans Can Still Block Obama's Judges: Blue Slips," Talking Points Memo, November 27, 2013, http://talkingpointsmemo.com/dc/how-republicans-can-still-block-obama-judges.

23. Charlie Savage, "Obama Lagging on Filling Seats in the Judiciary," *New York Times*, August 18, 2012, A1.

24. See, generally, Sheldon Goldman et al., "Obama's First Term Judiciary: Picking Judges in the Minefield of Obstructionism," *Judicature* 97, 1 (2014): 7–48.

25. Ibid.

26. Sam Stein, "Obama Left Largely Helpless as Judicial Vacancies Reach Crisis," *Huffington Post*, September 7, 2010.

27. Ian Millhiser, "Judicial Confirmation Rates Have Nosedived in the Obama Presidency" (Center for American Progress, September 10, 2010).

28. Jeffrey Toobin, "Bench Press: Are Obama's Judges Really Liberal?" *New Yorker*, September 21, 2009, 42.

29. Driver, "Obama's Law," 14.

30. Sheldon Goldman et al., "Obama's Judiciary at Midterm," *Judicature* 94 (2011): 272.

31. Michael Grunwald, "Did Obama Win the Judicial Wars?" politico.com, August 8, 2016, 2, http://www.politico.com/story/2016/08/obama-courts-judicial-legacy-226741.

32. Elliot Slotnick et al., "Writing the Book of Judges Part 1: Obama's Judicial Appointments Record after Six Years," *Journal of Law and Courts* 3, 2 (Fall 2015): 7.

33. Jeffrey Toobin, "The Obama Brief: The President Considers His Legacy," *New Yorker*, October 27, 2014.

34. Paul Kane, "Reid, Democrats Trigger 'Nuclear Option'; Eliminate Most Filibusters on Nominees," *Washington Post*, November 21, 2013.

35. "Trump Set to Reshape Judiciary after GOP Blockade," *Politico*, December 16, 2016.

36. Nancy Scherer, "Diversifying the Federal Bench: Is Universal Legitimacy for the U.S. Justice System Possible?" *Northwestern University Law Review* 5, 2 (2011): 588.

37. Slotnick et al., "Writing the Book," 2.

38. Grunwald, "Did Obama Win the Judicial Wars?" 2.

39. Matt Apuzzo, "Justice Dept. Presses Civil Rights Agenda in Local Courts," *New York Times*, August 19, 2015.

40. "Loretta Lynch's Parting Message," editorial, *New York Times*, December 17, 2016, A20.

41. Samuel R. Bagenstos, "Civil Rights Déjà Vu, Only Worse," Prospect.org, December 12, 2016.

42. Expedited judicial review provisions are routine in controversial laws that are expected to draw significant constitutional challenges, if only to reduce the uncertainty surrounding the implementation of such laws. For example, the McCain-Feingold Bipartisan Campaign Reform Act featured such a provision, as did the Line Item Veto Act (which the Supreme Court subsequently struck down in Clinton v. City of New York, 524 U.S. 417 [1998]).

OBAMA AND THE COURTS   185

43. Public Law 111-148, section 1332.
44. The final version of the health care legislation later passed by the Senate on December 24, 2009, did *not* call the failure to comply with the individual mandate a tax; instead, it was called a "penalty." The act reads in pertinent part: "If an applicable individual fails to meet the requirement of subsection (a) . . . there is hereby imposed a penalty." Act §1501(b)(1). Congress's conspicuous decision not to use the term "tax" (as it had done in at least three earlier incarnations of the legislation) proved significant to Judge Vinson's analysis; see Florida ex rel. McCollum v. US Dept. of Health and Human Services, 716 F. Supp. 2d 1120 (N.D. Fla. 2010). That decision did not sway Chief Justice Roberts or the rest of the majority from interpreting the penalty to be a tax in *NFIB v. Sebelius*.
45. Charles Fried, "The June Surprises: Balls, Strikes, and the Fog of War," *SCOTUSblog*, August 2, 2012, http://www.scotusblog.com/2012/08/the-june-surprises-balls-strikes-and-the-fog-of-war/Charles Fried.
46. See Wilson Ray Huhn, "Constitutionality of the Patient Protection and Affordable Care Act under the Commerce Clause and the Necessary and Proper Clause," *Journal of Legal Medicine* 32 (2011): 139–165.
47. U.S. v. Comstock, 560 U.S. 126 (2010).
48. Marcia Coyle, *The Roberts Court: The Struggle for the Constitution* (New York: Simon & Schuster, 2013), 294.
49. Gonzales v. Raich, 545 U.S. 1, 33 (2005) (Scalia, J. concurring).
50. Coyle, *Roberts Court*, 294.
51. Josh Blackman, *Unprecedented: The Constitutional Challenge to Obamacare* (New York: PublicAffairs, 2013), 80.
52. Coyle, *Roberts Court*, 295.
53. Ibid., 281–282.
54. Florida v. U.S. Dept. of Health and Human Services, U.S. District Court for the Northern District of Florida (Case No. 3:10-cv-91-RV/EM), filed January 31, 2011.
55. Coyle, *Roberts Court*, 296.
56. Michael Gerhardt, "Barack Obama," in *The Presidents and the Constitution*, ed. Ken Gormley (New York: NYU Press, 2016), 609.
57. King v. Burwell, 576 U.S. ___, 135 S. Ct. 2480 (2015).
58. Laurence Tribe and Joshua Maltz, *Uncertain Justice: The Roberts Court and the Constitution* (New York: Picador, 2014), 210.
59. See Jerry Markon and Michael Shear, "Justice Department Sues Arizona over Immigration Law," *Washington Post*, July 7, 2010, A1.
60. Anna Gorman, "Arizona's Immigration Law Isn't the Only One," *Los Angeles Times*, July 16, 2010, http://articles.latimes.com/2010/jul/16/nation/la-na-immigration-states-20100717.
61. Arizona v. U.S., 567 U.S. 387 (2012).
62. U.S. v. Texas, 579 U.S. ___, 136 S. Ct. 2271 (2016).
63. "Changing Attitudes on Gay Marriage," Pew Research Center, June 26, 2017, http://www.pewforum.org/2016/05/12/changing-attitudes-on-gay-marriage/.
64. 2008 Democratic Party Platform, "Renewing America's Promise," The American Presidency Project, August 25, 2008, http://www.presidency.ucsb.edu/ws/?pid=78283.
65. United States v. Windsor, 570 U.S. 744 (2013).
66. Obergefell v. Hodges, 576 U.S. ___, 135 S. Ct. 2584 (2015).

67. Obama, *Audacity of Hope*, 83.

68. Grunwald, "Did Obama Win the Judicial Wars?" 3.

69. Ibid.

70. Quoted in Adam Gopnik, "Liberal-in-Chief," *New Yorker*, May 23, 2016, 23–24.

71. Shep Melnick, "The Courts, Jurisprudence and the Executive Branch," in *The Executive Branch: Institutions of Democracy*, ed. Joel Aberbach and Mark Peterson (New York: Oxford University Press, 2005), 480.

CHAPTER NINE

Obama's Second-Term Domestic Agenda

Lessons and Legacies

Alyssa Julian and John D. Graham

President Obama's second term began after a decisive Electoral College victory over Republican challenger Mitt Romney and some modest Democratic gains in Congress. While the Democrats held a majority in the Senate, Obama's prospects for a progressive legislative agenda were dim due to the Republican House majority led by Speaker John Boehner (R-OH). Naturally, the president's focus gradually shifted to the use of executive power, and the House Republicans were unable to stop him due to the Democratic majority in the Senate and Obama's ability to veto legislation hostile to his agenda.

In this chapter, we compare Obama's second-term accomplishments in domestic policy with what he initially set out to do (table 9.4, at the end of this chapter, summarizes what we learned). Specifically, we focus on the economy, health care, gun control, climate change, and immigration—all well-known priorities for Obama that had international and transnational dimensions as well.

Overall, Obama's success rate with his second-term agenda was well below 50 percent due to adverse judicial rulings and legislative setbacks. We believe that this relatively ineffectual record contributed to Obama's poor job approval rating and difficulties for his party in the 2014 midterm elections. As expected, extreme partisan polarization of American politics was a barrier to many of Obama's initiatives.

Given the absence of personal scandal in the White House, it is reasonable to assume that the public's reaction to Obama's second term was largely conditioned by the state of the economy, the substance of his policy agenda, and perceptions of his effectiveness and competence. Although some results of the 2014 midterm elections were beyond Obama's control, his disappointing second-term record on domestic affairs contributed to the Democratic debacle that fall—most notably, the Democratic Party's loss of the Senate.

Throughout this chapter we draw on a theory of presidential effectiveness under conditions of partisan polarization, whereby the opposing leadership in Congress seeks to deny the president legislative success.[1] On some domestic issues, we suggest a counterfactual second-term scenario that might have enabled Obama to build a stronger policy legacy while minimizing electoral damage to congressional Democrats in 2014. In some cases, these counterfactual suggestions require a rethinking of Obama's first term as well. Although counterfactual thinking in presidential studies is inherently speculative, it is crucial if we want to move the field beyond description and toward practical lessons for future presidents.

The Economy

No incoming president since FDR had confronted an economic crisis like the one President Obama inherited in 2009. It was not apparent at the time, but the United States was in the midst of what we now call the Great Recession.[2] Obama's first-term policies sought to deliver short-term relief to prevent economic collapse (and a repeat of the Great Depression) and stimulate recovery of the economy. Although he was unable to enact all the measures he requested, Obama's first-term record in short-term economic policy-making was impressive.[3]

Deploying both executive and legislative powers, Obama took aggressive steps to ease the fiscal and economic crises. Under the leadership of chairman Ben Bernanke (originally an economic adviser to George W. Bush whom Obama reappointed), the Federal Reserve Board (the Fed) pumped huge volumes of money into the nation's credit system by essentially expanding the money supply. The Fed's action resulted in a sharp and sustained drop in interest rates, which played an important role in reviving the troubled auto and housing sectors of the US economy. The Obama-Bernanke collaboration produced a coordinated economic response to the financial meltdown: easy money at the Fed, coupled with fiscal stimulus by Congress. Through the $787 billion American Recovery and Reinvestment Act and other policies, Obama sought to lead the damaged economy on a path of recovery. Obama also helped engineer passage of the Dodd-Frank Wall Street reforms, which aimed to regulate the financial sector and prevent the practices that led to the Great Recession beginning in 2007.

As the economy slowly improved from 2009 to 2012, Obama supplemented his recovery agenda with an inequality agenda at the start of his second term. The Bush tax cuts for high earners were the primary target, as progressives were eager to see Obama deliver on his pledge, made four years earlier, to scuttle them. If the 2012 win over Romney did nothing else, it gave Obama the upper hand over Boehner, who chose quick concession rather than a prolonged public fight over tax cuts. The result was the American Taxpayer Relief Act of 2012. Enacted in January 2013, the act made permanent the Bush tax cuts for individuals earning less than $400,000 per year. It also permanently indexed for inflation the alternative minimum tax. For individuals making more than $400,000 per year, the tax rate increased from 35 to 39.6 percent. The act also limited deductions for individuals making more than $250,000, permanently capped estate tax exemptions at $5.2 million, and increased the top estate tax rate from 35 to 40 percent.[4] This significant achievement would prove to be one of the few legislative victories in Obama's second term. The ambitious tax reform legislation passed in late 2017, however, changed some of these provisions.

The rest of Obama's inequality agenda encountered effective resistance from the GOP. In 2013 and in each subsequent year, Obama asked Congress to raise the federal minimum wage. In his 2013 State of the Union address, he called for an increase in the federal minimum wage from $7.25 to $9.00 per hour. That proposal irritated some key congressional Democrats who were planning to bid for an even larger increase. In March 2013 House Republicans unanimously voted down the Fair Minimum Wage Act, which would have set the federal minimum wage at $10.10 an hour.[5] In April 2014 the Minimum Wage Fairness Act, another proposal to increase the federal minimum wage to $10.10 an hour, died in the Senate; the vote was 54–42, just 6 votes short of the 60 necessary to invoke cloture. There was only one Republican crossover, and one Democrat voted against it.[6]

Recognizing that his minimum wage agenda was not capturing anywhere near the 60 votes required in the Senate (let alone a majority in the House), Obama pivoted to a more limited executive action. In February 2014 he employed executive power to raise the minimum wage for federal contract workers from $7.25 to $10.10 per hour.[7] Obama's stance encouraged the states to act. Since 2013, eighteen states (mostly Democratic ones) and the District of Columbia have increased the minimum wage.[8] Obama later expressed support for the Raise the Wage Act proposed by Senator Patty Murray and Representative Bobby Scott, a bill that would have increased the minimum wage to $20 per hour by 2020. The measure was introduced in the Senate in 2015 but did not make it to the floor for a vote.[9] By the time the 2014 midterm elections were in sight, Obama's minimum wage agenda was more of a campaign stance for the Democrats than a serious legislative initiative. The minimum wage agenda had partisan value for the Democratic Party, as more congressional Republicans than congressional Democrats were cross-pressured.[10]

President Obama ran into a speed bump in 2013 when the House GOP staged a fiscal confrontation. From October 1 to 16, the federal government experienced a shutdown that curtailed most routine operations because Democrats and Republicans could not agree on a budget for 2014. When a conservative faction of the Republican-led House (overriding Boehner's reservations) tried to defund the Affordable Care Act, the Democrat-led Senate refused to go along, so nothing was sent to the president for approval.[11] After two weeks of negative press for the GOP (and, to a lesser extent, Obama), a continuing resolution was passed to reopen the government and suspend the debt ceiling. Obama won the confrontation, which put an end to GOP games involving shutdown threats for the remainder of his presidency.

President Obama devoted much political energy in his second term to an ambitious collaboration with House Speaker Boehner on a grand fiscal deal covering tax policy and entitlement reform. Neither politician had a clear electoral mandate to pursue such a deal; nor was either man in a strong position to deliver votes on a deal if they came up with one. The lack of tangible progress from these discussions with Boehner contributed to the second-term narrative of Obama's ineffectiveness in the domestic policy arena.[12]

In pursuit of economic growth, Obama advanced a new infrastructure agenda. His plan aimed to create jobs by attracting private investment in highways and public works. The agenda called for higher caps on "private activity bonds" to encourage more private spending on infrastructure projects. He also wanted to give foreign pension funds tax-exempt status when selling US infrastructure, property, or real estate assets, thereby hoping to gain more foreign investment. The plan called for $4 billion in new spending and a $10 billion national "infrastructure bank."[13] The president's focus on private-sector investment was designed to appeal to House Republicans, who were determined to block any new government spending. But the plan failed, as House Republicans engaged in strategic as well as ideological opposition. Lacking legislative success, Obama again shifted his infrastructure agenda to a campaign issue in 2014.

Another arm of President Obama's second-term pro-growth agenda was tax reform. Some of the proposed measures included cutting tax preferences for high-income households, eliminating special tax breaks for oil and gas companies, closing the carried interest loophole for investment fund managers, and eliminating benefits for those who bought corporate jets. In his fiscal year 2016 budget, Obama also proposed repealing the right to defer US corporate taxes on foreign profits. Without the deferral, companies would be forced to make locational decisions based on business factors rather than tax rates. The budget also called for a reduction in the corporate tax rate from 35 to 28 percent. This reduction would decrease tax revenue by $840 billion over the next ten years, but the lost revenue could be more than offset by the closing of tax loopholes. Additionally, the Obama budget proposed a global minimum tax of 19 percent on all foreign profits of US corporations. The global tax was intended to discourage US multinationals from shifting their foreign profits to tax havens around the world.

Although some of the president's tax agenda was appealing to the GOP (such as the cut in corporate income tax rates), Obama—urged on by Senate progressives—was looking for a net increase in revenue to the federal government. This was a fiscal outcome that Republican leaders and rank and file in Congress were not prepared to accept. Thus, Obama's ambitions for tax reform never came close to passage. His successor, Donald Trump, was able to rally the GOP to enact major tax reform, and in December 2017 Congress passed a massive tax reform bill costing roughly $1.46 trillion.[14] The bill permanently cut the corporate tax rate from 35 to 21 percent, gave a larger tax break to high earners, and eliminated the corporate alternative minimum tax, along with numerous other landmark provisions.[15]

President Obama also shifted his focus to international trade, as trade agreements have historically been appealing to Republican members of Congress. In February 2016 twelve Pacific Rim nations signed the Trans-Pacific Partnership (TPP) after more than five years of negotiations. The mission of the TPP was to promote economic growth, create jobs, enhance competition, and raise living standards. The agreement set high standards with regard to labor, the environment, intellectual property, and a free and open Internet.[16] The agreement also sought to eliminate or reduce tariffs on agricultural and industrial goods.

The TPP received a hefty dose of criticism from both the left and the right. For one, the negotiations were framed as secret endeavors. Organized labor was deeply suspicious that its members were being asked to compete against low-wage Asian labor. The Internet provisions were attacked as too extreme, putting unreasonable demands on Internet service providers. Environmentalists feared the agreement would lower, rather than raise, environmental standards for products and processes.[17] And the Tea Party—still a potent force in the GOP—feared that trade deals gave too much discretionary power to Obama.

Obama fought hard and won "fast-track" authority to negotiate the TPP (and a trailing European agreement), thereby allowing an "up or down" vote in Congress (no amendments and no filibusters) on each agreement. But the votes to approve fast-track authority were remarkably close. The measure barely passed in the Senate by a 60–38 vote (60 votes were required to invoke cloture) and narrowly passed in the House by a vote of 219–211. In the Senate, 13 Democrats voted in favor of the bill and 5 Republicans voted against it. In the House, 28 Democrats voted for the bill and 50 Republicans voted against it. The surprisingly large number of GOP members against fast-track authority was a signal that the TPP was in trouble.

As the 2016 elections approached, neither Democratic nor Republican members of Congress were looking forward to a vote on the TPP. The campaign rhetoric in both parties was highly hostile to previous trade agreements, especially the North American Free Trade Agreement (NAFTA). Indeed, Hillary Clinton, who had been a champion of the TPP while serving in the Obama administration, gradually turned against it in 2016 as a presidential candidate. When the TPP was delayed until after the 2016 elections, there was some hope that Congress might revisit it in the lame-duck session. But with Trump's surprising win based partly on an antitrade agenda, members of Congress from both parties seemed happy to let the initiative die. On the third day of his presidency, Trump issued an executive order formally withdrawing the United States from the TPP.[18]

Obama was correct to explore bipartisanship in the trade deals with Asian and European countries. The Tea Party's opposition to free trade, coupled with a sluggish economic recovery and a mistrust of Obama by organized labor and environmentalists, helped undermine these two promising free-trade initiatives. With the benefit of hindsight, it seems that Obama might have been better off leading with the European agreement, given that competition from low-wage laborers was less of a concern.[19]

Oil security was partly an Obama accomplishment. During the 2008 financial crisis and again in 2010, the average worldwide price of oil surged, with damaging economic consequences. The longest period of high oil prices in US history (defined as greater than $90 per barrel) was 2010 to 2014.[20] But in 2014 the price of oil collapsed due to increased production and decreased consumption. The consumption story was largely based on a rapid decline in the growth rate of Chinese consumption due to a slowdown of the Chinese economy. The production story involved the United States: in 2008 the United States produced 1.85 billion barrels of oil, but by 2016, US production was at 3.25 billion barrels.[21] Obama contributed to the increase in US production through his aggressive support of unconventional oil and gas technologies, such as fracking. Obama's pro-fracking stance isolated fracking opponents on the left, who believed the president's support for unconventional production was inconsistent with his climate-change agenda.[22]

In April 2011 crude oil prices hit a high of $111.68 per barrel. By 2016, oil prices had plummeted to between $29 and $53 per barrel.[23] The drop in oil prices paid off at the gas pump for US consumers, helping to intensify the economic recovery in 2015–2016. In 2012 the average retail gasoline price in the United States was $3.68 per gallon; by 2016, the average price per gallon was $2.25.[24] The impact of Obama's pro-fracking stance will not be short-lived, as the Energy Information Administration (EIA) has downgraded its gasoline price projections through 2025 (remaining at less than $3 per gallon).

As Obama's second term came to a close, there was good news about the state of the economy (see table 9.1). In January 2017 the Bureau of Labor Statistics reported that the official unemployment rate was 4.8 percent, down from a peak of 10.0 percent in October 2010.[25] The 2016 report of the US Census Bureau placed the nation's poverty rate at 11.6 percent and the median household income at $56,516.[26] In 2011 these figures had been 15.1 percent and $50,502, respectively.[27] The rise in median household income was the first increase since 2007. Gains in car sales and housing starts were impressive, as was the 2015–2016 drop in fuel prices. Whether the accelerated economic recovery was because of Obama's policies or in spite of them will be disputed for decades, but there is no question that the economy he left for Donald Trump was much stronger than the one he inherited from George W. Bush.

Table 9.1. Economic Trends, 2005–2017

Indicator	2005	2006	2007	2008	2009	2010	2011	2012	2013	2014	2015	2016	2017
December unemployment rate (%)	4.9	4.4	5.0	5.3	9.9	9.3	8.5	7.9	6.7	5.6	5.0	4.7	4.1
December jobs-to-people ratio	62.8	63.4	62.7	61.0	58.3	58.3	58.6	58.7	58.7	59.2	59.6	59.7	60.1
GDP growth rate (%)	3.3	2.7	1.8	−0.3	−2.8	2.5	1.6	2.2	1.7	2.4	2.6	1.6	2.3
December Dow Jones Industrial Average	10,718	12,463	13,265	8,776	10,428	11,578	12,218	13,104	16,577	17,823	17,425	19,763	24,232
New vehicle sales, annual average (million)	16.9	16.5	16.1	13.2	10.4	12.7	14.4	14.4	15.5	16.5	17.4	17.5	17.1
New housing starts, annual average (million)	2.07	1.81	1.34	0.90	0.55	0.59	0.61	0.78	0.93	1.00	1.11	1.18	1.20
Median household income (thousand $)	56.2	56.6	57.4	55.3	54.9	53.5	52.6	52.8	54.5	53.7	56.5	57.6	60.3
SNAP participation, average number of households (million)	25.6	26.5	26.3	28.2	33.5	40.3	44.7	46.6	47.6	46.7	45.8	44.2	42.1
Average retail gasoline price ($ per gallon)	2.31	2.62	2.84	3.30	2.41	2.84	3.58	3.68	3.58	3.44	2.52	2.25	2.53

Not all the economic news was highly favorable, however (see table 9.1). The best measure of the economy's job-producing performance (the jobs-to-people ratio) did not improve significantly until late in Obama's second term (2014–2016). The rate of participation in the Supplemental Nutrition Assistance Program (SNAP; formerly called food stamps) remained stubbornly high. And the annual rate of growth in gross domestic product (GDP) was sluggish, especially when compared with previous economic recoveries since World War II.

From a political perspective, Obama's second term—like his first one—was weak on centrist proposals that might have fostered bipartisan collaboration in Congress. Corporate tax reform showed some promise, but it was undermined by Obama's insistence on a net increase in federal revenue, something that GOP members could not support. If Obama had taken a revenue-neutral position from the start, bipartisan support in Congress might have been easier to achieve. Max Baucus (D-MT) in the Senate and Dave Camp (R-MI) in the House were well positioned to collaborate on tax reform in 2013–2014, and both were seasoned producers of bipartisan deals. Obama, however, chose to align the White House with progressives in the Senate rather than with Baucus. Knowing that he faced a tough reelection battle in Montana, Baucus ultimately decided to accept Obama's nomination to the post of ambassador to China, which effectively handed his Senate seat to the GOP.

Obama chose not to pursue regulatory reform in his second term, even though he had enjoyed some success in his first term. Obama could have built on that first-term success with a second-term legislative proposal, thereby providing centrist, pro-business Democrats in Congress (Mark Begich of Alaska, Kay Hagan of North Carolina, Mark Pryor of Arkansas, Mary Landrieu of Louisiana, Heidi Heitkamp of North Dakota, Mark Warner of Virginia) an appealing issue to run on in 2014, 2016, and 2018.

Another promising opportunity might have been expansion of the earned income tax credit, an issue of interest to both Obama and the new House Republican leader Paul Ryan. Yet Obama devoted most of his fiscal energies to the grand deal with Boehner, which caused more modest bipartisan reform opportunities to take a backseat.

In summary, Obama's big economic win at the beginning of his second term was repeal of the Bush tax cuts for high earners—the only tangible result of his inequality agenda. Also important was Obama's win on the government shutdown and confrontation with the GOP on the debt ceiling, removing what could have been a significant setback for the US economy (given that global confidence in US financial leadership would have been impaired). Most important was the continuing economic recovery throughout Obama's second term. Although it was not as robust, uniform, or steady as it could have been, it produced a US economy that was vastly stronger in January 2017 than it was in either January 2009 or January 2013.

Health Care

One of the biggest items on President Obama's first-term agenda was health care. As soon as he took office, he focused on passing the monumental Patient Protection and Affordable Care Act (ACA), also referred to pejoratively as Obamacare (although Obama and the rest of the country came to embrace the term). The ACA was intended to increase access to health care, enhance the quality of care, and lower costs.

Obama compromised on the ACA by not insisting on a single payer or a "public option" for insurance sponsored by the federal government. After a long and divisive journey through Congress, the ACA was signed into law on March 23, 2010. From a historical perspective, the ACA was a major achievement in social policy, but it was passed almost entirely with Democratic votes and came at a large political cost to Obama and the Democratic Party. The unpopularity of Obamacare was a key contributor to the devastating Democratic losses in the 2010 and 2014 midterm elections, including the loss of numerous state legislatures and governorships.[28]

The law required that all US citizens have health insurance by 2014 or else pay a fee for each month they were without minimum coverage—the so-called individual mandate. In addition, the ACA's employer mandate imposed a tax penalty on businesses with fifty or more workers if those companies did not offer adequate health insurance plans to their full-time employees. Under the ACA, people could purchase insurance through the traditional marketplace as well as through state or federal health insurance marketplaces (exchanges), which offered income-based subsidies. New regulations prohibited the denial of coverage based on preexisting conditions and allowed children to stay on their parents' insurance plans up to age 26.

During Obama's second term, the controversy over the ACA did not subside, in part due to embarrassing snafus during the complex implementation process. In October 2013 the Obama administration launched healthcare.gov, the federal portal for citizens to sign up for health care coverage. The initial launch was a disaster. The website malfunctioned due to the large volume of visitors to the page and faulty software. In the first month, nearly 27 million people visited the federal and state websites, but only 26,000 people managed to buy insurance. The White House had been hoping that half a million people would sign up during that first month.[29]

The main problem with the website was that several different government contractors had contributed parts of the system, but the parts did not work together. The entire healthcare.gov project was overseen by the Centers for Medicare and Medicaid Services (CMS), an organization that had only limited experience with large, complex software projects. Inexplicably, the Obama administration had not given priority to recruiting a leadership team with the necessary information tech-

Table 9.2. Delays in Implementation of the Affordable Care Act

Provision	Original Effective Date	Delayed Effective Date
Individual mandate	January 1, 2014	April 15, 2015
Employer mandate	January 1, 2014	For employers with 100 or more full-time employees: January 1, 2015
		For employers with 50–99 full-time employees: January 1, 2016
Start of exchanges	October 1, 2013 (website crashed)	December 23, 2013
Small-business program	October 1, 2013	January 1, 2014

nology (IT), management, and insurance industry experience.[30] The administration had received warnings months beforehand that the system was not ready, but no one anticipated the size and scope of the problems.[31] Eventually, most of the issues were resolved due to an IT "surge" ordered by the White House, but the damage done to the reputation of both the ACA and the president was considerable. For Democratic senators seeking reelection in November 2014, the timing of the debacle was quite unfortunate.

A related snafu emerged due to the rhetoric President Obama had used in his campaign speeches promoting the ACA. The president had repeatedly told people that they could keep their current insurance plans if they were happy with them. However, many current plans did not comply with the ACA's minimum standards. As a result, in the fall of 2013 millions of Americans received cancellation notices from their insurers because their plans did not comply with ACA requirements. Since the healthcare.gov site was not functioning properly during this period, many frightened and angry people did not know how to go about replacing the insurance coverage that had been canceled. Republicans in Congress seized on the issue to question both Obama's truthfulness and the ACA's workability. Obama apologized for the misinformation and approved a decision to temporarily permit substandard plans and to delay the effective dates of some ACA provisions to allow more time to resolve the confusion. Thus, during his second term, Obama spent as much time delaying ACA requirements as implementing them (see table 9.2).

Post enactment, the constitutionality of the ACA was tested several times. One of these challenges was resolved in the summer of 2012 when a divided Supreme Court made a landmark decision upholding the ACA's constitutionality in *National Federation of Independent Business v. Sebelius*. The National Federation of

Independent Business had claimed that both the ACA's individual mandate and the Medicaid expansion were unconstitutional. In a 5–4 decision, the Supreme Court held that the Tax Anti-Injunction Act did not apply to the individual mandate. Instead, it found that the individual mandate was a valid exercise of Congress's constitutional power to "lay and collect taxes." Thus, the tax power was seen as permissible by the Court, but the individual mandate was not a proper use of the Constitution's commerce clause or Congress's necessary and proper powers.[32]

In a separate part of the opinion, the Court determined that Congress exceeded its spending clause authority when it threatened to revoke a state's Medicaid funding if that state did not participate in the Medicaid expansion envisioned by the ACA. A majority of the justices agreed that the expansion was unconstitutionally coercive because it forced states to make expensive and transformative changes in their Medicaid programs. This was an unexpected setback for Obama, and—as we explore below—it complicated the ACA's implementation.

In 2015 the Supreme Court resolved a second constitutional challenge to the ACA. In a 6–3 decision in *King v. Burwell*, the Court upheld one of the main tenets of the ACA: that millions of Americans are entitled to federal tax subsidies to help them pay for health insurance.[33] The plaintiffs argued that, based on the precise language of the ACA, tax credits were to be distributed only through marketplaces "established by the state," not through the federal marketplace. The defendant argued that the language encompassed both state and federal exchanges. The Court agreed with the Obama administration, finding the disputed clause to be ambiguous and deferring to the judgment of the Department of Health and Human Services. Once again, Democrats praised the decision, while Republicans contested it.

Most of the ACA survived constitutional challenge (although additional cases are in the judicial pipeline), but the constant litigation received massive publicity and forced Democratic members of Congress into more ACA-related debates prior to the 2014 midterm elections. Perhaps more important, the Supreme Court's decision on the Medicaid expansion led to efforts in GOP-controlled states to block implementation of the ACA. Many Republican governors and state legislators feared that if they decided in favor of Medicaid expansion, they would be framed as supporters of Obamacare. Obama engaged in the creative use of executive power to negotiate expansion plans that were acceptable to Republicans in some states. As of July 2018, thirty-four states (including Washington, DC) had adopted the Medicaid expansion, and fourteen states had decided against it.[34]

Currently, the individual health insurance market is facing several challenges. The ACA requires insurers to sell insurance to everyone at the same price, regardless of medical history or risk. This presents a problem because insurance companies need young, healthy people to enroll in order to balance the costly claims of older, less healthy enrollees. However, young consumers are much less likely to be insured. According to an early 2016 study, 15.9 percent of 25- to 34-year-olds are uninsured, whereas only 8.1 percent of 45- to 64-year-olds are uninsured.[35] Premiums will rise unless young, healthy people enroll in the exchanges. And as premiums rise, participation becomes less appealing. The Obama administration redoubled its efforts to attract young, healthy people to the marketplace, realizing that otherwise, the program might not be sustainable.[36] Despite those best efforts, many young people simply claim waivers from the insurance mandate—waivers added by the Obama administration to reduce the controversy over the ACA.[37] Some young people simply prefer to pay the penalty and forgo insurance.[38] Ultimately, the tax cuts passed by Congress late in 2017 eliminated the individual mandate tax penalty, thus exacerbating the risk-pool problem.

The long-term viability of the health care marketplace is also uncertain because major health insurance companies and some states are dropping out of the ACA exchanges. Operating a state exchange is difficult and expensive, especially for smaller states.[39] Many insurance companies are withdrawing from the exchanges, fearing that participation will cause them to lose money (however, courts have found that some companies, such as Aetna and Centene, were actually making money off exchanges in some states).[40] Some of the largest companies, including Anthem Blue Cross, Aetna, United Health Group, and Humana, have stated that they will not participate in exchanges in certain states.[41] As these major companies withdraw, the marketplace becomes less competitive and consumers have less choice, negating one of the program's main objectives. Competition keeps costs low, so consumers lose when one company controls a large share of a specific marketplace. The exchange market faces even more uncertainty under Trump administration policies that terminated the payment of critical ACA subsidies to insurance companies to reduce deductibles and certain out-of-pocket costs for low-income customers. Without them, consumers could see large premium surges or loss of their insurance.[42]

As President Obama's second term came to a close, had the ACA achieved what it set out to do? A 2016 report from the US Department of Health and Human Services found that, between 2010 and 2016, 20 million Americans gained health care coverage.[43] The share of uninsured Americans peaked at 18 percent in the third quarter of 2013 but dropped to 10.9 percent in the third quarter of 2016.[44] Without question, the ACA increased access and coverage, though perhaps not as rapidly as initially envisioned.

Fears that the ACA would trigger a massive rise in health care spending have not been substantiated. Health care spending has actually increased at a lower rate since the ACA was enacted. The three years after 2010 (date of enactment of the ACA) saw the slowest growth (+1.1 percent) on record in real per capita national health expenditures. Between 1960 and 2010 the average annual growth rate was 4.6 percent.[45] Spending on Medicare beneficiaries exhibited a disproportionate slowdown, which is evidence that the overall decline in the rate of health care spending growth resulted at least in part from structural changes in the health care system, not just the recession.

The botched rollout of the ACA website, coupled with the insurance cancellation notices, temporarily hurt the president's credibility and raised doubts about the administration's competence and the ACA's workability. If the Obama White House had obtained the required expertise from CMS at the outset, preferably in the first term, implementation of the ACA might have proceeded more smoothly.[46] After the 2012 Supreme Court decision that clipped the Medicaid expansion, the viability of the federal exchange took on added significance, and the Obama administration's response needed to be more careful. The implementation schedule should have been adjusted to roll out the federal insurance exchange in January 2015, after the 2014 midterms. That schedule would have given CMS adequate time to do the proper testing and refinement of healthcare.gov before the first round of sign-ups. This aggressive use of executive power would have been good for Obama's agenda and good for the electoral future of vulnerable Senate Democrats in 2014.

Trump's election and the GOP takeover of the House put the ACA at considerable risk of partial or complete repeal. The GOP Congress was quick to eliminate penalties for noncompliance with the individual mandate (starting in 2019) through its 2017 tax reform bill, and Trump used executive authority to promote alternatives to other aspects of the law.[47] From a political perspective, passage and implementation of the ACA were more controversial than they needed to be, which helps explain some of the midterm losses in 2014 as well as in 2010. Thus, Obama's health care record, while accomplished, is also blemished because of the preventable damage inflicted on his party.[48]

Climate Change

President Obama entered his first term with an ambitious "green" agenda, especially as it related to climate change. He pledged in his first year to seek new legislation from Congress that would establish an economy-wide cap-and-trade system to reduce emissions of greenhouse gases (GHGs) such as carbon dioxide. The legislative focus was control of GHGs from stationary sources such as electric utilities, oil refineries, and manufacturing plants (e.g., steel, aluminum, cement).

Given the terrible condition of the economy and the many other legislative priorities, the Obama administration was encouraged to pursue the climate agenda administratively. For example, an April 2009 report from New York University made a creative legal case that the Environmental Protection Agency (EPA) had ample authority under the Clean Air Act to enact a cap-and-trade system, especially since the Supreme Court had ruled in 2007 that carbon dioxide is a pollutant within the meaning of the Clean Air Act. Nonetheless, Obama favored legislation over executive action, believing that would provide a more effective and durable solution.[49]

Cap and trade would consist of a national cap on GHGs coupled with a trading system that allowed companies facing high compliance costs to purchase emissions allowances from other companies that could reduce emissions at low cost. Instead of allocating allowances to companies at no charge (as had been done under the EPA's sulfur pollution trading program), Obama's first budget request to Congress proposed that the allowances be auctioned off to the highest corporate bidders. The result would be a large increase in federal revenue that could be used to support tax cuts or new spending initiatives to stimulate the economy.

The nascent Tea Party movement seized on the opportunity to label the new scheme "cap and tax." Although some large businesses worked with the Obama administration to pass the new climate plan, many businesses and trade associations organized strong opposition to it, including the coal industry and portions of the oil and gas industry. Some industrial labor unions joined businesses in a campaign to amend the plan so that imported goods would be subject to a border tariff if the producing country had weak controls on GHGs. Organized labor feared that the US manufacturing sector would be less competitive globally without the tariff.

Obama wanted the House to pass the ACA before his climate plan was debated, but Speaker Nancy Pelosi and senior Democrat Henry Waxman (chair of the Committee on Energy and Commerce) decided to pass the climate plan first. Despite a large Democratic majority (257–178), the climate plan passed the House in June 2009 by the slim margin of 219–212. And this occurred only after the addition of a border tariff provision the night before the vote, as Waxman and Pelosi set aside the Obama administration's strong opposition to the tariff. The House vote in favor of the climate plan ultimately became ammunition for Republican challengers in the 2010 midterm elections. One senior House Democrat from the coal region of Virginia, Rick Boucher, lost his bid for reelection in a campaign in which "cap and tax" was the central issue raised by his GOP challenger.

The struggle in the House should have been a signal that Senate passage would be extremely difficult and politically sensitive. In fact, a coalition of ten Democratic senators from the Midwest and the South were already on record as opposing a plan similar to the one Pelosi and Waxman were pushing.[50] Deliberations in the Senate were quite slow, and no progress was made in 2013 or in the first half of 2014. Few Republican senators expressed interest in collaborating with Obama on the climate issue, so the president intervened and hosted a meeting in the White House to stimulate Senate deliberations. A bipartisan group of senators, including Republican John McCain of Arizona, was urged to pass a climate plan, even if it differed significantly from the House plan. When no progress was made by October, Senate majority leader Harry Reid and President Obama publicly acknowledged that they did not have the votes to pass a climate plan in the Senate.[51] The idea was shelved indefinitely.

Meanwhile, in its first term, the Obama administration used executive power to make impressive progress on a plan to reduce GHG emissions from cars and light trucks. Twenty-five percent of all GHG emissions are from the transportation sector, and two-thirds of those emissions come from light-duty passenger vehicles (cars and light trucks).[52] President Obama instructed the Department of Transportation and the EPA to establish rules on mileage standards for light-duty passenger vehicles. These rules required the industry to increase average fuel economy from 29 miles per gallon (mpg) in model year 2012 to 34.5 mpg by 2016. Obama also established an aggressive regulatory plan for model years 2017–2025 to boost mileage to 54.5 mpg by 2025.[53] These improvements in fuel economy were expected to trigger steady reductions in GHG emissions over the thirty-year lives of the affected vehicles. It is unknown whether Obama's plan for 2017–2025 will survive the Trump administration. President Trump ordered the EPA to reopen a midterm review of GHG standards for model year 2022–2025 light trucks, arguing that Obama had hastily closed the review before leaving office.[54] The Trump administration has proposed to freeze the standards at 2021 levels rather than progressively increase them until 2025. Whether the freeze—and a bold preemption of California's regulations—will survive judicial review is far from clear.

Learning a lesson from his first term, President Obama chose executive power to advance his climate agenda during his second term. Collaborating with leaders from Europe and elsewhere, Obama helped make climate change a global priority. In 2014 the United States and China, the world's two largest economies, reached a historic agreement on climate change, vowing to cut carbon emissions over the next two decades. The United States pledged that it would cut its 2005 emissions level by 26 to 28 percent before 2025. China agreed to cap the growth of its carbon emissions and to derive 20 percent of its energy from zero-carbon sources by 2030.[55] This deal was important because China, the world's largest polluter, had previously been reluctant to act on climate change.

At the subsequent 2015 United Nations Climate Change Conference in Paris, Obama and his team worked with representatives of 195 nations to reach a landmark agreement, with nearly every nation committing to a reduction of GHG emissions to combat climate change. Each nation, rich and poor, devised its own voluntary plan to decrease emissions. The participating nations agreed to meet every five years to report on their progress and update their plans.[56] President Obama used the Paris agreement to lend greater credibility to his second-term climate change policies.

In 2013 President Obama announced that he would use executive power to direct the EPA to implement GHG limits on electric power plants, complementing his first-term actions on passenger vehicles. In 2015 Obama finalized the Clean

Power Plan (CPP), which called for a 32 percent reduction in GHG emissions by 2030. The program was designed to shift the generation of electricity from coal to cleaner energy sources such as natural gas, wind, and solar. It gave states flexibility on how to reduce power plant emissions within their borders but compelled sharp reductions in GHG emissions over time.[57] Congressional Democrats and Republicans from coal-producing and coal-using states attacked the CPP as a lawless effort, noting that Congress had not passed Obama's climate legislation in 2009–2010. More than twenty states and many business groups challenged the program, and the case ultimately reached the Supreme Court. In a 5–4 decision, the Supreme Court ordered a halt to implementation of the CPP until the US Court of Appeals for the District of Columbia could resolve some key issues. The case was decided eight months before the passing of conservative justice Antonin Scalia.

Similar to his executive rule-making on light-duty passenger vehicles, President Obama worked with the trucking industry in 2016 to implement a national policy to reduce GHG emissions from medium- and heavy-duty vehicles, which account for 20 percent of GHG emissions in the transportation sector. Through stricter standards and the development of new technology, Obama's plan would cut approximately 1.1 billion tons of carbon pollution, save vehicle owners up to $170 billion in fuel costs, and reduce oil consumption by 82 billion gallons by model year 2027.[58]

The Obama administration and the EPA also proposed regulations to reduce GHG emissions from airplanes. Aviation accounts for 2 percent of global emissions. The EPA expressed interest in working with the international community to establish global standards. Airlines have already begun reducing fuel use and increasing efficiency, since fuel is their largest cost. Given that rule-making processes are lengthy, the final aviation rule had not been completed by the time Obama left office.[59]

The Trump administration is certainly seeking to repeal or scale back much of Obama's climate agenda. It announced plans to formally withdraw from the Paris climate agreement. The EPA also plans to withdraw the CPP, and the federal courts are giving the agency time to decide whether this will be a complete repeal or a replacement of sorts. The standards for light trucks and cars could be relaxed or frozen for model years 2022–2025. However, judicial oversight of Trump's handling of the climate issue will be quite aggressive, and it remains to be seen whether the Trump administration has the rule-making competence to produce judicially defensible decisions on climate change.

In his second term, Obama was correct to pursue climate policy with executive power, given that legislative success was extremely unlikely. With the benefit of hindsight, it is clear that the CPP should have been launched in the first term, since there was insufficient time in the second term for it to be proposed, finalized, litigated, and refined to address judicial concerns. In contrast, Obama's GHG regulations in the transportation sector are much more likely to be retained in some form by the Trump administration, in part because the industry has already made some of the key capital investments to achieve compliance.

In summary, Obama committed a classic tactical error on climate policy in his first and second terms: he forced votes in Congress without a strong chance of victory, delaying an opportunity to make practical progress with executive power. In 2009 he forced a risky "cap and tax" floor vote on moderate Democrats in the House (with no realistic prospect of victory in the Senate) when he could have pursued much of his climate agenda with executive power. The CPP ran into litigation trouble in his second term, but that trouble was partly invited by Obama, as the administration had taken the position in the first term that the EPA lacked adequate statutory authority to address climate change effectively. The challenges to the CPP may have been resolvable with a revised proposal, but by the end of the second term, there was not enough time to fix the CPP. The Trump administration is now in a strong position to delay, weaken, or scuttle the CPP. It would have been much more difficult for the new administration to reverse a completed plan that had been refined and upheld in the federal courts, especially if the industry had already made significant investments to comply. Thus, the Obama legacy on climate change is high on ambition but limited on practical, durable effect.

Immigration

During the 2008 campaign, Barack Obama presented himself as a supporter of the Hispanic community and an advocate of the liberalization of federal immigration law. In fact, he pledged to make comprehensive immigration reform a first-year legislative priority (also see chapter 5 in this volume).

Obama's first term did not work out that way. Economic stimulus, health care, and climate change emerged as higher legislative priorities than immigration. The Department of Homeland Security (DHS) stunned the Hispanic community by tightening the screws on illegal immigration, resulting in many more deportations than took place under George W. Bush.[60] Tensions between the White House and the Hispanic community intensified in 2010 when Obama deployed 1,200 National Guard troops to help Arizona and other states secure the Mexican border.[61] Ambitious deportation quotas were established for each border agent; the capacity of detention centers was increased. As the 2010 midterm elections approached, Obama was widely criticized for not following through on his campaign promises. One leading Hispanic activist put it bluntly: "President Obama has earned the title 'Deporter in Chief.'"[62]

In fairness to Obama, during the lame-duck session of Congress in December 2010, he cooperated with Senate Democrats in a last-ditch effort to pass immigration reform legislation before the GOP took control of the House. Instead of advancing comprehensive reform, Obama and Capitol Hill Democrats proposed the modest Development, Relief, and Education for Alien Minors (DREAM) Act. Their theory was that a limited, targeted liberalization measure might attract sufficient votes in both the Senate and the House.

The DREAM Act had first been introduced in 2001 under the Bush administration. It provided a pathway to citizenship for those who had entered the country illegally before the age of 16 and had worked in the military or attended college for at least two years. It was believed that several hundred thousand young immigrants met the DREAM criteria.

The House, with its comfortable Democratic majority, passed the DREAM Act by a vote of 216–198, with 8 Republicans voting for it and 38 Democrats voting against it. In the Senate, the act fell 5 votes short (55–41) of the 60 needed to overcome a filibuster threat.[63] Three Republicans voted in favor of the bill, and 5 Democrats voted against it.[64] Although the DREAM Act failed to pass, Hispanics took note of Obama's efforts on its behalf and began to look more favorably on his reelection.[65]

In the wake of the DREAM Act's failure, President Obama turned to executive action to advance his immigration policy. In June 2012, several months before the presidential election, the Obama administration instituted the Deferred Action for Childhood Arrivals (DACA) program. DACA allowed certain undocumented immigrants who had entered the United States before their sixteenth birthdays and before June 2007 to receive renewable two-year work permits and exemption from deportation.[66] Early estimates suggested that more than 800,000 migrants were eligible to apply for these permits, which would then open the door to obtaining a Social Security number, a driver's license, professional certificates, and financial aid for college expenses.[67] By the end of 2014, nearly 702,000 unauthorized immigrants had applied for permits, and 87 percent of applicants had been approved.[68] DACA enabled President Obama to secure some of the benefits that would have flowed from passage of the DREAM Act.

Throughout much of his second term, Obama negotiated with House Speaker John Boehner to find a legislative compromise on immigration reform. However, for most House Republicans, who represented districts with few Hispanics, the case for compromise with Obama was weak.[69] A GOP split occurred between establishment Republicans and the Tea Party faction. House majority leader Eric Cantor of Virginia was working on a compromise plan, but in a vote that shocked establishment Republicans, he was defeated in the 2014 primary by a little-known challenger who objected to Cantor's efforts to collaborate with Obama on immigration. The White House, realizing that the GOP could not act, gave up on legislation. Instead, it pledged to the Hispanic community that executive action would be taken by September 2014. Several moderate Senate Democrats objected to this schedule, fearing that the publicity surrounding a pro-immigration plan would compromise their reelection prospects. Obama irritated Hispanics by delaying action until after the midterm elections.

Soon after the November 2014 elections, however, President Obama announced that he would expand DACA. The idea was to extend eligibility to undocumented immigrants who had entered the country before 2010, eliminate the requirement that applicants be younger than 31 years old, and lengthen the renewable deferral period to three years. A new program, Deferred Action for Parents of Americans and Lawful Legal Residents (DAPA), would allow parents of US citizens and lawful permanent residents to request deferred action and employment authorization for three years.[70] It was estimated that the program would shield nearly 5 million undocumented immigrants from deportation.[71]

Conservative activists attacked DAPA as excessive, invalid, and unconstitutional. They urged a federal judge to block implementation of the program, which was set to start in May 2015. On February 16, 2015, Judge Andrew Hanen of the US District Court for the Southern District of Texas issued a restraining order to stop implementation of the program. The injunction granted the request made on behalf of twenty-six states. The Department of Justice appealed the order to the Fifth Circuit Court of New Orleans, which denied the appeal, so the case went to the Supreme Court.[72] *United States v. Texas* resulted in a 4–4 tie (the death of Antonin Scalia had left the Court with only eight justices). The questions before the Court were whether DAPA violated the Administrative Procedure Act (APA), since it had been enacted without public comment, and the take-care clause of the Constitution, which imposed a duty on the president to take due care when executing laws.[73] Another question was whether the states actually had standing to challenge DAPA. Since the merits of the case had never been resolved in the lower courts, a Supreme Court opinion was considered crucial to decide the substantive issues. However, the tie vote in the Supreme Court left the issues unresolved and had the practical effect of upholding the district court's preliminary injunction, thereby blocking implementation of Obama's program. Undocumented immigrants could still apply for work permits under the original DACA program, but the DACA expansion and DAPA were effectively nullified. The judicial outcome was a big setback for Obama's legacy of liberalized immigration.

Obama's second-term executive agenda might have survived litigation under the APA if DAPA had been subject to public comment, conforming to standard rule-making procedures. By making such a brash assertion of constitutional power, the DHS invited judicial scrutiny under the APA, and the federal courts did not even have to address the tricky constitutional issues.

In contrast to the "deporter in chief" image acquired in his first term, President Obama worked with the DHS to slow the pace of deportations in his second term. Between 2009 and 2014 court-ordered deportations dropped 43 percent.[74] In 2015 US Immigration and Customs Enforcement (ICE) deported fewer people than it had since 2006.[75] The Obama administration accomplished this decline by shifting its focus and deporting only those immigrants who had committed crimes other than illegal entry. Although the Hispanic community praised the reduction in deportations, some of the system's serious deficiencies were exposed when a surge of illegal migrants (including many teenaged girls from Honduras) crossed the Mexican border. Many of these people were trying to escape gang violence and poverty and were seeking asylum, believing they would not be treated harshly in the United States.[76] House conservatives criticized the Obama administration for inviting this surge of migrants, a charge the White House denied.[77]

The Obama administration was slow to react to the surge of migrants that occurred during the second term. Large backlogs in the court system developed, and there was an acute shortage of proper detention facilities. As a result, the DHS began to release immigrants inside the United States temporarily, until they had their delayed day in court.[78] Flying the migrants back to their home countries had been standard practice, but that seemed inhumane; however, the schools and health clinics in many US communities were not equipped to handle the influx of migrants from Central America. The Obama administration was unable to persuade Congress to appropriate the funds and build the infrastructure necessary to deal with the surge of immigrants.[79] By the end of Obama's second term, it was apparent that any practical progress on the immigration issue had been limited at best.

In summary, Obama's pursuit of immigration reform with executive power was defensible, despite loss of the plan through subsequent litigation. If the DHS had sought public comment on the plan prior to issuing it, DAPA would have been less vulnerable to litigation under the APA and might have survived. If Obama had started with a DREAM executive order in 2009 (admitting that the Great Recession blocked any realistic prospect for comprehensive legislation), he could have followed up with a broader executive order in 2012, prior to his reelection. Even if the broader order had been set aside due to legal flaws, Obama would have had ample time in his second term to fix those flaws, repropose the plan, and secure judicial approval.

Gun Control

On the campaign trail in 2008, Obama sought common ground with both sides of the gun control debate. He recognized a right to bear arms under the Second Amendment, subject to reasonable regulation. But he also supported the Democratic Party's platform positions: close the gun show loophole, improve the background check system, and reinstate an assault weapons ban.[80] Obama did not emphasize the gun control issue during the 2008 campaign and never pledged to make it a first-year legislative priority on a par with health care, climate change, and immigration.

Not surprisingly, during Obama's first term, gun control was put on the back burner. Indeed, after his first year in office, the Brady Campaign to Prevent Gun Violence gave President Obama a grade of F on gun control.[81] What really annoyed gun control advocates was that Congress passed some measures that actually expanded gun rights. Specifically, in 2009 the Senate passed a bill requiring Amtrak to implement a system to check and track firearms so that passengers could lawfully carry weapons in their checked baggage; the guns had to be unloaded and placed in a securely locked container. The measure passed 68–30 as an amendment to a transportation and housing bill, without any strong opposition from the Obama administration.[82] After the Senate bill was reconciled with the House version, President Obama signed it into law.

In 2010 gun rights were expanded again when Congress voted to allow people to carry concealed weapons in national parks. Each park was authorized to follow the policy of the state where it was located. As a result, guns were permitted in all but 20 of the 392 National Park Service locations.[83] The measure passed the Senate 90–5 and the House 361–64 under the Credit Cardholders' Bill of Rights.[84] President Obama signed the bill into law, thereby making it easier for gun owners to travel between state and federal lands.

In his reelection bid against Mitt Romney in 2012, Obama did not place great emphasis on the gun control issue. But soon after his victory, he seized on tragedy to make a case for progress against gun violence. In December 2012 (after the election but before the start of Obama's second term), six adults and twenty children between the ages of 6 and 7 were fatally shot at Sandy Hook Elementary School in Newtown, Connecticut.[85] It was the third deadliest shooting in US history, and it received massive media attention throughout the country.

President Obama reordered his legislative priorities and launched an aggressive gun control agenda at the start of his second term. Vice President Joe Biden spearheaded a month-long review process, and then the administration released an ambitious legislative proposal.[86] The proposal required criminal background checks for all gun owners, reinstated a ban on assault weapons, restored a ten-round limit on ammunition magazines, and eliminated armor-piercing bullets. The proposal also increased mental health services in schools, allocated funds to hire more police officers, and implemented a federal gun trafficking statute. The total package was estimated to cost $500 million.[87]

Knowing that his proposal might be a hard sell in Congress, President Obama supplemented it with twenty-three executive actions in 2013. Many of them sought to improve the quality of the background check system and promote responsible gun ownership.[88] Other actions included greater school resources, enhanced mental health services, and better training in active shooting situations for law enforcement officers and first responders. The executive actions were limited in their practical impact. Some served only as guidance for federal agencies. The more ambitious measures required new legislation from Congress to obtain funding or acquire new regulatory authority.

By June 2016, President Obama had given fourteen speeches in response to a series of mass shootings. Nine people were killed in June 2015 during a prayer service at a church in Charleston, South Carolina. Fourteen people were killed in December 2015 in a terrorist attack at the Inland Regional Center in San Bernardino, California. In June 2016 forty-nine people were killed in an attack inside Pulse, a gay nightclub in Orlando, Florida.[89] President Obama addressed the nation after these and countless other incidents, urging Congress to act on gun control. In response to the Charleston shootings, Obama stated:

> I've had to make statements like this too many times. Communities have had to endure tragedies like this too many times. Once again, innocent people were killed in part because someone who wanted to inflict harm had no trouble getting their hands on a gun. . . . We as a country will have to reckon with the fact that this type of mass violence does not happen in other advanced countries.[90]

In contrast to his virtual silence from 2009 to 2012, President Obama made good use of the bully pulpit to highlight gun violence and to urge Congress to act. Still, despite repeated calls for legislative action, Obama could not persuade Congress to enact his gun control agenda. His efforts were defeated in 2013 when the Senate could not find the 60 votes necessary to block a filibuster of the agenda. When votes were taken on specific measures, only 40 senators voted in favor of an assault weapons ban, and only 46 senators supported limiting the size of ammunition magazines.

The proposal that came closest to success was the Manchin-Toomey plan to expand background checks to most gun sales. It was a genuinely bipartisan effort sponsored by Joe Manchin (a moderate Democratic senator from West Virginia) and Pat Toomey (a conservative senator from Pennsylvania). The proposal fell 6 votes short (54–46) of the 60 required to overcome the filibuster threat. It was largely a party-line vote, but 4 Democrats voted against the measure and 4 Republicans supported it. Public opinion polls showed that nine out of ten Americans supported the basic idea of expanding background checks.[91] President Obama blamed the National Rifle Association's campaign against the Manchin-Toomey bill for its defeat. But even if the Senate had passed the measure, it is highly unlikely that the GOP-controlled House would have followed suit.

President Obama announced another series of executive actions in January 2016, focused on five main goals: keeping guns out of the wrong hands through background checks, making communities safer from gun violence, increasing mental health treatment, expanding reports to the background check system, and shaping the future of gun safety technology.[92] But these actions were far short of what could be accomplished with legislative action.

In the summer of 2016 the Democrats again attempted to move legislative reform on gun control through Congress. Immediately following the Pulse nightclub shooting, Senator Chris Murphy from Connecticut staged a filibuster that lasted fourteen hours and fifty minutes, calling for action on gun violence. By disrupting Senate deliberations, Senator Murphy won promises that two measures would come to a vote: one to ensure that people on terrorist watch lists could not acquire guns, and the other to expand background checks to gun shows and internet sales.[93] A few days after the filibuster, House Democrats staged a sit-in for more than twenty-four hours to protest the lack of action on gun control. More than 170 lawmakers participated in the sit-in, but the House Republican leadership refused floor time for any votes on gun control.[94]

Over the course of the summer, the Senate voted on four gun control measures as amendments to HR 2578 (centered on improving background checks and preventing suspected terrorists from obtaining guns), but all were defeated.[95] None of the votes came any closer to passing than the Manchin-Toomey proposal. For gun control advocates, their disappointment was no longer with Obama; it was with Congress. Some hoped that, in light of public support for gun control and Obama's aggressive use of the bully pulpit, Republican votes against gun control would hurt GOP candidates in forthcoming elections. However, based on the 2014 midterm election results—another wave of success for the GOP—there was no evidence to support this theory.

Although President Obama was unable to get Congress to act on gun violence, his use of the bully pulpit helped shape the 2016 Democratic Party platform, which was much longer and more comprehensive than it had been in either 2008 or 2012. The platform drew attention to statistics on gun violence and urged even more aggressive countermeasures. From a counterfactual perspective, it is not clear what else Obama could have done in his second term to advance the cause of gun control.

The 2014 Midterms: Massacre Redux

During the 2010 midterm elections, the Democratic Party suffered a political massacre. The Democrats started with a 257–178 House majority and lost a net 64 seats, allowing the GOP to take over the House with a 242–193 majority. In the Senate, the Democrats lost 6 seats, reducing their majority from 59 to 53.[96] The GOP succeeded in nationalizing the 2010 midterm elections, making them a referendum on President Obama's policies and performance.[97]

Coming into the 2014 midterm elections, the Obama administration sought to protect congressional Democrats and prevent a repeat of the 2010 "shellacking." The White House focused on the nation's economic recovery and Obama's ambitious second-term agenda. As the economic recovery accelerated in 2013–2014, Democrats expected to reap some political benefit from the declining unemployment rate, the rise in consumer confidence, the surge in car and home sales, and the rising stock market (see table 9.1). However, the jobs-to-people ratio, a good indicator of job creation, was not improving rapidly; nor was household income increasing very fast. In addition, a persistently high rate of poverty was coupled with stubbornly high rates of household participation in SNAP. As a result, there was simply not much economic enthusiasm for Obama or for the Democrats in Congress. Voters were certainly unhappy with the obstructionism of the GOP leadership in Congress, but they were also discouraged by President Obama's ineffectiveness in moving an agenda through Congress.

President Obama started his second term with an approval rating of 46 percent.[98] However, 2013 was an unproductive and demoralizing year for the White House, as virtually none of Obama's initiatives made it through Congress. Obama started his sixth year in office with a job approval rating of 52 percent—lower than for all other presidents in their sixth years (except for Harry Truman and George W. Bush) since modern polling began in the 1930s.[99] Actually, Obama had received a temporary boost in public support by winning the budgetary confrontation with the House GOP in the fall of 2013. But before those gains could be solidified, embarrassing snafus in implementation of the ACA caused massive negative publicity for the president. In April and June 2014 Obama's approval rating continued to decline, dropping as low as 41 percent.[100] Lingering economic insecurity and inaction on Obama's second-term agenda contributed to these ratings. Recognizing Obama's vulnerabilities, the GOP set its sights on the big prize: majority control of the US Senate. Without Obama on the ballot to stimulate voting by African Americans and young people, the Democrats faced an electorate in 2014 that was predisposed to vote for the GOP.

Senate majority leader Harry Reid was in a difficult position coming into the 2014 midterm elections. He wanted to protect President Obama's first-term accomplishments (such as the ACA) and move his second-term agenda through the Senate, but he also wanted to protect the Democrats' 55–45 majority by avoiding any roll-call votes that would leave them vulnerable. (Reid himself was facing a tough reelection battle in Nevada.) Reid blocked votes on a variety of issues that would have resulted in a bipartisan group of senators defecting from the Obama administration.[101] Thus, Senate Democrats came into the election with apparent unity but also with little opportunity for moderate Democrats in GOP-leaning states to separate themselves from Obama's policies and low approval rating.

In the House, Republicans started with a 234–201 majority. The outcome of the 2014 election actually increased their majority to 247–188, despite having far more seats at risk than the Democrats. In the Senate, Democrats started with a 55–45 majority. The Republicans gained 9 seats, seizing control of the chamber by a 54–46 majority.[102] As had been the case in 2010, the GOP also made significant electoral gains in governorships and control of state legislatures. Taken together,

Table 9.3. Midterm Congressional Losses by the President's Party, 1946–2014

Year	President	Party	Net House Seats Gained/Lost	Net Senate Seats Gained/Lost
1946	Truman	D	−45	−12
1950	Truman	D	−29	−6
1954	Eisenhower	R	−18	−1
1958	Eisenhower	R	−48	−13
1962	Kennedy	D	−4	3
1966	Johnson	D	−47	−4
1970	Nixon	R	−12	2
1974	Ford	R	−48	−5
1978	Carter	D	−15	−3
1982	Reagan	R	−26	1
1986	Reagan	R	−5	−8
1990	G. H. W. Bush	R	−8	−1
1994	Clinton	D	−52	−8
1998	Clinton	D	5	0
2002	G. W. Bush	R	8	2
2006	G. W. Bush	R	−30	−6
2010	Obama	D	−63	−6
2014	Obama	D	−13	−9

the Democratic Party's losses in Obama's two midterm elections were among the largest in any administration since World War II (see table 9.3).

A Supreme Court Stalemate

For the first time since being elected in 2008, President Obama faced a Republican majority in both chambers in January 2015. The Republican majority in the Senate did not simply limit his ability to enact legislation. It made it difficult for him to appoint a new justice to the US Supreme Court.

Justice Antonin Scalia died in February 2016, creating a vacancy on the Supreme Court. Republican leaders vowed to block any nominee until after the next president was chosen. In March, President Obama nominated Merrick Garland, a centrist judge on the DC Circuit Court of Appeals, to fill the seat. Obama ignored supporters' advice to pressure Republicans by nominating a member of a racial minority, and liberals were upset that he did not nominate a more progressive voice.[103] Republicans simply refused to give Garland a hearing.[104] Even if the Democrats had held the Senate, it would have taken 60 votes to confirm Garland or any Obama nominee, and the GOP could have blocked the confirmation with a filibuster threat.[105] But if the Democrats had held the Senate, they could have changed the Senate rules and allowed Garland to be confirmed by majority vote. Thus, the Democrats' loss of the Senate majority in 2014 was a crippling blow to their prospects for filling another Supreme Court seat.

Conclusion: Obama's Domestic Legacy

The Democratic Party faced some promising opportunities coming into the 2016 elections. Throughout the year, the economy and Obama's approval rating had improved. Apart from focusing on the presidential election, Democrats hoped to take back the Senate and make significant gains in the House. After a bitter primary season, the GOP had nominated a controversial candidate, Donald Trump, who posted some of the most negative ratings for a presidential candidate in recent history.[106] As the general election drew closer, Hillary Clinton was the odds-on favorite to occupy the White House in 2017.

The November 2016 election was certainly a stunner. Trump managed a comfortable victory in the Electoral College (304 to 227), despite losing the popular vote to Clinton (48.03 to 45.94 percent). In the House, the GOP lost only six seats (although three other members later resigned to accept positions in the Trump administration). The Republicans thereby maintained control of the House by a margin of 241–194. In the Senate, the GOP lost two seats but kept control with a 52–48 majority.[107] The GOP's trifecta was unexpected.

Of course, it is not entirely clear how much President Obama's domestic policies affected the results of the 2016 election. For sure, Donald Trump ran a campaign that was diametrically opposed to Obama's policies in virtually all key respects. Trump succeeded in energizing an anti-Obama base, and his success in the election can be seen—at least in part—as a rejection of some of Obama's policies.[108] Yet Obama's popularity continued to rise during 2015–2016 and was close to 60 percent by early 2017.

There are plenty of alternative (or complementary) explanations for Trump's victory. Trump's focus on manufacturing and the loss of jobs to China and Mexico brought into play industrial states that had previously been safe country for Democrats. In addition, Hillary Clinton was a highly unpopular and uninspiring candidate, and some argued the country was not ready for a female president.[109] Another fundamental issue was that the Democratic Party could not energize its base to get out and vote as it had when Obama's name was on the ballot. Relatively low Democratic voter turnout (among African Americans, young people, and Hispanics) contributed to Clinton's loss (e.g., in Michigan, Pennsylvania, and Wisconsin) and to the Democratic Party's inability to achieve large partisan gains in the House and Senate.[110]

Table 9.4. Summary of Obama's Second-Term Initiatives

Initiative	Executive (E) or Legislative (L) Action	Enacted	Blocked/Defeated	Comment
Second stimulus package	L	American Taxpayer Relief Act of 2012 (January 2013) House: 257–167 Democrats: 172–16 Republicans: 85–151 Senate: 89–8 Democrats: 49–3 Republicans: 40–5		Repeal of Bush tax cuts for high earners
Minimum wage	L		Fair Minimum Wage Act defeated in House (March 2013) Minimum Wage Fairness Act defeated in Senate (April 2014) Raise the Wage Act introduced in Senate, not voted on (2015)	
Minimum wage	E	Executive Order 13658 (February 2014)		Raised minimum wage for federal contract workers
Infrastructure agenda	L	Introduced in 2013 budget	No congressional action	
Tax reform	L	Introduced in 2016 budget	No congressional action	

(continued on the next page)

Table 9.4. (*continued*)

Initiative	Executive (E) or Legislative (L) Action	Enacted	Blocked/Defeated	Comment
Trans-Pacific Partnership	L	Senate grants Obama fast-track authority by a vote of 60–38 (April 2015)		Asian and EU trade deals died in Congress
Launch of healthcare.gov	E	October 2013		Many implementation snafus
Climate deal with China	E	Signed 2014		
UN Climate Conference (Paris)	E	Agreement signed 2015		Congressional action required to meet objectives
Clean Power Plan (CPP)	E		Supreme Court halts implementation of CPP with 5–4 decision (2016)	
Rules on GHG emissions for heavy-duty vehicles	E	Standards issued August 2016 through EPA		
Regulation of GHG emissions for airplanes	E	Initial steps taken June 2015; rules not yet released		
Veto of Keystone Pipeline	E	Senate fails to override veto with 62–37 vote (2015)		
Immigration: expansion of DACA and implementation of DAPA	E		4–4 Supreme Court ruling in *United States v. Texas* blocks implementation of programs	
Gun control	L		Senate filibusters all major proposals; no House action	
Gun control	E	23 executive actions signed (January 2016)	Senate shuts down all major proposals	

So what is Obama's domestic legacy likely to be, given what we know today? What we can say for sure is that the state of the US economy improved significantly in the Obama years, especially during his second term. Economists will forever debate the causes of the recovery and whether—with different policies—it could have been stronger, faster, and more focused on the well-being of low-income and working-class Americans. Nonetheless, insofar as presidents are judged by what happens on their watch, Obama deserves some credit for the transition from a frightening economic mess to one of the healthiest economies in the world. Obama and the Democratic Party did not benefit as much as they might have from the economic progress, but positive economic indicators speak for themselves.

The conventional wisdom is that health care reform was Obama's signature domestic achievement. We urge caution with respect to this viewpoint. Multiple avenues of litigation against the ACA have continued during the Trump administration. For example, a federal judge in Texas ruled that the entire ACA is unconstitutional.[111] It remains to be seen how much of that opinion will hold up under judicial appeals. Even if the ACA survives the Trump years (which it may not), the ACA was much more politically costly to the Democratic Party than it needed to be. The link between Obama and the ACA—and the resulting decline in his popularity—was instrumental in the GOP's takeover of the House, the Senate, and many states and localities. With a better design and more competent implementation, the ACA could have been much less politically damaging to Obama and his party.

Obama was effective in a variety of domestic policy arenas, but his effectiveness was hampered by an extremely polarized political environment. Polarization preceded his presidency, but it became more intense during his two terms in office. The Trump administration is working to reverse, delay, or revise several of Obama's domestic accomplishments. Still, to the extent that these efforts also rest on executive action, it remains to be seen how durable Trump's changes will be.

Notes

1. John D. Graham, *Obama on the Home Front: Domestic Policy Triumphs and Setbacks* (Bloomington: Indiana University Press, 2016), chap. 2.
2. Kristin S. Seefeldt and John D. Graham, *America's Poor and the Great Recession* (Bloomington: Indiana University Press, 2013).
3. Graham, *Obama on the Home Front*, chaps. 3 and 4.
4. American Taxpayer Relief Act of 2012, H.R. 8, 112th Cong. §112-240.
5. Will Wrigley, "House Republicans Unanimously Vote down Minimum Wage Increase," *Huffington Post*, March 15, 2013, http://www.huffingtonpost.com/2013/03/15/gop -minimum-wage-increase_n_2884912.html.
6. Wesley Lowery, "Senate Republicans Block Minimum Wage Increase Bill," *Washington Post*, April 30, 2014, https://www.washingtonpost.com/news/post-politics/wp/2014

/04/30/senate-republicans-block-minimum-wage-increase-bill/?utm_term=.e71eb c8aadbb.

7. US Department of Labor, "Executive Order 13658 Fact Sheet," last modified June 2014, https://www.dol.gov/whd/flsa/nprm-eo13658/factsheet.htm.

8. "Raise the Wage," whitehouse.gov, accessed October 8, 2016, https://www.white house.gov/raise-the-wage.

9. Jared Bernstein, "The Raise the Wage Act: The New Proposal to Raise the Federal Minimum Wage to $12 in 2020," *Washington Post*, April 30, 2015, https://www.washing tonpost.com/posteverything/wp/2015/04/30/the-raise-the-wage-act-the-new-proposal-to -raise-the-federal-minimum-wage-to-12-in-2020/?utm_term=.18c6 51876855.

10. Graham, *Obama on the Home Front*, chap. 4.

11. Aaron Hellman, "Why Did the U.S. Government Shut down in October 2013?" *Huffington Post*, January 23, 2014, http://www.huffingtonpost.com/quora/why-did -the-us-government_b_4064789.html.

12. Graham, *Obama on the Home Front*, chap. 4.

13. Julie Pace, "Obama Promoting Public Works Plan in Miami," *Huffington Post*, March 29, 2013, http://www.huffingtonpost.com/2013/03/29/obama-miami_n_2978184 .html.

14. Heather Long, "The Final GOP Tax Bill Is Complete. Here's What Is in It," *Washington Post*, December 15, 2017, https://www.washingtonpost.com/news/wonk/wp/2017/12 /15/the-final-gop-tax-bill-is-complete-heres-what-is-in-it/?noredirect=on&utm_term =.b5ac35c3f47b.

15. Ibid.

16. John Kerry, "Successful Conclusion of Trans-Pacific Partnership Negotiations," US Department of State, October 5, 2015, http://www.state.gov/secretary/remarks/2015 /10/247870.htm.

17. "TPP: What Is It and Why Does It Matter?" BBC, July 27, 2016, http://www.bbc .com/news/business-32498715.

18. Adam Taylor, "A Timeline of Trump's Complicated Relationship with the TPP," *Washington Post*, April 13, 2018, https://www.washingtonpost.com/news/worldviews/wp /2018/04/13/a-timeline-of-trumps-complicated-relationship-with-the-tpp/?utm _term=.c44ee41fc2a4.

19. Graham, *Obama on the Home Front*, chap. 4.

20. Arthur Berman, "Why the Oil Price Collapse Is U.S. Shale's Fault," oilprice.com, April 6, 2015, http://oilprice.com/Energy/Oil-Prices/Why-The-Oil-Price-Collapse-Is -U.S.-Shales-Fault.html.

21. US Energy Information Administration, "U.S. Field Production of Crude Oil (Thousand Barrels)," Petroleum and Other Liquids, accessed June 6, 2017, https://www.eia .gov/dnav/pet/hist/LeafHandler.ashx?n=PET&s=MCRFPUS1&f=A.

22. Graham, *Obama on the Home Front*, chap. 8.

23. US Energy Information Administration, "Cushing, OK WTI Spot Price FOB," Petroleum and Other Liquids, accessed June 6, 2017, https://www.eia.gov/dnav/pet /hist/LeafHandler.ashx?n=PET&s=RWTC&f=D.

24. US Energy Information Administration, "US All Grades All Formulations Retail Gasoline Prices," Petroleum and Other Liquids, accessed June 6, 2017, https://www.eia .gov/dnav/pet/hist/LeafHandler.ashx?n=pet&s=emm_epm0_pte_nus_dpg&f=m.

25. US Department of Labor, Bureau of Labor Statistics, "Labor Force Statistics from the Current Population Survey," series LNS14000000, accessed December 20, 2016, http://data.bls.gov/timeseries/LNS14000000.

26. US Census Bureau, "Income, Poverty and Health Insurance Coverage in the United States: 2015," press release CB16-158, September 13, 2016, http://www.census.gov /newsroom/press-releases/2016/cb16-158.html.

27. Amanda Noss, "Household Income for States: 2010 and 2011," *U.S. Census Bureau American Community Survey Briefs*, September 2012, http://www.census.gov/prod /2012pubs/acsbr11-02.pdf; Annalyn Censky, "Poverty Rate Rises in America," CNN, September 23, 2011, http://money.cnn.com/2011/09/13/news/economy/poverty _rate_income/index.htm.

28. Graham, *Obama on the Home Front*, chap. 10; Michael K. Gusmano, "Health Care Reform," in *The Obama Presidency: A Preliminary Assessment*, ed. Robert P. Watson et al. (Albany, NY: SUNY Press, 2012), 199; Michael Lee, "Adverse Reactions: Structure, Philosophy, and Outcomes of the Affordable Care Act," *Yale Law and Policy Review* 29, 2 (2011): 559–602.

29. Steven Brill, *America's Bitter Pill* (New York: Random House, 2015); Maggie Fox, "26,000 Signed up on Federal Obamacare Website in First Month: Administration," NBC News, November 13, 2013, http://www.nbcnews.com/health/26 -000-signed-through-federal-obamacare-website-first-month-administration -2D11591428.

30. Graham, *Obama on the Home Front*, chap. 6.

31. Tim Carmody, "Inside the Failure of Healthcare.gov," *Newsweek*, October 31, 2013, http://www.newsweek.com/inside-healthcaregovs-failure-1449.

32. National Federation of Independent Business v. Sebelius, 200 U.S. 321 (2012).

33. King v. Burwell, 135 S. Ct. 2480 (2015).

34. "Status of State Medicaid Expansion Decisions," Kaiser Family Foundation, last modified July 27, 2018, https://www.kff.org/health-reform/slide/current-status-of-the -medicaid-expansion-decision/.

35. Ibid.

36. Louise Radnofsky and Stephanie Armour, "U.S. Health Law Faces Critical Year," *Wall Street Journal*, September 7, 2016, http://www.wsj.com/articles/u-s-health-law-faces -critical-year-1473262868.

37. Graham, *Obama on the Home Front*, chap. 6.

38. "Payments of Penalties for Being Uninsured under the Affordable Care Act: 2014 Update," Congressional Budget Office, 2014, https://www.cbo.gov/sites/default/files /113th-congress-2013-2014/reports/45397-IndividualMandate.pdf.

39. Dan Mangan, "States Shuttering Obamacare Exchanges, but Should They?" CNBC, July 22, 2015, http://www.cnbc.com/2015/07/22/states-shuttering-obamacare-ex changes-but-should-they.html.

40. Jonathan Cohn, "Why Some Obamacare Insurers Are Making Money, but Many Are Losing Big," *Huffington Post*, May 16, 2016, http://www.huffingtonpost.com /entry/obamacare-health-insurance_us_573a00dce4b060aa781ad6cc; Ron Hurtibise, "Aetna Was Actually Making Money off Obamacare in Florida, Ruling Reveals," *Sun Sentinel*, January 27, 2017, http://www.sun-sentinel.com/business/consumer /fl-aetna-humana-sofla-angle-20170127-story.html.

41. Jeffrey Young, "These Health Insurance Companies Are Winning at Obamacare," *Huffington Post*, January 27, 2014, http://www.huffingtonpost.com/2014/01/27/health-insurance-obamacare_n_4661164.html.

42. John Dawsey, Jennifer Haberkorn, and Paul Demko, "Trump Tells Advisers He Wants to End Key Obamacare Subsidies," *Politico*, May 19, 2017, http://www.politico.com/story/2017/05/19/donald-trump-end-payments-obamacare-subsidies-238616.

43. Department of Health and Human Services, "20 Million People Have Gained Health Insurance Coverage Because of the Affordable Care Act, New Estimates Show," HHS.gov, March 3, 2016, http://www.hhs.gov/about/news/2016/03/03/20-million-people-have-gained-health-insurance-coverage-because-affordable-care-act-new-estimates.

44. "U.S. Uninsured Rate at New Low of 10.9% in Third Quarter," Gallup, October 7, 2016, http://www.gallup.com/poll/196193/uninsured-rate-new-low-third-quarter.aspx?g_source=uninsured&g_medium=search&g_campaign=tiles.

45. Council of Economic Advisers, "Recent Trends in Health Care Costs," whitehouse.gov, September 24, 2014, https://www.whitehouse.gov/sites/default/files/docs/recent_trends_in_health_care_costs_9.24.14.pdf.

46. Graham, *Obama on the Home Front*, chap. 6.

47. Long, "Final GOP Tax Bill Is Complete"; Larry Levitt, "The Trump Administration's Hidden Attacks on the Affordable Care Act," *Washington Post*, January 5, 2018, https://www.washingtonpost.com/opinions/the-trump-administrations-hidden-attacks-on-the-affordable-care-act/2018/01/05/bd7002da-f237-11e7-97bf-bba379b809ab_story.html?utm_term=.56afd74e83eb.

48. Graham, *Obama on the Home Front*, chap. 6.

49. Ronald Brownstein, "Under Pressure," *National Journal*, May 17, 2014, 9.

50. Graham, *Obama on the Home Front*, chap. 7.

51. Carl Hulse and David M. Herszenhorn, "Democrats Call off Climate Effort," *New York Times*, July 22, 2009, http://www.nytimes.com/2010/07/23/us/politics/23cong.html.

52. "Sources of Greenhouse Gas Emissions," US Environmental Protection Agency, http://www3.epa.gov/climatechange.

53. Bill Vlasic, "US Sets Higher Fuel Efficiency Standards," *New York Times*, August 28, 2012, http://www.nytimes.com/2012/08/29/business/energy-environment/obama-unveils-tighter-fuel-efficiency-standards.html?_r=0.

54. Paul Eisenstein, "Trump Rolls Back Obama-Era Fuel Economy Standards," NBC, March 16, 2017, http://www.nbcnews.com/business/autos/trump-rolls-back-obama-era-fuel-economy-standards-n734256.

55. Matt Hoye and Holly Yan, "U.S. and China Reach Historic Climate Change Deal, Vow to Cut Emissions," CNN, November 12, 2014, http://www.cnn.com/2014/11/12/world/us-china-climate-change-agreement/index.html.

56. Coral Davenport, "Nations Approve Landmark Climate Accord in Paris," *New York Times*, December 12, 2015, http://www.nytimes.com/2015/12/13/world/europe/climate-change-accord-paris.html.

57. Brent Kendall and Amy Harder, "Obama Power Plant Emissions Rule Faces Key Test in Court," *Wall Street Journal*, September 26, 2016, A6.

58. "Fact Sheet: Obama Administration Announces New Actions to Spur Innovation and Promote More Efficient Cars and Trucks," whitehouse.gov, 2016, https://www.white

house.gov/the-press-office/2016/08/16/fact-sheet-obama-administration-announces
-new-actions-spur-innovation.

59. Jad Mouawad and Coral Davenport, "E.P.A. Takes Steps to Cut Emissions from
    Planes," *New York Times*, June 10, 2015, http://www.nytimes.com/2015/06/11/busi
    ness/energy-environment/epa-says-it-will-set-rules-for-airplane-emissions.html.

60. Frank James, "Deportations Higher under Obama than Bush," NPR, July 26, 2010,
    http://www.npr.org/sections/thetwo-way/2010/07/26/128772646/deportations
    -higher-under-obama-than-bush.

61. Michael Shear and Spencer Hsu, "President Obama to Send More National Guard
    Troops to U.S.-Mexico Border," *Washington Post*, May 26, 2010, http://www.wash
    ingtonpost.com/wp-dyn/content/article/2010/05/25/AR2010052503227.html.

62. Eyder Peralta, "National Council of La Raza Dubs Obama 'Deporter in Chief,'" NPR,
    March 4, 2014, http://www.npr.org/sections/thetwo-way/2014/03/04/285907255
    /national-council-of-la-raza-dubs-obama-deporter-in-chief.

63. Naftali Bendavid, "Dream Act Fails in Senate," *Wall Street Journal*, December 19,
    2010, http://www.wsj.com/articles/SB1000142405274870436800457602757084
    3930428.

64. "Removal Clarification Act of 2010: Roll Vote No. 278," H.R. 5281, December 18,
    2010, http://www.senate.gov/legislative/LIS/roll_call_lists/roll_call_vote_cfm.cfm?con
    gress=111&session=2&vote=00278.

65. Graham, *Obama on the Home Front*, chap. 9.

66. US Citizenship and Immigration Services, "Consideration of Deferred Action for
    Childhood Arrivals (DACA)," USCIS.gov, https://www.uscis.gov/humanitarian/con
    sideration-deferred-action-childhood-arrivals-daca#guidelines.

67. Julia Preston and John Cushman Jr., "Obama to Permit Young Migrants to Remain
    in U.S.," *New York Times*, June 15, 2012, http://www.nytimes.com/2012/06/16/us
    /us-to-stop-deporting-some-illegal-immigrants.html?_r=0.

68. Jens Manuel Krogstad and Ana Gonzalez-Barrera, "If Original DACA Program Is a
    Guide, Many Eligible Immigrants Will Apply for Deportation Relief," Pew Research
    Center, December 5, 2014, http://www.pewresearch.org/fact-tank/2014/12/05/if-orig
    inal-daca-program-is-a-guide-many-eligible-immigrants-will-apply-for-deportation
    -relief/.

69. Graham, *Obama on the Home Front*, chap. 9.

70. US Citizenship and Immigration Services, "Executive Actions on Immigration," US-
    CIS.gov, https://www.uscis.gov/immigrationaction.

71. David Leopold, "DAPA Eligible Immigrants Will Not Be Deported and 3 Other
    Things You Need to Know about the GOP Immigration Lawsuit," *Huffington Post*,
    February 23, 2015, http://www.huffingtonpost.com/david-leopold/dapa-eligible-im
    migrants-_b_6726192.html.

72. Adam Liptak and Michael Shear, "Supreme Court to Hear Challenge to Obama's
    Immigration Actions," *New York Times*, January 19, 2016, http://www.nytimes.com
    /2016/01/20/us/politics/supreme-court-to-hear-challenge-to-obama-immigration
    -actions.html.

73. United States v. Texas, 579 U.S. ___ (2016).

74. Julia Preston, "Court Deportations Drop 43 Percent in Last Five Years," *New York
    Times*, April 16, 2014, http://www.nytimes.com/2014/04/17/us/us-deportations
    -drop-43-percent-in-last-five-years.html.

75. Eyder Peralts, "In 2015, Deportations Reached Lowest Level since 2006," NPR, December 23, 2015, http://www.npr.org/sections/thetwo-way/2015/12/23/460797215/in-2015-deportations-reached-lowest-level-since-2006.

76. P. J. Tobia, "No Country for Lost Kids," PBS, June 20, 2014, http://www.pbs.org/newshour/updates/country-lost-kids/.

77. Leigh Caldwell, "Political Chatter: Obama Blamed for Immigration Influx," CNN, July 6, 2014, http://www.cnn.com/2014/07/06/politics/political-chatter-immigration/index.html.

78. Alicia Caldwell, "Obama Administration Sharply Reduces Number of Deportations," PBS, September 11, 2014, http://www.pbs.org/newshour/rundown/obama-administration-sharply-reduces-number-deportations/.

79. White House Office of the Press Secretary, "The Obama Administration's Government-Wide Response to Influx of Central American Migrants at the Southwest Border," press release, August 1, 2014, https://www.whitehouse.gov/the-press-office/2014/08/01/obama-administration-s-government-wide-response-influx-central-american-.

80. "2008 Democratic Party Platform," August 25, 2008, American Presidency Project, Gerhard Peters and John T. Woolley, http://www.presidency.ucsb.edu/ws/?pid=78283.

81. Mark Memmott, "Brady Campaign Gives President 'F' on Gun Control; Calls Him 'Abject Failure,'" NPR, January 18, 2010, http://www.npr.org/sections/thetwo-way/2010/01/brady_campaign_gives_obama_an.html.

82. Evan Glass, "Senate Passes Measure to Allow Gun Transport on Amtrak," CNN, September 16, 2009, http://www.cnn.com/2009/POLITICS/09/16/amtrak.guns/.

83. Ed O'Keefe, "National Parks Gun Law Takes Effect in February," *Washington Post*, May 22, 2009, http://voices.washingtonpost.com/federal-eye/2009/05/national_parks_gun_law_take_ef.html.

84. "Credit Cardholders' Bill of Rights Act of 2009: Roll Vote No. 194," *Congressional Record*, May 19, 2009, http://www.senate.gov/legislative/LIS/roll_call_lists/roll_call_vote_cfm.cfm?congress=111&session=1&vote=00194; "Credit Cardholders' Bill of Rights Act of 2009: Roll Vote No. 277," *Congressional Record*, May 20, 2009, http://clerk.house.gov/evs/2009/roll277.xml.

85. "Connecticut Shooting Fast Facts," CNN, October 24, 2016, http://www.cnn.com/2013/06/07/us/connecticut-shootings-fast-facts/index.html.

86. Sam Stein, "Obama Gun Control Proposals Unveiled, Marking Biggest Legislative Effort in Generation," *Huffington Post*, January 17, 2013, http://www.huffingtonpost.com/2013/01/16/obama-gun-control-proposals_n_2486919.html.

87. Ibid.

88. "List: Obama's 23 Executive Actions on Gun Violence," *Washington Wire* (blog), *Wall Street Journal*, January 16, 2013, http://blogs.wsj.com/washwire/2013/01/16/list-obamas-23-executive-actions-on-gun-violence/.

89. Gregory Korte, "14 Mass Shootings, 14 Speeches: How Obama Has Responded," *USA Today*, June 12, 2016, http://www.usatoday.com/story/news/politics/2016/06/12/14-mass-shootings-14-speeches-how-obama-has-responded/85798652/.

90. Barack Obama, "Statement by the President on the Shooting in Charleston, South Carolina," June 18, 2015.

91. Ed O'Keefe and Philip Rucker, "Gun-Control Overhaul Is Defeated in Senate," *Washington Post*, April 17, 2013, https://www.washingtonpost.com/politics/gun

-control-overhaul-is-defeated-in-senate/2013/04/17/57eb028a-a77c-11e2-b029-8fb 7e977ef71_story.html.

92. White House Office of the Press Secretary, "Fact Sheet: New Executive Actions to Reduce Gun Violence and Make Our Communities Safer," January 4, 2016, https:// www.whitehouse.gov/the-press-office/2016/01/04/fact-sheet-new-executive-actions -reduce-gun-violence-and-make-our.

93. Deirdre Walsh and Tom LoBianco, "Nearly 15 Hours Later, Democratic Senator Ends Filibuster over Guns," CNN, June 16, 2016, http://www.cnn.com/2016/06/15 /politics/gun-filibuster-senate-democrat/.

94. Deirdre Walsh, Manu Raju, Eric Bradner, and Steven Sloan, "Democrats End House Sit-in Protest over Gun Control," CNN, June 24, 2016, http://www.cnn .com/2016/06/22/politics/john-lewis-sit-in-gun-violence/.

95. Amber Phillips, "The Senate Voted on 4 Popular Gun Control Proposals Monday. Here's Why None of Them Passed," *Washington Post*, June 20, 2016, https://www.wash ingtonpost.com/news/the-fix/wp/2016/06/20/the-senate-will-vote-on-4-gun-control -proposals-monday-heres-everything-you-need-to-know/?utm_term=.5799c2f9393a.

96. Reuters, "Elections 2010," http://www.reuters.com/politics/elections-2010.

97. Gary Jacobson, "Polarization, Public Opinion, and the Presidency: The Obama and Anti-Obama Coalitions," in Watson et al., *Obama Presidency*, 98.

98. "Presidential Approval Ratings—Barack Obama," Gallup, 2016, http://www.gallup .com/poll/116479/Barack-Obama-Presidential-Job-Approval.aspx.

99. Neil King Jr. and Patrick O'Connor, "Poll Finds Americans Anxious over Future, Obama's Performance," *Wall Street Journal*, January 28, 2014, http://www.wsj.com /articles/SB10001424052702303277704579347030062444064.

100. Ibid.

101. Charlie Cook, "Blocking the Vote," *National Journal*, July 26, 2014, https://www .nationaljournal.com/s/43437.

102. "Results from the 2014 Midterm Election," WSJ News Graphics, http://graphics.wsj .com/midterm-election-results-2014/.

103. Michael Shear, Julie Hirschfield Davis, and Gardiner Harris, "Obama Chooses Mer-rick Garland for Supreme Court," *New York Times*, March 16, 2016, http://www .nytimes.com/2016/03/17/us/politics/obama-supreme-court-nominee.html?_r=0.

104. Karoun Demirjian, "Republicans Refuse to Budge Following Garland Nomination to Supreme Court," *Washington Post*, March 16, 2016, https://www.washingtonpost .com/news/powerpost/wp/2016/03/16/republicans-refuse-to-budge-following-gar land-nomination-to-supreme-court/?utm_term=.76d5e3efcf45.

105. The 2013 Senate rules change removing the filibuster from judicial appointment de-bates did not apply to the Supreme Court (see chapter 8 in this volume). However, in early 2017 the Republican Senate majority changed that rule as well in order to confirm Trump appointee Neil Gorsuch to the Court by a 54–45 vote.

106. Frank Newport, "Trump's Negative Image," Gallup, January 20, 2016, http://www .gallup.com/opinion/polling-matters/188936/trump-negative-image.aspx.

107. "Senate Election Results: G.O.P. Keeps Control," *New York Times*, August 1, 2017, http://www.nytimes.com/elections/results/senate.

108. David Jackson and Gregory Korte, "The Trump-Obama Rivalry Fuels 2016 Cam-paign, *USA Today*, November 3, 2016, http://www.usatoday.com/story/news/politics

/elections/2016/11/03/donald-trump-barack-obama-rivalry-miami-hillary-clinton/93156496/.

109. Gillian Mohney, "Understanding Gender Bias after Trump's Election Upset," ABC News, November 9, 2016, http://abcnews.go.com/Politics/understanding-gender-bias-trumps-election-upset/story?id=43416542.

110. Michael Regan, "What Does Voter Turnout Tell Us about the 2016 Election," PBS, November 20, 2016, http://www.pbs.org/newshour/updates/voter-turnout-2016-elections/.

111. Abby Goodnough and Robert Pear, "Texas Judge Strikes down Obama's Affordable Care Act as Unconstitutional," *New York Times*, December 14, 2018, https://www.nytimes.com/2018/12/14/health/obamacare-unconstitutional-texas-judge.html.

CHAPTER TEN

Obama and the Unilateral Presidency

Imperial or Imperiled?

Andrew Rudalevige

Barack Obama's presidency began with large Democratic majorities in Congress and an ambitious legislative agenda. It ended with Republicans in charge of both chambers and with renewed stress on the many tools of the administrative presidency. One result was that Obama's political opponents frequently charged him with presidential overreach, imperialism, and even dictatorship. In the wake of the decidedly unsympathetic outcome of the 2016 elections, another result was an unexpectedly fragile legacy, given a set of achievements established by executive action and thus constrained by the limits of statutory flexibility. As Obama told an NPR interviewer in December of that year, "My suggestion to the president-elect is, you know, going through the legislative process is always better, in part because it's harder to undo."[1]

Obama's tactical evolution was only partly a matter of choice. As had his predecessors before him, the president came to discover the useful range of executive actions available to him, allowing him to turn both domestic and foreign policy toward his preferences. Yet after the 2010 midterm elections—and certainly by the time the putative "grand bargain" over the budget was abandoned in the fall of 2011—his policy preferences had few other outlets. The reflexive obstructionism of his Republican opposition, which controlled the House after 2010 and the Senate after 2014, meant Obama's legislative program was dead on arrival. The 114th Congress managed to enact just 213 laws in 2016, a quarter of which were devoted to renaming federal facilities after favored deceased constituents. Even with those laws included in the total, the last *six* years of the Obama administration accounted for approximately the same number of statutes as the *two* years of the "Do Nothing" Congress of 1947–1948. Hence Obama's 2011 declaration that "we can't wait" and his 2014 pledge to utilize his "pen and phone" during a "year of action." As the president stated, "I can use that pen to sign executive orders and take executive actions and administrative actions that move the ball forward."[2]

The taxonomy of those actions and orders was quite extensive, and for the president's critics, they frequently went too far. The House of Representatives successfully sought standing to sue Obama over his health care and immigration initiatives. House Speaker John Boehner (R-OH) complained to his colleagues of an "aggressive unilateralism" that substituted for lawmaking: "President Obama has repeatedly run an end-around on the American people and their elected legislators."[3] House majority leader Eric Cantor produced a report, its cover drenched in funereal black, entitled (what else?) "The Imperial Presidency." Some went further still. "Let me be very clear," said Maine governor Paul LePage in October 2016. "I believe the President of the United States . . . is a dictator."[4]

Obama defended himself by claiming that he was using presidential power only because Congress was ignoring its responsibilities. "Our country and our economy would be stronger today if House Republicans had allowed a simple yes-or-no vote on this bill or, for that matter, any bill," Obama said about his immigration plan. "If Congress will not do their job, at least we can do ours."[5] In short, when Congress refused to pass new laws, the Obama administration looked to wring new authority from old ones. This meant aggressive statutory interpretation that could guide the implementation of policy to suit presidential preferences.

Obama argued that in so doing he was acting in the public interest. This, of course, was very much in the eye of the beholder. The actions justified by the Obama team's interpretations were frequently popular but rarely uncontested. In key areas such as health care, environmental protection, and immigration, the president mostly outflanked a polarized Congress—only to see his initiatives encounter an uneven reception in the federal courts to which his opponents inevitably appealed. Further, statutory interpretation, by its nature, can be changed by future interpreters. The administration's reliance on executive actions sometimes made the president seem "imperial," but it also risked imperiling his legacy. Both President Donald Trump and the Republican congressional majorities that returned to power after 2016 made early progress along these lines.

By contrast, Obama's aggressive—and far less challenged—use of the same basic tools in foreign policy will leave an important legacy to his successors. The administration's claims about the expansive scope of the 2001 Authorization for the Use of Military Force and the contrastingly narrow application of the 1973 War Powers Resolution were given much more leeway even by his partisan opponents—at a real cost to the powers and duties of Congress.

The bottom line is that the experience of the Obama administration affirmed the constraints on any individual actor in a separated system of powers. But, as James Madison warned long ago, that system works only when ambition actually functions to counteract ambition.[6]

From the Grand Bargain to Presidential Administration

"By the close of Clinton's presidency," Elena Kagan wrote (before her elevation to the Supreme Court), "a fundamental . . . transformation had occurred in the institutional relationship between the administrative agencies and the Executive Office of the President." The new relationship involved the use of a multitude of executive management tools to enhance presidential control of the bureaucracy—in Kagan's phrase, to create "presidential administration." Clinton had acted to expand executive management of the bureaucracy, Kagan wrote, because he was "faced for most of his time in office with a hostile Congress but eager to show progress."[7] That motivation rang equally true, and perhaps even louder, for the Obama administration.

True, polarization and gridlock did not seem to be of immediate concern as Obama entered office. From the White House to the House of Representatives, Democrats had swept the 2008 elections. The administration's first major legislative proposal, the $787 billion American Recovery and Reinvestment Act, was on the books less than a month after the president took office. So too were other initiatives, including an expansion of the state children's health insurance program (SCHIP) and a law addressing equal pay for female workers. By the end of 2010, the most comprehensive changes in Wall Street regulation since the Great Depression and an ambitious extension of health care coverage to 30 million uninsured Americans—inevitably termed Obamacare—had also become law. After two years in office, Barack Obama had the highest presidential rating for success on roll-call votes ever recorded by *Congressional Quarterly*.[8]

But in the 2010 midterm elections Republicans resurged, netting a stunning sixty-three seats to regain a majority in the House of Representatives while trimming six votes from the Democratic margin in the Senate. The Republicans' antigovernment Tea Party wing would have important sway over both new and returning members of both chambers, who showed few signs of compromising their putative mandate. Senate minority leader Mitch McConnell had declared immediately after the election that "the single most important thing we want to achieve is for President Obama to be a one-term president"; in early 2011 McConnell likewise defined bipartisanship as "see[ing] if [Obama] actually wants to work with us to accomplish things that we're already for."[9]

On the whole, Obama did not. In the summer of 2011 he discovered that no one was already for, or even ready for, the "grand bargain" he sought to craft— that is, an umbrella package of fiscal responsibility that would have pulled off a three-way trade involving revisions to Social Security and Medicare, higher taxes, and spending cuts. Democrats objected to the first leg, and Republicans objected to the second; while both claimed to like the third, this was only in the abstract, not when popular programs were specifically threatened. In the end, the mindless bludgeon of an across-the-board "sequester" was the only solution that could be reached. Given lawmakers' inability to put their votes where their rhetoric was, the president declared that "we can't wait" for "an increasingly dysfunctional Congress to do its job."[10]

This rallying cry gave its name to a White House website and to a broad collection of executive actions. By the summer of 2012, Obama's inability to wait totaled forty-plus initiatives, from cutting lending fees on government-backed mortgages to creating a new national park in Virginia. And unilateralism would remain a cornerstone of Obama's agenda to the end of his administration. Key arenas for action included health care, labor law, and environmental protection. The president also stressed his prosecutorial discretion, which included the decision not to defend the Defense of Marriage Act (DOMA) in court in advance of the *Obergefell* decision legalizing same-sex marriage, wide use of his commutation power to shorten jail terms for those convicted of nonviolent drug crimes, and the constraint of federal enforcement of drug laws in states that had legalized recreational marijuana use. Perhaps Obama's most sweeping and most controversial actions—discussed in greater depth later—dealt with immigration and deportation.

It is worth noting that Obama's brand of "presidential administration" included many different tools. Executive orders got most of the press and the opprobrium, but in fact, many actions that were not executive orders were wrongly identified as such. When Obama announced a package of gun control measures in February 2016, former Florida governor Jeb Bush, then a candidate for president, tweeted, "I'll repeal his executive orders and protect [the] 2nd amend[ment]." But the package did not contain a single executive order. Likewise, in July 2014 Speaker Boehner observed that "every president issues executive orders," but "most of them . . . do so within the law"—charging that Obama had failed to do so when enacting educational waivers, environmental regulations, and a prisoner exchange involving Taliban detainees and a US serviceman. Yet none of these were achieved by executive order; rather, Obama used other sorts of administrative documents and directives—studies have tracked more than two dozen.[11]

What these actions had in common was their goal of executing the law according to the Obama administration's preferences. As Obama political aide David Axelrod noted in late 2010, "The next phase is . . . less about legislative action than it is about managing the change that we've brought about"—implementing laws passed in 2009–2010, including the Affordable Care Act and the Dodd-Frank financial sector reforms.[12] But the idea of "managing change" developed to include longer-standing laws, especially when newer ones could not be passed—for example, when large-scale legislation to forestall climate change or comprehensive immigration reform stalled. Martha Derthick could have been speaking of the Obama years when she observed (about the 1990s), "Much of the activity of American policymaking consists of attempts not to pass new laws but to invest old ones with new meanings."[13]

This is possible because, although the Constitution enjoins the president to "take care that the law be faithfully executed," such fidelity is hard to define. If nothing else, presidents have many laws to choose among—some of them contradictory, and others just sitting in the statute books awaiting rediscovery. Given the difficulty of passing laws and the multiplicity of circumstances to which they must apply, it rarely makes sense to try to anticipate every possible outcome in legislative language. Thus, Congress routinely delegates power to executive departments and agencies so that they can promulgate regulations specifying how a given law will work in practice.

Further, complex substantive debates tend to generate complex statutes: the Affordable Care Act ran to more than 900 pages, containing vague provisions, multiple drafting errors, and any number of unintended consequences. Even in the best circumstances, maneuvering a bill through Congress requires ambiguous statutory language, which allows all sides to point to the same language as supporting their ideals and thus claim victory. The discretion granted to the executive branch by statute aggregates with the growth of the US Code itself.

Statutory Interpretation, in Theory and Practice

The result is that the specifics of policy implementation are often up for grabs. We often think of statutory interpretation as a judicial function, and courts—drenched in the perfumed home brew of *Marbury v. Madison*—constantly claim that it is their job to determine "what the law is."[14] But Congress and the executive branch have a role to play as well. Questions over the president's interpretation of the Constitution date back to the Washington administration.[15]

Applying this to George W. Bush and Barack Obama, *New York Times* reporter Charlie Savage wrote, "Many of the lawyers [Bush and Cheney] surrounded themselves with . . . embraced such sweeping views of executive power that the law was not a factor. They dispatched every hard problem with the same easy answer: The president could do whatever he deemed necessary to protect national security."[16] Obama, by contrast, declared in 2009 that he would act "with an abiding confidence in the rule of law and due process; in checks and balances and accountability."[17] That is, he did not want to claim presidential prerogative to override statutory constraints; he intended to ground each action in some sort of legal authority. One result, as Savage put it, was that "lawyerliness suffused the Obama administration. . . . Obama's governance . . . cannot be seen clearly without looking at it through a legal lens."[18]

But a legal lens does not mean a limited scope for unilateralism. As Bush administration official John Graham noted, "creative lawyers can find lots of lawful ways for a determined president to advance an agenda."[19] The president's lawyers, of course, work for the president, incurring the risk that (as law professor Bruce Ackerman put it) the "authoritative-looking opinions" they produce may favor "short-term presidential imperatives" rather than "sober legal judgments."[20] Historically, administration attorneys have shown great talent in finding statutory interpretations that justify presidential preferences. Indeed, there is something of a market for presidential legal advice, and the president can choose the "product"—the legal conclusion—that most empowers his policy choices.

To see this at work in the Obama years, consider four contentious domestic policy areas in which Obama made aggressive claims about his ability to act in creative ways under statutory authority: health care, labor, the environment, and immigration. Long-term results on the ground—and on Capitol Hill—have been decidedly mixed.

Health Care

"This Administration's lawlessness has been most widely noticed with President Obama's implementation of Obamacare," complained Representative Diane Black (R-TN) in 2014.[21] Much of that implementation involved the issuance of tax regulations or interpretations of the law's text. Treasury officials considered these tasks to be well within their ongoing statutory authority under the Internal Revenue Code. Assistant Secretary Mark Mazur framed it as a simple "exercise of the Treasury Department's longstanding administrative authority to grant transition relief when implementing new legislation."[22] An additional package of rules changes was announced in March 2014 by an administrative bulletin released by the Centers for Medicaid and Medicare Services.

Black's reference was to a series of delays in the implementation of Affordable Care Act (ACA) requirements beginning in February 2013. In July of that year the administration put off the employer mandate portion of the bill for twelve months; in February 2014 that deadline was extended yet again for medium-sized companies. Other shifts included the deadline for imposition of the individual mandate; adjustments to the online marketplace for small businesses; and, with the health care.gov website still in tatters, extension of the general deadline for enrollment online. When insurance companies (quite properly) began to cancel plans that did not meet the ACA's minimum requirements, this undermined the president's pledge that "if you like your plan, you can keep it." Obama thus gave insurers the discretion to extend those plans for an additional year—and did so again in early 2014, pushing such cancellations all the way past the 2016 elections. It was not clear whether these changes were in fact lawful, given the specificity of the deadlines in the law. But since those affected could hardly claim to have suffered "harm" in a legal sense (indeed, they welcomed the delays), there were no real court challenges.

That was not the case, though, when the Internal Revenue Service (IRS) announced that it would read the ACA to include individuals enrolled via federal- as well as state-run insurance exchanges as eligible for tax credits subsidizing their policies. *King v. Burwell* centered on this question, since one section of the law seemed to state that subsidies could be given only to those purchasing coverage from an exchange run by one of the states. The ACA, thanks in part to the tortuous legislative process leading to its passage, suffered from (as the *King* majority gently put it) "inartful drafting." Some, including the IRS, argued that the section in question was simply an elaborate typographical error.[23] But it became a crucial issue when about two dozen states refused to set up their own exchanges, forcing the federal government to do the work. Thus, unlike the 2010 test of the ACA in *NFIB v. Sebelius*, which was about the scope of the commerce clause, *King v. Burwell* dealt not with interpreting the Constitution but with interpreting the ACA's text.

The Supreme Court has long preached judicial deference to an executive branch department's or agency's reading of a vague law, assuming that such reading is based on reasonable grounds. Following this logic, the Fourth Circuit Court of Appeals ruled in favor of the government, but the DC Circuit Court of Appeals thought the law was clear and ruled the other way. The Supreme Court, for its part, decided that the agency should not make the call at all: "This is not a case for the IRS," Chief Justice John Roberts wrote for the majority. "It is instead our task to determine the correct reading of [the relevant section]." Having done so, the Court found that the notion of "State," with regard to an exchange "established by the State," was indeed ambiguous when taken in the context of the ACA as a whole. If federal exchanges were unworkable, the health care marketplaces that were so central to the law would collapse in a "death spiral"—something Congress could not have meant to do. Thus, although it was a close call, the key section "can fairly be read consistent with what we see as Congress's plan, and that is the reading we adopt."[24]

Others, of course, were unimpressed with this line of reasoning. Justice Antonin Scalia's instantly famous dissent in *King* accused his colleagues of judicial malpractice, plain stupidity, and something he called "jiggery-pokery." But the ACA lived to fight another day—for example, when opponents charged that Obama was spending money on certain provisions of the law without that money being specifically appropriated by Congress. That case never came to decision, since President Trump used his own administrative discretion to discontinue the spending—prompting yet another round of lawsuits, this time by insurance companies that had used the payments to subsidize consumers' out-of-pocket costs.[25]

Labor

As noted, executive orders constituted a relatively small proportion of Obama's executive actions overall. But they did play an important role in shaping the administration's policies toward the American workforce.

Recall that executive orders affect the private sector only indirectly: they address government officials and agencies. However, the US government buys over $500 billion worth of contracted products and services every year, and requiring the businesses receiving those contracts to meet certain basic conditions can have an important impact on the wider economy.[26] Although Obama could not issue an order raising the federal minimum wage, he could order that the contracts negotiated with private-sector companies doing business with the federal government include that higher minimum wage. And he did.

Obama's broader strategy sought to rework the relationship between the federal government and the private contractors it relies on. His executive orders (EOs) not only limited government procurement to providers that agreed to pay a higher minimum wage (EO 13658, February 2014), they also banned discrimination on the basis of sexual orientation or identity (EO 13672, July 2014); required full compliance with laws mandating "integrity and business ethics" to ensure "fair pay and safe workplaces" (EO 13673, July 2014; EO 13738, August 2016); and provided for paid sick leave (EO 13706, September 2015). The Department of Labor then developed regulations to implement these requirements. For example, the rules governing EO 13706 were issued in final form in early September and took effect on January 1, 2017.

These accompanying rules gave the orders more stability than the orders themselves could claim. An EO, after all, can be reversed by a subsequent EO issued by a new president. President Trump in fact rolled back some of Obama's EOs in early 2017, including EO 13673 (fair pay and safe workplaces). But even the rules did not escape controversy or pushback. In late October 2016 a district court judge in Texas issued an injunction holding up the implementation of EOs 13673 and 13738.[27] In a lawsuit brought by trade associations representing builders and security guard companies, the judge ruled that the orders' provisions went too far in requiring companies to report charges (as opposed to convictions) of workplace law violations. The case was mooted when President Trump revoked the orders.[28] The third branch of government weighed in too: even before agencies could move to rescind the rules they had promulgated, legislators voided them by passing a resolution under the Congressional Review Act (CRA). The CRA had been passed in 1996 but rarely used, since activating it required that both Congress and the president be hostile to a given regulation; with those conditions met, fifteen rules were repealed in 2017 and another in 2018.[29]

Other Obama efforts to boost workers' rights also stalled as his administration wound down. In March 2014 a presidential memorandum directed the Department of Labor to update its interpretation of the 1938 Fair Labor Standards Act so that more white-collar workers would be eligible for overtime pay.[30] The Labor Department issued a proposed regulation in July 2015, greatly expanding eligibility for overtime pay, and then a final regulation in May 2016; the final regulation rolled back the draft proposal somewhat, but the department still estimated that its new salary threshold would apply to 4.2 million workers.[31]

Businesses, which had provided most of the 270,000 public comments received by the Labor Department concerning the rule, were not happy; nor were some state governments. In September 2016 the US Chamber of Commerce sued, as did public officials in twenty-one states, arguing that, "once again, President Obama is trying to unilaterally rewrite the law." They argued that the new regulation raised the threshold too much and improperly indexed it to inflation—which meant that the regulation would change over time without advance notice and without the ability to comment on the change.[32] The rule was set to take effect on December 1, 2016, but on November 22 a district court issued an order suspending it. The judge agreed with the plaintiffs that the department had gone beyond its statutory authority. The Labor Department quickly appealed, but the Trump administration switched sides when the case was heard again in 2017, successfully blocking the new rule and promising to work with business to develop a less burdensome version.[33]

Environmental Protection

The Obama administration had more, but hardly universal, success in the environmental arena. Although the administration's carbon "cap and trade" bill aimed at combating global warming passed the House in June 2009, the Senate never voted on it. Thus Obama turned to administrative action.

In May 2010 the president sent a memorandum to four agency heads, directing (technically, "requesting") them to tighten greenhouse gas and fuel efficiency standards such that "coordinated steps . . . produce a new generation of clean vehicles." One result came in March 2014, when the Environmental Protection Agency (EPA) announced new rules that would reduce sulfur in gasoline and drive changes in both automotive and oil refinery technology. More broadly, after a slow drafting process—and some additional stalling meant to ensure that controversial rules were not issued right before the 2012 elections—the rule-writing project also resulted in efforts to extend Clean Air Act (CAA) authority to existing power plants, especially those fueled by coal, and to limit greenhouse gases produced by new development. Even EPA attorneys considered their legal interpretation of the CAA "challenging," so it was no surprise when lawsuits resulted, questioning that interpretation.[34]

The first case to make its way to the Supreme Court in 2014 was *Utility Air Regulatory Group (UARG) v. EPA*, involving the regulation of larger industrial plants emitting greenhouse gases. The Court largely upheld the EPA's substantive position, noting that "Congress's profligate use of [the phrase] 'air pollutant' is not conducive to clarity." Here, as it so often does, vague law led to administrative discretion. However, the EPA regulations had sought to change the threshold for regulating carbon emissions produced by new (as opposed to existing) facilities. Under the CAA, regulation kicked in when a facility generated more than 250 tons of a given pollutant—but that is a tiny amount of greenhouse gases. The EPA's new regulation raised the limit for carbon pollutants to 75,000 tons per year—which was better for industry but disregarded language in the act that was *not* vague. In oral argument, Justice Elena Kagan—that erstwhile proponent of "presidential administration"—mused disapprovingly that "the solution that EPA came up with actually seems to give it complete discretion to do whatever it wants, whenever it wants." As Justice Antonin Scalia later wrote in the decision, "An agency may not rewrite clear statutory terms to suit its own sense of how the statute should operate."[35]

In *Michigan v. Environmental Protection Agency* (2015), though, Kagan and Scalia disagreed about how to interpret the letter of the law. Scalia (and four others) and Kagan (and three others) differed on what constituted a "reasonable" interpretation of the Clean Air Act when it came to regulating the specific type of power plants under review in the case. Scalia accused the EPA of "interpretive gerrymanders" that "keep parts of statutory context it likes while throwing away parts it does not." Kagan and the dissenters complained about judicial "micromanagement."[36]

Michigan was a loss for the administration, but with limited practical effect (as detailed below). However, the third round to reach the Court was more problematic for Obama's efforts to combat climate change. Just a few days before Justice Scalia's unexpected death in February 2016, he cast the deciding vote forcing a delay in the administration's Clean Power Plan (CPP) regulations.[37] The problem for the administration was severalfold—starting with yet another typographical error introduced when the CAA was amended in 1990. Could the electricity grid as a whole be treated as a "system," in the act's language? And since the aim was to reduce reliance on coal-fired electricity generation, standards drawn from renewable energy sources were used as the goal for reducing emissions. Was this allowed, or was it a sort of extrastatutory bait and switch? The administration's position constituted "an aggressive argument," one scholar noted, "and if the courts reject it, there is no CPP."[38] Reflecting the importance of the case, a ten- (rather than three-) judge panel of the DC Circuit Court of Appeals heard an astonishing seven hours of oral argument in September 2016.[39] But no decision was handed down during the Obama administration. This allowed Trump's EPA to ask the court to defer its decision until a new, less stringent rule could be drafted; this replacement draft did not emerge until the summer of 2018, with months of public comment still to come.[40] Environmental groups hoped to turn the tables by delaying any new rule in court until after the 2020 election and, they fervently hoped, a new administration that would be more sympathetic to their aims.

The fact that the CPP regulations were blocked so early gave its saga more substantive resonance. The regulations ultimately overturned in *Michigan* had been in effect long enough to shape industry decisions about what kind of power plants to build or expand. Those decisions involved high infrastructure costs ($10 billion, according to one estimate) and were unlikely to be reversed even when the rules were set aside. By contrast, the CPP was not yet embedded in private-sector decision-making. Still, with the cost of coal far higher than the cost of natural gas or even wind power, the CEO of Michigan's largest utility announced in late 2016 that all eight of the state's coal-fired plants were on the road to retirement, even if the CPP was shelved. "I don't know anybody in the country who would build another coal plant," he said.[41]

Immigration

As noted in chapter 5, the 2012 campaign season and the failure of the Development, Relief, and Education for Alien Minors (DREAM) Act in Congress prompted President Obama to announce the Deferred Action for Childhood Arrivals (DACA) program. DACA aimed to protect from deportation about 1.2 million people who were in the country illegally: young people who had been brought to the United States before they were 16 years old, who were high school students or graduates or had served in the armed forces, and who had no criminal record. DACA's beneficiaries were a sympathetic group that (helpfully for legal purposes) could be clearly delineated to fit within the discretion granted the executive branch by the Immigration and Nationality Act (INA).

After Obama's reelection, action on immigration seemed likely to move to the legislative arena. After all, even key Republicans blamed their 2012 losses on the party's lack of appeal to minority voters. But a comprehensive immigration reform bill passed by the Senate in June 2013 was never even debated in the House. In response, Obama took to the national airwaves in November 2014 to announce a large expansion of his earlier initiative. Saying that he wanted to deport "felons, not families," the president announced that he would extend and expand the DACA program and create a far broader variant called Deferred Action for Parents of Americans (DAPA). The upshot was that, in certain circumstances, the deportation of as many as 4 million parents of US citizens would be deferred, and in the meantime, they could work legally in the United States. The burden of the change rested on enforcement of the INA by the Department of Homeland Security (DHS), which issued guidance reshaping law enforcement officers' "removal priorities."

Did the INA allow so much prosecutorial discretion? Obama's instructions to DHS, and DHS's instructions to officials on the ground, did not change the law per se; rather, they set forth who was to be prosecuted (deported) first—or, rather, last. The Justice Department's analysis emphasized the INA's goal of keeping families together. It was true that discretion in immigration cases had a strong jurisprudential pedigree—as recently as 2012, in *Arizona v. United States*, the Court had held that "[a] principal feature of the removal system is the broad discretion exercised by immigration officials" in order to deal with "immediate human concerns" as well as "policy choices that bear on this Nation's international relations" and "other realities." The administration also took solace in Justice William Rehnquist's claim in *Heckler v. Chaney* (1985): "an agency's decision not to prosecute or enforce, whether through civil or criminal process, is a decision generally committed to an agency's absolute discretion."[42]

Congress could, of course, make that discretion less absolute. But since the polarized 114th Congress was unable to agree on a response to Obama's move (or much of anything else), opponents of the president's agenda again turned to the courts. Texas, along with two dozen other states and state officials, argued that the "brazen lawlessness" of the president's administrative actions actually changed the substance of the law. They claimed that, in practice, he had not made individual exceptions through prosecutorial discretion but had instead affirmatively bestowed new rights on large groups of people. In February 2015 a Texas district court judge issued an injunction blocking the DAPA program, and that injunction was upheld in May by the Fifth Circuit Court of Appeals.

Neither court directly addressed the merits of the question, although the circuit court noted that "the United States has not made a strong showing that it [was] likely to succeed." Rather, they addressed procedural concerns about rule-making and standing. Could these states even sue? Had they been harmed by the new policy? Texas argued that it would incur costs in issuing driver's licenses to the newly nondeported, while the administration countered that the states did not *have* to subsidize licenses and the like but could change their laws to recover the costs. In oral argument at the Supreme Court, the justices split on this point. "Isn't losing money the classic case for standing?" asked Chief Justice John Roberts. Justice Sonia Sotomayor asked the states, however, "Can we give you standing just on the basis of you saying, 'I'm going to do this when it makes no sense?'" (She also argued that Texas did not need to spend more money on its Department of Motor Vehicles, on the grounds that DMV customer service was generally so terrible that no one would notice if the DAPA population just got in the existing long lines.)[43]

The substance of the question, again, was whether the Obama administration had properly interpreted the powers provided by the INA. The president's lawyers argued that he had no choice but to set priorities: Congress's annual appropriations for dealing with "removable aliens" was only 3.5 percent of the amount needed to actually remove them. But Justice Anthony Kennedy worried that "what we're doing is defining the limits of discretion. And it seems to me that that is a legislative, not an executive act." The administration argued, of course, that Congress had already defined those limits in a way that allowed the president's actions. In the end, the Court—at that point with only eight members—could not reach a decision. The holding, issued on June 23, 2016, was just one sentence long: "The judgment is affirmed by an equally divided Court." This meant that the injunction issued by the lower courts remained in place, and DAPA would not be implemented.[44]

Still, through all this, the original DACA program remained intact, an example of the president's power to create new political facts on the ground that are costly for his successor to undo. In the fall of 2017 President Trump said he would rescind

DACA after a six-month grace period. But he claimed he was taking this action only because the law did not give him the power to implement it, and he asked Congress to help the DACA population. As 2019 dawned, legislators had not provided a statutory fix, but several federal court rulings had kept the program alive well past Trump's stated deadline.

Foreign Policy and the War Powers

These mixed results in the domestic realm are in contrast with Obama's legacy in foreign policy. The Obama administration emphasized that its actions in that sphere would not rely on broad claims of inherent presidential power or prerogative: the president vowed to act only when he had specific statutory or constitutional authority to do so. Therefore, affirmative congressional action could and did block presidential preferences at times. The Guantanamo Bay detention facility, for instance, was still open for business on Obama's last day in office, despite his order, on nearly his first day, that it be closed.[45] That effort was blocked by repeated statutory bans on spending any funds to move the detainees or build a new prison in the United States. Obama did manage, though, to build on George W. Bush's policy of transferring detainees to other countries, where possible; just forty-one detainees, the hardest cases of all, remained in Cuba by January 2017.

Still, as in the domestic arena, laws can be vague. As Jack Goldsmith, who headed the Justice Department's Office of Legal Counsel for part of the Bush 43 administration, noted, "a president has enormous unilateral authority to alter how the United States sees its international law commitments by merely interpreting those commitments."[46] For present purposes, the statutes of most interest are the 1973 War Powers Resolution (WPR) and the 2001 Authorization for the Use of Military Force (AUMF). Under Obama, the first was bypassed, and the second was greatly expanded. Other significant issues of executive unilateralism in the Obama years—the use of drones, for example, especially when used to target American citizens—flow largely from the prior question of whether the United States is at war, with whom, and where. That is, if the United States is at war, the use of instruments in that war—whether drones or indefinite detention—is largely delegated to the president.

The power to initiate war seems clear enough: it is specifically granted to Congress by Article I of the Constitution. Yet presidents have garnered a good deal of discretionary autonomy in this area as well, abetted by both congressional inaction and the vagaries of past delegations of power.[47] And the administration had many resources for interpreting past statutes in the way it preferred, starting with a large and acronym-laden population of foreign policy lawyers. In a 2010 speech, State Department legal adviser Harold Koh listed a subset of his interagency colleagues, including attorneys in the State Department, the White House, the National Security Council, the Office of the US Trade Representative, the Department of Defense (from its general counsel to the JAG Corps), the Department of Justice (across five different divisions), the Department of Homeland Security, the Director of National Intelligence, and the Central Intelligence Agency.

The War Powers Resolution: No Hostilities?

When Arab Spring uprisings threatened the regime of Libyan dictator Muammar al-Qaddafi in 2011, the venerable dictator threatened a "bloodbath" in retaliation. A UN Security Council resolution urged the prevention of a humanitarian disaster, a mission that quickly expanded to provide military support for rebel forces that overthrew Qaddafi's government and executed Qaddafi himself.[48]

Many strands were woven into the US decision to support military action in Libya, but none of them ran through Congress—even though the WPR envisions explicit congressional authorization for any US involvement in "hostilities, or into situations where imminent involvement in hostilities is clearly indicated by the circumstances." To be sure, the WPR was never a triumph of careful legal drafting, and its vague language has made enforcement problematic.[49] Still, it clearly prohibits unauthorized involvement after a sixty- to ninety-day "clock" has expired. As the Libya operation approached the two-month mark, the Obama administration needed to decide on a course of action.

Obama did not argue that the WPR was unconstitutional, as some of his predecessors had done; however, his loose array of "lawfare" attorneys had diverging views on the legality of using the American military in Libya after the WPR clock ran out. Libya serves as a reminder that statutory interpretation is a product available through an intra-administrative market for legal advice. Most of the president's lawyers (including those in the Office of Legal Counsel in the Justice Department and at the Pentagon) seemed to think that, at the very least, the "operational tempo" would have to be dialed back. In this scenario, the United States would provide logistical support for NATO attacks but would not do the attacking itself.

However, White House counsel Robert Bauer, along with Koh at the State Department, developed what Charlie Savage termed "a very aggressive interpretation" of the War Powers Resolution.[50] They argued that the Libya operation did not constitute "hostilities" under the terms of the WPR; therefore, that law and its limits simply did not apply. In this reading, as Obama himself later said at a press conference, the WPR was meant only for wars on the scale of Vietnam.[51]

Legislative (and legal) critics were not hugely impressed with this logic. Congress, however, did not act; it was too divided on the merits of the policy to take firm action regarding its legality.

ISIS and the AUMF: No Limits?

The use of American forces in Syria and Iraq against the so-called Islamic State (ISIS) generated another creative exegesis of statute and even less political opposition—thanks in part to the group's brutal tactics both in the Levant and around the globe.

Given the extensive use of air strikes and the creeping use of ground forces in the Middle East, Obama did not deny that the WPR applied. But under the WPR, presidents are authorized to use force when there is (1) a declaration of war; (2) a specific statutory authorization; or (3) "a national emergency created by attack upon the United States, its territories or possessions, or its armed forces." The first two options are self-explanatory, but they did not seem to apply to ISIS.

Presidential use of force under option 3—without specific authorization—tends to fall into two categories: cases of self-defense (sometimes imaginatively defined), cases with wide multilateral support (often owing to humanitarian concerns or treaty obligations), or both.[52] Obama's early arguments in 2014 regarding ISIS feinted toward both categories: the mission originally focused on the Mosul Dam, whose breach "could threaten the lives of large numbers of civilians, endanger U.S. personnel and facilities, including the U.S. Embassy in Baghdad." But he did not try very hard to establish the facts of a "national emergency" and simply argued in general terms that "these actions . . . are in the national security and foreign policy interests of the United States, pursuant to my constitutional authority to conduct U.S. foreign relations and as Commander in Chief and Chief Executive." (Why the last mattered was never explained.)

But in September 2014 Obama changed gears and argued that he did in fact have the specific authorization mandated by the WPR to expand air attacks on ISIS in Iraq and even to extend them into Syria.[53] First, the *Washington Post* reported that "the White House's belief that it has authority to act is based on the reports Obama has filed with Congress under the War Powers Act [*sic*] and the earlier congressional authorization for the war in Iraq."[54] But the administration's "reports," as just noted, simply claimed that the president was acting "pursuant to [his] constitutional authority," and the 2002 congressional authorization to use force in Iraq was for the use of force *against* the state of Iraq, not a blank check for the use of force *in* Iraq. Potential attacks within Syria's borders seemed even more removed from the authorization's intent.

Thus, the Obama administration soon settled on a different legal justification: the Authorization for the Use of Military Force, passed three days after the September 11, 2001, terrorist attacks. As White House press secretary Josh Earnest framed it, "The answer simply is that Congress, in 2001, did give the executive branch authorization to take this action, and there's no debating that."[55] The AUMF's text is indeed very broad: "the President is authorized to use all necessary and appropriate force against those nations, organizations, or persons he determines planned, authorized, committed, or aided the terrorist attacks that occurred on September 11, 2001, or harbored such organizations or persons, in order to prevent any future acts of international terrorism against the United States by such nations, organizations or persons." But it is explicitly linked to the 9/11 attacks and, presumably, to al-Qaeda. Al-Qaeda, in turn, is not ISIS.

Or is it? As Earnest stated: "It is the view of the . . . Obama administration that the 2001 AUMF continues to apply to [ISIS] because of their decade-long relationship with Al Qaida, their continuing ties to Al Qaida; because . . . they have continued to employ the kind of heinous tactics that they previously employed when their name was Al Qaida in Iraq. And finally, because they continue to have the same kind of . . . aspiration that they articulated under their previous name."[56] The Pentagon's general counsel put it this way in April 2015: "the name may have changed, but the group . . . has been an enemy of the United States within the scope of the 2001 AUMF continuously since at least 2004."[57]

As with Libya, this argument did not receive stellar external reviews. Goldsmith called it "presidential unilateralism masquerading as implausible statutory interpretation."[58] John Bellinger, a veteran of the State Department and National Security Council, called it a "very strained legal interpretation."[59] The clearest critique was that ISIS was not associated with the 9/11 attacks because it did not exist in 2001. In addition, it had broken rather firmly with al-Qaeda and thus was not an "associated force," even under the administration's earlier definition of that term. "'Associated' does not mean 'not associated' or 'repudiated by' or 'broken with' or even 'used to be associated with.'"[60] Did splinter groups from ISIS count? Groups that splintered from splinter groups? Were there any limits at all?

Indeed, the administration argued that the March 2016 air strikes that killed about 150 al-Shabab militants in Somalia also fell under the AUMF. A June 2016 "supplemental consolidated report" to Congress listed operations in Afghanistan, Iraq, Syria, Yemen, Somalia, Djibouti, and Libya as part of the AUMF umbrella. And in November the administration announced a legal opinion assigning culpability for the 9/11 attacks not just to al-Shabab leaders but to the entire group.[61] Yet al-Shabab did not exist until 2006.

Still, as the Obama term wound down, Congress showed little inclination to get involved. The ISIS attacks in Paris in November 2015 and in Brussels in March 2016—and the alleged allegiance to ISIS of American murderers in California and Florida—prompted both bellicose rhetoric and the use of special forces as "advisers" on the ground in Syria and Iraq. They did not prompt Congress, however, to deliberate matters of war and peace.

In February 2015 President Obama sent Congress a new draft AUMF to cover the ISIS war. Obama's version would have repealed the 2002 Iraq authorization but kept the 2001 version in place. It provided a three-year window in which the president was authorized "to use the Armed Forces of the United States as the President determines to be necessary and appropriate against ISIL [aka ISIS] or associated persons or forces," but it did not allow for the use of American troops in "enduring offensive ground combat operations." The proposal received no serious legislative consideration; in this sense, Earnest was right: there was "no debating that." Senate Foreign Relations Committee chair Bob Corker, among others, agreed and stated, "I believe the administration has the authorit[y] to do what they're doing against ISIS." Senate minority leader Harry Reid had a more faith-based approach: "I don't believe in AUMFs."[62] His colleagues seemed to share his existential doubts.[63]

Into this vacuum, the American commitment kept ramping up. During Obama's last year in office, internal rules governing drone strikes—in zones of self-declared "active hostilities" and elsewhere—were loosened. The administration promised to avoid "boots on the ground," but hundreds of special ops advisers (perhaps in different footwear) were very much on the front lines again by 2016. By the end of the year, at least sixteen Americans had been killed in anti-ISIS operations in Iraq, and one in Syria.[64]

This brought the story back to a familiar place: the courtroom. In May 2016 army captain Nathan Smith filed a lawsuit asking a US district court to declare that "President Obama's war against ISIS is illegal because Congress has not authorized it."[65] He argued that the WPR's requirements had not been met and that, as far back as the 1804 case *Little v. Barreme*, the judiciary has required that presidential orders be "strictly warranted by law." Smith's attorney argued that "this is a garden variety statutory construction case," not a political question that the courts should or could avoid; this was "precisely the kind of 'undeclared war' that the [War Powers] Resolution aimed to avoid." And "if the Justice Department succeeds in denying Smith a judicial hearing on the merits, this will make it impossible for anybody to appeal to courts to prevent future presidents from treating the War Powers Resolution with impunity."[66] Nevertheless, the district court dismissed the case in November, holding that Smith did not have standing to sue and that the case involved a political question beyond the court's competence.[67] After a long delay, in July 2018, Smith's appeal was also dismissed—because by then, he had left the army. The Trump administration, free of judicial oversight, continued to expand the war against ISIS.[68]

A Lasting Legacy?

Cementing a substantive legacy requires substantive achievements, and for Barack Obama, at least after 2010, that seemed to require detours around congressional gridlock. In the *King v. Burwell* oral arguments, the solicitor general was asked why legislators could not simply fix any problems with the ACA that stemmed from drafting errors. He replied, to knowing laughter, "*this* Congress?" As Obama put it in his 2014 immigration address, almost as a taunt, "to those members of Congress who question my authority . . . , or question the wisdom of me acting . . . , I have one answer: Pass a bill."[69]

Congress's ability to do that was limited, as Obama well knew. In any case, his actions ensured that Congress would be reacting to an altered political and substantive environment. As Alexander Hamilton wrote, "the Executive in the exercise of its constitutional powers, may establish an antecedent state of things which ought to weigh in the legislative decisions." That "antecedent state" comes with its own constraints, including political barriers to tearing down the new status quo. In these cases, if Congress does not act, the president wins. If it does act, he might still win. For this reason, political scientist William Howell argues that presidents are almost always better off politically when they take decisive action, even if that action is not obviously legal.[70]

In this context, when was Obama—and more broadly, the presidency—strongest? The answer: when Congress was most irresponsible in carrying out its constitutional duties in the arena of war powers. That enabled Obama to change facts both in legal textbooks and on the ground. Likewise, this was generally true when government regulation shaped private action over time in ways that made subsequent reversal unlikely, because changing course would be too expensive. As a result, the Obama administration pushed hard to "flood the zone," publishing a slew of new rules before the president's term ended; not surprisingly, this spurred criticism of "midnight regulations" rushed out without sufficient analysis.[71] The resurrection of the Congressional Review Act, though notable, managed to roll back only a small number of finalized rules.[72]

But if the use of statutory interpretation was inevitable, it was also invitational; it attracted both political flak and, perhaps more crucially, challenges from other political institutions. This was especially true in domestic policy, where interests are thick on the ground and can shop around for sympathetic venues—whether in courtrooms or in Congress. A united legislative majority can certainly block presidential actions, such as Obama's effort to close Guantanamo Bay. Courts were active (and frankly activist) players in the administrative arena during the Obama years, stepping in to affirm—but also to delay or reverse—numerous executive orders and regulations and the statutory interpretations that undergirded them. Finally, of course, executive actions can be reversed not just by new laws or court rulings but also by future executives. This is exactly what President Trump promised to accomplish.

As Obama himself observed:

What I didn't fully appreciate, and nobody can appreciate until they're in the position, is how decentralized power is in this system. . . . You realize, "Okay, not only do I have to persuade my own party, not only do I have to prevent the other party from blocking what the right thing to do is, but now I can anticipate this lawsuit, this lobbying taking place, and this federal agency that technically is independent, so I can't tell them what to do." . . . A lot of the work is not just identifying the right policy but now constantly building these ever-shifting coalitions.[73]

In short, administrative action is inherently fragile compared with legislative change. Obama's unilateralism may have been necessary to make progress on his agenda. Important changes in environmental protection, workplace culture, immigration, civil rights, and law enforcement will likely have a lasting if uneven impact. But another part of the Obama legacy highlights the brittle nature of unilateral change in a system that demands, but can rarely induce, consensus and coalition building to achieve permanent reform.

Notes

1. "NPR's Exit Interview with President Obama," December 19, 2016, http://www.npr .org/2016/12/19/504998487/transcript-and-video-nprs-exit-interview-with-presi dent-obama.
2. Barack Obama, "Remarks by the President before Cabinet Meeting," January 14, 2014, http://www.presidency.ucsb.edu/ws/?pid=104598. This and other presidential documents quoted here are from the American Presidency Project at the University of California, Santa Barbara, curated by Gerhard Peters and John T. Woolley.
3. Memo from Speaker Boehner to House Colleagues, "That the Laws Be Faithfully Executed . . . ," June 25, 2014, http://www.scribd.com/doc/231315267/Boehner-memo -to-House-members.
4. Eugene Scott, "Maine Gov. Paul LePage: Barack Obama Is a Dictator," CNN.com, October 12, 2016, http://www.cnn.com/2016/10/12/politics/paul-lepage-donald -trump-obama-dictator/.
5. Barack Obama, "Remarks on Immigration Reform," June 30, 2014, http://www.pres idency.ucsb.edu/ws/?pid=105370.
6. Andrew Rudalevige, *The New Imperial Presidency: Renewing Presidential Power after Watergate* (Ann Arbor: University of Michigan Press, 2005).
7. Elena Kagan, "Presidential Administration," *Harvard Law Review* 114 (June 2001): 2385. Clinton was also aggressive in his use of unilateral tools in foreign policy; see, e.g., Ryan Hendrickson, *The Clinton Wars: The Constitution, Congress, and War Powers* (Nashville, TN: Vanderbilt University Press, 2002).
8. Andrew Rudalevige, "'A Majority Is the Best Repartee': Barack Obama and Congress, 2009–2012," *Social Science Quarterly* 93 (December 2012): 1272–1294.
9. Jeff Winkler, "McConnell Skeptical of Obama's Centrist Rhetoric Ahead of State of the Union," *Daily Caller*, January 25, 2011, http://dailycaller.com/2011/01/25/mc connell-skeptical-about-obamas-centrist-rhetoric-ahead-of-state-of-the-union/.
10. Barack Obama, "Remarks in Las Vegas," October 24, 2011, http://www.presidency .ucsb.edu/ws/?pid=96941.
11. Andrew Rudalevige, "The Obama Administrative Presidency: Some Late-Term Patterns," *Presidential Studies Quarterly* 46 (December 2016): 868–890; Harold C.

Relyea, *Presidential Directives: Background and Overview* (Washington, DC: Congressional Research Service, 2008); Graham G. Dodds, *Take up Your Pen: Unilateral Presidential Directives in American Politics* (Philadelphia: University of Pennsylvania Press, 2013), 6.

12. Quoted in Peter Nicholas and Christi Parsons, "Rebuilding Staff, Obama Charts New Course," *Philadelphia Inquirer*, October 10, 2010.

13. Martha Derthick, *Up in Smoke*, 3rd rev. ed. (Washington, DC: CQ Press, 2011), 56.

14. R. Shep Melnick, *Between the Lines* (Washington, DC: Brookings Institution, 1994).

15. Harold H. Bruff, *Untrodden Ground: How Presidents Interpret the Constitution* (Chicago: University of Chicago Press, 2015). See also Keith E. Whittington, *Constitutional Construction: Divided Powers and Constitutional Meaning* (Cambridge, MA: Harvard University Press, 2001).

16. Charlie Savage, *Power Wars: Inside Obama's Post-9/11 Presidency* (Boston: Little, Brown, 2015), 63.

17. Barack Obama, "Remarks at the National Archives," May 21, 2009, http://www.presidency.ucsb.edu/ws/?pid=86166.

18. Savage, *Power Wars*, 67.

19. Quoted in Rebecca Adams, "Lame Duck or Leapfrog?" *CQ Weekly*, February 12, 2007, 450.

20. Bruce Ackerman, *The Decline and Fall of the American Republic* (Cambridge, MA: Harvard University Press, 2010), 88. See also Chris Edelson, "In Service to Power: Legal Scholars as Executive Branch Lawyers in the Obama Administration," *Presidential Studies Quarterly* 43 (September 2013): 618–640.

21. Hearing of the Committee on the Judiciary, US House of Representatives, "Enforcing the President's Constitutional Duty to Faithfully Execute the Laws," February 26, 2014, http://judiciary.house.gov/index.cfm/2014/2/enforcing-the-president-s-constitutional-duty-to-faithfully-execute-the-laws.

22. Quoted in Andrew Rudalevige, "Constitutional Structure, Political History, and the Invisible Congress," in *The Imperial Presidency and the Constitution*, ed. Gary Schmitt, Joseph M. Bessette, and Andrew E. Busch (Lanham, MD: Rowman & Littlefield, 2017), 59.

23. Robert Pear, "Four Words Imperil Health Law; All a Mistake, Its Writers Say," *New York Times*, May 26, 2015, A1. For a detailed examination of the ACA's convoluted passage through Congress, see Barbara Sinclair, *Unorthodox Lawmaking*, 5th ed. (Washington, DC: Sage/CQ Press, 2017), chap. 7.

24. King v. Burwell, 576 U.S. ___ (2015).

25. Since the Trump administration and the 115th Congress failed to repeal the ACA in 2017–2018, the administration implemented a wide range of executive actions designed to destabilize the exchange markets created by the law. The 2017 Tax Cuts and Jobs Act set the ACA's tax penalty for failing to obtain insurance to zero, leading one conservative district court judge in Texas to rule (implausibly) that the entire ACA had been rendered unconstitutional. That ruling is expected, though not guaranteed, to be overturned on appeal. See, e.g., Michael Hiltzik, "Trumpcare Sabotage #1: Trump Reneges on Obamacare Payments," *Los Angeles Times*, October 13, 2017, http://www.latimes.com/business/hiltzik/la-fi-hiltik-trump-csr-20171013-story.html; Dylan Scott, "The Trump Administration's Latest Steps to Undermine the Affordable Care Act, Explained," vox.com, July 12, 2018, https://www.vox.com/policy-and-politics/2018

/7/12/17561214/obamacare-open-enrollment-2019-premiums-trump; Abby Good-nough and Robert Pear, "Texas Judge Strikes down Obama's Affordable Care Act as Unconstitutional," *New York Times*, December 14, 2018, https://www.nytimes.com /2018/12/14/health/obamacare-unconstitutional-texas-judge.html.

26. Daniel P. Gitterman, *Calling the Shots: The President, Executive Orders, and Public Policy* (Washington, DC: Brookings Institution Press, 2017).

27. Texas was a highly favored site for "venue shoppers" filing suit against the Obama ad-ministration because many judges there were unsympathetic to aggressive regulatory behavior, because it had a fast "rocket docket," and because the Fifth Circuit Court of Appeals, which covers Texas, was dominated by Republican appointees. As one reporter noted, "Another day, another Obama administration regulation blocked na-tionwide by a federal court in Texas." Josh Gerstein, "Judge Blocks Obama Contract-ing Rules Nationwide," *Politico*, October 25, 2016, http://www.politico.com/blogs /under-the-radar/2016/10/obama-government-contractors-regulation-blocked-texas -court-230295.

28. See Executive Order 13782, March 27, 2017.

29. Paul J. Larkin, "The Trump Administration and the Congressional Review Act," *Georgetown Journal of Law and Public Policy* 16 (Summer 2018), https://papers.ssrn .com/sol3/papers.cfm?abstract_id=3172775.

30. The salary cutoff had not been seriously examined since the 1960s. In 1975 more than 60 percent of full-time workers could receive overtime, but this number had dropped to only 7 percent by 2015.

31. For this rule, see the Department of Labor website: https://www.dol.gov/WHD/over time/final2016/.

32. Daniel Wiessner, "States, Interest Groups Sue U.S. Government on Overtime Pay Rule," Reuters.com, September 20, 2016, http://www.reuters.com/article/us-over time-lawsuit-idUSKCN11Q2E2.

33. Melanie Trottman, "Federal Judge Issues Nationwide Injunction," *Wall Street Journal*, November 23, 2016, http://www.wsj.com/articles/federal-judge-issues-nationwide -injunction-putting-overtime-pay-regulation-on-hold-1479857762; Daniel Wiessner, "U.S. Judge Strikes down Obama Administration Overtime Pay Rule," Reuters.com, August 21, 2017, https://www.reuters.com/article/us-usa-overtime/u-s-judge-strikes -down-obama-administration-overtime-pay-rule-idUSKCN1BB2Y8.

34. Coral Davenport, "E.P.A. Staff Struggling to Create Pollution Rule," *New York Times*, February 4, 2014, http://www.nytimes.com/2014/02/05/us/epa-staff-struggling-to -create-rule-limiting-carbon-emissions.html; Coral Davenport and Gardiner Harris, "Obama to Unveil Tougher Environmental Plan with His Legacy in Mind," *New York Times*, August 2, 2015, http://www.nytimes.com/2015/08/02/us/obama-to-unveil -tougher-climate-plan-with-his-legacy-in-mind.html.

35. Utility Air Regulatory Group (UARG) v. Environmental Protection Agency, 573 U.S. ___ (2014).

36. Michigan v. Environmental Protection Agency, 576 U.S. ___ (2015).

37. Jonathan H. Adler, "Supreme Court Puts the Brakes on the EPA's Clean Power Plan," *Volokh Conspiracy* (blog), *Washington Post*, February 9, 2016, https://www.washing tonpost.com/news/volokh-conspiracy/wp/2016/02/09/supreme-court-puts-the -brakes-on-the-epas-clean-power-plan/?utm_term=.4a359fb75e87.

38. Jonathan H. Adler, "Placing Obama's Clean Power Plan in Context," *Volokh Con-*

spiracy (blog), *Washington Post*, February 10, 2016, https://www.washingtonpost.com/news/volokh-conspiracy/wp/2016/02/10/placing-the-clean-power-plan-in-context/?utm_term=.bc1435759a3f. See also Coral Davenport, "Obama Climate Plan, Now in Court, May Hinge on Error in 1990 Law," *New York Times*, September 25, 2016, http://www.nytimes.com/2016/09/26/us/politics/obama-court-clean-power-plan.html?_r=0.

39. Jonathan H. Adler, "The En Banc D.C. Circuit Meets the Clean Power Plan," *Volokh Conspiracy* (blog), *Washington Post*, September 28, 2016, https://www.washingtonpost.com/news/volokh-conspiracy/wp/2016/09/28/the-en-banc-d-c-circuit-meets-the-clean-power-plan/?utm_term=.8a76b4c05c12.

40. Lisa Friedman and Brad Plumer, "E.P.A. Drafts Rule on Coal Plants to Replace Clean Power Plan," *New York Times*, July 5, 2018, https://www.nytimes.com/2018/07/05/climate/clean-power-plan-replacement.html.

41. Brad Plumer, "Want to Know Why Trump Will Struggle to Save the Coal Industry? Look at Michigan," vox.com, November 28, 2016, http://www.vox.com/energy-and-environment/2016/11/28/13763728/trump-coal-industry-michigan. The economic realities were such that the Trump administration explored a variety of means to prop up fossil fuels, including the dubious use of the 1950s Defense Production Act to require that utilities purchase power from coal-fired plants.

42. Arizona v. United States, 567 U.S. 387 (2012); Heckler v. Chaney, 470 U.S. 821 (1985).

43. U.S. v. Texas, US Supreme Court, docket no. 15-674, April 18, 2016, 40, 58, 60, https://www.supremecourt.gov/oral_arguments/argument_transcripts/2015/15-674_b97d/pdf.

44. Ibid., 24; U.S. v. Texas, 579 U.S. ___ (2016), https://www.supremecourt.gov/opinions/15pdf/15-674_jhlo.pdf.

45. Executive Order 13492, January 22, 2009.

46. Jack Goldsmith, "The Contributions of the Obama Administration to the Practice and Theory of International Law," *Harvard International Law Journal* 57 (Spring 2016): 456.

47. See, e.g., Rudalevige, *New Imperial Presidency*.

48. Jo Becker and Scott Shane, "Clinton, 'Smart Power,' and a Dictator's Fall," *New York Times*, February 28, 2016, A1; Chris Edelson, *Emergency Presidential Power* (Madison: University of Wisconsin Press, 2013); Louis Fisher, "Military Operations in Libya: No War? No Hostilities?" *Presidential Studies Quarterly* 42 (March 2012): 176–189.

49. Louis Fisher and David Gray Adler, "The War Powers Resolution: Time to Say Goodbye," *Political Science Quarterly* 113 (Spring 1998): 1–20.

50. Savage, *Power Wars*, 645.

51. Barack Obama, "The President's News Conference," June 29, 2011, http://www.presidency.ucsb.edu/ws/?pid=90590.

52. However, the WPR specifically rules out using treaty obligations, by themselves, to justify the use of force.

53. "*Meet the Press* Transcript," NBC News, September 7, 2014, http://www.nbcnews.com/meet-the-press/meet-press-transcript-september-7-2014-n197866.

54. Juliet Eilperin and David Nakamura, "Obama Ready to Strike at Islamic State Militants in Syria, He Tells Policy Experts," *Washington Post*, September 9, 2014.

55. Daily press briefing by the White House press secretary, October 31, 2015, https://

www.whitehouse.gov/the-press-office/2015/10/30/daily-press-briefing-press-secre
tary-josh-earnest-103015.

56. Quoted in Steven T. Dennis, "Here's Obama's Legal Justification for ISIS War," *Roll Call*, September 11, 2014, http://www.rollcall.com/news/home/heres-the-adminis
trations-legal-justification-for-isis-isil-war.

57. Stephen Preston, "The Legal Framework for the United States' Use of Military Force since 9/11" (speech delivered to the annual meeting of the American Society of International Law, Washington, DC, April 10, 2015), http://www.defense.gov/News
/Speeches/Speech-View/Article/606662.

58. Jack Goldsmith, "Obama's Breathtaking Expansion of the President's Power to Make War," *Time*, September 11, 2014, http://time.com/3326689/obama-isis-war-powers
-bush/.

59. John Bellinger's Salzburg Global Seminar speech, November 20, 2016, quoted in Lexington, "The Dark Side," *Economist*, November 26, 2016, 30.

60. Benjamin Wittes, "AUMF: Scope and Reach: Not Asking the Girl to Dance," *Lawfare* (blog), September 10, 2014, https://www.lawfareblog.com/not-asking-girl-dance. See also Robert Chesney, "The 2001 AUMF: From Associated Forces to (Disassociated) Successor Forces," *Lawfare* (blog), September 10, 2014, https://www.lawfareblog
.com/2001-aumf-associated-forces-disassociated-successor-forces.

61. Charlie Savage, Eric Schmitt, and Mark Mazzetti, "Obama Expands War with al-Qaeda to Include al-Shabab in Somalia," *New York Times*, November 28, 2016, A8.

62. Corker quoted in David Welna, "GOP Lawmakers Reluctant to Act on ISIS War Authorization Request," NPR, November 5, 2015, http://www.npr.org/2015/11/05
/454829097/gop-lawmakers-reluctant-to-act-on-isis-war-authorization-request;
Reid quoted in Burgess Everett, "New War Authorization Left for Dead," *Politico*, September 11, 2015, http://www.politico.com/story/2015/11/syria-corker-veterans
-day-war-authorization-215702.

63. Rep. Jim McGovern (D-MA) did manage to force a roll-call vote on the question of withdrawing forces from Syria and Iraq altogether; this was rejected, with 288 members voting against withdrawal.

64. Brendan McGarry, "1st US Service Member Killed Fighting ISIS in Syria," military.com, November 25, 2016, http://www.military.com/daily-news/2016/11/25/2-us
-servicemembers-killed-in-syria-iraq.html.

65. Charlie Savage, "Soldier Sues Obama over ISIS War Policy," *New York Times*, May 5, 2016, A14.

66. Bruce Ackerman, "Is Obama Enabling the Next President to Launch Illegal Wars?" *Atlantic*, August 24, 2016, http://www.theatlantic.com/politics/archive/2016/08
/obama-illegal-wars/497159/.

67. Marty Lederman, "Judge Kollar-Kotelly Dismisses Captain Smith's Suit," JustSecu
rity.org, November 22, 2016, https://www.justsecurity.org/34778/judge-kollar-kotel
ly-dismisses-captain-smiths-suit/.

68. Daniel J. Rosenthal and Loren DeJonge Schulman, "Trump's Secret War on Terror," *Atlantic*, August 10, 2018, https://www.theatlantic.com/international/archive
/2018/08/trump-war-terror-drones/567218/.

69. Barack Obama, "Address to the Nation on Immigration Reform," November 20, 2014, http://www.presidency.ucsb.edu/ws/?pid=107923.

70. William Howell with David Milton Brent, *Thinking about the Presidency: The Primacy of Power* (Princeton, NJ: Princeton University Press, 2013).

71. See, e.g., Dave Boyer, "The 'Most Transparent' Administration in History Issues Record Number of 'Midnight' Regulations," *Washington Times*, January 5, 2017, http://www.washingtontimes.com/news/2017/jan/5/obama-issuing-record-number-midnight-regulations/.

72. Proponents of more aggressive employment of the Congressional Review Act suggest that it can be used for guidance documents too, where those amount to substantive regulation. If so, this would expand both the scope of the CRA oversight power and the time allowed to use it. See Larkin, "Trump Administration and the CRA."

73. Bill Simmons, "President Obama and Bill Simmons: The GQ Interview," *GQ*, November 2015, http://www.gq.com/story/president-obama-bill-simmons-interview-gq-men-of-the-year.

CHAPTER ELEVEN
"Don't Do Stupid Shit"
Obama's Foreign and National Security Policy

David Patrick Houghton

Assessing the legacies of presidents is a difficult task, for a number of reasons. For one thing, success or failure in foreign policy—as in any area of policy-making—is in part a matter of perception. In one interesting study, researchers found that perceptions of victory are critically affected by how the issue or problem is framed by the mass media and others.[1] For instance, the United States unquestionably came out on top in the 1968 Tet Offensive, but TV viewers did not see it that way. Already distrusting Lyndon Johnson, they saw the Vietcong running around the US embassy in Saigon and asked themselves what had been achieved in the last four years.

And just as victory can be seen as defeat, the opposite is also true. During the *Mayaguez* hostage crisis of 1975, Gerald Ford pressed military planners to conduct a rescue mission and raid before they were ready to do so, and more US marines died in that operation than the number of *Mayaguez* crewmen held hostage (and the captives were released anyway, before the operation even began). But the public perception was that this was a needed "shot in the arm" after the withdrawal from Vietnam that year, and Ford's opinion poll ratings went up.

Compounding the perceptual nature of success and victory is the fact that we often make decisions comparatively, judging the worth of something by comparing it to something else (rather than to a hypothetical list of all possible alternatives).[2] This is true not only in fields like aesthetics—where we might judge the beauty of an individual by reference to other human comparators—but also when we assess the domestic and foreign policy legacy of a president of the United States. Put differently, the presidency of Barack Obama will inevitably look better or worse than it otherwise might have when compared with readily available alternatives, such as the (chaotic) approach of Donald Trump or the (much criticized) perspective of George W. Bush. Put simply, the context of the times or the environment in which a president works matters, as does the political fate of predecessors and successors.

Second, we should note that—at the time of writing, at least—we lack any real historical perspective on Obama or his legacy. To use one (often mentioned) example from US politics, Harry Truman was seen as a rather weak president by many of his contemporaries in the 1940s (perhaps because he looked bad in comparison to the more politically astute Franklin Roosevelt). But then revisionists began to recast his presidency in a much better light, and both historians and political scientists saw attributes in Truman that had been unnoticed or obscured before. By the time of the 1992 presidential election, all three of the main contenders—George H. W. Bush, Bill Clinton, and H. Ross Perot—were competing to appear the most Trumanesque, something that was decidedly not true of presidential races in the 1950s and 1960s. And as Jonathan Chait suggests, 100 years from now, probably the main fact most Americans will learn about Obama is that he was the first African American president—even though the man himself often avoided discussion of racial issues.[3]

A third problem is that what a president *tried* to do also matters. Obama's foreign policy agenda was, on the whole, a modest one. He was seeking not to transform the outside world—as his predecessor had attempted to do in many ways—but to draw back into the domestic arena of the United States itself. Should presidents be judged on their own merits—by their success or failure at attaining stated objectives—or based on our judgments of what we think they ought to have been doing? Have they really failed if they succeed in meeting their own objectives but do not live up to our standards? As David Mervin notes, critics of George H. W. Bush often accused him of lacking the "vision thing," but he was being assessed relative to a model of presidential activism handed down by scholars like Richard Neustadt, rather than being considered on his own merits.[4] Internal criteria for judging presidential performance can be as useful as the more commonplace external ones.

A fourth problem is that presidents inevitably become drawn into conflicts—and sometimes "wicked problems"—that they no doubt wished never existed, and they may be judged by their performance in areas they did not choose to become involved in. It seems that Obama wanted a domestic legacy far more than he wanted a foreign one, and he might reasonably note that he did not start the wars in Iraq and Afghanistan but was forced to confront their ongoing effects; they had been "handed off" to him by his predecessor, as he often put it during the final months of his presidency. But expectations of what a president should be doing in the world are not easily thrown off, and liberal idealism is arguably more natural to Americans than bald pragmatism. Many countries in Europe and elsewhere look to the United States as the defender of Western values, so presidents who take a more withdrawn approach inevitably pay a political price of some sort. Obama clearly realized this immediately, acknowledging, "After the election the world's problems were seen as his responsibility. 'People are saying, you're the most powerful person in the world, why aren't you doing something about it?'"[5] In this vein, Obama repeatedly faced accusations that he was "leading from behind" on all manner of foreign policy issues, but was such an assessment fair?

This issue is related to the stubborn indeterminacy of counterfactuals. If the United States had intervened in the civil war still raging in Syria, for instance, would we have seen even greater US military casualties or more civilian casualties? Would Syria have proved to be a quagmire similar to Vietnam, Iraq, or Afghanistan, into which American blood and treasure were poured to little or no avail? Would US intervention have led to clashes with Russian or Iranian troops, and perhaps even to World War III? Did Obama's unwillingness to get involved actually save many lives? Or was inaction the product of overly cautious and risk-averse behavior on the part of a president who was unwilling to use American force? Our cognitive difficulty in conceiving of possible alternative worlds hinders our capacity to accurately judge presidential performance.

Last, determining a legacy is complicated by the fact that some administration members have a strong incentive to sugarcoat past performance, exaggerating successes and downplaying failures. This may be especially true of those who work on the White House staff, such as national security assistants, White House chiefs of staff, and White House press secretaries. Asked to speak about the Obama administration in 2016, for instance, Ben Rhodes—deputy national security assistant from 2009 to 2017—pointed to myriad accomplishments, including "[the] Paris climate agreement, Iran deal, Cuba opening, dramatically reducing the number of U.S. troops serving in harm's way while sustaining pressure on terrorists, taking out Osama bin Laden, reaching young people all around the world, stamping out Ebola."[6] Cabinet secretaries, in contrast, are less prone to view failure as success, being somewhat less proximate to the White House and its interests. Both Robert Gates and Leon Panetta served as Obama's secretary of defense, and both ended up being critical of the president's performance (at least as measured by the memoirs they wrote afterward).[7] In short, where you sit often determines how you judge, and we have to distinguish hyperbole from honest assessment.

All these factors affect how we perceive the foreign policy legacy of presidents. The difficulty of assessing this legacy does not imply impossibility, however. In this case, it seems reasonable to examine Obama's conduct of the wars in Iraq and Afghanistan by both internal and external criteria, as well as other issues such as the proposed closure of the US base at Guantanamo Bay, better relations with Cuba, the negotiation of the Iran nuclear deal, the decision to intervene in Libya, the Asian "pivot," the decision not to intervene decisively in Syria, and the ongoing war against the so-called Islamic State, or ISIS. It is not possible to discuss all these issues in depth here. Some are inevitably accorded more space than others. It seems reasonable, though, to first look in an overall sense at what Obama was trying to achieve (or not achieve) as president.

The Obama Foreign Policy Style

Although he enjoyed a meteoric rise to power, having briefly served as a state leg-islator and US senator, Barack Obama came to the presidency with little foreign policy experience. He was the first president since John F. Kennedy to move to the White House directly from the US Senate, but he spent less than four years in that chamber. Like the former state governors who preceded him—Jimmy Carter, Ronald Reagan, Bill Clinton, and George W. Bush—as well as the nonpolitician Donald Trump who came afterward—he essentially had to learn foreign policy on the job. He may not have been as effective as Abraham Lincoln in this task, but he was more effective than most.[8]

Many commentators attest to Obama's highly deliberative style in foreign pol-icy.[9] Although he was capable of "blink" decisions on occasion, he was renowned for gathering all the relevant information before making key decisions, in a way that approximated the rational actor model. But given human beings' cognitive limitations, this model can only mimic real behavior. Thorough debate was one hallmark of Obama's approach, as he explained early on:

> I think that's how the best decisions are made. One of the dangers in a White House, based on my reading of history, is that you get wrapped up in group-think and everybody agrees with everything and there's no discussion and there are no dissenting views. So I'm going to be welcoming a vigorous debate inside the White House. But understand, I will be setting policy as president. I will be responsible for the vision that this team carries out, and expect them to imple-ment that vision once decisions are made.[10]

Many observers, however, mention the relatively cold or passionless character of Obama's decision-making. According to Panetta, Obama is "supremely intelli-gent," but "he does . . . sometimes lack fire. Too often, in my view, the president relies on the logic of a law professor rather than the passion of a leader."[11] Similarly, Gates observes, the "one quality I missed in Obama was passion, especially when it came to the two wars." He notes that, unlike the Bushes, he never saw Obama on the verge of tears. "I worked for Obama longer than [George W.] Bush, and I never saw his eyes well up."[12]

During his presidency, Obama drew back from something that resembled a team of rivals in his first term, embracing what became a more clearly centralized foreign policy style in his second.[13] Early on in the administration, the team of rivals notion—very much akin to the "spokes in the wheel" approach to managing presidential advisers utilized by FDR and Kennedy—exerted a particular effect on the composition of the foreign policy team. Most notably, Obama included Hillary Clinton as secretary of state and Republican Robert Gates as secretary of defense.

Although foreign policy-making was always somewhat centralized, in the second term Obama relied more overtly on an inner circle of advisers within the White House. Like most presidents before him, he really wanted to be his own secretary of state. As detailed in the discussion of Afghanistan below, an unhealthy relationship would also develop with the US military, which may have led Obama to take power away from the agencies and centralize it in the White House again.

Obama's—and Americans'—Foreign Policy Beliefs

The irony of the Obama presidency was that while he possessed the oratorical skills of a gifted Wilsonian, his temperament was very much that of a cold-eyed realist. But what was the administration's foreign policy strategy? What was it ultimately trying to achieve in the world?[14] One popular answer was suggested by Obama himself in his 2009 Nobel Prize speech:

> Where force is necessary, we have a moral and strategic interest in binding ourselves to certain rules of conduct. And even as we confront a vicious adversary that abides by no rules, I believe the United States of America must remain a standard bearer in the conduct of war. That is what makes us different from those whom we fight. That is a source of our strength. That is why I prohibited torture. That is why I ordered the prison at Guantanamo Bay closed. And that is why I have reaffirmed America's commitment to abide by the Geneva Conventions. We lose ourselves when we compromise the very ideals that we fight to defend. And we honor—we honor those ideals by upholding them not when it's easy, but when it is hard.[15]

Put differently, a hard-headed realism, combined with a basic commitment to American ideals, was the basic approach.

But a strategy is about more than goals or objectives; it is also about how those goals are achieved (about ends, ways, and means). Put in those terms, Leslie Gelb, former president of the Council on Foreign Relations, claimed that Obama actually had no strategy at all. By this reading, the president was nothing more than an ultrapragmatist who bounced from one tactical issue to another, with no real compass or guide to what he truly believed. As Gelb puts it, "while Obama saw what American power could not do, he failed to appreciate what American power could do, especially when encased in good strategy. Thus his principal shortcoming was failing to formulate strategy and understand its interplay with power. . . . To this day, Obama's Afghanistan strategy seems little more than a disjointed list of tactics."[16] Yet as Paul Pillar notes, "it is hard to distinguish something that stands out as a strategy from what [are] simply skilful responses to the particular opportunities and problems that happened to confront particular presidents at the times they were in office."[17] What is clear is that the Obama administration did have a strategy of sorts, and to some extent, it did *constrain itself* between 2009 and 2017. It was a rather unadventurous strategy—especially when compared with, and in no small part *because of*, its predecessor—and it sought to address America's internal problems rather than external issues.[18]

Bert Rockman has suggested that Obama had "a relatively successful but not transformational presidency."[19] Indeed, it is questionable whether he even tried to be transformational in a foreign policy context. Obama sought to create a domestic legacy rather than a foreign policy one, and the president himself said that he wanted to focus on "nation building here at home" rather than foreign adventures. His strategy was therefore one of realist retrenchment.[20] Many have argued against retrenchment, while others have argued for it.[21] But it was fairly clear that this was Obama's foreign policy strategy. Obama chose a more restrained foreign policy than his predecessor, mostly because he genuinely believed that military adventurism overseas was not in America's best interest. He also thought that securing liberal legacies at home—a kind of *reculer pour mieux sauter*—was.[22]

Coming on the heels of two phases of idealism that were seen in some quarters as failed experiments—one from the left, the other from the right—it was natural that a period of realism and pragmatism should come next.[23] As David Milne has argued, Barack Obama is essentially a realist of the Reinhold Niebuhr stripe, and the former president himself has admitted the influence of that thinker on his foreign policy philosophy.[24] The son of German immigrants, Niebuhr was an American theologian who believed that evil lies in the human heart—a very Christian assumption—but he departed from his more liberal colleagues in justifying both killing and war as necessary in some circumstances to uphold values such as democracy and peace. Obama, Milne notes, is inherently pragmatic rather than dogmatic, preferring a case-by-case approach to ideological dogmas or blueprints. He also surrounded himself with people who were similarly nonideological, keeping idealists at arm's length. At times, liberal idealists in the administration had their way, most notably during the Libyan intervention in 2011. But Obama played a far less active role in Syria, which, on its face, was a largely similar case. He also retained the national security apparatus of the conservative idealists and waged the war on terror even more ardently and aggressively in some ways than the Bush administration did. For all the attempts to label Obama and his administration, he remained exceptionally difficult to categorize.

With the possible exception of Samantha Power—who was a somewhat less visible US ambassador to the United Nations than she might have been in the second term—there was no Madeleine Albright figure in the administration during the last few years of its existence.[25] If national security assistant Susan Rice played this role at all, she did so very quietly and behind the scenes. With the possible exception of the 2011 Libyan intervention—an exercise in regime change—there was not a lot of evidence that strong interventionists held much sway in the administration. Although Obama deliberately created a team of rivals during his first term, there was no hawkish or muscular advocate of armed liberal intervention around the president in his second term. John Kerry was a more cautious manager of the State Department than a radical figure in his own right. It is difficult to imagine him ever challenging a Colin Powell figure over the use of military power, for instance, or anyone having an "aneurysm" over his (very rare) advocacy of military force.[26]

It is worth noting that this tendency toward pragmatism was supported, if not reinforced, by changes in public opinion that occurred during Obama's presidency. After Harry Truman's adventures during the Korean War, Dwight Eisenhower sought to retrench American involvement in the rest of the world, although one can argue that his "rollback" perspective—meaningful to some, mere rhetoric to others—constituted a departure from containment.[27] The end of the Cold War also had a clear effect on public opinion, making it especially difficult for Bill Clinton to commit US troops to hot spots overseas. In more recent times, moreover, there has been a counterreaction to the adventurism of the Iraq and Afghanistan years.[28] Broadly speaking, Barack Obama was elected to get America *out* of wars, not into them.

Of course, this approach had its costs. As already noted, the president was often accused of "leading from behind," and he once unwittingly said into an open microphone that his foreign policy was simply "don't do stupid shit."[29] Getting hit from both directions, Obama was caught between liberal interventionists on the left and neoconservative adventurists on the right, neither of whom approved of his cautious and pragmatic approach. But looking at recent public opinion data, what is most striking is that Obama's approach fit the tenor of the times. In terms of his overall foreign policy strategy, the limited agenda he was pursuing meshed with an increasingly inward-looking citizenry; US public opinion is at its most isolationist since the 1930s (a trend that Trump capitalized on in 2016).

But what do ordinary Americans want out of foreign policy? First of all, it has to be conceded that most Americans know little about the topic. Adam Berinsky, for instance, follows a long line of research in this area. As he puts it, in the case of both World War II and Iraq, "there is little evidence that citizens had the information needed to make cost/benefit calculations when deciding whether to support or oppose military action."[30] The public often expects easy solutions to thorny problems, and it sometimes believes that hard power alone is the answer. Nevertheless, there is evidence that ordinary people do pay attention to the *effects* of foreign policy. Voters may vote in a retrospective manner, for instance.[31] In other words, they may not seek to prevent wars from occurring in the first place, but they can play a significant role after the fact when judging actual performance.

One consequence of the disastrous interventions in Iraq and Afghanistan is that there has been a clear turning away from the rest of the world, leading to a strong measure of isolationism in US public opinion.[32] Indeed, the effect of those wars on ordinary Americans seems to be equivalent to that of Vietnam or even greater. The proportion of Americans saying that the United States should "mind its own business internationally" rose by just over 20 percent between 1964 and 1974, about the same as the rise between 2002 and 2013. This is greater than the effect of the end of the Cold War; the proportion of people favoring a smaller US role in international affairs rose by only about 10 percent between 1989 and 1994. And for the first time in forty years of polling, the Pew Research Center found in 2013 that a *majority* of Americans—about 52 percent—believed the country should "mind its own business," the most striking finding of all.[33]

This figure did not change a great deal between 2013 and 2016, although the data were somewhat mixed. About 57 percent of Americans continued to believe in 2016 that the United States should "deal with its own problems and let other countries deal with their own problems as best they can." A mere 37 percent expressed the view that the United States ought to assist other countries with their various problems. Despite Trump's victory in 2016, *fewer* US citizens actually said the United States does too much (41 percent) rather than too little (27 percent) to help solve the world's problems, down from about 51 percent three years before.[34]

At the same time, there was clearly a continuing desire between 1993 and 2013 to *share* American leadership, along with a concomitant desire to embrace multilateralism rather than unilateralism. Over that ten-year span, the proportion of people who wanted America to play no leadership role at all almost doubled, from about 7 percent to 12 percent. In the early stages of the Trump administration, Americans may not want the United States to lead from behind, but they do want it to lead collectively (only a minority want no leadership role at all). Moreover, the Trump administration's policies may have produced a counterreaction among Democrats. By 2017, 47 percent of Americans believed the United States should play an active global role, although that increase was almost entirely attributable to Democrats and Democratic-leaning independents, rather than Republicans.[35]

How, then, can we assess the Obama administration's performance across a range of foreign policy issues? Although it is not possible to do full justice to all the issues that were central to his presidency, the sections below deal with some of them. Obama's major objective was withdrawal from the "idealist" wars of his predecessor, George W. Bush, and I turn to these next.

Iraq and Afghanistan

By purely internal criteria, and strictly speaking, the wars in Iraq and Afghanistan eventually came to an end as promised, and this will undoubtedly be part of Obama's foreign policy legacy. Although Obama had pledged during the 2008 campaign that all troops would be withdrawn from Iraq within sixteen months, this commitment proved unrealistic. Despite the delay, Obama deserves much credit for ending the expansive involvements his predecessor had saddled him with. In December 2011 official US involvement in the Iraq war ended. Official American involvement in Afghanistan, as part of a NATO mission, ended in December 2014. It is important to recall that there were once 60,000 American troops in Afghanistan. This was one of the longest and most expensive commitments in US history, and it ended under President Obama. A different interpretation might be that the withdrawal of US troops only necessitated their return later, if on a smaller scale, after ISIS in Iraq and the Taliban in Afghanistan began to fill the vacuum left by the thinning of US forces.

Of course, the overall picture is rather complicated. As his successor took office in 2017, there were still at least 5,000 US troops in Iraq and 9,800 in Afghanistan (officially, in a purely training capacity).[36] When Obama took office in 2009, it was not clear what America was doing in Afghanistan, reminiscent of the "why are we in Vietnam?" question asked by earlier generations. Bob Woodward writes about discussions between Joe Biden and US troops on a visit to Afghanistan in early 2009, illustrating the wholesale confusion rather well:

> The vice president–elect believed that off-the-cuff conversations often yielded more insights than formal presentations. As he made the rounds with the troops, after asking the basic "How's it going?" he then slipped into a "What are we trying to do here." Everyone—colonels, lieutenants, sergeants—gave a different answer. "Basically, we're trying to rebuild this country," said one, "so that it can stand on its own two feet."
>
> Another said, "We're trying to get al Qaeda."
>
> Biden replied, "But I was just told they're not here."[37]
>
> A more common answer from the front-line troops was, "I don't know."[38]

Asking ten people the same question would yield ten different answers, Biden maintained.

We can question whether a real strategy was forthcoming under Obama, though. Afghanistan has a well-justified reputation as the "Graveyard of Empires," and Obama's overall approach was marred by conflicts between the White House and the Pentagon and by the emergence of profound mistrust between Obama and his generals.[39] Afghanistan was supposedly Obama's "good war"—although he never used that phrase in public—in contrast to what he saw as the wasteful diversion of the war in Iraq.[40] But the White House—especially Biden—repeatedly complained that the military was boxing the president in. Obama constantly asked for more options from the military. He complained (rightly or wrongly) that the military really gave him only one choice: send in more troops. The two options offered were both troop increases—one was woefully insufficient to do the job, and the other was so excessive that Congress would never approve it. In the end, Obama split the differ-ence and chose a "surge" of 30,000 troops, but he was never sold on the core coun-terinsurgency campaign favored by Generals David Petraeus, Stanley McCrystal, and Mike Mullen. Based on the model of the British in Malaya during the 1950s, a counterinsurgency often takes ten to twelve years to be successful. With one eye on the next election, the president feared that he was being sucked into a commitment without end, and there was no guarantee that a counterinsurgency campaign would even work.

The morphing of the Iraq insurgency into the ISIS problem made it difficult if not impossible to end America's involvement in the Iraq war completely. ISIS used brutal and spectacular online videos to broadcast the practice of executing anyone who did not buy into its uncompromising distortion of Islam, and this heaped pressure on elected officials to do something about the problem. Of course, one could argue that these were two entirely separate problems. However, there was a more or less seamless connection between the Sunni insurgency that occurred after the 2003 invasion of Iraq and the emergence of ISIS, which was a splinter group of the former. Arguably, the number of US troops in Iraq was expanding in the last days of the Obama presidency, and this was a natural outcome of the need to bolster the American military presence against ISIS. By its own internal criteria, the administration had reopened the Iraq war. However, it cannot be blamed for the fact that the fight against ISIS is likely to take many years, far exceeding Obama's time in office.

In the end, there was no solution in either Iraq or Afghanistan that all parties found acceptable. It was never clear what the strategic objective behind interven-tion was, and Obama was not prepared to countenance the long-term counter-insurgency commitment recommended by General Petraeus in both countries. Such a commitment, the president judged, would leave US forces bogged down for years, while he was committed to "winding the war down, not ratcheting it up."[41]

Cuba and Guantanamo

Obama pledged to shutter the US military base at Guantanamo Bay, Cuba, during the 2008 campaign, but no closure ever occurred during his presidency, and the base is still being used to hold prisoners at the time of this writing. His successor, meanwhile, pledged in 2016 not only to keep the base open but also to fill it with what he called "some real bad dudes." Resistance from his own party and from the bureaucracy inhibited Obama's ability to close the base, and domestic opposition to having al-Qaeda suspects housed on the US mainland proved decisive, as did the legal-constitutional argument that those same suspects would benefit from the provisions of US law if they were moved.

In contrast, restoring relations with Cuba will probably be seen as one of Obama's great successes in the long run, even though Trump has made it more difficult for US citizens to travel to the island (in addition to expelling Cuban diplomats from Washington and bringing American ones back home). Still, it will be difficult for the Trump administration to fully reverse the tide on this issue. During the Cold War, the outsized power of the Cuban lobby made it all but impossible for any US president to extend an olive branch to Fidel Castro's Cuba. But by the time of the Obama administration, that power had been reduced by competing commercial interests, which saw the potential profit to be gained from doing business in an underdeveloped country close to American shores. The aging of the population also meant that there were more younger Cuban Americans who could not even remember the pre-Castro days of Batista and were less likely to vote Republican.

The Cuban American National Foundation (CANF) is in many ways the functional equivalent of the American Israel Public Affairs Committee (AIPAC), and it has long pressed for maintenance of the harsh sanctions against Cuba's communist regime that have been in place since 1961. Until recently, hard-line members of Congress—such as Republican Illeana Ros-Lehtinen, former chair of the House Foreign Relations Committee—even continued to press for the assassination of the Castro brothers,[42] an indicator of the ongoing hostility. CANF is not against all linkages between the United States and Cuba or more open travel, but it strongly opposed lifting the long-established embargo. Commentators frequently attribute great electoral power to the Cuban lobby; Cuban Americans account for less than 1 percent of the US population as a whole, but they are concentrated in "swing states" such as Florida and New Jersey, and in principle, this gives them great sway over US policy-making. Tony Smith argues that CANF demonstrated "real power over American foreign policy" during passage of the Helms-Burton bill in 1996, and a survey of Washington elites shows that they regard Cuban Americans as the second most influential ethnic lobby in America.[43] There is also some evidence that campaign contributions may influence US policy toward Cuba.[44]

The Cold War ended many years ago, and tiny, isolated Cuba no longer represents a threat to US security interests. But there remains a danger that ethnic lobbies may "distort" foreign policy, ensuring that it fails to reflect America's underlying security interests. Under Barack Obama, however, we saw increased *marginalization* of the Cuban American lobby. In part, this was a result of the emergence of significant commercial interests as a rival or alternative lobby. These interests see the island's potential as a "playground" for Americans abroad, and they suggest that the country is overdue for significant economic development.[45] The change in attitude is also a product of the shrinking Cuban population that remembers the Cold War.

Obama capitalized on both developments, engineering a gradual change in US-Cuban relations. In 2015 diplomatic ties were restored, and the United States reopened its embassy in Havana for the first time since 1961, when relations were broken in the waning days of the Eisenhower administration. Obama also called for the lifting of the trade embargo and was clearly on a mission to liberalize relations between the United States and Cuba.[46] To be sure, many Cuban Americans in Congress are Republicans, such as Senators Ted Cruz and Marco Rubio, and they were implacably hostile to Obama's agenda. Likewise, Cuban Americans have a strong tendency to vote Republican.[47] As Noah Feldman puts it, "Obama's opening to Raul Castro's regime is precisely what the Cuba lobby has long feared and opposed. Its two leading voices in the Senate, New Jersey Democrat Robert Menendez and Florida Republican Marco Rubio, immediately condemned Obama's apparent swap of three convicted Cuban spies for convicted American Alan Gross and another unnamed American held on espionage charges in Cuba."[48] Trying to end the embargo will likely result in a similar effort by the lobby, if indeed there is such an effort under Donald Trump (which seems unlikely).

The Asian Pivot

In retrospect, there was less to Obama's Asian pivot than met the eye. Critics questioned whether US policy really changed as a result of it, and they alleged that it left China ascendant.[49] It may well be true, as Jeffrey Michaels suggests, that we took the pivot too seriously and that it was primarily a shift in *rhetoric* rather than policy:

> In Europe, a belief emerged that the Administration's rhetoric constituted a major new development in US policy and would actually place meaningful restrictions on America's willingness and capability to deal with European security problems. This belief has now become dogma, and its institutionalization is evident in the mainstream political, bureaucratic and expert discourse. Moreover, the "pivot" was not only accepted as a fact in its own right, but it became the prism through which US foreign policy behaviour has been viewed more generally. Unfortunately, as is the case with most accepted wisdom, it is rarely challenged, despite the existence of considerable evidence and credible alternative interpretations that would call it into question. . . . In contrast to the mainstream interpretation, the Asia "pivot" or "rebalancing" is mostly a rhetorical construct that has very little meaning for US security policy, and it has served to mislead analysts trying to understand that policy.[50]

Similarly, Victor Cha of the Center for Strategic and International Studies notes that "in polite company people won't say it, but behind closed doors I think they'll openly ask where the pivot is."[51]

From China's perspective, the arrangement was intended as a "balance" against its growing power in the region. Obama countered that the pivot was designed to manage China's inevitable evolution to superpower status. In the end, it amounted to a few troop movements in Australia. To have real teeth, it would have required passage of the Trans-Pacific Partnership (TPP), but Obama's advisers conceded that this was all but dead by the time he left office. Donald Trump made it clear that presidential support for the TPP would not be forthcoming, and he formally abandoned the arrangement in 2017.

Kurt Campbell and Brian Andrews argue that there was a high degree of unanimity at all levels of the Obama government and among numerous organizations in generating the pivot. "To develop and implement it, the government's national security leaders showed strong cooperation and team work," they contend. "Secretary [Hillary] Clinton, Secretary of Defense Robert Gates and his successor Leon Panetta, and National Security Assistant Tom Donilon worked closely and effectively together, with the full range of US agencies and departments and a host of supporting characters, to realize the president's vision through six key efforts."[52] Hillary Clinton's memoir *Hard Choices* makes it clear that much of the policy was developed within the State Department early in 2009 (a noted contrast to the Nixon and Kissinger "triangular diplomacy" of 1971–1972, which was developed in the White House and by conscious design wholly *without* the State Department). Clinton writes that she and her deputy, James Steinberg, considered three main options for a reassessment of US policy toward China, in concert with Kurt Campbell, the assistant secretary of state for East Asian and Pacific affairs:

> One option was to focus on broadening our relationship with China, on the theory that if we could get our China policy right, the rest of our work in Asia would be so much easier. An alternative was to concentrate our efforts on strengthening America's threat alliances in the region (with Japan, South Korea, Thailand, the Philippines, and Australia), providing a counterbalance to China's growing power. A third approach was to elevate and harmonize the alphabet soup of regional multilateral organizations, such as ASEAN (the Association of Southeast Asian Nations) and APEC (the Asia-Pacific Economic Cooperation organization). Nobody was expecting anything as coherent as the European Union to spring up overnight, but other regions had learned important lessons about the value of well-organized multinational organizations.[53]

Clinton decided not to choose among the three options but to pursue all of them simultaneously, arguing that "the smart power choice was to meld all three approaches."[54]

Was the Asia policy successful, then? Certainly, the substantive changes were modest. Clinton in particular engaged in a burst of foreign travel, racking up the air miles in a flurry of diplomatic activity. In concrete terms, the clearest result was that 2,500 US marines would be stationed in Australia by 2016, but it could be argued that little had changed. The pivot continued a trend in policy-making that had been evident across a number of previous administrations, as opposed to being something entirely new. Nevertheless, in a world of perceptions, even changes in rhetoric can have substantive consequences, increasing the comfort of allies while discomforting adversaries or enemies. There is a well-known adage that if you want peace, prepare for war. But we also know that the psychological belief that war is inevitable—often fueled by such preparations—can be one of its major causes, and conflict thereby becomes self-fulfilling. More than one observer has noted that Chinese policy-makers were deeply uneasy about the pivot policy, believing that the whole thing was targeted at them. But for eight years the Obama administration managed to avoid a major showdown with China similar to the Hainan island incident confronted by the George W. Bush administration in its first year.[55]

The Iran Nuclear Deal

Early in 2012 Israeli premier Benjamin Netanyahu's assessment suggested that Iran was no more than a few months from being able to make a nuclear weapon (a judgment that proved to be wrong, or at least exaggerated). This view was apparently shared by Israeli defense minister Ehud Barak. However, it was not shared by US intelligence, which estimated that Iran was at least twelve months away and perhaps a good deal longer. Netanyahu and Obama met in Washington, DC, in 2012, and there were reports of tension between the two and a wide-ranging debate about the wisdom of bombing Iran. Netanyahu may or may not have asked the United States to provide the "bunker-busting" technology to make an attack on Iran possible, but it is clear that Obama was not convinced of the necessity of a preemptive strike. He even berated reporters who speculated that such an attack was imminent, and Netanyahu went back to Israel essentially empty-handed.

Nevertheless, there was a clear impetus to act, and the Obama administration announced in 2015 that it had reached a nuclear deal with Iran, designed to forestall the regional arms race that would inevitably follow if Iran were to develop a nuclear bomb.[56] The Israeli government and AIPAC were virtually ignored in this rapprochement. Although the Israeli lobby enjoyed even greater electoral advantages and levels of organization than the Cuban American one, fears that the lobby would exert a pernicious influence on policy-making during the Obama years were mostly unrealized. This is because a majority of Jewish voters still overwhelmingly supported the president and the Democratic Party, while AIPAC and the Likud administration in Israel increasingly appealed to only very conservative Jewish Americans. A clear majority of Jewish Americans—a group with especially high levels of voter turnout—actually *supported* the Iran nuclear deal. As Scott Clement notes, "Jewish support for the deal was 20 percentage points higher than for Americans overall [in 2015], according to a side-by-side poll of the general public."[57]

Ultimately, of course, the proof of the pudding is in the eating, and it is unclear at this time whether the deal will lead to some sort of long-lasting change or rapprochement. The Trump administration formally abandoned the Iran nuclear deal in May 2018, but the president seemed more intent on simply throwing it out as opposed to negotiating something else in its place. Moreover, France, Germany, and the United Kingdom remain committed to the deal, making it unclear how much difference US opposition will make. Perhaps to Trump's frustration, whether to retain the deal is only partially an American decision to make. But if the arrangement is retained or revived by a later administration, it may form a lasting part of Obama's legacy. To Obama's credit, he realized that there was little alternative to some sort of peace deal, even though conservative forces in both Iran and the United States decried it. It is widely known today that some of Iran's nuclear facilities are many miles underground, and it is thought that only the United States possesses the kind of bunker-busting bombs capable of destroying them. But any US or Israeli bombing of the site at Natanz—reportedly many miles underground—would be an uncertain military task at best, and there is no guarantee that Obama could have destroyed Iran's nuclear program from the air. Opposition in Washington has centered on the claim that this is supposedly a "bad deal" for the United States, but the real problem is that the deal may be too good to be true (it promises to get rid of 98 percent of Iran's enriched uranium, for instance). But there is an ongoing fight between conservatives and reformers within Iran itself to shape the identity of the nation, and the deal may be hijacked by Iranian hard-liners opposed to closer ties with the West. The deal also lacks any real enforcement mechanism, relying on Iranian goodwill (although military options remain on the table as punishment for noncompliance).

The Libyan Intervention

One place where the wars in Iraq and Afghanistan might have been expected to in-fluence President Obama was Libya during the 2011 NATO intervention. Indeed, these wars did have an effect on the foreign policy realist and on the character of his response. The phrase "leading from behind" was an unfortunate term initially used by an Obama staffer to describe the US intervention in Libya.[58] It was, however, somewhat apt in this case—empirically, if not politically—since France and Britain took the lead in launching that intervention, and the United States provided much of the military backing and support. Leery of being seen as intervening in the fortunes of yet another Arab state, the Obama administration encouraged the perception that America was really just assisting its allies in Libya, not leading "another Iraq."

It was sometimes alleged that the out-of-character intervention was the product of some sort of "CNN effect." Paul Miller, for instance, claimed in the pages of the influential US journal *Foreign Policy* that the administration took action in Libya simply because of the harrowing images shown on television. Similarly, Joshua Gleis asserted that the military intervention in Libya was sparked by media coverage and that the comparative absence of such coverage explains the weak US response to the Syrian crisis.[59] While the truth may remain obscure for years to come, the real reasons for the different approaches were likely the relative difficulty of the tasks and the available intelligence about the probable consequences. Libya would be easy, in a military sense; the situation allowed for a quick intervention from the air based on the Afghan model, whereby a friendly force on the ground (such as the Northern Alliance) could capitalize on allied control of the air. It was consistent with the Vietnam syndrome as well, which suggested the strong inadvisability of putting US boots on the ground. Moreover, despite many years in power, Muammar Qaddafi had isolated himself from potential international allies, somewhat like Slobodan Milosevic had done in 1999 after the Russians withdrew their support. When the West intervened in Libya in 2011, China and Russia basically sat on their hands.

Somewhat unfairly, events in Libya became associated in the public's mind with the attack on the embassy in Benghazi, where US Ambassador Christopher Stevens and an associate were killed at the hands of Islamic terrorists. Despite unrelenting and repeated investigations by a Republican-led Congress, there was no evidence of wrongdoing by Secretary of State Hillary Clinton. The real purpose of these investigations seems to have been to discredit Clinton's presidential candidacy in 2016, since there was little or no mention of the matter once the election was over. But the investigations took their toll, and many apparently concluded that there *had* been some wrongdoing. This was unfortunate because, looked at objectively, the intervention represented a policy success. US policy-makers no doubt shied away from images of the brutal killing of Qaddafi at the hands of his own people, but judged on its own merits, the intervention clearly achieved its intended objectives. And for once, critics on the progressive left could approve of an Obama intervention to uphold the right of a sovereign people to decide their own fate.

The Syrian Nonintervention

If the Libyan intervention was somewhat out of character for a foreign policy realist, Obama's response to events in Syria was not. The civil war in Syria became a constant presence on the evening news in America, with harrowing images of human suffering filling the screen as dictator Bashar al-Assad—supported by his close allies in Russia and Iran—mercilessly bombed and gassed his own people in an effort to cling to power. One image of a little boy sitting bloodied in the back of an ambulance, for example, was especially memorable. The United States would not intervene during the Obama years, however, and it is instructive to note that the administration did not bow to considerable pressure from Congress. The late

Senator John McCain, for instance, repeatedly urged Obama to launch military action, but the administration did very little in response.[60]

Why was there no intervention in Syria under Obama, similar to that undertaken in Libya in 2011? Again, it is not entirely clear at this time, but the president's realist-style reasoning was obvious enough. One major concern was the apparent absence of "friendly" forces within Syria. Intelligence sources suggested that a "moderate" force on the ground either was not present at all or had been disillusioned into nonexistence by Obama's failure to act after stating that the use of chemical weapons would be a "red line" for the administration.[61] The relatively sophisticated nature of Syrian air defenses made an air-based intervention difficult. Russia and Iran were also offering close support, in contrast to the diplomatic and military isolation of Qaddafi. Lyndon Johnson had reportedly been haunted by mental images of triggering World War III in Vietnam if a stray bullet hit a Soviet or Chinese operative, and it would be surprising if the supposedly "cold" Obama did not have similar dreams. Most tellingly, from Obama's perspective, the United States lacked any compelling national interest in Syria, beyond the fact that inaction might embolden the country's allies. This itself was a kind of "red line" for realists.

And yet the fact of nonintervention remained. By the internal criteria, it was "mission accomplished," or perhaps "mission nonexistent." For Obama's idealist critics, however, this will always be the president's greatest foreign policy failing. He will likely be haunted by the ghosts of Syria long after his presidency is over, just as the US failure to intervene in Rwanda prior to the 1994 genocide reportedly haunted Bill Clinton. From an external perspective, the results of America's nonintervention were not at all satisfying, yet by staying out of Syria, Obama might have prevented an even greater slaughter in that country.

Obama's Foreign Policy Legacy

This was in some ways a presidency of great contradictions.[62] As Rosa Brooks notes, Obama "accelerated a covert drone war that has so far killed an estimated 4,000 people in Pakistan, Somalia and Yemen."[63] By the same token, he was accused of being feckless by the right and unwilling to use America's vast military resources for good. He was hit by criticisms coming from both directions, as most centrists are. But Obama quickly discovered that there is a kind of "damned if you do, and damned if you don't" quality to being the commander in chief. On the one hand, if you go into one of the world's hot spots with guns blazing and capitalize on America's massive conventional superiority, you are accused of acting in a hasty or precipitate way, before all the facts are known. On the other hand, if you stay out of those same hot spots and cite the lack of a national interest, you may be accused of acting callously and ignoring humanitarian tragedy. There is, of course, a middle ground here, and Obama often tried to find a foreign policy that met this criterion. But in Syria, for instance, critics will always argue that he got the balance wrong. By the Obama administration's own internal criteria, he did quite well on the realist scorecard overall, and in terms of foreign policy, his presidency will be judged mainly a success. Outside the administration, critics on both the left and the right will judge him more harshly, arguing that he failed in some way. Realists will applaud his restraint when compared with his predecessor, George W. Bush—and perhaps when contrasted with his successor, Donald Trump—but liberal interventionists will rue the opportunities they think he lost.

Few presidents have witnessed a more overt desire on the part of his successor to reverse his whole foreign policy legacy and agenda. In this respect, Obama has been somewhat unlucky, especially with regard to a Republican Senate (as of early 2019) that showed little inclination to rein in President Trump's power. But so far, the Trump administration has been unable to reverse everything Obama did by executive order, least of all to remake the world order that underpinned the foreign policies of his predecessors. As the founding fathers intended, the power of the American presidency is far from limitless.

The most central question, however, is whether Obama diminished or enhanced America's position in the world. The answer, of course, depends on who you ask. Perceptions of the US position in the world have changed greatly over time, implicitly calling into question whether unipolarity is (at least partly) in the eye of the beholder. In the 1980s conventional international relations theory usually portrayed the United States as having entered a process of terminal hegemonic decline, partly due to "imperial overstretch."[64] By the 1990s, though, hegemonic stability theory was no longer in vogue, and some observers—many of them on the political right—were talking about the "benevolent empire" and the "unipolar moment."[65] Stephen Brooks and William Wohlforth, writing before Iraq and Afghanistan, were impressed with the reach of American power, claiming that "vulnerability to terror has few effects on U.S. strength in more traditional interstate affairs." They argued that "the United States has no rival in any critical dimension of power. There has never been a system of sovereign states that contained one state with this degree of dominance."[66] After Iraq and Afghanistan became (rightly) viewed as failures, the dominant view changed yet again. Liberal observers such as Joseph Nye, for instance, argued that the system is unipolar in only one respect but multipolar in others.[67] Yet Richard Haass was surely still correct in 1999 when he wrote, "the reality is that the United States is first among unequals. This is and will likely remain a world of distinct American primacy."[68] According to most estimates, though, this state of affairs is unlikely to persist forever, and the US role will decline at some point during the next twenty to thirty years. As Nye notes, primacy "seems like a more accurate description of a country's disproportionate (and measurable) share of all three kinds of power resources: military, economic, and soft."[69] This primacy continued under Barack Obama, and his withdrawal from the costly intervention in Afghanistan and semiwithdrawal from Iraq helped ensure that the United States will remain a central player in international politics for some years to come. President Trump can sign executive orders that partially negate the Iranian and Cuban initiatives, but the signature achievements of the Iran nuclear deal and the opening to Cuba will be difficult to reverse in practice, as will the phenomenon of a "China rising" and the need to respond to this.

Obama was not as constrained in foreign policy as he was in domestic affairs. Indeed, we may have been too hasty in our dismissal of Aaron Wildavsky's famous two presidencies thesis.[70] Public opinion about America's role in the world—at least at the time—was quite consistent with where Obama wanted it to be, providing a permissive environment for a strategy of disengagement. There was little public appetite for what might be called military adventurism, and this has been a major legacy of Iraq, Afghanistan, and Obama's time in office. Of course, foreign policy in the United States is shaped mainly by elites. But Trump inherited an America that was bolstered by eight years of the Obama presidency, even if the still-divided country was not entirely happy with itself as a "shining city upon a hill." Overturning that legacy will certainly take more than the stroke of a presidential pen. Yet Trump has made others' faith in the credible commitments made by the United States more perilous with respect to both allies and adversaries. In that sense, it might be said that Obama's legacy is being slowly but surely erased.

Notes

1. Dominic Tierney and Dominic Johnson, *Failing to Win: Perceptions of Victory and Defeat in International Politics* (Cambridge, MA: Harvard University Press, 2006).
2. Philip Crowley and Thomas Zentall, eds., *Comparative Decision Making* (New York: Oxford University Press, 2013).
3. Jonathan Chait, interview with Jim Acosta about the book *Audacity*, CSPAN2, January 22, 2017.
4. David Mervin, *George Bush and the Guardianship Presidency* (London: Palgrave Macmillan, 1996). See also Fred Greenstein, *The Hidden-Hand Presidency: Eisenhower as Leader* (Baltimore: Johns Hopkins University Press, 1982).
5. Bob Woodward, *Obama's Wars* (New York: Simon & Schuster, 2010), 12.
6. Barbara Maranzani, "White House Q&A: President Obama's Foreign Policy Legacy," November 30, 2016, http://www.history.com/news/white-house-qa. Ben Rhodes offers a longer and more detailed defense of Obama's foreign policy achievements in *The World as It Is: A Memoir of the Obama White House* (New York: Simon & Schuster, 2018).
7. Robert Gates, *Duty: Memoirs of a Secretary at War* (New York: Alfred Knopf, 2014); Leon Panetta, *Worthy Fights: A Memoir of Leadership in War and Peace* (New York: Penguin Books, 2014).
8. See Elliot Cohen, *Supreme Command: Soldiers, Statesmen and Leadership in Wartime* (New York: Free Press, 2012).

9. See, e.g., Gates, *Duty*, 299.

10. Quoted in Fred Greenstein, *The Presidential Difference: Leadership Style from FDR to Barack Obama*, 3rd ed. (Princeton, NJ: Princeton University Press, 2009), 216–217.

11. Panetta, *Worthy Fights*, 442.

12. Gates, *Duty*, 298–299.

13. Doris Kearns Goodwin, *Team of Rivals: The Political Genius of Abraham Lincoln* (New York: Simon & Schuster, 2006); Andrew Rudalevige, "Rivals, or a Team?" in *The Obama Presidency: First Appraisals*, ed. Bert A. Rockman, Andrew Rudalevige, and Colin Campbell (Washington, DC: Sage/CQ, 2012).

14. Jeffrey Goldberg, "The Obama Doctrine," *Atlantic*, April 2016, http://www.theatlan tic.com/magazine/archive/2016/04/the-obama-doctrine/471525/.

15. See https://www.nobelprize.org/nobel_prizes/peace/laureates/2009/obama-lecture _en.html.

16. Leslie Gelb, "The Elusive Obama Doctrine," *National Interest*, September–October 2012, 18. See also Adam Quinn, "The Art of Declining Politely: Obama's Prudent Presidency and the Waning of American Power," *International Affairs* 87, 4 (July 2011): 803–824.

17. Paul Pillar, "What Is a Strategy?" *National Interest* (blog), August 22, 2012, http:// nationalinterest.org/blog/paul-pillar/what-strategy-7388.

18. Colin Dueck, *The Obama Doctrine: American Grand Strategy Today* (New York: Oxford University Press, 2015). Neoclassical and other realists are apt to describe realism and retrenchment as something fundamentally different, but they are actually very similar, since looking inward when there are few compelling threats abroad *is* a realist tactic.

19. Bert Rockman, "The Obama Presidency: Hope, Change, and Reality," *Social Science Quarterly* 93, 5 (December 2012): 1077. As Henry Nau argues, Obama did not try to "stop the pendulum." Henry Nau, "Obama's Foreign Policy," *Policy Review* 160 (April 1, 2010), https://www.hoover.org/research/obamas-foreign-policy.

20. Nau, "Obama's Foreign Policy," 2–3.

21. See, e.g., Stephen Brooks, John Ikenberry, and William Wohlforth, "Don't Come Home, America: The Case against Retrenchment," *International Security* 37, 3 (Winter 2012–2013): 7–51; Joseph Parent and Paul MacDonald, "The Wisdom of Retrenchment: America Must Cut Back to Move Forward," *Foreign Affairs* 90, 6 (November–December 2011): 32–47.

22. See Parent and MacDonald, "Wisdom of Retrenchment." The French phrase *reculer pour mieux sauter* means "taking one step back to take two steps forward."

23. Leslie Gelb, *Power Rules: How Common Sense Can Rescue American Foreign Policy* (New York: HarperCollins, 2009).

24. David Milne, "Pragmatism or What? The Future of US Foreign Policy," *International Affairs* 88, 5 (July 2012): 935–951. See also Paul Pillar, "Obama's Realism," *National Interest* (blog), April 20, 2015.

25. See, e.g., Samantha Power, *A Problem from Hell: America and the Age of Genocide*, 2nd ed. (New York: Basic Books, 2013).

26. This is a widely cited reference to a confrontation between Madeleine Albright and Colin Powell during the early Clinton administration; see, e.g., Christopher O'Sullivan, *Colin Powell: A Political Biography* (London: Rowman & Littlefield, 2010), 111.

27. For one argument that Truman created containment and Eisenhower continued

it, see John Lewis Gaddis, *Strategies of Containment: A Critical Reappraisal of American National Security Policy during the Cold War*, rev. ed. (New York: Oxford University Press, 2015). Truman's "adventure'" in Korea was a UN-sponsored action, and he actually tried to limit General MacArthur's desire to eliminate the new communist regime in China. For his part, Eisenhower encouraged the internationalist wing of the Republican Party, which may have contributed to the intervention in Lebanon and to John Foster Dulles's efforts to forge regional security pacts around the globe.

28. For an especially cogent analysis in this vein, see Gian Gentile, *Wrong Turn: America's Deadly Embrace of Counter-Insurgency* (New York: New Press, 2013).

29. See, e.g., David Rothkopf, "Obama's 'Don't Do Stupid Shit' Foreign Policy," *Foreign Policy* (blog), June 4, 2014, http://foreignpolicy.com/2014/06/04/obamas-dont-do-stupid-shit-foreign-policy/.

30. Adam Berinsky, "Assuming the Costs of War: Events, Elites and American Public Support for Military Conflict," *Journal of Politics* 69, 4 (November 2007): 975–997.

31. See V. O. Key, *The Responsible Electorate* (Cambridge, MA: Belknap Press, 1966).

32. See Max Fisher, "American Isolationism Just Hit a 50-Year High: Why that Matters," *Washington Post*, December 4, 2013, https://www.washingtonpost.com/news/world views/wp/2013/12/04/american-isolationism-just-hit-a-50-year-high-why-that-mat ters/.

33. See Pew Research Center, "Public Sees U.S. Power Declining as Support for Global Engagement Slips," December 3, 2013, http://www.people-press.org/2013/12/03/public-sees-u-s-power-declining-as-support-for-global-engagement-slips/.

34. See Pew Research Center, "Key Findings on How Americans View the U.S. Role in the World," May 5, 2016, http://www.pewresearch.org/fact-tank/2016/05/05/key-findings-on-how-americans-view-the-u-s-role-in-the-world/.

35. See Pew Research Center, "The Partisan Divide on Political Values Grows Even Wider: Foreign Policy," October 5, 2017, http://www.people-press.org/2017/10/05/3-foreign-policy/.

36. Missy Ryan, "The US Military Has a Lot More People in Iraq than It Has Been Saying," *Washington Post*, March 21, 2016, https://www.washingtonpost.com/news/checkpoint/wp/2016/03/21/the-u-s-military-has-a-lot-more-people-in-iraq-than-it-has-been-saying/?utm_term=.1f5267b41d43.

37. Intelligence suggested that al-Qaeda was, by then, more of a presence in Pakistan than Afghanistan.

38. Woodward, *Obama's Wars*, 71.

39. Rosa Brooks, "Obama vs. the Generals," *Politico Magazine*, November 2013, http://www.politico.com/magazine/story/2013/11/obama-vs-the-generals-099379.

40. Jack Fairweather, *The Good War: Why We Couldn't Win the War or the Peace in Afghanistan* (New York: Basic Books, 2014).

41. Panetta, *Worthy Fights*, 253.

42. Fidel Castro died in 2016.

43. Tony Smith, *Foreign Attachments: The Power of Ethnic Groups in the Making of American Foreign Policy* (London: Harvard University Press, 2000), 69; David Paul and Rachel Anderson Paul, *Ethnic Lobbies and US Foreign Policy* (London: Lynne Rienner, 2009), 137, 141. The Israel lobby was considered the most influential.

44. See Trevor Rubenzer, "Campaign Contributions and U.S. Foreign Policy Outcomes:

An Analysis of Cuban American Interests," *American Journal of Political Science* 55, 1 (January 2011): 105–116.

45. Philip Brenner, Patrick Haney, and Walter Vanderbush, "Intermestic Interests in US Policy towards Cuba," in *The Domestic Sources of American Foreign Policy: Insights and Evidence*, 5th ed., ed. Eugene Wittkopf and James McCormick (Lanham, MD: Rowman & Littlefield, 2008), 71.

46. Daniel Dombey, "Anti-Castro Politicians Frozen out as US Eases Island's Isolation," *Financial Times*, June 3, 2009.

47. Noah Feldman, "Obama Takes on the Cuba Lobby," *BloombergView*, December 17, 2014, http://www.bloombergview.com/articles/2014-12-17/obama-takes-on-the-cuba -lobby.

48. Ibid.

49. See, e.g., Simon Tisdall, "Barack Obama's 'Asian Pivot' Failed. China Is in the Ascendancy," *Guardian*, September 25, 2016, https://www.theguardian.com/commentis free/2016/sep/25/obama-failed-asian-pivot-china-ascendant.

50. Jeffrey Michaels, "America's Global Defence Predicament—Why the Asia 'Rebalancing' Has Little Significance for European Security," Egmont Paper 72 (Egmont Royal Institute of International Relations, December 2014).

51. Quoted in Jamie Muller, "Four Factors Shaping President Obama's Visit to Asia," *Washington Post*, April 23, 2014, http://www.washingtonpost.com/blogs/the-fix /wp/2014/04/23/four-factors-shaping-president-obamas-visit-to-asia/.

52. Kurt Campbell and Brian Andrews, "Explaining the US 'Pivot' to Asia," Chatham House, Royal Institute of International Affairs, August 1, 2013, https://www.cha thamhouse.org/publications/papers/view/194019.

53. Hillary Clinton, *Hard Choices* (New York: Simon & Schuster, 2014), 44.

54. Ibid., 45. See also Kurt Campbell quoted in "JoongAng-CSIS Forum Debates U.S. Pivot to Asia," May 28, 2014, CSIS website.

55. In April 2001 an American EP3 aircraft collided with a Chinese plane, and the former was forced to land in Chinese territory.

56. Rhodes, *The World as It Is*, offers an interesting insider's perspective on the genesis of Obama's approach to Iran.

57. Scott Clement, "Jewish Americans Support the Iran Nuclear Deal," *Washington Post*, July 27, 2015, http://www.washingtonpost.com/news/the-fix/wp/2015/07/27/jewish -americans-support-the-iran-nuclear-deal/.

58. Ryan Lizza, "Leading from Behind," *New Yorker*, April 26, 2011, http://www.newyo rker.com/news/news-desk/leading-from-behind.

59. Paul Miller, "Obama Lip-Syncs a Neocon Tune on Libya," *Foreign Policy*, March 3, 2011, http://foreignpolicy.com/2011/03/03/obama-lip-syncs-a-neocon-tune-on-libya/; Joshua Gleis, "The Syrian Anomaly," *Huffington Post*, April 18, 2011, http://www .huffingtonpost.com/joshua-gleis/the-syrian-anomaly_b_849762.html.

60. The Trump administration embarked on a very limited bombing campaign of a single target in Syria on April 17, 2017.

61. This was a (perhaps) careless utterance by President Obama toward the end of a press conference, but the US unwillingness to act on this "red line" was rendered less relevant by a Russian-brokered "peace deal" signed by the parties shortly thereafter.

62. Goldberg, "Obama Doctrine."

63. Brooks, "Obama vs. the Generals."

64. See, in particular, Paul Kennedy, *The Rise and Fall of the Great Powers: Economic Change and Military Conflict from 1500 to 2000* (New York: Random House, 1987).

65. Robert Kagan, "The Benevolent Empire," *Foreign Policy* 111 (June 1998): 24–35; Charles Krauthammer, "The Unipolar Moment," *Foreign Affairs* 70, 1 (1990–1991): 23–33.

66. See Stephen Brooks and William Wohlforth, "American Primacy in Perspective," *Foreign Affairs* 81, 4 (July–August 2002): 20–33.

67. Joseph Nye, *The Paradox of American Power* (New York: Oxford University Press, 2002).

68. Richard Haass, "What to Do with American Primacy," *Foreign Affairs* 78, 5 (September–October 1999): 35–40.

69. Joseph Nye, "American Hegemony or American Primacy?" *Project Syndicate* (blog), March 9, 2015.

70. See Steven A. Shull, ed., *The Two Presidencies: A Quarter Century Assessment* (Belmont, CA: Wadsworth, 1991).

CHAPTER TWELVE

The Leadership Style and Legacy of Obama

Comparisons and Complexities

Bert A. Rockman

There is a perennial question about leaders and the times in which they serve: which has the greatest impact on success—the person, or the conditions under which he or she serves? This question may still be an open one in many circles of popular writing on leadership, and especially on the US presidency. Political scientists, however, have concluded that the structural conditions and political circumstances under which leaders serve are the dominant forces dictating the relative success of their agendas. Of course, this does not mean that personal characteristics are unimportant—but it means that their importance may be limited to those matters on which leaders have leeway. Leaders' ability to make the kind of substantial "pie in the sky" changes they usually campaign on is largely dependent on forces beyond their control. Mostly, these circumstances tend to powerfully constrain the exercise of presidential power. Sporadically, they enable it. Despite the audacious claim that the US presidency is the most powerful office in the world, the reality is that only under rare circumstances is this even remotely true. In fact, a good bit of evidence suggests that the American presidency is one of the weakest among presidential systems.[1]

The complex institutions of American government and its splintered electoral and fragmented representational system make the office of the president considerably less powerful than the popular rhetoric implies. One possible inference is that the bargaining skills emphasized by Richard Neustadt in his pathbreaking book *Presidential Power* and elaborated by Robert Caro in his multivolume work on Lyndon Johnson are less important now, in a far less fluid political system, than they once were, even though the actual impact of such political acumen has always been overestimated.[2] Currently, brute partisan force (up to a point) seems to have more utility, at least in regard to a president's relationship with the legislative branch. To be sure, Congress is only one of the actors a president has to deal with; there are also organized interests, state and local political leaders, the bureaucracy, and, above all, international leaders and organizations. But the relationship with Congress is the one most likely to determine the president's programmatic fate.

Obviously, the complicated institutional arrangements of separation of powers, checks and balances, and federalism hinder any president's ability to do more or less whatever he or she wants. Accordingly, institutional hindrances to presidential power are perceived as the main entities we need to understand, and ultimately, presidents will look for ways to circumvent these institutional obstacles in order to meet public demands and expectations and to satisfy their own policy and legacy ambitions. Richard Neustadt, who is often credited with originating the study of the modern American presidency, took the institutional constraints on presidential leadership as a given and asked the question: what can a president do to enhance his prospects for success? His answer was by no means clear-cut, but it rested on the political instincts a president brings to the job. To some degree, this involves luck in being able to sustain support among the populace. Neustadt conceived of this support as a form of currency that enables a president to navigate the complex relationships with other actors in Washington. To do so successfully, however, a president needs an arsenal of skills to convert the currency of public standing into power relative to other actors on whom the president is dependent (just as they are dependent on him). Neustadt did not have a precise formula for this conversion, except to point out that political amateurs are likely to fail, and only those experienced in politics and savvy in its ways are likely to succeed. He did, of course, identify points of leverage, but the nature of leverage and the opportunities to employ it vary over time and may be greater or lesser in any particular political moment or political epoch.

Neustadt's ideas about how to succeed in the presidency contain not only considerable ambiguities but also biases toward presidents with active legislative agendas. That tends to work against the outlook of traditional conservative presidencies such as those of Dwight Eisenhower (1953–1961) and George H. W. Bush (1989–1993), whose views of the office leaned toward consolidation and national integration rather than policy entrepreneurship.[3] It is also dismissive of the popularity of some leaders whose conventional political experience was meager (Eisenhower), and it fails to anticipate that some of those who were deeply experienced in the ways of Washington, such as Lyndon Johnson (1963–1969) and Richard Nixon (1969–1974), would squander their accomplishments and substantial electoral victories through poor judgment or, in Nixon's case, illegal behavior. The first George Bush (41) liked to talk about unwise courses of action being imprudent, the implication being that prudence is essential to avoiding costly disasters. Bush 41's wisdom may have been underappreciated, because one thing is surely true: presidents can hurt themselves more readily than they can help themselves.[4]

That observation provides a clue as to how individuals can impact the presidency. This ability may well depend on their capacity to understand both their limits and the country's. Given citizens' extraordinary expectations of the office and the person who occupies it, the assertion that the US presidency is the most powerful office in the world should be viewed with skepticism.[5] So should the corresponding expectation that the United States can dramatically alter events and forces at great distances from its shores. Even so, all presidents seem to suffer from exuberant hubris, perhaps as a consequence of the mythology invested in the office. Some presidents understand their limits better than others, but nearly all try to alter the balance of forces in their favor and to master these forces rather than submit to them. Some do this in bold and irretrievable steps that lead to catastrophe, such as Johnson's escalation in Vietnam and George W. Bush's uninformed and ill-planned venture in Iraq. Others find themselves sucked into smaller commitments that later bind their successors, such as John F. Kennedy's small-scale efforts to protect the governments in Laos and Vietnam that grew into much larger efforts under his successors, Johnson and Nixon.

Presidents who dare to undertake multiple "transformative" projects and significant policy shifts are likely to fail in proportion to the magnitude and scope of the changes they propose. The American political system does not readily countenance large-scale change or an overloaded agenda. Obstacles are everywhere. Veto players are omnipresent. Big things happen only rarely, and typically only when the political forces are largely in alignment. This is the system the constitutional framers created and bequeathed to us, whether or not it is in accord with modern demands on leadership. Such demands are often vaguely articulated by the public as a plea to "make things better," which can be loosely translated as an appeal to "please make a miracle—or else."

Altered States

However complicated our political system is, conditions vary over time that may either benefit presidents or disadvantage them. It is noticeable, for example, that the more fluid political circumstances of the 1950s and 1960s began to give way, first gradually and then rapidly, to the fiercely combative party alignments characteristic of the early twenty-first century.[6] Actually, as Morris Fiorina points out, the rigidity of the party positions may well be a function of the "unstable majorities" characteristic of recent decades in American politics.[7] In the mid-twentieth century a president's political coalition might be forged across party lines to achieve the president's goals. The parties of the mid-twentieth century were composed mostly of alliances of convenience filled with contradictory coalitions generated by regional differences. This internal heterogeneity made interparty bargaining more palatable because the fluidity of political alignments meant that like minds could be found across the aisle. And in an era in which congressional politicians could be praised for bringing home the proverbial bacon, particularistic (constituency-specific) goods could be ladled out unashamedly to sweeten the pot in order to seal deals.

Now, however, the political battle lines are more clearly defined. Parties are more internally homogeneous. The "goods" used to cajole buy-ins to political bargains are mostly, but not completely, gone; when available, they are likely to generate as much bad publicity as good for congressional politicians. As a result of more stringent efforts to remove the temptation to use taxpayer funds to buy out politicians, along with the general diminution of discretionary spending through the appropriations process, there is more rigidity in the system.[8] Consequently, bargaining is largely confined to one's party mates. Politicians are more dependent on their own party's base than on the median voter, and they are increasingly reliant on financing and pressure from sources outside of their party structures that pull them right (Republicans) and left (Democrats).

With less in play, presidents need to have cohesive majorities, even supermajorities, in Congress to align with them. The main problem is that the larger the majority, the less cohesive it may be because attaining a majority depends on winning seats in what is normally hostile territory. House members and senators from the increasingly fewer swing districts and states are often conflicted as to whether to appeal to the median voter, which may be perceived as a winning strategy in a general election, or to appeal to their rabid political base to deter internal challenges during the party's primary. And should they survive the primary, will they receive only lukewarm support from party enthusiasts in a general election if they pitch their appeals to the median voter? Politicians usually deal with their ambitions sequentially.[9] First things first. Once they gain their party's nomination, then they can figure out a general election strategy. In most, but not all, deep red or deep blue districts or states (now the vast majority), the strategy of appealing to the party base is not likely to hurt the candidate in a general election. The consequence is that parties are now highly cohesive, which is more appropriate to a majority government parliamentary system, such as the Westminster system, than to the multiple veto system created by the constitutional framers. Furthermore, parties are more cohesive in opposition than in governance simply because it is easier to knock down a proposal that threatens the status quo than to generate support for such a proposal.

These rigid political alignments among legislators make legislating more difficult, with the possible exception of having strong majorities in both chambers. Thus, presidents are often forced to apply their executive authority wherever they can.[10] However, they do not get much of a free pass on the use of these tactics either. Because party cohesion and ideology are more evident now than in the mid-twentieth century, lawsuits against presidential actions or agency interpretations of statutory provisions are increasingly subjected to organized political litigation—

much of it coming from opposition state attorneys general, and some of it coming from Congress. The courts' reluctance to adjudicate such disputes under what was once known as the "doctrine of political questions" has largely disappeared, especially as judicial alignments have also become notably more consistent with party. Even when presidents win in the courts, they are, for better or worse, continually being challenged in this venue.

Given that presidents are likely to be swallowed up by these constraining forces, where can presidential leadership style possibly make a difference? And how can we conceptualize individual differences among presidents? More specifically, how can we conceptualize the leadership style of Barack Obama as president? It is best to think of any president's leadership characteristics in comparison with those of other presidents, especially immediate predecessors and successors, and in several dimensions. The aspects emphasized here are character, temperament, and intellect. The method utilized is to compare how different presidents focused on similar problems. But first, it is useful to note some generic differences in how presidents behave and the "metrics"—such as they are—of individual and ideological predispositions.

Leadership Style

The most ephemeral aspect of any presidency is the style of leadership the individual brings to the office. Presidents often operate in starkly different ways from their immediate predecessors. This can be partly explained by several factors. First, when campaigning for office, the aspirant typically needs to differentiate him- or herself from the incumbent, even when they are of the same party. Despite his service as vice president under Ronald Reagan, George H. W. Bush felt the need to present himself as a softer, kinder version of his more ideologically driven predecessor. Reagan, in turn, had presented himself as a decisive and certain leader driven by broad principles (ideology), in contrast to Jimmy Carter's relatively nonideological style of decision-making. Where Carter tended to see ambiguity and to focus on discrete problem-solving,[11] Reagan saw certainty and his straightforward ideology as the solution to any problems that could be bent into his ideological framework.[12] Similarly, whereas Bill Clinton tended to address the complexity and nuances of problems in skull sessions, without coming to clear decisions,[13] his successor George W. Bush (43) seldom relitigated his decisions or tempered his commitment to them, even in the face of apparent failure. Bush 43 noted that no one is likely to follow a leader who lacks confidence in his own decisions.[14] Bush's instinctive approach was displaced by Barack Obama's inclination to conduct a thorough search of alternatives and to encourage advisers to offer him different perspectives to mull over.[15] In turn, Obama's tendency to carefully assess his choices has been replaced with the ad hoc decision-making style preferred by his successor, Donald Trump.

Second, presidents of different parties tend to take different approaches to leadership, at least in the modern era, where the parties are more definitively aligned along liberal-conservative dimensions. Social and political psychologists have identified a set of foundational traits that they hypothesize are characteristic of liberal and conservative predispositions. These traits—sometimes referred to as the "Big Five"—are agreeableness, openness to experience, emotional stability/neuroticism, conscientiousness, and extraversion/introversion. Several studies indicate that liberals are more open-minded and value creativity, novelty, and diversity, whereas conservatives are more orderly, more conventional, and better organized.[16] It is possible (though not certain) that these differences are even more robust at the elite level. If so, they could be a crucial component of the differences in both managerial organization and cognitive tendencies of presidents of different parties, especially as the divide between Democrats and Republicans has widened. Gerber and colleagues note in particular the robust effects (except for African Americans) of the so-called Big Five traits in differentiating the cognitive ordering propensities of liberals and conservatives.[17]

This distinction provides some systemic order in what is otherwise a hopelessly subjective assessment of individual propensities. Openness and order, novelty and tradition, exploration and definable moral codes are among the traditional antinomies that characterize classical understandings of liberalism and conservatism.[18] That said, we can better understand why Democratic and Republican presidents organize their White House operations in such different ways (looser and more open among Democrats; more organized and hierarchical among Republicans).[19] That also explains why Democratic and Republican presidents tend to have different operational leadership styles. As time goes on, however, all administrations become more centralized and narrower in terms of trusted personnel.[20] This may occur because, over time, the pressures of leadership, plus the inevitable sorting out—that is, who can be trusted and who cannot—eventually overwhelm any presidential administration, altering how it organized itself at the beginning. Put somewhat differently, leadership style matters, but circumstances might matter even more.[21]

Although there are important tendencies and differences in leadership style across the political spectrum—and although these should not be underestimated— there are still important differences within each point on that spectrum. Next, therefore, I examine three traits that characterize any given president and how they define an administration, with special attention to President Obama.

Leadership Characteristics

Three elements of a leader's psyche—character, temperament, and intellect—have some influence on how a president behaves in office, how opportunities and constraints are assessed, and the extent to which the consequences of decisions are taken into account (if at all). The importance of these elements, however, is almost directly inverse to any consensus about their definition.

Character

James Pfiffner notes that while there is no consensus about what character is, there are various dimensions that relate to one's conduct in office: truth versus lying, sexual fidelity, consistency and follow-through with regard to campaign promises, and self-propelled scandals caused by presidential action.[22] Additionally, something less clearly defined—or perhaps more obvious—might be called upholding the dignity of the office. Most presidents do reasonably well in this regard, although Donald Trump may be setting a new and lower standard for such behavior. Much of this conduct has to do with personal self-discipline, and in this case, Obama likely would be considered to have upheld standards of presidential dignity.

Everyone, though, has flaws. To what extent do they influence the course of a president's tenure in office? Inevitably, we are more forgiving of presidents who share our political predispositions and more hostile toward those who do not. A few presidents have self-destructed—most obviously, Nixon. His downfall was the Watergate break-in—less the event itself than the criminal misconduct to cover it up, along with other illegal actions. In Nixon's case, some of this questionable behavior was foretold by his intervention during the 1968 presidential campaign, when he urged, through a surrogate, the South Vietnamese government to back away from the Paris peace talks because, if he were elected, he would offer more favorable terms to the Saigon regime.[23] Whatever Nixon's assets, his willingness to not merely bend the norms of democratic politics to achieve his personal ambitions but, in fact, to break the law to advance and protect his own interests at the expense of the country's strongly suggests that he deserved the sobriquet "Tricky Dick."

Both Johnson and Nixon soured their presidencies and damaged public confidence in government by failing to legitimate the high costs of military ventures in Southeast Asia with candid assessments of the likelihood of success. Once an administration is committed to a military venture and, above all, to its escalation, path dependency makes it difficult to pull back, especially in the case of an unyielding foe.

Sexual temptations can also affect presidencies, notably, those of Clinton and Kennedy. While both men were apparently quite indiscreet, the norms governing their escapades changed dramatically between the 1960s and 1990s. Kennedy's indiscretions came to public attention only after his death, even though they were common knowledge among Washington insiders and many of the journalists covering the White House. Clinton already had an independent counsel on his tail, looking into a different matter altogether, and that investigation uncovered not only an affair with a young intern but also inconsistencies in Clinton's testimony under oath. The attempted cover-up gave rise to jokes about Clinton's clever eva sions in his sworn testimony based on what constitutes sex and what the meaning of "is" is. Clinton's character flaws were offset by the nation's prosperity and by his high level of public approval as the economy gained momentum, but he remains only one of two presidents to be impeached by the House of Representatives (Andrew Johnson was the other). Everyone has flaws, but how much is made of them is a function of time and context and changing norms about their relevance to presidential behavior.

In contrast to Clinton, and similar to his immediate predecessor, Bush 43 (with the exception of prepresidential bouts of rowdiness and alcohol use), Obama's domestic life seemed remarkably tranquil, even blissful. Conservative author J. D. Vance observed in a *New York Times* column during the final days of the Obama presidency, "It is one of the great failures of recent political history that the Republican Party was too often unable to disconnect legitimate political disagreements from the fact that the president [Obama] himself is an admirable man."[24] There was little room for personal scandal, although there were scandals affecting the Veterans Administration and, more questionably, the Internal Revenue Service. But none of these issues appeared to emanate from the White House.

Obama's early career as a community organizer in Chicago, however, made some on the political right paint him as a nefarious, disruptive radical. Aside from this farcical characterization, other, more legitimate concerns were voiced about Obama's resort to unilateral executive power to work his will in a resistant political climate, his administration's opaqueness in contrast to promises of transparency, aggressive efforts to restrict journalists' reliance on confidential sources for national security reasons, and a record number of deportations of undocumented immigrants. Some of the most withering criticisms came from within Obama's own support base on the political left, which felt that he was coming up short of expectations. All these issues are complex. On some, Obama backed away; on others (especially immigration), he sought legislative remedies and, in their absence (and in some cases the absence of even legislative consideration), utilized executive means to avoid executing the letter of certain laws that, in his opinion, encouraged either discriminatory or punitive actions that elevated categorical judgment over compassion and discretionary justice.

Since Eisenhower, some presidents stand out for their character. Their presidencies either had no major scandals or addressed them promptly. This list likely would include Eisenhower, Ford, Carter, Bush 41 (putting aside recent accusations of sexual indiscretions at an advanced age and an unseemly appeal to link crime and race in his 1988 campaign), and Obama.[25] This list is notable for the fact that three of the five presidents served one term or less, having been defeated in their quest to extend their time in office. The presidency of Donald Trump makes it startlingly obvious that character may not count for much in the voting booth or in the opinion polls. Notably, Carter always received much higher ratings for personal approval than he did for job approval as president. On the other side of the coin, public approval of Clinton's presidential performance was close to 70 percent on the day the House of Representatives approved articles of impeachment against him deep into his second term, but his personal approval rating was much lower. Carter's character did not help him politically, and Clinton's did not hurt him.

Obama's presidency was largely scandal free, despite some executive agency missteps and the botched rollout of the Affordable Care Act. His personal behavior was beyond reproach (putting aside controversies over policies and his campaign's effort in 2012 to tar Mitt Romney's association with Bain Capital for throwing people out of work). Yet his administration was nowhere near as transparent as he claimed it would be during the campaign. What looks reasonable as a campaign promise often looks very different once an individual is inside the Oval Office. However, by contrast with his successor—against whom every president is judged—Obama's presidency now looks remarkably transparent. In fact, whatever their flaws, nearly every president looks better than Trump, for whom this could be his singular contribution to history. Obama, with his sense of grace and style and absence of personal or executive scandal, scores especially high on the character dimension.

In the end, presidential character is far more important normatively than politically. It provides a normative expression of how officeholders should conduct themselves in office and in their personal lives. Character is important for upholding republican norms and virtues—no minor matter—but in the short run, it has relatively little political importance.

Temperament

If character is a concept that is hard to nail down with precision, temperament may be even more challenging to define. A statement often attributed to journalist Walter Lippmann characterized Franklin D. Roosevelt as having a second-rate intellect but a first-rate temperament.[26] Richard Neustadt concluded that only individuals with a temperament forged in the arena of politics are likely to be fit for the presidency. Both Lippmann and Neustadt left us to decide more precisely what those traits of temperament are, having left only scattered and indefinite clues.

Neustadt's conception of temperament implies that a president must have an instinct for power, an opportunistic mind-set to exploit available options, and an aptitude for enhancing leverage. This aspect of temperament is an actionable component that enables one to employ whatever power resources are available to achieve one's goals. Such opportunities were present in the first two years of Obama's two-term presidency, but they were few and far between over the following six years as a consequence of Republican control of the House and later the Senate.

In popular lore, the ability to schmooze with other politicians is a key component of a political temperament. Lyndon Johnson and Bill Clinton were thought to be well endowed with this skill. Obama, like Carter and Nixon before him, is not a gregarious personality—and certainly not with other politicians, for whom all three may have had a healthy (or unhealthy) disrespect. In Obama's case, this was partly a function of the new political order and its rigid alignments and partly a function of his temperament, which tended more toward intellectual detachment. But in this regard, Obama was essentially following (whether he knew it or not) what political scientists have been saying for some time: personal influence, which is widely celebrated, is in reality very narrowly constricted.[27]

There is another facet of temperament, however, that is characterized by prudence—a word that Bush 41 often invoked as his personal signature. A key element, after all, of "guarding one's stakes" with regard to power (another Neustadtian conception of wise presidential behavior) is to avoid painting oneself into a corner and thus foreclosing options. But there is a fine line between keeping one's options open and being indecisive. History, however, is replete with leaders who made commitments they could not keep or could keep only at great cost to the country and to their own political standing. Inevitably, they were sucked into commitments that extracted great costs and yielded few, if any, gains. The contrast between Bush 41 and Bush 43 in the Persian Gulf illustrates the wisdom (or lack thereof) of setting limited objectives and forging broad alliances. Bush 41 firmly grasped political reality; Bush 43 fell victim to overreach and an inability to understand the complexities on the ground.

It is no easy matter for leaders to strike the right balance between an entrepreneurial ability to exploit opportunities and an understanding of the limits of power. One path involves taking risks; the other requires a consideration of all that can go wrong. Among presidents since Eisenhower, perhaps Kennedy, Bush 41, and Obama came closest to striking this balance. To illustrate this point, I examine the critical choices made by these three presidents as they took advantage of strategic opportunities or exhibited the due diligence that enabled them to avoid costly, even tragic, mistakes. These illustrations are not definitive evidence that these three got everything right or that others got it all wrong. All presidents have their moments of success and failure. Rather, these examples show that these particular presidents were open to critical opportunities and careful to avoid catastrophic choices. It goes without saying that not everyone will see things precisely as I do.

John F. Kennedy

However reluctant he may have been politically, Kennedy's response to the protests against racial segregation and the violent counterprotests was to initiate the civil rights legislation that would later be enacted during the Johnson administration. A number of modest civil rights measures had been passed during the Eisenhower administration, but local authorities' brutal reaction to civil rights protests in Birmingham, Alabama, led Kennedy to make a crucial choice between two important but opposing Democratic constituencies: African Americans and southern segregationists. Kennedy was cautious about broad-scale civil rights legislation until events built momentum for such an effort. But that effort was also impeded by the complex task of finding an appropriate constitutional rationale for asserting federal authority in what were theoretically private and localized decisions to deny accommodations based on race. The Fourteenth Amendment to the Constitution provides for equal standing before the law but does not prevent private discrimination, such as denying service in a restaurant or lodging in a hotel. Consequently, the Kennedy administration took the highly controversial step of subjecting these service providers' discriminatory behavior to federal law through the Constitution's commerce clause, which grants the federal government jurisdiction over interstate commerce. The expansion of federal jurisdiction through means of constitutional provisions continues to reverberate many decades later. For instance, in June 2012 Chief Justice John G. Roberts wrote an opinion justifying the individual mandate of President Obama's Affordable Care Act, finding that it fell under the federal government's taxation power rather than its power to regulate interstate commerce.

During the Cuban missile crisis of 1962, Kennedy's instincts led him to search for opportunities to de-escalate a situation that had the potential to result in nuclear conflagration between the United States and the Soviet Union. Kennedy wisely removed himself from the deliberations among a group of key national security officials and diplomats that came to be known as the EXCOM, recognizing that his presence might inhibit a free and unbridled discussion of options. A particularly important moment occurred in the EXCOM deliberations nearly a week after President Kennedy had announced the naval quarantine of Cuba. The EXCOM had been presented with two contradictory messages from the Kremlin—an initial conciliatory one, and a subsequent hard-line one. To the untrained eye, it seemed clear that the later message was the one to respond to, as concluded by Attorney General Robert F. Kennedy, who chaired the EXCOM. But sitting on the committee was Llewellyn Thompson, a career foreign service ambassador to the Soviet Union. Wise in the ways of Soviet political factions and decision-making inside the Kremlin, Thompson noted that the attorney general's conclusion might be faulty, opening the way for a potential deal with the Soviet leadership. Of course, luck played a role in the deliberations, but this episode also illustrates the importance of listening to diplomatic and military experts and engaging a strategy designed to avoid premature, irrevocable decisions. At moments like these, presidential temperament and due diligence are crucial. Avoiding premature closure on a decision is essential, and enabling free discussion is critical to avoiding an unfortunate outcome.

George H. W. Bush

In 1990 the large budget deficits at the end of the Reagan administration led President Bush to begin a dialogue and negotiation with the Democratic majorities in Congress, in particular, Daniel Rostenkowski (D-IL), chair of the House Ways and

Means Committee. To generate enthusiasm for his nomination as the Republican standard-bearer in 1988, Bush had made red-meat promises to the Republican base, which had been thrilled by Reagan's tax cuts but was less committed to the more moderately conservative Bush. In accepting his nomination in 1988, Bush had promised "no new taxes," and for emphasis he added, "read my lips." That pledge was undoubtedly the triumph of exigency over long-term viability. By 1990, it was clear that the fiscal status quo was unsustainable. Bush commissioned his budget director, Richard Darman, to set up discussions with Rostenkowski, who had sent signals to the administration that he (and likely his party) was amenable to working together to resolve the deficit problem. Many months of discussions and negotiations eventually led to a compromise in which a coalition of majority Democrats and minority Republicans passed legislation in 1991 (opposed by a majority of Republicans and a minority of Democrats) that provided new revenue and new rules regarding offsets on spending. Bush exploited this opportunity to work across party lines to achieve a positive result. In return, of course, he lost standing within his own party, which was drifting rightward, as a stalwart for an uncompromising right-wing agenda. Bill Clinton later followed Bush's bipartisan strategy to reach agreement on fast-tracking NAFTA, the trade agreement with Canada and Mexico, against the sentiments of a core Democratic Party constituency—labor unions— and the majority of Democrats in Congress.

Bush's cautious temperament was evident in meeting the challenges posed by the Iraqi regime's 1990 invasion of Kuwait and the potential threat to Saudi Arabia. All three countries, but especially Saudi Arabia, were major oil producers. As US ambassador to the United Nations, Bush had enjoyed a reputation as a skilled diplomat. That was useful in forming a broad coalition to support the rolling back of the Iraqi incursion and its threat to other Persian Gulf states. More than fifty countries provided some type of support for the operation, which was undertaken only after negotiations with the Iraqi government of Saddam Hussein failed. A key to forming this broad coalition was to keep the objectives limited. That meant no invasion of Baghdad, no externally imposed overthrow of the despotic Saddam regime, and the limited objective of reducing the threat to Saudi Arabia and pushing Iraqi troops out of Kuwait. The strategy achieved its objectives in a short time, including a no-fly zone.

Subsequent rebellions took place between the Shiite-majority Arabs in southern Iraq and the Sunni Saddam regime, and between the Kurds in the north and the Baghdad government. Protective measures were taken on behalf of the Kurds, but nothing was done to protect the Shiite Arabs, and the Saddam regime brutally quashed their rebellion. For this, Bush came under great criticism. But the wisdom of Bush's prudence was confirmed by his son's subsequent and largely disastrous efforts to right all these earlier wrongs with an open-ended invasion of Iraq. George W. Bush's objective of overthrowing the Saddam government would necessitate governing the country directly, with only limited support from others (mostly from Britain). Bush 41 achieved an imperfect peace; Bush 43 brought turmoil and far greater civil strife to the region, at considerable cost to the United States. One president's temperament allowed him to understand the limits of power; the other president's temperament led him to engage in impossible quests based on obviously false and inadequately vetted justifications, at significant costs to both Iraq and the United States. Prudence was a word that easily rolled off George H. W. Bush's often ineloquent tongue, but its virtues were reflected in the conduct of his presidency, and never more so than in his decision to limit American objectives in the first Iraq war.

Barack Obama

Like Kennedy, President Obama inspired followers with his soaring words and his vision for the country. In reality, he understood that the politics of governing was very different from motivating an audience of supporters. The speeches set forth ideals (often powerfully but vaguely articulated). Governing, however, proved to be a hard slog.

In most respects, Obama's ideals were progressive in the contemporary political parlance. There was certainly massive political opposition from the right against his proposals and even his rhetoric. But even though his ideals were on the left, his initial instinct was to find areas where he thought there could be agreement—until, after much experience, he concluded that agreement was impossible. Put somewhat differently, Obama looked for opportunities for progressive achievement, but his search was tempered by the institutional and political realities of the political system. Obama eventually conceded that these realities constricted what he could do and how he could do it, after which he went full-force unilateral.

How best to describe Obama's political temperament? For someone with such striking political rhetoric, he was not fundamentally enamored of other politicians. In that respect, he was more like Jimmy Carter. His administration emphasized evidence-based policy,[28] although he was not above cutting transactional political deals when warranted. It was a necessary, if sometimes repugnant, cost of doing business. He was often described as detached in his dealings with others, focusing on rational arguments rather than personal relationships. New York Times columnist Maureen Dowd characterized him as akin to Mr. Spock, the coldly rational character from Star Trek.[29] Unlike Carter, however, Obama possessed a keenly acerbic wit that he used to belittle his opponents. He joked at a White House correspondents' dinner in his second term (2013) about his relationship with an implacable opponent, Senator Mitch McConnell (R-KY). Early on, McConnell's prophetic advice to his Republican cohorts in the Senate had been to oppose everything on Obama's agenda as the way back to power. Some had advised the president that he should just sit down and have a drink with McConnell, but Obama sarcastically countered that if anyone thought the major problem in their relationship was personal rather than deeply political, *they* "should go have a drink with Mitch McConnell." It turned out that both figures had accurately summed up their political situations. After a few election cycles, the Republicans regained the Senate majority, and Obama came to realize that there was virtually no give in his relationship with congressional Republicans. Early in his administration, Obama had still believed in compromises, until he concluded that the only deals the Republican leadership would accept were exclusively on their terms—thus, no compromise at all. This, of course, was a reflection of the deep partisan polarization that had been gathering strength for decades.

Taking office in the early stages of the worst economic crisis since the Great Depression, Obama did several things that were unpopular among both his left-wing party mates and right-wing Republicans. This included rescuing the financial institutions whose lending had been more or less frozen because of uncertainty over the value of each institution's assets. The Bush administration had begun this process in its last few months, once it became clear that major economic failure was at hand. Populist forces on the left and right opposed it. Eventually, this rescue gained some traction, but as the economic crisis worsened, the Obama administration moved to assert more control over the banks and some key failing industries (automakers, insurance companies) in return for more financial support to sustain them. This proved to be highly controversial among Republicans, but the control, however temporary, was essential to gain the support of left-wing populists among the Democrats, who blamed the financial institutions' irresponsible behavior for the economic chaos.

At the outset of his presidency, Obama concluded that a stimulus package was necessary to get the economy moving. He wanted to gain Republican support for the stimulus, but to have any chance of that, he had to limit the stimulus amount to the more politically palatable figure of less than $1 trillion. Some of his advisers and would-be advisers among Democratic economists thought the figure Obama settled on ($787 billion) was too low to have the necessary impact.[30] But Obama was hoping this figure would draw some Republican support, at least symbolically. The package was broadly divided into three parts: (1) traditional hard-hat infrastructure improvement projects; (2) rescues of state and local governments' budgets by sustaining funds to deter layoffs of police, firefighters, and teachers; and (3) temporary tax cuts on withdrawn income in salary checks. The last of these, which was also the single largest allocation, was designed to attract Republican support. In the end, no Republicans in the House voted for the bill, and only three Republicans in the Senate (Arlen Specter of Pennsylvania and Olympia Snowe and Susan Collins of Maine) did so. Only one of these senators (Collins) remains in the Senate.

The Affordable Care Act (ACA), Obama's legislative crown jewel, was designed to widen the availability of health insurance. However, it was built on the very complex system of private insurance that already existed. More radical options, such as single-payer insurance, were not on the table, except in marginal ways. The price of buying off the key interests in health care—insurance companies, pharmaceutical manufacturers, and health care systems and providers—was to essentially retain the existing complicated system of health care insurance and service distribution. However imperfectly designed, the ACA sought to greatly expand insurance coverage, balance the insurance risk pool with the inclusion of healthy young people, alter the methods of compensating health care providers (from procedures to results), and make the overall health care system more efficient and less costly. The ideas behind the ACA had originated with Republicans nearly a generation earlier, including Stuart Butler of the Heritage Foundation and Speaker of the House Newt Gingrich. Mitt Romney, the 2012 Republican presidential nominee, had instituted the forerunner of the ACA in Massachusetts during his term as governor. Obama's instinct to settle for what was less than ideal,[31] and his willingness to bargain with the affected interests to at least neutralize opposition, led to legislation that was extremely complex and interdependent in its varied parts. It was not easy to understand, and it would prove to be politically fragile. But Obama saw that the health care plan set forth early in the Clinton administration, though very ambitious, had been noticeably vague in several respects and never had the tacit support of the key actors. In addition, Obama waited patiently for the legislative committee process to play out in both chambers, hoping to get some buy-in from the opposition. But that support failed to materialize, and the delay almost resulted in legislative failure. In the end, the ACA received zero Republican votes, a sign that Obama's gestures were inadequate in the polarized political environment, which has only worsened.

Foes of his administration criticized Obama's alleged radical overreach on the health care effort. Those sympathetic to his administration criticized his failure to focus exclusively on the economy and for potentially alienating support he would need for the rest of his agenda and for the remainder of his administration. George C. Edwards, for example, has argued that Obama's pursuit of health care reform cost his party dearly in subsequent elections.[32] John Graham has similarly contended that whatever the value of the health care legislation, its unpopularity eroded the Democratic Party's strength in Congress.[33]

In sum, Obama had a "brief shining moment" when he had sizable congressional majorities. There is certainly much debate about whether he chose his priorities wisely. There was, however, an economic crisis that commanded his immediate attention; in particular, he had to lubricate the frozen economy he had inherited as a consequence of lax oversight of the international banking system. But he also pursued a signature piece of legislation that had been on his party's wish list for many decades. The US health care system is complicated, expensive, inefficient, and inadequate in its coverage. And at a time when employers were seeking to shed costs and unemployment was rising, leaving many vulnerable to the vagaries of the private health insurance market, it could be argued that health care reform was no less a priority than economic stimulation. Obama chose to tackle this issue as the hallmark of his presidency. Doing so may have been a fatal attraction from a short-term political standpoint, as the new law was unpopular and contributed to the Democrats' heavy losses in the 2010 midterm elections. Under the ACA, most of the existing complicated health care system was kept in place; in fact, it became even more complicated. However, about 20 million people gained coverage—far from universal, but a major improvement over the status quo. Within his own party, there was some desire for a more radical, if fundamentally simpler, single-payer system, and most Democrats supported at least a public option or a partial buy-in to Medicare. Obama may have preferred to go that route, but ultimately, he accepted what was possible rather than what was desirable. The Affordable Care Act was a complicated morass of regulations, incentives, subsidies, and taxes that was hard to digest or explain. But ultimately, a significant number of people gained benefits that they would later worry about losing.

At least until the last two years of his administration, Obama largely proved to be a political progressive with a conservative temperament. In the last quarter of his presidency, however, that conservative temperament was largely abandoned in the face of implacable resistance by a rejuvenated Republican majority in both houses of Congress. At this point, Obama went solo, doing what he could through executive action, even though such acts were more easily reversible than statutory enactment.

Obama's cautionary style, especially on matters of race, drew criticism from his constituencies on the left. As the first American president of color, Obama was well positioned to understand the long and tortured history of racism in the United States. As an American president, however, he could not identify himself exclusively with the aspirations of any single constituency. From the standpoint of his critics, he had to be "respectable," which, ironically, conflicted with more radical prescriptions on behalf of the African American population.[34] Rather, Obama's rhetoric to largely African American audiences emphasized the sacrifices of the civil rights generation, the racial progress made, personal and familial responsibilities, empathy toward others, and the civic obligation to participate in the political process. These themes were prominent in Obama's commencement addresses at two historically black colleges and universities.[35] Probably these themes would have been articulated by any president of color; otherwise, that person would have been unlikely to attain the presidency. Obama was especially mindful of the historical role he played. However, these themes were also consistent with the keynote speech he delivered at the 2004 Democratic National Convention in Boston, which was a fundamentally aspirational view of the diverse threads making up the fabric of American society.

Intellect

Another dimension in which presidents differ is their intellectual curiosity and ability to learn over time. It is usually helpful if an incoming president possesses knowledge of the institutions for which he or she is responsible (the executive branch) and those with which a president must interact (the legislative and judicial branches). But by itself, this is insufficient. Institutional experience did not prevent Lyndon Johnson from getting sucked further into the deadly morass of the Vietnam War. In fact, it may have led him into it; he adhered too easily to the assumptions he and his fellow politicians and experts had derived from their Cold War experience. Reading about history and understanding it can be valuable if this induces reflection. But George W. Bush, who was apparently an avid reader of history, failed to develop sufficient skepticism about the depth of a leader's ability to influence events in a positive way or to reflect about the complexity and perversity of a leader's choices.

Skepticism may be a crucial element of intellect, in the sense that one must understand the uncertainty attached to all plausible alternatives and their likely ramifications. It means questioning conventional assumptions as well as one's own. It means being one's own toughest critic. That, of course, can lead to "paralysis by analysis." Evidence, though, is crucial to the decision-making process. As the conservative *New York Times* columnist David Brooks noted early in the Obama administration, the president was in command of the evidence and in control of the room during a meeting with congressional leaders of both parties over health care legislation.[36] That, unfortunately, did not persuade anyone who was not already on board with Obama's health care proposal. Prior assumptions and commitments and dependence on interests dictate the stark limits of persuasion.

Obama's cool, detached intellectual style made him less than beloved by other politicians. He did not cozy up to them, nor they to him. But part of this aloofness was Obama's recognition that after his early attempts to accommodate the opposition, there was very little room for persuasion and few instruments with which to achieve it. The myth of Lyndon Johnson as the Great Persuader in Chief does not fully take into account the outsized Democratic majorities and undivided government during his administration. Further, there was more overlap between the parties in that era than during Obama's presidency. Party was only one of several sources of issue cleavage (though still the most important one). Action in Congress (or the lack thereof) was still in the hands of powerful committee chairs, whose grip on power was more likely to be limited by mortality than by political challenges in an era when seniority determined accession up the ladder of authority.

Obama's intellect and penchant for thinking through options often led him to minimize risk-taking, particularly in matters of foreign policy. He grew skeptical of escalating commitments made in earlier administrations. He also became skeptical of increasingly open-ended commitments, and especially of counterinsurgency tactics predicated on the defense of societies that, in his view, were unlikely to develop resiliency.[37] Deep down, he became a realist in international affairs and eschewed idealism that led to deepening commitments.[38] For this, he was criticized by more interventionist figures such as the late Senator John McCain (R-AZ) as having a "feckless foreign policy."

Skepticism does not necessarily lead to a correct policy—whatever that may be. And it may potentially induce an excess of caution. However, it is likely to avoid entanglements for which there is no reasonable exit and to avoid tactics that have a significant risk of being counterproductive. Obama characterized his own foreign policy in pithy terms: "Don't do stupid shit."[39] More realism and less idealism became the motif of Obama's foreign policy. Avoiding entanglements in the multisided civil war in Syria was an inevitable outcome of Obama's thought process. There were likely voices encouraging him to do more, including some from within his own administration, as though unilateral military power always achieves desirable outcomes in complicated civil struggles. What some like Senator McCain might have seen as feckless, others might see as wise and judicious. Being smart does not guarantee an optimal decision. Nor does it necessarily guarantee a good decision, even if there were some way to discern what that is. However, it likely minimizes foreseeable risks. Sometimes the least bad decision appears to be sensible in retrospect. But getting there requires introspection and a serious vetting of alternatives.[40]

Leaders and Their Times: The Interplay of Leadership and Opportunity

Historians' analysis of leaders and their performance is a continuous quest and never reaches finality. This statement should provide a cautionary note about this assessment of President Obama's style of leadership. This is true because history, and certainly contemporary history, can reach few definitive conclusions and because human beings, especially those in leadership roles, respond in a highly complex manner to political incentives and imperatives; at the same time, they want to leave their mark on the future. Yet each president has a signature style of operation, even if that style is altered over the course of an administration by circumstances.

When Obama had the political opportunities to achieve his agenda, he was largely successful. In the early days of his presidency, however, he was on the prowl for a buy-in from affected interests and, where possible, from Republican members of Congress. As events transpired, Obama grew increasingly skeptical about the possibility of dealing with the Republicans in Congress. The final straw probably occurred during the debt ceiling negotiations of 2011 between the president and House Speaker John Boehner. If only these two politicians had been involved, a deal probably could have been struck. But reaching a compromise required both leaders to get concessions from their parties, and in the end, neither could do it.

From that point on, Obama abandoned efforts to bring along congressional Republicans. The level of distrust between the Obama White House and the Republicans in Congress was too great and too deep to be reconciled.

Obama's policy success in his first two years, and especially his controversial health care reform, may have precipitated large political losses in the 2010 midterm elections, rendering remote the likelihood of legislative achievement in his next six years in office.[41] By the last two years of his second term, when Republicans gained control of both chambers of Congress, Obama was forced into a purely defensive mode and pursued unilateral executive authority—authority he may or may not have actually possessed.[42]

What Is Obama's Legacy?

By definition, leadership style is ephemeral and, in some measure, unique to the individual. In most instances, any given president is apt to be most unlike his immediate predecessor and immediate successor. This is because, since the presidency of Franklin Roosevelt, presidents of one party who have completed their terms in office have been, with only one exception, from a different party than their immediate successors and hence their immediate predecessors as well. In these times, party makes a difference in leadership style that, to some extent, coincides with the party's approach to government. The nature of the political campaign also emphasizes a contrast in styles; that is, candidates seek differentiation from the preceding administration. These two elements—party and the need for differentiation—tend to be interactive. As such, comparisons across presidents help elucidate key characteristics of presidential leadership style.

It is quite likely, however, that a president's leadership style will vary during an administration, depending on circumstances, point in time within the president's term,[43] and the ability to learn from prior failures. Clearly, Obama's respect for the institutional constraints that bind presidents diminished in the latter stages of his presidency as he grew increasingly impatient with a dysfunctional Congress. It is reasonable to believe that virtually all presidents desire to leave a mark, and that desire is enhanced over time as their degrees of freedom dwindle. But some dominant traits are ultimately unveiled across events and over time. Some of what we think we know today may be uprooted by additional evidence as archival documents become available and as an administration recedes into the historical horizon. History itself is a variable, not a constant. Time changes the lens through which we view events. Different norms and judgments are inevitable as they are applied retroactively to past presidencies. For example, recent historical judgment has been less kind to Andrew Jackson and Woodrow Wilson because certain aspects of their presidencies, especially those related to race, took on more importance as a function of altered norms in society.

There is inevitably more than a modest measure of subjectivity in assessing how a president conducts himself in office, especially when that experience is fresh in the observer's mind and thus sharply influenced by existing political controversies. That is especially true because this aspect of a presidency lacks a clear set of metrics. All contemporaneous judgments are fallible but not necessarily implausible. With these cautions in mind, this chapter has assessed Barack Obama's presidential character, his temperament, and his intellect. Such assessments are, of course, comparative and hence controversial. Accordingly, it has been Obama's personal good fortune, but not necessarily the country's, that his successor's conduct in office is about as diametrically opposite as it is possible to be. The conclusion here is that Obama is an individual of considerable intellect, which he applied to presidential decision-making; he was a president of high personal character and prudential temperament, yet one who was willing to exploit political opportunities to make profound policy changes. None of this implies that his policies are incontestable or that his decisions were good ones, but prudence, intellectual acuity, and honorable behavior in office are the necessary ingredients from which good outcomes are more likely to be baked than when these elements are lacking. A reasonable summation of Obama's style of leadership would be *progressive ambitions through conservative means*. As the clock ticked toward the end of his term, however, the means became increasingly unilateral and subject to judicial interpretation of his authority. And in matters of foreign policy, he became more minimalist than ambitious.

As his administration concluded, Obama's presidential approval rating closed at a high level (59 percent), but he was never an unusually popular or unpopular president. His average approval rating (47.9 percent) places him ninth among the twelve presidents since Truman. He is also third from the bottom in his highest approval rating (69 percent), with only Reagan (yes, Reagan!) and Nixon failing to exceed that. However, his lowest approval rating (38 percent) is better than that of all other presidents since Truman except for Kennedy and Eisenhower.[44] In sum, Obama had a low ceiling but a relatively high floor, with only modest fluctuations. In the current political climate in the United States, strong partisan support sustains a president, while strong partisan opposition enfeebles him. Obama encountered a frozen economy when he became president, but there is now an equally frozen sphere of politics. He did not create this situation, but in some views, he reinforced it, while his partisans were often disappointed that he did not do more. Unless more fluidity and bargaining possibilities arise in the political system, the tendency toward unilateral executive politics will likely continue its upward spiral. Even Obama's respect for institutional constraints had its limits.

Notes

The author is greatly indebted to Andrew Rudalevige and Ignacio Araña for their astute comments and suggestions.

1. See Matthew S. Shugart and John M. Carey, *Presidents and Assemblies: Constitutional Design and Electoral Dynamics* (Cambridge: Cambridge University Press, 1992); Lee K. Metcalf, "Measuring Presidential Power," *Comparative Political Studies* 33, 5 (2000): 661–685; Timothy Frye, "A Politics of Institutional Choice: Post-Communist Presidencies," *Comparative Political Studies* 30, 5 (1997): 523–552.

2. Richard E. Neustadt, *Presidential Power* (New York: John Wiley, 1960); Robert A. Caro, *Master of the Senate: The Years of Lyndon Johnson* (New York: Vintage, 2002); Robert A. Caro, *The Passage of Power* (New York: Knopf, 2012).

3. This point is driven home by Greenstein in his analysis of Eisenhower's presidential style. See Fred I. Greenstein, *The Hidden Hand Presidency: Eisenhower as Leader* (Baltimore: Johns Hopkins University Press, 1994).

4. For example, see Richard M. Pious, *Why Presidents Fail: White House Decision-Making from Eisenhower to Bush II* (Lanham, MD: Rowman & Littlefield, 2008); Elaine Kamarck, *Why Presidents Fail and How They Can Succeed Again* (Washington, DC: Brookings Institution Press, 2016).

5. Anthony King asked, "Whoever said the U.S. Presidency was powerful?" as quoted in Charles O. Jones, "The American Presidency: A Separationist Perspective," in *Presidential Institutions and Democratic Politics: Comparing Regional and National Contexts*, ed. Kurt von Mettenheim (Baltimore: Johns Hopkins University Press, 1997), 22. For skeptical views of the actual extent of presidential power versus presidential expectations, see Terry M. Moe and William G. Howell, *Relic: How Our Constitution Undermines Effective Government—And Why We Need a More Powerful Presidency* (New York: Basic Books, 2016); Terry M. Moe and Michael Caldwell, "Political Institutions: The Neglected Side of the Story," *Journal of Law, Economics, and Organization* 6 (1990): 213–254; Terry M. Moe, "The Institutional Foundations of Democratic Government: A Comparison of Presidential and Parliamentary Systems," *Journal of Institutional and Theoretical Economics* 150 (1994): 171–195.

6. See Frances E. Lee, *Insecure Majorities and the Perpetual Campaign* (Chicago: University of Chicago Press, 2016). Also see Gregory Koger and Matthew J. Lebo, *Strategic Party Government: Why Winning Trumps Ideology* (Chicago: University of Chicago Press, 2017).

7. Fiorina notes that this shifting began with the 1992 election, when both parties' grip on power became volatile, leading to an unwillingness to cooperate across party lines because the current "outs" might soon become the "ins." Fiorina attributes this partisan rigidity to each party's activist base. An unstable grip on power in the electorate leads to rigid party positions as the parties become focused on the political mobilization of their activist bases and the consequent need to cater to them. See Morris P. Fiorina, *Unstable Majorities: Polarization, Party Sorting, and Political Stalemate* (Stanford, CA: Hoover Institution Press, 2017). Also see Lee, *Insecure Majorities*.

8. The overall diminution of discretionary spending was a function of its being impacted by high-cost mandated social insurance programs and by the unanticipated default position in 2011 to sequester funds for both domestic programs and defense. This sequester was an indication that the only thing the parties agreed on was taking the other side's favored programs prisoner. They agreed in 2018, however, to "release the prisoners" and increase discretionary funding for both defense and domestic programs. Of course, the consequence of all this—along with a large tax cut, much of

which is permanent—is to put the federal government on the path of unsustainable indebtedness.

9. Joseph A. Schlesinger, *Ambition and Politics: Political Careers in the United States* (Chicago: Rand McNally, 1966).

10. See, e.g., Terry M. Moe, "The Politicized Presidency," in *The New Direction in American Politics*, ed. John E. Chubb and Paul E. Peterson (Washington, DC: Brookings Institution, 1985), 235–271; William G. Howell, *Power without Persuasion: The Politics of Direct Presidential Action* (Princeton, NJ: Princeton University Press, 2003); Andrew Rudalevige, *The New Imperial Presidency* (Ann Arbor: University of Michigan Press, 2005).

11. James Fallows, "The Passionless Presidency: The Trouble with Jimmy Carter's Administration," *Atlantic*, May 1979, https://www.theatlantic.com/magazine/archive/1979/05/the-passionless-presidency/308516.

12. Greenstein's contrast of presidential leadership styles along six dimensions is likely the single best assessment of the strengths and weaknesses of presidents as leaders. See, especially, his contrast between Carter and Reagan—one with the capacity and analytic ability to decompose the big picture into its discrete parts, and the other with little knowledge but the ability to focus on the big picture. See Fred I. Greenstein, *The Presidential Difference: Leadership Style from FDR to Barack Obama* (Princeton, NJ: Princeton University Press, 2009), 127–159.

13. On Clinton's decisional tendencies, see Greenstein, *Presidential Difference*, 160–172.

14. A quote from President George W. Bush is instructive here. Meeting with university students on May 25, 2003, Bush stated: "A leader must be willing and then be decisive enough to make a decision and stick by it. . . . To lead, you've got to know what you believe. . . . You have to believe in certain values, and you must defend them at all costs. . . . You must set clear goals and constantly lead toward those goals." As quoted in Greenstein, *Presidential Difference*, 191.

15. For contrasts between George W. Bush and Barack Obama, see Greenstein, *Presidential Difference*, 173–218. Also see John W. Dean, "How Our Decider-in-Chief Decides: Decisionmaking and the Obama Presidency," *FindLaw for Legal Professionals*, August 6, 2010; George W. Bush, *Decision Points* (New York: Crown, 2011), chap. 9. For two interesting and different, but sometimes coincident, points of view about Bush's leadership style, see Nicholas Lemann, "The Will to Believe," *New Republic*, January 27, 2011, https://newrepublic.com/article/82220/decision-points-book-review-bush; Richard Brookhiser, "Close Up: The Mind of George W. Bush," *Atlantic*, April 2003, https://www.theatlantic.com/magazine/archive/2003/04/close-up=the-mind-of-george-w-bush/303399/.

16. See Jesse Graham, Jonathan Haidt, and Brian A. Nosek, "Liberals and Conservatives Rely on Different Sets of Moral Foundations," *Journal of Personality and Social Psychology* 96 (2009): 1029–1046; Alan S. Gerber, Gregory A. Huber, David Doherty, and Shang E. Ha, "Personality and Political Attitudes: Relationships across Issue Domains and Political Contexts," *American Political Science Review* 104 (2010): 111–133; Dana R. Carney, John T. Jost, Samuel D. Gosling, and Jeff Potter, "The Secret Lives of Liberals and Conservatives: Personality Profiles, Interaction Styles, and the Things They Leave Behind," *Political Psychology* 29 (2008): 807–840.

17. Gerber et al., "Personality and Political Attitudes."

18. See Morgan Marietta, *A Citizen's Guide to American Ideology: Conservatism and Liberalism in Contemporary Politics* (New York: Routledge Press, 2011).

19. See, e.g., Colin Campbell, *Managing the Presidency: Carter, Reagan, and the Search for Executive Harmony* (Pittsburgh: University of Pittsburgh Press, 1986); Bert A. Rockman, "Organizing the White House: On a (West) Wing and a Prayer," *Journal of Managerial Issues* 5 (1993): 453–464.

20. Thomas E. Cronin, "'Everybody Believes in Democracy until He Gets to the White House . . .': An Examination of White House–Departmental Relations," *Law and Contemporary Problems* (1970): 573–625, https://scholarship.law.duke.edu/cgi/view content.cgi?article=3301&context=1cp.

21. Walcott and Hult argue that in recent times there is less variability in the organization of presidential administrations and, consequently, less variability across party lines. See Charles E. Walcott and Karen M. Hult, "White House Structure and Decision Making: Elaborating the Standard Model," *Presidential Studies Quarterly* 35, 2 (2005), https://doi.org/10.1111/j.1741-5705.2005.00250.x.

22. James P. Pfiffner, *The Character Factor: How We Judge America's Presidents* (College Station: Texas A&M University Press, 2004).

23. John A. Farrell, *Richard Nixon: The Life* (New York: Doubleday, 2017), especially 342–345.

24. J. D. Vance, "Barack Obama and Me," *New York Times*, January 2, 2017, A15, national edition.

25. There were actually two publicized scandals during the Eisenhower and Carter administrations. In Eisenhower's second term, the president's long-serving chief of staff, Sherman Adams, accepted an expensive gift (a vicuna coat) from businessman Bernard Goldfine, who was seeking to curry influence. Ike considered Adams indispensable, but the political pressure to part ways with him became too great. Relatively early in the Carter administration, Bert Lance, director of the Office of Management and Budget and the president's close confidant, became involved in a possible bribery scandal. Carter was also reluctant to let Lance go, but ultimately the president was compelled to show him the door; Lance was later acquitted. In each case, the accused (Adams and Lance) were guilty of bad judgment but no actual crimes.

26. Though often attributed to Walter Lippmann, the quote might have originated with Supreme Court justice Oliver Wendell Holmes Jr. Prior to the 1932 election, Lippmann apparently remarked that FDR was a "pleasant man who without any important qualifications for the office would very much like to be President." See James Chace, "The Winning Hand," *New York Review of Books*, March 11, 2004.

27. See George C. Edwards, *At the Margins: Presidential Leadership of Congress* (New Haven, CT: Yale University Press, 1989); George C. Edwards, *On Deaf Ears: The Limits of the Bully Pulpit* (New Haven, CT: Yale University Press, 2003). Also see Stephen Skowronek, *Presidential Leadership in Political Time: Reprise and Reappraisal*, 2nd ed. (Lawrence: University Press of Kansas, 2011). A measured counter to the limitations of presidential persuasion can be found in Brandon Rottinghaus, *The Provisional Pulpit: Modern Presidential Leadership of Public Opinion* (College Station: Texas A&M University Press, 2010).

28. See Ron Haskins and Greg Margolis, *Show Me the Evidence: Obama's Fight for Rigor and Results in Social Policy* (Washington, DC: Brookings Institution Press, 2015).

29. President Obama's resemblance to the half Vulcan, half human character in the *Star*

Trek series was first brought to public attention in a *New York Times* op-ed on May 9, 2009. In a column entitled "Put Aside Logic," Maureen Dowd described Obama as "a control freak who learned to temper, if not purge, all emotion" but who, like the hybrid Spock, "was more adept . . . at learning to adjust his two sides to charm both worlds, and to balance his cerebral air with his talent for evoking intense emotion." Later that year, other commentators in the *Atlantic* (December 1, 2009) weighed in on the Spock-Obama analogy. Of particular note was the observation by Seth Borenstein of the Associated Press, who wrote, "Obama's Spock-like qualities have started to cause him political problems in real world Washington. Critics see him as too technocratic, too deliberative, too lacking in emotion." Dowd may have been closer to the truth, depicting Obama as both cerebral *and* emotional. He exhibited the latter after the senseless slaughter of young schoolchildren and school personnel in Newtown, Connecticut, and after a white supremacist murdered clergy and members of a Bible study group at a historic African American church in Charleston, South Carolina.

30. The Obama administration proposed a $787 billion package; however, Congress appropriated only $720 billion. The stimulus was carried into an additional year. Consequently, the total amount appropriated was $816 billion. See Kimberly Amadeo, *The Balance*, https://www.google.com/url?ct=abg&q=https.

31. On June 30, 2003, speaking to the Illinois AFL-CIO, Obama said, "I happen to be a proponent of a single payer health care program." Physicians for a National Health Program, "Barack Obama on Single Payer in 2003," www.pnhp.org/news/2008/june/barack_obama_on_sing.php. Later, as the presidency came into view, Obama backed off this position, saying that if he were starting a system "from scratch," he would favor a single-payer system, but under existing circumstances, it would be too disruptive. See Angie Drobnic Holan, "Obama Statements on Single-Payer Have Changed a Bit," *Politifact*, July 16, 2009, www.politifact.com/truth-o-meter/statements/2009/jul/16/barack-obama/obama-statements-single-payer-have-changed-bit/ys.

32. George C. Edwards III, *Overreach: Leadership in the Obama Presidency* (Princeton, NJ: Princeton University Press, 2012).

33. John D. Graham, *Obama on the Home Front: Domestic Policy Triumphs and Setbacks* (Bloomington: Indiana University Press, 2016). Also see chapter 9 in this volume.

34. See, e.g., Frederick G. Harris, *The Price of the Ticket: Barack Obama and the Rise and Decline of Black Politics* (New York: Oxford University Press, 2012).

35. See Obama's commencement address remarks at Morehouse College on May 19, 2013, and at Howard University on May 7, 2016.

36. David Brooks, "Not as Dull as Expected," *New York Times*, February 26, 2010, A23, national edition.

37. Mark Landler, "Fractured World Tested the Hope of a Young President," *New York Times*, January 2, 2017, A1, A5, national edition.

38. See chapter 11 in this volume for evidence of Obama's realist turn in foreign policy.

39. Mike Allen, "Don't Do Stupid Sh—— 'Stuff,'" *Politico*, June 1, 2014, https://www.politico.com/story/2014/06/dont-do-stupid-shit-president-obama-white-house-107293.

40. John R. McAndrews, Bert A. Rockman, and Colin Campbell, "The Causes and Consequences of Career Bureaucratic Influence," in *Canada and the United States in Comparative Perspective*, ed. Paul J. Quirk (Oxford: Oxford University Press, 2019).

41. Graham, *Obama on the Home Front*. Also see chapter 9 in this volume.

42. Louis Fisher, *President Obama: Constitutional Aspirations versus Executive Actions* (Lawrence: University Press of Kansas, 2018).

43. Bert A. Rockman, *The Leadership Question: The Presidency and the American System* (New York: Praeger, 1984), 83–129.

44. Gallup Historical Presidential Job Approval Statistics, January 18, 2018, http://news.gallup.com/poll/116677/presidential-approval-ratings-gallup-historical-statistics-trends.aspx.

ABOUT THE CONTRIBUTORS

Julia R. Azari is associate professor, assistant chair, and director of graduate studies for the department of political science at Marquette University.

Matt A. Barreto is professor of political science and Chicana/Chicano studies at the University of California, Los Angeles, and cofounder of the research and polling firm Latino Decisions.

John D. Graham is dean of the School of Public and Environmental Affairs at Indiana University and former administrator of the federal Office of Information and Regulatory Affairs.

Angela Gutierrez is a graduate student in the department of political science at the University of California, Los Angeles.

David Patrick Houghton is professor of national security affairs at the US Naval War College.

Alyssa Julian is research assistant to the dean of the School of Public and Environmental Affairs at Indiana University and a JD candidate at Vanderbilt University Law School.

Angela X. Ocampo is an LSA collegiate postdoctoral fellow in political science at the University of Michigan.

Molly E. Reynolds is a fellow in governance studies at the Brookings Institution.

Bert A. Rockman is professor emeritus of political science at Purdue University and visiting scholar in political science at the University of Pittsburgh.

Brandon Rottinghaus is Pauline Yelderman Endowed Chair and professor of political science at the University of Houston.

Andrew Rudalevige is Thomas Brackett Reed professor of government at Bowdoin College.

Sharece Thrower is assistant professor of political science at Vanderbilt University.

Alvin B. Tillery Jr. is associate professor of political science and director of the Center for the Study of Diversity and Democracy at Northwestern University.

David A. Yalof is professor and head of the department of political science at the University of Connecticut.

INDEX